Lonely Planet Publications
Melbourne | Oakland | London

W9-BYZ-677

Chris Rowthorn

Kyoto

The Top Five

1 Kyoto Imperial Palace Park
From blazing leaves to cherry blossoms, every season is special (p75)
2 Nanzen-ji
In a city of temples, this stands out as a beauty (p58)
3 Nishiki Market
Colourful, lively and bustling, this is easily Kyoto's best market (p57)
4 Fushimi-Inari-taisha
Tunnels of torii make this a magical spot (p86)
5 Kurama-dera
This mountaintop temple is the perfect escape from the city (p91)

Contents

Published by Lonely Planet Publications Pty Ltd
ABN 36 005 607 983

Australia Head Office, Locked Bag 1, Footscray,
Victoria 3011, ☎ 03 8379 8000, fax 03 8379 8111,
talk2us@lonelyplanet.com.au

USA 150 Linden St, Oakland, CA 94607,
☎ 510 893 8555, toll free 800 275 8555,
fax 510 893 8572, info@lonelyplanet.com

UK 72–82 Rosebery Ave, Clerkenwell, London,
EC1R 4RW, ☎ 020 7841 9000, fax 020 7841 9001,
go@lonelyplanet.co.uk

© Lonely Planet 2005
Photographs © Phil Weymouth and as listed (p202)
2005

Printed through The Bookmaker International Ltd
Printed in China

The Authors

CHRIS ROWTHORN

Born in England and raised in the United States, Chris has lived in Kyoto since 1992. Soon after his arrival in Kyoto, Chris began studying the Japanese language and culture, while supporting himself by teaching English and working as an editor. In 1995 he became a regional correspondent for the *Japan Times*, a national English-language newspaper published in Tokyo.

Chris joined Lonely Planet in 1996 and has worked on a total of 17 Lonely Planet travel guides, including *Japan, Hiking in Japan, Tokyo, Kyoto* and *Read This First: Asia & India*. Despite all of his work-related travel, Chris still takes every opportunity to explore the world, in particular the Himalayas and Southeast Asia. When he's not on the road, he spends his time seeking out Kyoto's best restaurants, temples, hiking trails and various other *anaba* (secret places known only to the locals). He also conducts walking tours of Kyoto and the rest of Kansai. For more on Chris, check out his website at www.chrisrowthorn.com.

PHOTOGRAPHER
PHIL WEYMOUTH

In the back lanes of Kyoto, Phil spotted a geisha. The sight actually made him take a breath – she was stunning. Walking through the busy shops she seemed to sum up the contrast of Japan, old and new. Phil found Kyoto a joy to travel around: the trains ran on time, the food was exceptional and the history of this cultural city was fascinating.

Australian born, Phil's family moved to Iran in the late 1960s. They called Tehran home until the revolution in 1979. Phil then studied photography in Melbourne, and returned to the Middle East to work as a photographer in Bahrain. Phil's Lonely Planet commissions include *Hong Kong, Beijing* and *Shanghai*.

Introducing Kyoto

With over 1600 Buddhist temples, more than 400 Shintō shrines and 17 Unesco World Heritage sites, Kyoto is one of the world's most culturally rich cities. These riches are the legacy of the 1000-plus years that Kyoto was the capital of Japan, the very stage on which Japanese history unfolded. And even though the capital has long since migrated to Tokyo, Kyoto remains the heart and soul of Japan, the place that modern Japanese visit to discover what it means to be Japanese.

But Kyoto is far more than just temples, shrines and history; it's also one of the loveliest cities in Asia. It's home to the world's most sublime gardens and an array of traditional architecture unmatched by any city outside Europe. Perhaps more importantly, Kyoto is a city that is designed to make the most of the beauty of the changing seasons. From the riot of cherry blossoms in spring, to the lush green of summer, to the blazing maples of autumn and the snow-covered landscapes of winter, Kyoto is a place where the pageantry of the seasons is given full reign.

Of course, having heard so much about the wonders of Kyoto, the first glimpse of the city is a profound letdown for most visitors. The eye-smartingly ugly expanse of concrete and neon that greets you as you leave Kyoto Station is enough to make you think you've been had – that all this talk of 'beautiful Kyoto' is just a bunch of tourist-literature hype. But the discerning eye will pick out some hints of Kyoto's beauty even among the concrete that surrounds the station: the soaring pagoda of Tō-ji and the gentle curves of Higashi Hongan-ji, two of Kyoto's lovely ancient temples.

Heartened by these first glimpses, the determined visitor can venture out into the city and find endless pockets of beauty: ancient teahouses that are sandwiched between high-rise apartment buildings, sacred shrines tucked neatly into modern shopping

Lowdown

Population 1.4 million

Time zone GMT plus 9 hours

Three-star hotel room ¥10,000

Coffee ¥350

Bowl of rāmen ¥600

Bus fare ¥220

No-no Shoes on the tatami

arcades, and exquisite traditional restaurants competing for customers with a growing legion of fast-food restaurants.

Indeed, Kyoto, perhaps more than any other city in Asia, rewards the determined explorer. Whether you've been in the city for two days, two years or two decades, you can still take a short stroll and make new discoveries, often right around the corner. This may well be Kyoto's most endearing quality: the feeling that the closer you look, the more there is to see.

Those who take the time to look closely will find that Kyoto is one of the world's most aesthetically refined cities. The reason for this is simple: in addition to being the home of Japan's imperial court for over 1000 years, Kyoto is also the home of most of Japan's major Buddhist sects and its most prestigious families. Much of Kyoto's traditional industry was geared to serving the demands of these elite groups. It is only natural, then, that the most esteemed artists and craftspeople from all over the country migrated to Kyoto. Even today, the city is home to thousands of small workshops turning out the best in Japanese traditional arts and crafts.

Essential Kyoto

- Kurama (p91)
- Nanzen-ji (p58)
- Nishiki Market (p57)
- Shōren-in (p60)
- Tetsugaku-no-Michi (p64)

From the echoes of ancient courtly speech that can still be heard in the diction of modern-day Kyoto geisha, to the manner in which even humble Kyoto citizens decorate their homes, every aspect of the city's cultural life bears the stamp of its imperial past. Of course, with such a long and proud history, it's hardly surprising that Kyotoites consider themselves something of a breed apart. Indeed, other Japanese find them frustratingly inscrutable and sometimes even arrogant. This haughty demeanour is the result of having to live for so long among different political factions – a situation that called for extreme delicacy and indirectness.

While many Kyotoites may seem a little cold to their fellow Japanese, the typical foreign visitor to the city will find them incredibly gracious and eager to please. From the kindly old gentleman who goes out of his way to show you how to get to a temple, to the gracious hospitality of the kimono-clad woman who welcomes you to your ryokan (traditional Japanese inn), visitors to the city will experience countless instances of kindness.

To visit Kyoto is to experience the best of all things Japanese. You can sample all the wonders of Japanese cuisine, drink to the early hours in a perfect little bar and then soak your cares away in some of Japan's best baths. And once you've done all that, you can lay your head to rest in an atmospheric old ryokan, the pinnacle of Japanese hospitality. All told, we are inclined to repeat what was once said about another great city: if you don't love Kyoto, you don't love life.

CHRIS' TOP KYOTO DAY

I grab a quick breakfast at my ryokan, the Yachiyo, on the southeast side of town. Then I head up to Nanzen-ji or the Tetsugaku-no-Michi (Path of Philosophy) for a contemplative stroll in the early morning light. I make my way downtown and grab some eel for lunch at Kane-yo, my favourite eel place in Kyoto. Next, I hit Teramachi-dōri to poke among the shops there, before making my way south for a leisurely pass through Nishiki Market. Following that, I head over to Maruzen bookshop. After browsing, I stop in at a nearby coffee shop for a quick pick-me-up and a read. It's then time to visit a good local *sentō* (public bath) for a soak. Clean and refreshed, I head out to meet friends for dinner, perhaps some sushi at Tomi-zushi, if there's room at the counter. After dinner we stroll along the Kamo-gawa between Shijō-dōri and Sanjō-dōri and then cross the bridge and soak up the evening ambience of Gion. Finally, we head to Tadg's Irish Pub to catch up with friends and reflect on the day.

City Life

City Life

KYOTO TODAY

The first decade of the 21st century finds Kyoto struggling to find a happy middle ground between two sometimes conflicting desires: on one hand it yearns to be a modern metropolis on a par with Tokyo; on the other, it wants to hold onto its unique cultural identity.

The past several years have witnessed major additions to the city's infrastructure. The ultra-modern Kyoto Station opened in 1997, while a new east–west line has expanded the city's modest, yet efficient, subway system. Foreign visitors will now find most major streets marked with roman-letter signs, and bus announcements are also made in English. The government has also made great efforts to make it easier for the visually and physically handicapped to navigate the city.

In spite of these accomplishments, the shrinking of the city's economic base and the high percentage of elderly citizens are drawbacks. How it will fund further development presents a serious challenge to the city's leaders.

At the same time, Kyoto's leaders have demonstrated a marked disregard for the preservation of traditional architecture, and the unfortunate results of this can be seen in an increase in the number of high-rise buildings, some of which now block views of the surrounding mountains. Where once stood rows of wooden *machiya* (traditional Kyoto townhouses), there are now coin parking lots and nondescript concrete apartment buildings. However, in spite of official indifference, what *machiya* are left have suddenly found favour with the city's visitors, and this new-found popularity may save them.

These days, not only foreigners, but Japanese flock to Kyoto in search of the essence of Japan. After having been denigrated as stodgy and stuffy, Kyoto, with its quirky customs, its odd foodstuffs, and its sometimes inscrutable dialect, is suddenly seen as exotic and alluring. Funky old Kyoto has suddenly become chic and has captured the imagination of the rest of the country, which is finally wondering if, in its rush to industrialise, it hasn't thrown out the baby with the bathwater. In brand-obsessed Japan, Kyoto is the brand of the moment. Will this go to the Old Capital's head? Probably not – Kyoto always knew it was special.

> ### Top Five Kyoto Books
>
> - **Kyoto, Seven Paths to the Heart of the City** (Diane Durston) An informative and beautifully illustrated guide to Kyoto's still unspoiled districts.
> - **Old Kyoto, A Guide to Traditional Shops, Restaurants, and Inns** (Diane Durston) Introduces Kyoto through its long-established shops known as *shinise*. A must for connoisseurs of things Kyoto.
> - **Lost Japan** (Alex Kerr) A loving and at times highly critical examination of modern Japan.
> - **A Guide to the Gardens of Kyoto** (Mark Treib and Ronald Herman) A compact and authoritative guide to Kyoto's gardens.
> - **Meeting with Japan** (Fosco Maraini) Long out of print (but a staple of used-bookshops), this classic account by an Italian Japanologist still packs a punch. The chapters on Kyoto are incredibly erudite yet never dry.

CITY CALENDAR

Kyoto, like the rest of Japan, follows the Gregorian calendar. Many traditional events, however, are based on the old lunar calendar. As in the rest of Japan, the school year starts on 1 April. This is also the time when college graduates start working and when company workers are transferred to new locations.

The Kyoto yearly cycle features a wealth of traditional events, which range from the awesome to the arcane. Many originated as Shintō rites of purification or exorcism, or as Buddhist memorial services. No matter how large or small, each event is regarded as vital to the well-being of those involved. Because of their religious underpinnings, such events tend to be characterised by decorum rather than delirium.

Two flea markets play a major role in the life of the city: nicknamed Kōbō-san, the market at Tō-ji is held on the 21st of each month, while Tenjin-san, the market at Kitano Tenmangū, takes place on the 25th of every month (for more on these markets, see p131).

Kyoto's busiest tourist seasons are early April, when the *sakura* (cherry blossoms) are in bloom, and late October and early November, when the fall colours are at their crimson best. If you're planning on coming anytime around those dates, be sure to book accommodation well in advance. Golden Week, a series of national holidays stretching from the end of April through to the first week of May, is also peak tourist time, as is O-shogatsu (New Year's).

For information on public holidays in Japan, see p186. For details on Kyoto's climate, see p182.

JANUARY

HATSU-MŌDE (FIRST SHRINE VISIT OF THE NEW YEAR)
1 January
People visit shrines to pray for health and prosperity in the New Year. Many go to Yasaka-jinja, where nō is performed in the morning, and in the afternoon 14 women dressed in Heian-period costume play a card game called *karuta*. Visitors buy lengths of rope called *okera*, which they light at fires on the shrine grounds and take home to light the kitchen fire.

HATSU EBISU
8–12 January
People flock to Ebisu-jinja to pray for prosperity (see also the listing for Hatsuka Ebisu in October on p10).

COMING OF AGE DAY
15 January
A festival for those who turned 20 during the previous year. Young women participate in an archery contest at Sanjūsangen-dō.

FEBRUARY

SETSUBUN
2–4 February
Shrines and temples hold rites to exorcise demons – an event marking the start of spring according to the lunar calendar. Setsubun festivities at Yoshida-jinja are especially lively.

BAIKA-SAI (PLUM FESTIVAL)
25 February
Geisha of the Kamishichiken district hold an outdoor tea ceremony in the Kitano Shrine precinct. The shrine's plum garden is open to the public. The event coincides with the shrine's monthly flea market.

MARCH

HINA MATSURI (DOLL FESTIVAL)
3 March
Families with young girls display dolls representing the Heian court and serve special dishes.

OHIGAN
20 or 21 March
Called *higan*, the week surrounding the vernal equinox is a time when families visit their ancestral grave and hold memorial services. During March, Tōfuku-ji, Sennyu-ji and Shinnyō-dō Temples commemorate the death of Buddha by displaying large *nehan-zu* (scrolls) that show his passing into nirvana.

APRIL

SAKURA MADNESS
Early April
During the first week of the month, people flock to Maruyama-kōen and other locations. Ostensibly they go to engage in *hanami* (cherry-blossom viewing), but activities such as sake-drinking and karaoke are not neglected.

GEISHA DANCES
Throughout April
The geisha of Gion perform Miyako Odori, the Miyagawa-chō geisha hold the Kyō Odori, and the geisha of Kamishichiken put on the Kitano Odori. For exact dates, see p123.

APRIL/MAY

GOLDEN WEEK
Late April–5 May
A series of national holidays from the end of April until 5 May means about five days off for most of the working populace.

MAY

KODOMO NO HI (CHILDREN'S DAY)
5 May

Families with male children fly carp banners and eat special sweets.

KAMOGAWA ODORI
1–24 May

Every day of the month, up to the 24th, the geisha of Pontochō hold dances for the public at the Pontochō Kaburen-jō Theatre.

AOI MATSURI
15 May

One of Kyoto's biggest festivals, the Aoi Matsuri consists of a procession of beautifully decorated oxcarts attended by some 400 people dressed in Heian-period costume. The parade leaves the Old Imperial Palace in the morning and heads north to Shimogamo-jinja, reaching the shrine around noon. It then proceeds to Kamigamo-jinja, arriving there late in the afternoon.

JUNE

TAKIGI NŌ
1–2 June

Nō is performed by firelight in the precincts of Heian-jingū.

JULY

GION MATSURI
10–17 July

Kyoto's biggest festival. On 17 July, 32 fantastically decorated floats head east from Karasuma-dōri along Shijō-dōri. At Kawaramachi-dōri the parade heads north to Oike-dōri, where it turns west. At Muromachi-dōri and Shinmachi-dōri the floats turn south and return to their various neighbourhoods.

AUGUST

TOKI MATSURI (POTTERY FESTIVAL)
7–10 August

Stalls along Gojō-dōri, from the river to Higashiyama-dōri, offer pots and porcelain. Those on the north side sell Kiyōmizu-yaki, those on the south side sell pottery made outside the city.

GOZAN OKURIBI (FIVE MOUNTAIN SEND-OFF BONFIRES)
16 August

Five bonfires in the shape of *kanji* (Chinese characters) are lit on the mountainsides surrounding the city to send the ancestral spirits that had returned to this world back to the 'other side'. An ancient folk festival that marks the end of Obon, the Buddhist Festival of the Dead.

JIZŌ-BON
23–27 August

Neighbourhoods around the city hold a festival for their stone image of bodhisattva Jizō, a deity thought to watch over children. Kids play games and eat sweets.

SEPTEMBER

OHIGAN
22 or 23 September

Called *higan*, the week surrounding the autumnal equinox is a time for families to visit their ancestral grave and hold memorial services.

OCTOBER

HATSUKA EBISU
19–21 October

A festival celebrating Ebisu, one of the Seven Gods of Good Fortune and the patron deity of merchants. Business people flock to Ebisu-jinja to buy *fukuzasa* (branches of bamboo festooned with miniature treasure ships, rice bales, gold coins and other lucky charms). Held only in Kyoto, the festival originated in the Edo

Pots, Toki Matsuri (right)

period, when Kyoto merchants returning from business trips to Edo would visit this shrine to give thanks for a successful journey.

JIDAI MATSURI & KURAMA HI MATSURI
22 October
During the day, one of Kyoto's biggest *matsuri* (festivals), the Jidai Matsuri (Festival of the Ages), takes place. Part costume show, part history lesson, the procession winds from the Old Imperial Palace to Heian-jingū. Several hundred marchers dress in exquisite costumes from the various periods of Kyoto history.

In the evening, flaming torches are paraded through the village of Kurama (p91) in one of Kyoto's most exciting festivals, the Kurama Hi Matsuri (Kurama Fire Festival). If you're in town on this day, we highly recommend making the trek to Kurama. The fun starts around dusk.

OCTOBER/NOVEMBER
KAMOGAWA ODORI
15 October–7 November
Between October and November, Pontochō geisha hold dances for the public at the Pontochō Kaburen-jō Theatre.

NOVEMBER
SPECIAL TEMPLE OPENINGS
Throughout November
Temples not normally open to the public display their gardens and treasures.

DECEMBER
KAOMISE (GRAND KABUKI)
1–26 December
The country's most famous kabuki actors put on a month-long kabuki extravaganza at the Minami-za.

KOTO-HAJIME
13 December
Geisha and *maiko* (apprentice geisha) pay formal visits to their teachers between 10am and noon. It's a good opportunity for photos, especially in Gion.

JOYA NO KANE (NEW YEAR'S EVE BELL RINGING)
31 December
Temple bells are solemnly rung 108 times at midnight to atone for the 108 evil passions to which humankind is prone.

CULTURE

Like many an old capital city, Kyoto clings to a core of values that has served it well generation after generation. The concepts described below are more or less commonly shared by all Japanese, but seem to apply especially to Kyotoites.

INTRODUCTIONS

In Kyoto, nobody gets anywhere without the proper *shokai* (introduction). This is especially true of geisha teahouses, where *'Ichi-gen-san okoto-wari'* is the unwritten rule (*'Ichi-gen-san'* means 'Mr First Sight', ie a person who walks in off the street, and *'okoto-wari'* means 'honourable refusal'). While this is usually applied to geisha teahouses and formal restaurants, it seems to hold true for other aspects of Kyoto life as well. The corollary of this is that Kyotoites tend to be quite protective of their connections.

INDIRECTNESS

In Kyoto, being vague is generally considered a virtue, while directness is thought to be the sign of a coarse and simplistic way of thinking. Living in what was a volatile political centre, Kyoto's citizens learned the art of stating their opinions as obliquely as possible so as not to offend any faction; now it's an ingrained habit. Kyotoites sometimes take this to a perverse extreme by even preferring to insult indirectly.

UNDERSTATEMENT & REFINEMENT

Kyoto is where the tea ceremony originated and its values of *wabi* and *sabi* ('spare and lonely beauty') carry over into many aspects of life. Showiness is considered vulgar. Sensitivity to detail and appreciation of subtle beauty are highly valued. Likewise, frugality is a virtue.

ENRYŌ, KI O TSUKAU & WA

Enryō, meaning a tactful sense of the need to refrain or hesitate, is a virtue that the Japanese feel they have in abundance. Kyotoites especially seem to feel they possess superior powers of *enryō*. A classic anecdote tells the story of an out-of-town guest being entertained in a Kyoto household. After a long and delicious meal, the man looks at his watch and says it's time for him to be hitting the road. 'Oh,' the housewife says, offering the traditional late-night snack of rice with tea and pickles, 'Won't you have some *ocha-zuke* before you go?' A local would realise that she's only making a pretence of being gracious and, demonstrating *enryō*, would decline. The man, however, takes the offer at face value, and sitting back down, unwittingly violates Kyoto etiquette.

Ki o tsukau, another valued trait, means to be sensitive to the needs of others and to anticipate their desires. For example, if you are going to have a party that might run late and get noisy, you might visit your neighbours beforehand and offer them a small gift. The neighbours will then go into the *enryō* mode and assure you that it's not necessary for you to *ki o tsukau* in such a fashion, but after you insist they will eventually accept. Thus, everyone has observed the proper forms of behaviour, and *wa* (harmony) reigns.

IMPORTANCE OF WORK

One's work is considered to be more important than one's family, and it is expected that one's personal life will be sacrificed accordingly. In addition, your own worth is gauged by the importance of the organisation or company to which you belong. An example of this is the pride that ordinary Kyotoites take in Kyoto University (usually abbreviated to Kyōdai). After Tokyo University, Kyōdai is rated the second most prestigious university in Japan, and the average Kyotoite, even though he or she may have no connection whatever with the institution, feels some degree of importance by virtue of its presence in town.

IDENTITY

The gap between how Kyotoites view themselves and how other Japanese view them is large and illuminating. Kyotoites view their penchant for avoiding direct expression as an admirable trait: it avoids causing offence and suggests subtle profundities. Deep down they also realise it allows them to cleverly hide their true feelings. To the more forthright Osakans and Tokyoites, however, it's an endless source of frustration, especially when conducting business.

The closed nature of Kyoto society is also frequently commented on. An old rule of thumb says that your family must be here for five generations before it is truly accepted. Indeed, Japanese from outside Kyoto who move here because of work or marriage often find it extremely hard to fit in. However, Kyoto society is sometimes likened to a *machiya*: the entrance is long and narrow, but once you're in, you're in deep. In fact, this writer has often noticed that it generally takes three visits to a Kyoto restaurant or bar before one is accepted. The initial visits form a kind of interview; if you pass then you are treated like a member of the family.

Both born-and-bred Kyotoites and those who have come here from elsewhere agree on one thing: the city is sometimes uncomfortably small. It takes two strangers only a few minutes before discovering they have a mutual friend or relative. Hence the common wisdom that if you want to do something naughty, you better go to Osaka or further afield. Trying to do something on the sly in Kyoto will only get you in trouble.

Kyoto has some complex divisions in its racial makeup. An estimated 33,000 Japanese-Koreans have made their homes here, especially in the neighbourhoods south of Kyoto Station. Many are children or grandchildren of Koreans who were brought to Japan as slave labourers following Japan's annexation of Korea in 1905. Though born and raised in Japan, these *zai-nichi-kankoku-jin* (resident Koreans) were only recently released from the obligation of carrying fingerprinted ID cards at all times. They still face severe job discrimination, especially when applying to public universities or for civil service positions. 'Prestigious' Japanese companies often refuse to hire them. Middle- and upper-middle class Kyotoites are known to hire detectives from special agencies to ensure that potential marriage partners are not of Korean heritage.

Another 'hidden' group in Kyoto is the *buraku-min*, an untouchable class whose members traditionally worked in unclean trades such as butchering, leather tanning, undertaking or sewage disposal. Many *buraku-min* reside in south Kyoto and, although their situation has vastly improved over the last 20 years, they still face conspicuous discrimination, from schools to the workplace.

LIFESTYLE

Until very recently, the seasons were the defining element in the Kyoto lifestyle. When people lived in non-air-conditioned wooden houses, for example, homes were 'summer-ised' to create a feeling of coolness. *Fusuma* (sliding doors) were taken out and replaced with indoor screens called *misu*. Rugs were rolled up and *goza* (woven mats) or rattan mats were placed over the tatami. Winter ceramics were replaced with glass dishware. Menus changed with the seasons, as did the scrolls and flower arrangements displayed in the *tokonoma* (sacred alcove).

Nowadays the average Kyoto family lives in a modern, Western-style *mansion* (condominium) with a climate-controlled environment. Only one room is likely to have tatami, and it may or may not feature a *tokonoma*.

The seasons' role in the Kyoto lifestyle is much diminished but not entirely forgotten. The city's restaurants still pay much attention to serving seasonal ingredients and the city's gourmets eagerly await the first *matsutake-gohan* (rice cooked with *matsutake* mushroom) of the fall or the first crab of winter.

Much of the mundane affairs of Kyoto daily life are administered by *chōnai* (neighbourhood associations). Each *chōnai* is subdivided into *kumi* (groups composed of four or five households). Periodically, the various *kumi* get together in a *chōnai-kai* (neighbourhood association meeting), which deals with such matters as recycling and neighbourhood festivals. In Kyoto a major responsibility of the *chōnai* is organising the neighbourhood's Jizō-bon festival in August (see p10).

The *chōnai* system encourages a stable, conformist pattern of life that suits Kyoto's generally conservative outlook.

Men, especially oldest sons, are expected to marry around the age of 30. Daughters are supposed to do so earlier. Many sons find work in Tokyo or other large cities, but it is understood that they will eventually return to Kyoto upon retirement.

ECONOMY & COSTS

Because of Kyoto's role as the historical and cultural centre of Japan, much of the city's economy is dependent on tourism. Its tourism and related retail and service industries presently employ about 65% of the workforce, down from about 70% in 1988. Due to a strong yen, the number of tourists visiting Kyoto plummeted in the middle of the last decade, but recent figures show the number of visitors is at an all-time high. Many of these visitors come from other Asian countries, which the national government has been targeting with a heavy promotional campaign.

With the construction of the enormous Kyoto International Conference Hall (p65) in the far northeastern area of the city,

How Much?

One night in a guesthouse dorm room ¥2500

One night in a basic ryokan ¥8,000

Beer in a bar ¥600

Cup of green tea in a teahouse ¥500

Bowl of rāmen ¥600

Set meal in a shokudō (standard eatery) ¥800

Sushi feast in a good restaurant ¥6000

Taxi ride across town ¥1500 to ¥2000

Newspaper ¥130

Public-bath entry ¥350

Kyoto has had some success in drawing international conventions and it continues to enthusiastically promote itself as 'Conference City Kyoto'.

Recent economic trends show that Kyoto is continuing to lose business to Osaka, especially in low-tech industries. In manufacturing, the Kyoto economy is heavily dependent on the textile and machinery industries, which account for almost half of its wholesale industry. In 2001 the gross economic product of Kyoto was estimated at ¥5.6 trillion. Per-capita income in the city was just over ¥3 million (around US$25,000).

While many of Kyoto's traditional industries such as silk-weaving, fabric-dyeing and cabinet-making have been in steady decline, several of its high-tech companies are thriving, including international camera giant Kyocera and video-game trailblazer Nintendo.

Kyoto's business and civic leaders today face a dilemma: how to keep tourism and the traditional industries as an integral part of the economy while modernising to remain competitive. Some effort is under way to preserve parts of traditional Kyoto (perhaps those most profitable to tourism), and as part of its plan to boost local infrastructure the city has invested heavily in creating world-class science facilities and joint private-public ventures, such as Kyoto Research Park, Kyoto Science City and Kansai Science City on the border of Kyoto and Nara Prefectures.

GOVERNMENT & POLITICS

The Kyoto city council is made up of 69 members elected by majority vote. Council members serve a four-year term, and elections are held every four years. Despite its post as prefectural capital, the city assembly is completely autonomous from the Kyoto prefectural assembly, which handles prefectural issues and is set up like a state government with an elected governor.

The Kyoto city assembly is dominated by the Liberal Democratic Party (LDP), the same party that has dominated Japanese national politics since the end of WWII. The conservative LDP has the support of local businesses and Kyoto's traditional power base.

Kyoto is also well known as a stronghold of the Japan Communist Party (JCP). As the second-largest party in the city council, it has the ability to check the LDP's power and initiatives. The JCP is known for its straight-talking politicians, an emphasis on social welfare programmes and a lack of scandal and corruption. These days, however, many of Kyoto's young people are switching their support to the relatively new Democratic Party of Japan (DPJ).

Voter frustration at the failure of the LDP and the JCP to halt Kyoto's economic slide resulted in a victory for independent candidate Masumoto Yorikane in the 1996 mayoral election. Promising to halt wasteful construction projects and revitalise the city's economy, the centrist Masumoto won by a narrow 0.9%. Re-elected by a more comfortable margin in 2004, Masumoto is now focussing his energies on improving the city's educational system (he used to be head of the Kyoto Board of Education).

ENVIRONMENT

Landlocked and surrounded by mountains to the north, east and west, the city of Kyoto sits in the southeast of Kyoto-fu (Kyoto Prefecture) at 135° east longitude and 35° north latitude. About 370km west of Tokyo and 45km northeast of Osaka, present-day Kyoto occupies what was once a massive lake bed. When the city was first established it occupied just 30 sq km, but over the centuries it has spread outward, incorporating several surrounding towns and villages. Today Kyoto-shi (Kyoto City) covers more than 600 sq km and is divided into 11 wards, extending some 50km north to south and 25km east to west.

The mountains that surround the city are the Kitayama (Northern Mountains), the Higashiyama (Eastern Mountains) and the Arashiyama (Stormy Mountains). Only the city's south side is free of mountains and is consequently one of the most heavily developed areas. Kyoto basin itself is relatively flat, with only a few hills cropping up here and there.

Kyoto has two major rivers flowing north to south: the Kamo-gawa and Katsura-gawa. Traditionally these rivers and their tributaries played a crucial role in the lives of the people, both as a means of transportation and as a vital source of water for drinking and irrigation. The purity of the water was highly praised for the production of Fushimi sake and also for use in traditional fabric-dyeing. In times of heavy rains, however, the rivers frequently wreaked havoc when major floods struck the city. Today, the problem has been solved primarily by concrete reinforcement of the river banks and improved drainage.

Arts & Architecture

Arts & Architecture

Invariably described as Japan's cultural heart and soul, Kyoto is justly famous for keeping alive the flame of Japanese tradition. However, the city also boasts a long history of eagerly embracing the new, the exotic and the experimental. Cases in point are the Persian carpets and Flemish tapestries that decorate the Gion Matsuri floats. Kyoto's savvy silk merchants managed to obtain these Silk Road products even after the Tokugawa Shōgunate clamped its lid on the country in the mid-17th century. When the Meiji Restoration of 1868 once again opened Japan to the world, Kyoto's culturally astute citizens quickly demonstrated as much enthusiasm for European classical music and painting as they did for Western science and technology.

The present moment finds Kyoto, along with the rest of Japan, showing a renewed interest in the arts and crafts of its Asian neighbours. Kyotoites' taste in art continues to follow an eclectic path. The current artistic scene shows a new willingness to combine elements heretofore considered incompatible. In one of the city-sponsored art festivals, for instance, a Brahms quintet might take place on the nō stage of a Shintō shrine, or an Edo-period Buddhist temple might host a performance of *butō* (a form of Japanese modern dance). Likewise, the Kyoto Art Center, a city-sponsored project, has turned an unused elementary school (several of Kyoto's central elementary schools have closed due to a lack of students) into a centre for the performing and visual arts. Built in 1931, this structure now hosts a variety of artistic offerings, from kabuki lecture demonstrations to installations by foreign artists.

Meanwhile, on the architectural front, *machiya* (traditional Kyoto townhouses) are enjoying a comeback. On the verge of extinction, these venerable structures, which for centuries defined the lifestyle of the city's inhabitants, have been given a new lease of life in the guise of boutiques and restaurants. For more on *machiya*, see the boxed text on p25.

Unfortunately, most of Kyoto's craft traditions are in crisis. The silk-weaving industry, which for centuries supported the city's economy and gave work to countless artisans, is in decline as fewer and fewer Japanese wear kimono. In fact, all crafts tied to the traditional Japanese lifestyle are in similar danger of disappearing.

Whatever the future holds, the legacy of Kyoto's glorious past – its temples, shrines and gardens – will remain to delight the visitor. And, in spite of *pachinko* parlours, parking lots and other forms of urban ugliness, such things as the maple leaf garnish on your lunch-set tofu or the Nishijin-obi (decorative belt) of your waitress' kimono prove that an artistic sensibility shaped by 1,200 years of tradition is still alive.

PERFORMING ARTS

Nō and kabuki, Japan's best-known theatrical traditions, can both be viewed in Kyoto. The city is home to several schools of nō and performances are frequent. Kyōgen, an offspring of nō, is well represented in Kyoto by the Shigeyama family. Performances of kabuki, however, are rather infrequent, as the city does not have a resident troupe. Unless your visit coincides with *kaomise*, the annual year-end kabuki extravaganza, Osaka's Shochikuza theatre might be the only place in Kansai to catch this spectacular drama.

NŌ

Nō seems to have originated from the happy combination of indigenous Shintō-related dance and mime traditions, and dance forms that originated elsewhere in Asia. It owes its form and repertory to the artistic dynasty of Kannami Kiyotsugu, which flourished in Kyoto between 1350 and 1450. Rather than a drama in the usual sense, a nō play seeks to express a poetic moment by symbolic and almost abstract means. The actors wear masks and perform before an unchanging set design, which features a painting of a large pine tree. The elegant language used is that of Kyoto's 14th-century court. Obviously, nō's rather esoteric qualities make having some previous understanding of the play to be performed especially helpful. An exception to this might be the open-air Takigi Nō, performed in the precincts of Heian-jingū (p59) on the evenings of 1 and 2 June. Here, the play of firelight on brocade costumes will captivate even the most untutored viewer.

KYŌGEN

Designed to provide comic relief during a programme of nō plays, kyōgen is farce that takes the spectator from the sublime realm of nō into the ridiculous world of the everyday. Using the colloquial language of the time, kyōgen pokes fun at such subjects as samurai, depraved priests and faithless women. Masks are not worn and costumes tend to feature bold, colourful patterns.

The recent years have witnessed a boom in kyōgen's popularity, largely thanks to the influence of the mass media and the appearance of a new generation of photogenic young actors. In Kyoto the Shigeyama family is the foremost practitioner of the art. To see kyōgen in its original folk-art form, try to catch a performance of Mibu Kyōgen. These mimed Buddhist morality plays are today performed at Mibu-dera (p78) just as they were in Kyoto's early medieval period.

KABUKI

While nō was patronised by the Ashikaga shōguns who created Ginkaku-ji and Kinkaku-ji, kabuki, which developed much later, was a plebeian form of entertainment supported by the merchant class that came to prominence during the long and peaceful Edo period. It is as vibrant and brash as the former is austere and refined.

Kabuki evolved mainly in Edo (present-day Tokyo), but Kyoto played a big part in its beginnings. It was here, around 1600, that an Izumo shrine priestess called Okuni and her troupe of dancers started entertaining crowds on the banks of the Kamo-gawa with a new type of dance that people dubbed 'kabuki', a slang expression that meant 'cool' or 'in vogue'. Okuni was the Madonna of her day and knew how to please a crowd. At a time when 'Southern Barbarian' (ie European) fashion was all the rage, she is reported to have sometimes danced in Portuguese garb with a crucifix around her neck.

Okuni's dancers were not above prostituting their talents, and when fights for the ladies' affections became a bit too frequent, the order-obsessed Tokugawa officials declared the entertainment a threat to public morality. When women's kabuki was banned, troupes of adolescent men with unshorn forelocks took it over, a development that only fed the flames of samurai ardour. Finally, in 1653, the authorities mandated that only adult men with shorn forelocks could perform kabuki, which gave rise to one of kabuki's most fascinating and artistic elements, the *onnagata* (an actor who specialises in portraying women).

Ingenious features of kabuki include the revolving stage (a kabuki invention), the *hanamichi* (a raised walkway connecting the stage to the back of the theatre, which is used for dramatic entrances and exits), *koken* (on-stage assistants) and *hiki-nuki* (on-stage costume changes).

Unlike Western theatre, kabuki is an actor-centred, actor-driven drama. It is essentially the preserve of a small number of acting families, and the Japanese audience takes great enjoyment in watching how different generations of one family perform the same part.

A kabuki programme generally lasts five hours and is made up of sections of four or five different works. One of the pieces is often a dance-drama. Only the most diehard fans sit through an entire programme. Many spectators slip out to enjoy a *bentō* (boxed lunch or dinner) or a cigarette, returning to their seats to catch the scenes they like best.

Kyoto boasted seven kabuki theatres in the Edo period. Now only one, the Minami-za (p122), remains. Completely renovated in 1990, it stands just east of Shijō-Ōhashi, the same site it occupied back in 1615. Every December (and sometimes also November) it hosts *kaomise*, during which Tokyo's most famous kabuki actors come to Kyoto to show *(mise)* their faces *(kao)*. Kyoto's newest kabuki showcase is located on the campus of Kyoto Zokei Daigaku. This state-of-the-art theatre was built mainly to showcase the talents of the school's professor, famous kabuki actor and innovator, Ichikawa Ennosuke, and his troupe.

A statue of Okuni, fan in hand and a samurai sword slung over one shoulder, stands at the east end of Shijō-Ōhashi, diagonally across from the Minami-za.

TEA CEREMONY

As much a philosophy as an art, *sadō*, or The Way of Tea, requires familiarity with a host of related arts and crafts: ceramics, kimono, calligraphy, flower arrangement, food and cooking, traditional architecture, garden design and incense, just to name a few. No wonder a tea-ceremony license has always been considered a desirable quality in a prospective Kyoto bride.

Originally the pastime of samurai and Zen priests, *sadō* placed great emphasis on the aesthetic qualities of simplicity and naturalness. Tea master Sen no Rikyū codified the practice in the Momoyama period, and three of his descendants established schools based on his precepts. In today's Kyoto their three schools – Urasenke, Omotesenke and Mushanokojisenke reign supreme. Of the three, Urasenke has been especially successful at spreading the gospel of tea around the world. The Zen temple complex of Daitoku-ji has been closely connected with the tea world ever since the days of Sen no Rikyū.

FLOWER ARRANGEMENT

In Kyoto, the foremost school of flower arrangement (ikebana) is Ikenobo, whose sumptuous headquarters stand on Karasuma-dōri, just north of Rokkaku-dōri, and which hosts exhibitions several times a year. Ikenobo has branches all over Japan, as well as in many countries around the world. Many other schools of ikebana exist as well, and the popularity of this art form is evident in the eye-pleasing creations that are found in the city's shop windows and the *tokonoma* (sacred alcoves) of its private residences. A recent trend, hopefully a short-lived one, combines plastic and other shiny artificial objects with natural materials.

PAINTING

Until WWII the history of painting in Kyoto was essentially the history of painting in Japan. By the end of the Heian period the emphasis on religious themes painted according to Chinese conventions gave way to a purely Japanese style, known as *yamato-e*. During the Muromachi period the Chinese influence returned, as monochrome ink paintings by Sung-dynasty artists were imported and avidly copied by Japanese artists. Shokoku-ji, one of Kyoto's main Zen temples, became the centre of this artistic activity, which gave rise to the great landscape painters Sesshū, Shūbun, Sesson and Motonobu.

The short-lived but brilliant Momoyama period heralded the arrival of the Great Decorators such as Kanō Eitoku and other artists who adorned the castles and palaces of their *daimyō* patrons. Hasegawa Tōhaku tried to combine boldness of design with a sensibility reminiscent of Sesshū.

The 250 years of the ensuing Edo period witnessed a wide range of competing styles, some of which were influenced by European painting that had been introduced in the 16th century by the Jesuits. The Kanō school became the official favourite of the Tokugawa Shōgunate for its depiction of Confucian subjects, while the Tosa school, whose members followed the *yamato-e* style, were commissioned by the nobility to paint scenes from the classics of Japanese literature.

A rival school, the Sōtatsu, or Rimpa school, clung to native Japanese tradition and produced a strikingly original decorative style. The works produced by Tawaraya Sōtatsu, Honami Kōetsu and Ogata Kōrin from this school rank among the finest of the period.

While the Kanō and ukiyo-e (wood-block print) schools flourished in Edo, a style of painting called *bunjin-ga*, or 'gentlemen's painting', was popular in Kyoto. Strongly influ-

Top Five Kyoto Museums

- Kyoto National Museum (p63)
- National Museum of Modern Art (p59)
- Kyoto Municipal Museum of Art (p59)
- Kawai Kanjirō Memorial Hall (p62)
- Fureai-kan Kyoto Museum of Traditional Crafts (p60)

enced by Chinese art and ideals, these *bunjin-ga*, or *nanga*, painters considered calligraphy equally as important as painting. Ike no Taiga and Yosa Buson are this movement's most representative artists.

Another painter, Maruyama Ōkyo, combined Western perspective and Ming realism with decorative Japanese painting to become one of the most influential artists of the time. His follower, Goshun, went on to found the Shijō school.

The Meiji era ushered in a golden age of Kyoto painting. Meji artist Takeuchi Seiho and other members of the Kyoto school of Japanese-style artists united Maruyama and Shijō traditions with Western-style oil painting. In the Taisho era (1911–26), Tsuchida Bakusen, Chikkyo Ono and others sought to make *nihonga* a modern art movement. (*Nihonga* is a unique Japanese painting technique that relies on a fresco-like layering of mineral pigments.) The creations of this innovative period can be viewed at Kyoto's National Museum of Modern Art (p59).

CRAFTS

Kyoto's crafts were created to please a demanding clientele that at one time or another in the city's history has included Buddhist clergy, the imperial court and nobility, samurai, tea masters and other practitioners of the traditional arts, and merchants. Not surprisingly, they attained a level of refinement rarely seen in other parts of Japan, so much so that today a craft object labelled with the prefix *kyō* (eg *kyō-yūzen* – Kyoto dyed silk, *kyō-ningyo* – Kyoto dolls) is synonymous with excellence. As a result, craftspeople here are held in high esteem and many of their creations are considered to be fine art. The high level of contemporary Kyoto crafts can be verified at the Museum of Kyoto (p57). The Kyoto Handicraft Center (p129) is also a good place to view craft items. The crafts mentioned below can be found in speciality shops throughout the city. Department stores are also dependable outlets. For information on where to see craftspeople at work or take courses in traditional crafts, see p182.

KIMONO TEXTILES

The end product of many steps involving the hands of a number of different artisans, the Kyoto kimono is one of Japan's most elegant craft items. However, the product's labour-intensive nature, as well as Kyoto's complex, many-tiered distribution system have conspired to make it an expensive item at a time of falling demand. During the post-war years, Japanese women gradually stopped wearing kimono, but by the time Kyoto's hidebound and complacent kimono merchants noticed, Nishijin, the city's silk-weaving and dyeing district – long a driving force of the Kyoto economy – was in deep trouble. The bursting of Japan's asset-inflated economy in the late 1980s accelerated the area's decline, and one after another the city's kimono wholesalers went belly up.

The kimono will no doubt survive, but perhaps only as formal wear – something to be worn at wedding receptions and other important events. Unfortunately, such high-end kimono represent only a small fragment of what was once a fabulous assortment of styles and designs. In addition, more and more of Kyoto's kimono-makers have been farming out steps of the dyeing or weaving process to Chinese factories in order to cut costs.

On the bright side, young Japanese have recently been demonstrating a new interest in their native costume. To encourage this trend, some of the city's taxicab companies and restaurants offer discounts to kimono-clad customers. It remains to be seen what effect, if any, this trend will have on the fortunes of Nishijin.

Kyō-yūzen, a silk-dyeing technique perfected by the 17th-century fan painter Miyazaki Yūzen, is one of Kyoto's most important contributions to the art of the kimono. This elaborate and ingenious technique was devised to circumvent the sumptuary laws imposed on the merchant class, members of which were prohibited from wearing embroidered brocades.

Utilising brightly coloured dyes, *kyō-yūzen* typically features simple circular flower designs *(maru-tsukushi)*, and bird and landscape motifs. By means of a technique demanding great brushwork skill, designs are hand-traced on to the silk, after which rice paste is applied like a stencil in order to prevent colours from bleeding into other areas of the fabric. By

Kimono textiles

repeatedly changing the pattern of the rice paste, very complex and painterly designs can be achieved.

Kyoto is also famed for such techniques as stencil-dyeing *(kyō-komon)* and tie-dyeing *(kyō-kanoko shibori)*, although the latter, a notoriously time-consuming process, is now largely performed in China and other Asian countries where labour is cheaper.

Woven textile for kimono generally goes by the name Nishijin-ori, named after the district where weavers established a community on the ruins left behind by the disastrous Onin War (1467–77). Kyoto's first woven textiles were developed to satisfy the tastes of the nobility. Over time Nishijin's weavers expanded their techniques and began to experiment with materials such as gauze, brocade, damask, satin and crepe to satisfy a variety of clients.

The best-known Nishijin product is the exquisite *tsuzure*, a tightly woven tapestry cloth produced with a hand loom *(tebata)*, on which detailed patterns are preset. Kyoto's weavers, however, have continually introduced new styles, such as Japanese brocade *nishiki* (woven on Jacquard looms first imported from France around 1900). Today, computers are used to create new designs and to pilot automated looms.

Orinasu-kan (p76), established in 1915, is a textile museum that exhibits fine Nishijin silk fabrics and embroidery. Nishijin Textile Center (p75) stocks a wide selection of Nishijin products at reasonable prices.

POTTERY & CERAMICS

Pottery, a highly esteemed craft in Japan, is especially revered in Kyoto, where tea bowls are the most coveted of *chadō-gu* (tea-ceremony utensils). In addition, Kyoto's culinary traditions, especially its banquet-style *haute cuisine* known as *kaiseki*, place great emphasis on tableware, and even in restaurants serving *obanzai* (Kyoto home-style fare), dishes of every size and shape are carefully chosen to complement the food put in them. This is a city where ceramic art plays an active part in everyday life, and where a knowledge of pottery traditions is the mark of a cultivated person.

The first Kyoto wares *(kyō-yaki)* date to the early 8th century, the reign of Emperor Shōmu. By the mid-1600s there were more than 10 different kilns active in and around the city. Of these, only Kiyomizu-yaki remains today. Potter Nonomura Ninsei (1596–1660), who developed an innovative method of applying enamel overglaze to porcelain, was largely responsible for this kiln's rise to prominence. The technique he developed was further refined by the addition of other decorative features.

Kiyomizu-yaki is still actively produced, and examples of this colourful, highly decorative porcelain can be found in many of Kyoto's tea-ceremony rooms, restaurants and private kitchens. To comply with air-pollution regulations, the kilns relocated to Yamashina Ward many years ago, but their products are still sold in the many shops lining the roads leading up to Kiyomizu-dera. Every summer, just prior to the Bon holiday (a Buddhist festival in which people honour the souls of their departed ancestors), a lively pottery festival is held here, and pottery stalls line both sides of Gojō-dōri, from Kamo-gawa east to Higashiyama-dōri.

Kyoto is also the home of *raku-yaki*, a type of tea-ceremony ware that originated in the Momoyama period when Toyotomi Hideyoshi encouraged master potter Chōjiro to create tea bowls from clay found near his palace. His creations, which he stamped with the character *raku* (enjoyment), soon became prized possessions, examples of which are on display at the intimate Raku Museum.

A must-see museum for Japanese-pottery lovers is the home of Kawai Kanjirō (p62), a potter who was one of the leaders of the *mingei* folk-art revival. The museum houses the climbing kiln *(noborigama)*, which he used to fire his pieces.

Takashimaya and Daimaru department stores regularly hold exhibitions of ceramics.

OTHER CRAFTS

Lacquerware *(shikki* or *nurimono)* is made using the sap of the lacquer tree. In the better pieces, multiple layers of lacquer are painstakingly applied to a wood surface, left to dry, and finally polished to a luxurious shine. *Kyō-shikki* (Kyoto lacquerware) is highly regarded for its elegance and sound construction. A decorative lacquer technique called *maki-e* involves the sprinkling of silver and gold powders on to liquid lacquer to form a picture. After the lacquer dries, another coat seals the picture. The final effect is often dazzling. Kodai-ji, the Momoyama-period temple mausoleum of Hideyoshi's widow, Ne-Ne, is especially famous for its *maki-e* decoration.

Kyō-sashimono (Kyoto wood products) are among the best in the country. Woodworkers use superior woods, such as cedar *(sugi)*, cherry *(sakura)*, zelkova *(keyaki)*, mulberry *(kuwa)* and paulownia *(kiri)*. Once a variety of wood types has been carefully chosen, preparations to properly season them can take up to 10 years. Many types of finishes, including oils, wax, lacquer and persimmon tanin, are employed. Other famous Kyoto wood products include *sadō-sashimono* (tearoom fittings and tea-ceremony utensils). High-quality wooden trays, shelves and delicately shaped water containers play an important role in the tea ceremony.

Bamboo crafts *(take-seihin)*, especially tea-ceremony ladles and whisks, and bamboo baskets, are another speciality of Kyoto. Remarkable for their complexity and delicacy, baskets are used in flower arrangements during the warm-weather months. Much bamboo was transported from neighbouring Shiga Prefecture into the Old Capital along the old Tōkkaidō highway, which terminated at Sanjō-Ōhashi. Even today several bamboo speciality shops ply their trade just east of the bridge.

You can admire *kyō-ningyō*, Kyoto's refined dolls, but don't try to play with them. Kyoto dolls, noted for their detailed workmanship and fine brocade costumes, are not toys. Other well-known doll types include chubby plaster babies called *gosho-ningyō* and *ishō-ningyō*, elaborately costumed dolls often based on kabuki characters.

Folding fans *(sensu)* are still a practical and fashionable way of dealing with Kyoto's sweltering summers, and both men and women carry them. Several shops in Kyoto specialise in the large, elaborate types used in nō drama and classical dance. The meticulous, step-by-step process of making *kyō-sensu* is fascinating to watch and can be observed at one of the Kyoto fan-making studios open to the public.

Washi (traditional Japanese handmade paper) was introduced from China in the 5th century. By the Heian era, Kyoto's aristocrats were using it for their poetry and diaries. The introduction of Western paper in the 1870s caused the number of families involved in the craft to plummet. However, *washi* has enjoyed a revival, and a fine selection is available in several speciality stores.

Incense, which Heian nobles used to perfume their robes and Buddhist priests to accompany their sutras, is another of Kyoto's specialities. The city's incense shops carry both varieties for the family altar, as well as types to be burned for simple enjoyment, in stick, coil, cone and pellet form.

LITERATURE

Japan's first real literature, the *Kojiki* (Record of Ancient Matters) and *Nihon Shoki* (Chronicle of Japan), were written in the 8th century in emulation of Chinese historical accounts. Later, Japanese literature developed its own voice, when male members of the court, preoccupied with copying Chinese styles and texts, left the more humble *hiragana* (Japanese script) to their female counterparts. Thus it was that the ladies ended up producing Japan's first truly Japanese literature. Chief among these female authors is Murasaki Shikibu, a minor lady-in-waiting who wrote *Genji Monogatari* (The Tale of Genji). Sei Shonagan's catty *Pillow Book* offers another fascinating glimpse into the world of the Heian court.

Heike Monogatari (The Tale of the Heike) relates the saga of the destruction of the Taira clan by the Genji clan at the end of the 12th century. Possibly set down in the early 13th century, the tale was transmitted orally by blind, mendicant monks who accompanied themselves on the *biwa* (Japanese lute). By turns heroic and heartbreaking, the episodes illustrate the Buddhist teaching that all is suffering and illusion.

Kenkō, a Buddhist priest and court poet composed his *Tsurezuregusa* (Essays in Idleness) sometime around 1331. Like Emily Dickinson, Kenkō left his pithy observations on scraps of paper – only his were pasted to the walls of his cottage somewhere in Kyoto's Yoshida district. Mentioning two of Kyoto's burial and cremation places, he wrote: 'If man were never to fade away like the dews of Adashino, never to vanish like the smoke over Toribeyama, but lingered on forever in the world, how things would lose their power to move us!' (Donald Keene, trans.). In other words, cherry blossoms are beautiful because they fall.

In 1691 haiku master Bashō Matsuo, author of *The Narrow Road to the Deep North*, composed his *Saga Diary* at Rakushisha (House of the Fallen Persimmons; p81), which still stands in Kyoto's Sagano district. In the 18th century Kyoto was home to Yosa Buson, one of Japan's most famous haiku poets and literati painters.

Twentieth-century author Tanizaki Junichirō spent approximately seven years in Kyoto in a house near Shimogamo-jinja. He produced only one work here, a novella titled *Yume no Ukihashi* (The Bridge of Dreams). Apparently Tanizaki couldn't stand Kyoto's hot summers and freezing winters and spent those seasons at the hot springs resort of Atami.

Only one of Nobel Prize winner Kawabata Yasunari's novels, *Koto* (The Old Capital), is set in Kyoto. One of its female protagonists tries to be respectable and free at the same time, 'a combination which never works' according to Donald Richie in his review of the movie version (*The Japanese Movie*, Kodansha International, 1966).

Mishima Yukio, author of *The Temple of the Golden Pavilion*, is probably the most controversial of Japan's modern writers and is considered unrepresentative of Japanese culture by many Japanese.

Top Five Kyoto Novels

- **The Tale of Genji** (Murasaki Shikibu) A detailed, highly poetic chronicle of Heian court life centred on the life and loves of Prince Genji. Considered the world's first novel and regarded as the greatest single work in Japanese literature, it continues to inspire romantic novels and TV dramas.
- **The Old Capital** (Kawabata Yasunari) One of the three works that garnered Kawabata the 1968 Nobel Prize in Literature.
- **The Temple of the Golden Pavilion** (Mishima Yukio) A novel depicting the true story of a troubled young Buddhist priest who burns down Kinkaku-ji, Kyoto's prized Golden Pavilion.
- **Memoirs of a Geisha** (Arthur Golden) The bestselling debut novel about the world of the geisha will be released as a movie.
- **The Tale of Murasaki** (Liza Dalby) Dalby's historical novel takes up where Lady Murasaki left off. Dalby is an anthropologist specialising in Japanese culture and the only Westerner to have become a geisha.

CINEMA & TV

Motion pictures came to Japan in 1896, and, by 1899, the Japanese were making their own. In the early 1900s, Kyoto became the centre of Japan's motion-picture industry. Dubbed Japan's Hollywood, the city at one time boasted 15 movie studios. In the 1920s swashbuckling samurai films *(chanbara)* became an enduring staple of Japanese cinema. After WWII, however, such feudalistic films were banned by the Allied authorities, and motion-picture companies turned to making animated films, monster movies and comedies.

The 1950s were a golden age of Japanese cinema. Kurosawa Akira's *Rashōmon* (1950) took top prize at the 1951 Venice Film Festival. This was followed by such Kurosawa classics

Four Classic Kyoto Films

Conflagration (1958) Based on Mishima Yukio's novel depicting the true story of a troubled young Buddhist priest who burns down Kinkaku-ji, Kyoto's prized Golden Pavilion.

Late Spring (1949) A young woman refuses to get married and leave her widowed father. Finally, she relents, and father and daughter go to Kyoto for a final farewell. This film defines Ozu Yasujiro's interpretation of what it means to be truly Japanese.

Sisters of Gion (1936) A landmark of realism in Japanese cinema, this is a tale of a geisha who initiates her sister into the 'floating world' of Gion. The only time Mizoguchi Kenji was awarded Japan's prize for Best Film.

Sisters of Nishijin (1952) A family of Kyoto silk-weavers cannot adapt to industrialisation; the father-patriarch kills himself, and his widow, daughter and assistants try to carry on. Directed by Yoshimura Kozaburō.

as *Shichinin-no-Samurai* (Seven Samurai, 1954); *Yōjimbō* (1961), the tale of a masterless samurai who single-handedly cleans up a small town bedevilled by two warring gangs; and *Ran* (1985), an epic historical film.

In the 1970s and '80s, Japanese cinema went into a decline, partly due to the overwhelming strength of international movie-making, and partly due to a failure to develop new independent film-making companies. Now only two movie companies, Shochiku and Toho, continue to do business in Kyoto.

Movie scenes and TV shows are occasionally shot at Kyoto's Tōei Uzumasa Movie Village (p84), now also a popular theme park, and the city is frequently used as a location for both period and contemporary films.

TV dramas set in Kyoto generally portray the city and its inhabitants in stereotypical fashion. A typical whodunit might open with a beautiful kimono-clad geisha found murdered on the banks of the Kamo-gawa. Many of the characters in these nationally aired programmes are played by Tokyo actors and actresses, whose attempt at Kyoto dialect is not always convincing.

ARCHITECTURE
RELIGIOUS ARCHITECTURE
Temples

Temples *(tera* or *ji)* vary widely in their construction, depending on the type of school and historical era of construction. From the introduction of Buddhism in the 6th century until the Middle Ages, temples were the most important architectural works in Japan, and hence exerted a strong stylistic influence on all other types of building.

There were three main styles of early temple architecture: *tenjikuyō* (Indian), *karayō* (Chinese) and *wayō* (Japanese). All three styles were in fact introduced to Japan via China. *Wayō* arrived in the 7th century and gradually acquired local character, becoming the basis of much Japanese wooden architecture. It was named so as to distinguish it from *karayō* (also known as Zen style), which arrived in the 12th century. A mixture of *wayō* and *karayō* known as *setchuyō* eventually came to dominate, and *tenjikuyō* disappeared altogether.

With their origins in Chinese architecture and emphasis on other-worldly perfection, early temples were monumental and symmetrical in layout. A good example of the Chinese influence can be seen in the famous Phoenix Hall (p89), a Tang-style pavilion at Byōdō-in.

The Japanese affinity for asymmetry eventually affected temple design, leading to the more organic – although equally controlled – planning of later temple complexes. An excellent example in Kyoto is Daitoku-ji (p76), a Rinzai Zen monastery, which is a large complex containing a myriad of subtemples and gardens.

Temples generally have four gates, oriented to the north, south, east and west. The *nandai-mon* is the southern gate, and usually the largest one. There is also a central gate, *chū-mon*, which is sometimes incorporated into the cloister. The *niō-mon* (guardian gate) houses frightful-looking statues of gods such as Raijin (the god of thunder) and Fū-jin (the god of wind).

The *gojū-no-tō*, or five-storey pagoda, is a major component of temple design. These are elegant wooden towers, symbolising Shaka, the Buddha. Their design is a variation of the Indian stupa, a structure originally intended to hold the remains of Shaka (sometimes with an actual tooth or chip of bone, more often represented by crystal or amber). The spire on top usually has nine tiers, representing the nine spheres of heaven.

Kyoto contains a number of excellent examples of five-storey pagodas. The pagoda at Tō-ji (p79) is the best known and the tallest in Japan. Other impressive pagodas are those at Daigo-ji (p87) and Kiyomizu-dera (p61).

Shrines

Shrines can be called *jinja*, *jingū*, *gū* or *taisha*. The original Shintō shrine is Izumo Taisha in Shimane Prefecture, which has the largest shrine hall in Japan. It is said to have been modelled on the Emperor's residence, and its style, known as *taisha-zukuri*, was extremely influential on later shrine design. Shrines tend to use simple, unadorned wood construction and are built raised above the ground on posts. The roof is gabled, not hipped as with temple architecture. The entrance is generally from the end, not the side, again distinguishing it from temple design. The distinctive roof line of shrine architecture is due to an elaboration of the structural elements of the roof. The crisscross elements are called *chigi* and the horizontal elements are called *katsuogi*.

As Buddhism increased its influence over Shintō, it also affected the architecture. The clean lines of the early shrines were replaced with curving eaves and other ornamental details. Worshippers were provided with shelter by extending the roof or even building a separate worship hall. This led to the *nagare* style, the most common type of shrine architecture. Excellent examples in Kyoto can be found at Shimogamo-jinja (p64) and Kamigamo-jinja (p75).

Torii in front of Heian-jingū (p59)

Machiya: Kyoto's Traditional Townhouse

One of the city's most notable architectural features is its *machiya*, which are long and narrow wooden row houses that functioned as both homes and workplaces. The shop area was located in the front of the house, while the rooms lined up behind it formed the family's private living quarters. Nicknamed *'unagi no nedoko'* (eel bedrooms), the *machiya*'s elongated shape came about because homes were once taxed according to the amount of their street frontage.

A *machiya* is a self-contained world, complete with private well, store house, Buddhist altar, clay ovens outfitted with huge iron rice cauldrons, shrines for the hearth god and other deities, and interior minigardens.

Although well suited to Kyoto's humid, mildew-prone summers, a wooden *machiya* has a limited lifespan of about 50 years. Thus, as the cost of traditional materials and workmanship rose, and as people's desire for a more Western-style lifestyle increased, fewer and fewer people felt the urge to rebuild the old family home, as had been the custom in the past. Those considerations, plus the city's high inheritance tax, convinced many owners to tear down their *machiya*, build a seven-story apartment building, occupy the ground floor, and live off the rent of their tenants.

The result is that Kyoto's urban landscape – once a harmonious sea of clay-tiled two-story wooden townhouses – is now a mish-mash of ferro-concrete offices and apartment buildings.

Ironically, however, *machiya* are making a comeback. After their numbers have drastically declined, the old townhouses have began to acquire an almost exotic appeal. Astute developers began to rehab them, converting them into restaurants, clothing boutiques, even hair salons. Today, such shops are a major draw for the city's tourist trade, and not only foreign visitors, but the Japanese themselves (especially Tokyoites), love their old-fashioned charm.

As for Kyotoites, their reaction is mixed. A friend born and raised here had this to say about the *machiya*-restaurant experience: 'I just feel like I'm in one of my childhood friend's houses,' he said. 'What's the big deal?'

The *gongen* style uses a H-shaped plan, connecting two halls with an intersecting gabled roof and hallway called an *ishi no ma*. This element symbolises the connection between the divine and the ordinary worlds. The best example of this style in Kyoto is at Kitano Tenman-gū (p76).

At the entrance to the shrine is the torii (gateway), which marks the boundary of the sacred precinct. The most dominant torii in Kyoto is in front of Heian-jingū (p59). It's a massive concrete structure located a considerable distance south of the shrine. Fushimi-Inari-taisha (p86) in southern Kyoto has thousands of bright vermilion gates lining paths up the mountain to the shrine itself.

GARDENS

Many of Japan's most famous gardens are to be found in Kyoto, and no trip here would be complete without a visit to at least a few of them. Most of the well-known ones, whose characteristics are described below, are connected to temples or imperial villas. In addition to these, Kyoto's traditional dwellings and shops feature another type of garden called *tsubo-niwa*, which are tiny inner gardens that bring light into the building and provide its inhabitants with a sense of the seasons.

Japanese gardens fall into four basic types: *funa asobi* (pleasure boat), *shūyū* (stroll), *kanshō* (contemplative) and *kaiyū* (varied pleasures).

Popular in the Heian period, *funa asobi* gardens featured a large pond used for pleasure boating. Such gardens were often built around noble mansions. The garden which surrounds Byōdō-in (p89) in Uji is a vestige of this style of garden.

The *shūyū* garden is intended to be viewed from a winding path, allowing the garden to unfold and reveal itself in stages and from different vantages. Popular during the Heian, Kamakura and Muromachi periods, *shūyū* gardens can be found around many noble mansions and temples from those eras. A celebrated example is the garden of Ginkaku-ji (p64).

The *kanshō* garden is intended to be viewed from one spot. Zen rock gardens, also known as *karesansui* gardens, are an example of this type, which were designed to aid contemplation. Ryōan-ji (p83) is perhaps the most famous example of this type of garden. Although various interpretations of the garden have been put forth (eg the rocks 'represent a tiger and her cubs'), the garden's ultimate meaning, like that of Zen itself, cannot be expressed in words.

The *kaiyū* garden features many small gardens with one or more teahouses surrounding a central pond. Like the *shūyū* garden, it is meant to be explored on foot and provides the viewer with a variety of changing scenes, many with literary allusions. The imperial villa of Katsura Rikyū (p85) is a classic example of this type of garden.

Japanese gardens make use of various ingenious devices to achieve their effect. *Shakkei*, or 'borrowed scenery', is one such clever design ploy, by which a distant object, such as a mountain or volcano cone, is incorporated into the garden's design, adding depth and impact. Kyoto's garden designers obviously never anticipated urban sprawl. If plans for a high-rise apartment building go through, the view from Entsū-ji's (p82) famous *shakkei* garden will feature more than Mt Hiei.

Food & Drink

Food & Drink

Those familiar with *nihon ryōri* (Japanese cuisine) know that eating is half the fun of being in Japan. Even if you've already tried some of Japan's better-known specialities in restaurants in your own country, you're likely to be surprised by how delicious the original is when served on its home turf. More importantly, the adventurous eater will be delighted to find that Japanese food is far more than just sushi, tempura or sukiyaki. Indeed, it is possible to spend a month here and sample a different speciality restaurant every night.

This variety is fairly new to Japan. Until the beginning of the 20th century, Japanese food was spartan at best (at least among the farming masses) and the typical meal consisted of a bowl of rice, some miso soup, a few pickled vegetables and, if one was lucky, some preserved fish. As a Buddhist nation, meat was not eaten until the Meiji Restoration of 1868. Even then, it took some getting used to: early accounts of Japan's first foreign residents are rife with horrified stories of the grotesque dietary practices of 'the barbarians' – including the 'unthinkable' consumption of milk.

These days the Japanese have gone to the opposite extreme and have heartily embraced foreign cuisine. Unfortunately this often means a glut of fast-food restaurants in the downtown areas of most cities. In fact, there are so many McDonald's that the president of McDonald's Japan once remarked that it was only a matter of time before Japanese youth started growing blonde hair!

Those in search of a truly Japanese experience will probably want to avoid such fast-food emporiums and sample some of Japan's more authentic cuisine. Luckily this is quite easy to do, although some may baulk at charging into an unfamiliar restaurant where both the language and the menu are likely to be incomprehensible. The best way to get over this fear is to familiarise yourself with the main types of Japanese restaurants so that you have some idea of what's on offer and how to order it. Those timid of heart should take solace in the fact that the Japanese will go to extraordinary lengths to understand what you want and will help you to order.

With the exception of shokudō (Japanese-style cafeterias) and *izakaya* (Japanese pubs/eateries), most Japanese restaurants are speciality restaurants serving only one type of cuisine. Naturally, this makes for delicious eating, but does limit your choice. This chapter will introduce the main types of Japanese restaurants (see p30), along with the most common dishes served (see p36). With a little courage and effort you will soon discover that Japan is a gourmet paradise where good food is taken seriously.

CULTURE
ETIQUETTE

When eating in Kyoto there are some implicit rules, but they're fairly easy to remember. If you're worried about putting your foot in it, relax – the Japanese don't expect you to know everything and are unlikely to be offended as long as you follow the standards of politeness of your own country. For many rules (eg lifting soup bowls, slurping noodles) just follow the locals.

Among the more important eating 'rules' are those regarding chopsticks. Don't stick them upright in your rice – that's how rice is offered to the dead! Passing food from your chopsticks to someone else's is a similar no-no. When taking food from shared plates, avoid using the business end of your chopsticks – invert them before reaching for that tasty morsel.

Before digging in, it's polite to say *'itadakimas'* (literally, 'I will receive'). At the end of the meal you should say *'gochisō-sama deshita'*, a respectful way of saying that the meal was good.

If you're out for a few drinks, remember that you're expected to keep the drinks of your companions topped up. Don't fill your own glass: wait for someone to do this for you. It's polite to hold the glass with both hands while it is being filled. The Japanese equivalent of cheers is *'kampai'*.

If someone invites you to eat or drink with them, they will be paying. In any case, it's unusual for bills to be split. Generally at the end of the meal, something of a struggle ensues to see who gets the privilege of paying. If this happens, it is polite to at least make an effort to pay the bill, though it is extremely unlikely that your host will acquiesce. Exceptions to this are likely among younger Kyotoites.

HOW LOCALS EAT

Kyotoites generally eat breakfast at home, where a few slices of bread and a cup of coffee are quickly taking over from the traditional Japanese breakfast of rice, fish and miso soup as the breakfast of choice. If they don't eat at home, a *mōningu setto* (morning set) of toast and coffee at a coffee shop is the norm.

Lunch is often eaten at a shokudō or a noodle restaurant, usually in the company of co-workers or alone if a partner can't be found.

Evening meals are a mixed bag. Many people, of course, eat at home, but the stereotype of the 'salaryman' (male company worker) heading out for drinks and dinner every evening after work with his workmates has some basis in fact.

Weekends are when almost everyone, if they can afford it, heads out for dinner with friends, and almost all of Kyoto's restaurants are packed with groups of people eating, drinking and conversing, and generally having a ball.

Meal times are pretty much the same as in many parts of the West: breakfast is eaten between 6am and 8am, lunch is eaten between noon and 2pm, and dinner is eaten between 7pm and 9pm.

EATING IN A JAPANESE RESTAURANT

When you enter a restaurant in Japan, you'll be greeted with a hearty *'irasshaimase!'* (Welcome!). In all but the most casual places the waiter will next ask you: *'nan-mei sama?'* (How many people?). Answer with your fingers, which is what the Japanese do. You will then be led to a table, a place at the counter or a tatami (straw mat) room.

Rāmen *restaurant, downtown Kyoto*

At this point you will be given an *o-shibori* (hot towel), a cup of tea and a menu. The *o-shibori* is for cleaning your hands (and while actually considered bad form, many Japanese men fancy wiping their faces with these as well). When you're done with it, just roll or fold it up and leave it next to your place. Now comes the hard part: ordering. If you don't read Japanese, you can use the romanised translations in the Food Glossary (p37), or direct the waiter's attention to the Japanese script. If this doesn't work, there are two phrases that may help: *'o-susume wa nan desu ka?'* (What do you recommend?) and *'o-makase shimasu'* (Please decide for me). If you're still having problems, you can try pointing at other diners' food or, if the restaurant has them, dragging the waiter outside to point at the plastic food models in the window.

When you've finished eating you can ask for the bill by saying *'o-kanjō kudasai'*. Remember that there is no tipping in Japan and tea is free of charge. Usually you will be given a bill to take to the cashier at the front of the restaurant. At more upmarket places the host of the party will discreetly excuse themself to pay before the group leaves. Unlike in the West, don't leave cash on the table by way of payment. Only the bigger and more international places take credit cards, so cash is always the surer option.

When leaving, it is polite to say to the restaurant staff, *'gochisō-sama deshita'*, which means 'It was a real feast'.

STAPLES

RICE

The word 'rice' *(gohan)* is interchangeable with the word 'meal' in Japanese. Thus, the word for breakfast, *'asagohan'*, literally translates to 'morning rice'. Though cosmopolitan Kyotoites have adopted a taste for many Western culinary habits (such as having toast for breakfast), rice, especially at dinner, is still the done thing.

FISH

One need only visit any Kyoto supermarket or market street to see just how much Kyotoites love fish – there will inevitably be a wide range of fresh, delicious choices. Almost every meal you eat in Kyoto will probably include something fishy.

NOODLES

It's hard to imagine how the city could function without *soba* (brown buckwheat noodles), *udon* (white wheat noodles) and *rāmen* (noodles in meat broth with toppings). In addition to being the world's healthiest fast food, these basics keep bodies and schedules running smoothly.

STANDARDS

In this section we introduce some of the more common types of Japanese cuisine. In the Food Glossary section (p37) we provide sample menus, with the Japanese and romanised names of the most typical dishes served at restaurants that specialise in these types of cuisine.

SUSHI & SASHIMI

Most sushi restaurants specialise in two main dishes: sashimi and sushi. Sashimi refers to pieces of raw fish. Sushi actually refers to the rice on which pieces of (usually) raw fish are eaten, but, as in the West, the word 'sushi' has now come to mean both the rice and the fish. There are two main types of sushi: *nigiri-zushi* (served on a small bed of rice – the most common variety) and *maki-zushi* (served in a seaweed roll). Lesser-known varieties include *chirashi-zushi* (a layer of rice covered in egg and fish toppings), *oshi-zushi* (fish pressed in a mould over rice) and *inari-zushi* (rice in a pocket of sweet, fried tofu). Whatever kind of sushi you try, it will be served with lightly vinegared rice. In the case of *nigiri-zushi* and *maki-zushi*, it will contain a bit of wasabi (hot green horseradish).

Sushi is not difficult to order. If you sit at the counter of a sushi restaurant you can simply point at what you want, as most of the selections are visible in a refrigerated glass case located between you and the sushi chef. You can also order à la carte from the menu. When ordering, you usually order *ichi-nin mae* (one portion), which usually means two pieces of sushi. If ordering à la carte feels like a chore, you can take care of your whole meal by ordering a *mori-awase* (assortment plate of *nigiri-zushi*). These usually come in three grades: *futsū nigiri* (regular *nigiri*), *jō nigiri* (special *nigiri*) and *toku-jō nigiri* (extra-special *nigiri*). The difference is in the type and quality of fish used. Most *mori-awase* contain six or seven pieces of sushi.

Before popping the sushi into your mouth, dip it in *shōyu* (soy sauce), which you pour from a small decanter into a low dish that is specially provided for the purpose. If you're not good at using chopsticks, don't worry, sushi is one of the few foods in Japan that is perfectly acceptable to eat with your hands. Slices of *gari* (pickled ginger) will also be served to help refresh the palate. The beverage of choice with sushi is beer or sake (hot in winter and cold in summer), with a cup of green tea at the end of the meal.

Kyoto's Best ...

Kushiage & Kushikatsu Kushi Hachi (p112)

Okonomiyaki Chabana (p111)

Shokudō Kuishinbō-no-Mise (p114); Eating House Hi-Lite (p114)

Soba & Udon Omen (p113); Misoka-an Kawamichi-ya (p106); Gonbei (p107); Tagoto Honten (p109); Hinode (p112)

Sukiyaki & Shabu-Shabu Morita-ya (p106); Mishima-tei (p105)

Sushi Den Shichi (p115); Tomi-zushi (p106); Ganko Zushi (p105)

Tempura Ōzawa (p106); Yoshikawa (p107)

Yakitori Ichi-ban (p105); Daikichi (p109)

RĀMEN

This dish was imported from China and has gradually become one of the world's most delicious fast foods. *Rāmen* dishes are big bowls of noodles in a meat broth, served with a variety of toppings, such as sliced pork, bean sprouts and leeks. In some restaurants you may be asked if you'd prefer *kotteri* (thick) or *assari* (thin) soup. Other than this, ordering is simple: just sidle up to the counter and say *rāmen*, or ask for any of the other choices usually on offer (see p38). Since *rāmen* is derived from Chinese cuisine, some *rāmen* restaurants also serve *chāhan* or *yaki-meshi* (fried rice), *gyōza* (dumplings) and *kara-age* (deep-fried chicken pieces).

Rāmen restaurants are easily distinguished by their long counters lined with customers hunched over steaming bowls. You can sometimes hear a *rāmen* shop as you wander by – it's considered polite to slurp the noodles, and *rāmen* aficionados claim that slurping brings out the full flavour of the broth.

See the boxed text on p109 for a list of some of Kyoto's best *rāmen* restaurants.

YAKITORI

Yakitori (skewers of grilled chicken and vegetables) is a popular after-work meal. It is not so much a full meal as an accompaniment to beer and sake. At a *yakitori-ya* (*yakitori* restaurant) you sit around a counter with the other patrons and watch the chef grill your selections over charcoal. The best way to eat here is to order several varieties, then order seconds of the ones you really like. Ordering can be a little confusing since one serving often means two or three skewers (be careful – the price listed on the menu is usually that of a single skewer). In summer, the beverage of choice at a *yakitori-ya* is beer or cold sake, while in winter it's hot sake.

TEMPURA

Tempura consists of portions of fish, prawns and vegetables cooked in fluffy, nongreasy batter. When you sit down at a tempura restaurant, you will be given a small bowl of *ten-tsuyu* (a light-brown sauce) and a plate of grated *daikon* (white radish) to mix into the sauce. Dip each piece of tempura into this sauce before eating it. Tempura is best when it's hot, so don't wait too long – use the sauce to cool each piece, and dig in.

While it's possible to order à la carte, most diners choose to order a *teishoku* (set-course meal), which includes rice, *miso-shiru* (miso soup) and Japanese pickles. Some tempura restaurants offer tempura courses that are differentiated by how many pieces they include.

SUKIYAKI & SHABU-SHABU

Restaurants usually specialise in both sukiyaki and *shabu-shabu*. Popular in the West, sukiyaki is a favourite of most foreign visitors to Japan. Sukiyaki consists of thin slices of beef cooked in a broth of soy sauce, sugar and sake and is accompanied by a variety of vegetables and tofu. After cooking, all the ingredients are dipped in raw egg before being eaten. When made with high-quality beef, such as that from Kōbe, it is a sublime experience.

Shabu-shabu consists of thin slices of beef and vegetables cooked by swirling the ingredients in a light broth, then dipping them in a variety of special sesame-seed and citrus-based sauces. Both of these dishes are prepared at your table in a pot over a fire; a waiter or waitress will usually help you get started, and keep a close watch as you proceed. The key is to take your time, add the ingredients a little at a time and savour the flavours as you go.

Sukiyaki and *shabu-shabu* restaurants usually have traditional Japanese décor and sometimes a picture of a cow to help you identify them.

SOBA & UDON

Soba and *udon* are Japan's answer to Chinese-style *rāmen*. *Soba* are thin, brown buckwheat noodles and *udon* are thick, white wheat noodles. Most Japanese noodle shops serve both *soba* and *udon* in a variety of ways. Noodles are usually served in a bowl containing a light, bonito-flavoured broth, but you can also order them served cold and piled on a bamboo screen with a cold broth for dipping.

By far the most popular type of cold noodles are *zaru soba*, which is served with bits of *nori* (seaweed) on top. If you order *zaru soba*, you'll receive a small plate of wasabi and sliced spring onions – put these into the cup of broth and eat the noodles by dipping them in this mixture. At the end of your meal, the waiter will give you some hot broth to mix with the leftover sauce, which you drink like a kind of tea. As with *rāmen*, you should feel free to slurp as loudly as you please.

Fresh sushi (p30)

TONKATSU

Tonkatsu is a deep-fried crumbed pork cutlet served with a special sauce, usually as part of a *tonkatsu teishoku* (set meal). *Tonkatsu* is served both at speciality restaurants and at shokudō. Naturally, the best *tonkatsu* is found at the speciality places, where you are able to choose between *rōsu* (a fatter cut of pork) and *hire* (a leaner cut).

KUSHIAGE & KUSHIKATSU

This is the fried food to beat all fried foods. *Kushiage* and *kushikatsu* are deep-fried skewers of meat, seafood and vegetables that are eaten as an accompaniment to beer. *Kushi* means 'skewer' and if a piece of food can fit on one, it's probably on the menu. Cabbage is often eaten with the meal.

You order *kushiage* and *kushikatsu* by the skewer (one skewer is *ippon*, but you can always use your fingers to indicate how many you want). Like *yakitori*, this food is popular with after-work salarymen and students.

OKONOMIYAKI

The name means 'cook what you like', and an *okonomiyaki* restaurant provides you with an inexpensive opportunity to do just that. Sometimes described as Japanese pizza or pancake, the resemblance is in form only. At an *okonomiyaki* restaurant you sit around a *teppan* (iron hotplate), armed with a spatula and chopsticks to cook your choice of meat, seafood and vegetables in a cabbage and vegetable batter.

Some restaurants will do most of the cooking and bring the nearly finished product over to your hotplate for you to season with *katsuo bushi* (bonito flakes), soy sauce, *ao-nori* (an ingredient similar to parsley), Japanese Worcestershire-style sauce and mayonnaise. Cheaper places, however, will simply hand you a bowl filled with the ingredients and expect you to cook it yourself. If this happens, don't panic. First, mix the batter and filling thoroughly, then place it on the hot grill, flattening it into a pancake shape. After five minutes or so, use the spatulas to flip it and cook it for another five minutes. Then dig in. Most *okonomiyaki* places also serve *yaki-soba* (fried noodles) and *yasai-itame* (stir-fried vegetables). All of this is washed down with mugs of draught beer. Also look for *okonomiyaki* served at festivals and street fairs.

COMMON RESTAURANT TYPES

SHOKUDŌ

A shokudō is the most common type of restaurant in Japan, and is found near train stations, tourist spots and just about any other place where people congregate. Easily distinguished by the presence of plastic food displays in the window, these inexpensive places usually serve a variety of *washoku* (Japanese) and *yoshoku* (Western) dishes.

At lunch, and sometimes dinner, the easiest meal to order at a shokudō is a *teishoku*, which is sometimes also called *ranchi setto* (lunch set), or *kōsu* (set meal). This usually includes a main dish of meat or fish, a bowl of rice, miso soup, shredded cabbage and some *tsukemono* (Japanese pickles). In addition, most shokudō serve a fairly standard selection of *donburi-mono* (rice dishes) and *menrui* (noodle dishes). When you order noodles, you can choose between *soba* and *udon*, both of which are served with a variety of toppings.

IZAKAYA

An *izakaya* is the Japanese equivalent of a pub. It's a good place to visit when you want a casual meal, a wide selection of food, a hearty atmosphere and, of course, plenty of beer and sake. When you enter an *izakaya*, you are given the choice of sitting around the counter, at a table or on a tatami floor. You usually order a bit at a time, choosing from a selection of typical Japanese foods such as *yakitori*, sashimi and grilled fish, as well as Japanese interpretations of Western foods such as French fries and beef stew.

Izakaya can be identified by their rustic façades and the red lanterns outside their doors bearing the kanji for *izakaya*. Since *izakaya* food is casual fare to go with drinking, it is usually fairly inexpensive. Depending on how much you drink, you can expect to spend ¥2500 to ¥5000 per person.

SPECIALITIES

UNAGI

Even if you can't stand the creature, you owe it to yourself to try *unagi* (eel) at least once while in Japan. It's cooked over hot coals and brushed with a rich sauce composed of soy sauce and sake. Most *unagi* restaurants display plastic models of their sets in the front windows, and may have barrels of live eels to entice passers-by.

FUGU

The deadly *fugu* (pufferfish) is eaten more for the thrill than the taste. It's actually rather bland – most people liken the taste to chicken – but is acclaimed for its fine texture. Nonetheless, it makes a good 'been there, done that' story back home.

Although the danger of *fugu* poisoning is negligible, some Japanese joke that you should always let your dining companion try the first piece of *fugu* – if they are still talking after five minutes, you can consider it safe and have some yourself. If you need a shot of liquid courage in order to get you started, try a glass of *hirezake* (toasted *fugu* tail in hot sake) – the traditional accompaniment to a *fugu* dinner.

Fugu is a seasonal delicacy best eaten in winter. *Fugu* restaurants usually serve only *fugu*, and can be identified by a picture of a *fugu* on the sign out the front.

KAISEKI

Kaiseki (Japanese *haute cuisine*) is the pinnacle of Japanese cuisine, where ingredients, preparation, setting and presentation come together to create a dining experience quite unlike any other. Born as an adjunct to the tea ceremony, *kaiseki* is a largely vegetarian affair (though fish is often served, meat never appears on the *kaiseki* menu). One usually eats *kaiseki* in the private room of a *ryōtei* (an especially elegant style of traditional restaurant), often overlooking a private, tranquil garden. The meal is served in several small courses, giving the diner an opportunity to admire the plates and bowls, which are carefully chosen to complement the food and season. Rice is eaten last (usually with an assortment of pickles) and the drink of choice is sake or beer.

VEGETARIAN OPTIONS

Kyoto has several good vegetarian restaurants. In addition to these speciality restaurants, you can usually find vegetarian choices at standard Japanese shokudō and other restaurants. These include noodle, rice and vegetable dishes.

If you eat fish, you'll have plenty to choose from. If you don't, you'll have to forgo even the ubiquitous miso soup, which is usually made from fish broth. Nonfish-eating vegetarians can get their protein from tofu, which comes in a variety of forms in Japan, and can often be ordered raw, with a dash of soy sauce and ginger (ask for *hiyayako*). If it arrives with *katsuobushi* (shaved bonito flakes) on top, simply remove them before eating.

SWEETS

Although most restaurants don't serve dessert (plates of sliced fruit are sometimes served at the end of a meal), there is no lack of sweets in Japan. Most sweets (known generically as *wagashi*) are sold in speciality stores for you to eat at home. Many of the more delicate-looking ones are made to balance the strong, bitter taste of the special *matcha* (powdered green tea) served during tea ceremonies.

Even if you have the sweetest tooth in the world and have sampled every type of sweet that's come your way, you may find yourself surprised by Japanese confectionery. Many sweets contain the unfamiliar red adzuki-bean paste called *anko*. This earthy, rich filling turns up in a variety of pastries, including those you pick up at bakeries.

With such a wide variety of sweets, it's impossible to list all the names. Sweet shops are easy to spot; they usually have open fronts with their wares laid out in wooden trays to entice passers-by.

DRINKS

Drinking plays a big role in Japanese society, and there are few social occasions where beer or sake is not served. Alcohol (in this case sake) also plays a ceremonial role in various Shintō festivals and rites, including the marriage ceremony. As a visitor to Kyoto you'll probably find yourself in situations where you are invited to drink, and tipping back a few beers or glasses of sake is a great way to get to know the locals. However, if you don't drink alcohol, it's no big deal to order *oolong cha* (oolong tea) or a soft drink.

ALCOHOLIC DRINKS

Beer

Introduced at the end of the 1800s, *bīru* (beer) is now the favourite tipple of the Japanese. The quality is generally excellent and the most popular type is light lager, although recently some breweries have been experimenting with darker brews. The major breweries are Kirin, Asahi, Sapporo and Suntory. Beer is dispensed everywhere, from vending machines to beer halls, and even in some temple lodgings. A standard can of beer from a vending machine is about ¥250, although some of the gigantic cans cost over ¥1000. At bars, a beer starts at ¥500 and the price climbs upwards, depending on the establishment. *Nama bīru* (draught beer) is widely available, as are imported beers.

Sake

Rice wine has been brewed for centuries in Japan. Once restricted to imperial brewers, it was later produced at temples and shrines across the country. In recent years, consumption of beer has overtaken that of sake, but it's still a standard item in homes, restaurants and drinking places. Large casks of sake are often seen piled up as offerings outside temples and shrines, and the drink plays an important part in most celebrations and festivals.

There are several types of sake, including *nigori* (cloudy), *nama* (unrefined) and regular, clear sake. Of these, clear sake is by far the most common. Clear sake is usually divided into three grades: *tokkyū* (premium), *ikkyū* (first grade) and *nikkyū* (second grade). *Nikkyū* is the routine choice. Sake can be further divided into *karakuchi* (dry) and *amakuchi* (sweet). As well as the national brewing giants, there are thousands of provincial brewers producing local brews called *jizake*.

Sake is served *atsukan* (warm) or *reishu* (cold), with warm sake not surprisingly more popular in winter. When you order sake, it will usually be served in a small flask called *tokkuri*. These come in two sizes, so you should specify whether you want *ichi-gō* (small) or *nigō* (large). From these flasks you pour the sake into small ceramic cups called *o-choko* or *sakazuki*. Another way to sample sake is to drink it from a small wooden box called *masu*, with a bit of salt on the rim.

With a 17% alcohol content, sake, particularly the warm stuff, is likely to go right to your head however you drink it. After a few bouts with sake you'll come to understand why it's drunk from such small cups. Particularly memorable is a sake hangover born of too much cheap sake, something you'll particularly want to avoid before getting on to a plane.

Shōchū

For those looking for a quick and cheap escape route from the sorrows of the world, *shōchū* is the answer. It's a distilled spirit, with an alcohol content of about 30%, and has been resurrected from its previous lowly status (it was used as a disinfectant in the Edo period) to become a trendy drink. You can drink it *oyu-wari* (with hot water) or *chūhai* (with soda and lemon).

Wine, Imported Drinks & Whisky

Japanese wines are available from areas such as Yamanashi, Nagano, Tōhoku and Hokkaidō and are often blended with imports from South America or Eastern Europe. The major producers are Suntory, Mann's and Mercian.

Whisky is also available at most drinking establishments and is usually drunk *mizu-wari* (with water and ice) or *onzarokku* (on the rocks). Local brands, such as Suntory and Nikka, are sensibly priced, and most measure up to foreign standards. Expensive foreign labels are popular as gifts.

Japanese tea

Most other imported spirits are available at drinking establishments in Japan. Bars with a large foreign clientele, including hotel bars, can usually mix anything you request. If not, they will certainly tailor a drink to your specifications.

NONALCOHOLIC DRINKS

Most of the drinks you're used to at home will be available in Japan, with a few colourfully named additions, such as Pocari Sweat and Calpis Water. One convenient aspect of Japan is the presence of drink vending machines on virtually every street corner, and with six million of them in the city, refreshment is rarely more than a few steps away.

Coffee & Tea

When ordering *kōhī* (coffee) at a coffee shop in Japan, you'll be asked whether you like it *hotto* (hot) or *aisu* (cold). Black tea also comes hot or cold, with *miruku* (milk) or *remon* (lemon). Hot and cold coffee are also widely available in vending machines.

Japanese Tea

You're probably already familiar with green tea, which contains loads of vitamin C and a good dose of caffeine. The powdered form used in the tea ceremony is called *matcha* and is drunk after being whipped into a frothy consistency. The more common form, a leafy green tea, is simply called *o-cha*, and is drunk after being steeped in a pot. In addition to green tea, you'll probably drink a lot of a brownish tea called *bancha*, which restaurants serve for free. In summer a cold beverage called *mugicha* (roasted barley tea) is served in private homes.

MENU DECODER
USEFUL WORDS & PHRASES

(Note that letters within square brackets are not pronounced.)

A table for two/five people, please.	*(futari/go-nin) onegai shimas[u]*	(2人／5人)お願いします。
Do you have an English menu?	*eigo no menyū ga arimas[u] ka?*	英語のメニューがありますか？
Can you recommend any dishes?	*osusume no ryōri ga arimas[u] ka?*	お勧めの料理がありますか？

Is this self-service?	*koko wa serufu sābis[u] des[u] ka?*	ここはセルフサービスですか？
Is service included in the bill?	*sābis[u] ryō wa komi des[u] ka?*	サービス料は込みですか？
Cheers!	*kampai!*	乾杯！

Please bring (a/an) ...	*... o onegai shimas[u]*	... をお願いします。
the bill	*o-kanjō*	お勘定
chopsticks	*hashi*	箸
fork	*fōku*	フォーク
glass (of water)	*koppu (ippai no mizu)*	コップ (一杯の水)
knife	*naifu*	ナイフ
spoon	*supūn*	スプーン

I'm a vegetarian.	*watashi wa bejitarian des[u]*	私はベジタリアンです。
I don't eat meat.	*niku wa tabemasen*	肉は食べません。
I don't eat chicken, fish or ham.	*toriniku to sakana to hamu wa tabemasen*	鶏肉と魚とハムは食べません。
I'm allergic to (peanuts).	*watashi wa (pīnattsu) arerugī des[u]*	私は (ピーナッツ) アレルギーです。

FOOD GLOSSARY

RICE DISHES

katsu-don	カツ丼	rice topped with a fried pork cutlet
niku-don	肉丼	rice topped with thin slices of cooked beef
oyako-don	親子丼	rice topped with egg and chicken
ten-don	天丼	rice topped with tempura shrimp and vegetables

NOODLE DISHES

kake	かけ	*soba* or *udon* noodles in broth
kitsune	きつね	*soba* or *udon* noodles with fried tofu
soba	そば	buckwheat noodles
tempura	天ぷら	*soba* or *udon* noodles with tempura shrimp
tsukimi	月見	*soba* or *udon* noodles with raw egg on top
udon	うどん	thick, white wheat noodles

SUSHI & SASHIMI

ama-ebi	甘海老	sweet shrimp
awabi	あわび	abalone
ebi	海老	prawn or shrimp
hamachi	はまち	yellowtail
ika	いか	squid
ikura	イクラ	salmon roe
kai-bashira	貝柱	the adductor muscle of shellfish
kani	かに	crab
katsuo	かつお	bonito
maguro	まぐろ	tuna
tai	鯛	sea bream
tamago	たまご	sweetened egg
toro	とろ	a choice cut of fatty tuna belly
unagi	うなぎ	eel with a sweet sauce
uni	うに	sea-urchin roe

RĀMEN

chānpon-men	ちゃんぽんメン	Nagasaki-style *rāmen* (noodles in meat broth with toppings)
chāshū-men	チャーシューメン	*rāmen* topped with slices of roasted pork
miso-rāmen	味噌ラーメン	*rāmen* with miso-flavoured broth
rāmen	ラーメン	soup and noodles with a sprinkling of meat and vegetables
wantan-men	ワンタンメン	*rāmen* with meat dumplings

YAKITORI

gyū-niku	牛肉	pieces of beef
hasami/negima	はさみ/ねぎま	pieces of white meat alternating with leek
kawa	かわ	chicken skin
pīman	ピーマン	small green peppers
rebā	レバ	chicken livers
sasami	ささみ	skinless chicken-breast pieces
shiitake	しいたけ	Japanese mushrooms
tama-negi	たまねぎ	white onion
tebasaki	手羽先	chicken wings
tsukune	つくね	chicken meat balls
yaki-onigiri	焼きおにぎり	triangle of rice grilled with *yakitori* sauce
yakitori	焼き鳥	plain, grilled white meat

TEMPURA

kaki age	掻き揚げ	tempura with shredded vegetables or fish
shōjin age	精進揚げ	vegetarian tempura
tempura moriawase	天ぷら盛り合わせ	selection of tempura

SOBA

zaru soba	ざるそば	cold noodles with seaweed strips served on a bamboo tray

TONKATSU

hire katsu	ヒレカツ	*tonkatsu* (crumbed pork) fillet
kushi katsu	串カツ	deep-fried pork and vegetables on skewers
minchi katsu	ミンチカツ	minced pork cutlet
tonkatsu teishoku	トンカツ定食	set meal of *tonkatsu*, rice, *miso-shiru* and shredded cabbage

KUSHIAGE & KUSHIKATSU

ebi	海老	shrimp
ginnan	銀杏	ginkgo nuts
gyū-niku	牛肉	beef pieces
ika	いか	squid
imo	いも	potato
renkon	レンコン	lotus root
shiitake	しいたけ	Japanese mushrooms
tama-negi	たまねぎ	white onion

OKONOMIYAKI

gyū okonomiyaki	牛お好み焼き	beef *okonomiyaki* (meat and vegetables cooked in a cabbage and vegetable batter)

ika okonomiyaki	イカお好み焼き	squid *okonomiyaki*
mikkusu	ミックス焼き	mixed filling of seafood, meat and vegetables
modan-yaki	モダン焼き	*okonomiyaki* with *yaki soba* and a fried egg
negi okonomiyaki	ネギお好み焼き	thin o*konomiyaki* with scallions

IZAKAYA

agedashi-dōfu	揚げだし豆腐	deep-fried tofu in a fish stock soup
chīzu-age	チーズ揚げ	deep-fried cheese
hiya-yakko	冷奴	cold block of tofu with soy sauce and scallions
jaga-batā	ジャガバター	baked potatoes with butter
kata yaki-soba	固焼きそば	hard fried noodles with meat and vegetables
niku-jaga	肉じゃが	beef and potato stew
poteto furai	ポテトフライ	French fries
sashimi mori-awase	刺身盛り合わせ	selection of sliced sashimi
shio-yaki-zakana	塩焼魚	whole fish grilled with salt
tsuna sarada	ツナサラダ	tuna salad over cabbage
yaki-onigiri	焼きおにぎり	triangle of grilled rice with *yakitori* sauce
yaki-soba	焼きそば	fried noodles with meat and vegetables

UNAGI

kabayaki	蒲焼	skewers of grilled eel without rice
unadon	うな丼	grilled eel over a bowl of rice
unagi teishoku	うなぎ定食	full-set *unagi* meal with rice, grilled eel, eel-liver soup and pickles
unajū	うな重	grilled eel over a flat tray of rice

FUGU

fugu chiri	ふぐちり	stew made from *fugu* (pufferfish) and vegetables
fugu sashimi	ふぐ刺身	thinly sliced raw *fugu*
fugu teishoku	ふぐ定食	set course of *fugu* served several ways, plus rice and soup
yaki fugu	焼きふぐ	*fugu* grilled on a *hibachi* (small clay pot containing burning charcoal or wood) at your table

SWEETS

anko	あんこ	sweet paste or jam made from adzuki beans
mochi	餅	pounded rice cakes made of glutinous rice
wagashi	和菓子	Japanese-style sweets
yōkan	羊羹	sweet red-bean jelly

ALCOHOLIC DRINKS

amakuchi	甘口	sweet sake
atsukan	熱燗	warm sake
bīru	ビール	beer
chūhai	チューハイ	*shōchū* with soda and lemon
ikkyūshu	一級酒	first-grade sake
jizake	地酒	local brew
karakuchi	辛口	dry sake
mizu-wari	水割り	whiskey, ice and water
nama	生	unrefined sake
nama bīru	生ビール	draft beer
nigori	にごり	cloudy sake

nikkyūshu	二級酒	second-grade sake
o-choko	お猪口	ceramic sake cup
onzarokku	オンザロック	whiskey with ice
oyu-wari	お湯割り	*shōchū* with hot water
reishu	冷酒	cold sake
sakazuki	杯	ceramic sake cup
sake	酒	Japanese rice wine
shōchū	焼酎	distilled grain liquor
tokkyūshu	特級酒	premium-grade sake
whisky	ウイスキー	whiskey

NONALCOHOLIC DRINKS

american kōhī	アメリカンコーヒー	weak coffee
bancha	番茶	ordinary-grade green tea, has a brownish colour
burendo kōhī	ブレンドコーヒー	blended coffee, fairly strong
kafe ōre	カフェオレ	*café au lait*, hot or cold
kōcha	紅茶	black, British-style tea
kōhī	コーヒー	regular coffee
matcha	抹茶	powdered green tea used in tea ceremonies
mugicha	麦茶	roasted barley tea
o-cha	お茶	green tea
orenji jūsu	オレンジジュース	orange juice
sencha	煎茶	medium-grade green tea

History

History

THE RECENT PAST

Battles in Kyoto today are fought not with swords, but with pens, as preservationists desperately struggle to save the city from a coalition of local government forces and commercial interests who seem bent on the heedless modernisation of the city at the expense of its traditional architecture. While there has been a handful of tenuous victories in the efforts to protect Kyoto's surviving heritage, such triumphs are few and far between.

Marking the 1200th anniversary of the founding of Kyoto, 1994 was a monumental year. Developers capitalised on this proud milestone by further exploiting the city. Controversy swelled over the blatant bending of city construction ordinances, which allowed projects such as Kyoto Hotel and Kyoto Station to be built higher than previous legal limits, setting a frightful precedent for the future.

Fuelling the rush to develop Kyoto is the knowledge that the city can no longer depend on tourist revenue as its main source of income. Thus, the city is desperately trying to shift its economic focus from tourist-related service industries to manufacturing and research. Unfortunately, efforts by the city fathers to increase the city's industrial base have met with only limited success.

Still, the city remains an important cultural and educational centre. Today over 60 museums and 37 universities and colleges are scattered throughout the city, and it houses more than 200 of Japan's National Treasures and nearly 1700 important Cultural Properties.

The city also continues to expand its infrastructure. In 1997 two transportation milestones were reached: the new Tōzai subway line was opened and the giant new Kyoto Station building was unveiled.

As Kyoto heads into the new millennium, the city hangs in a limbo, torn between the desire to preserve its heritage and the need to develop its economy. The real challenge for Kyoto is to find ways to survive in the modern world without sacrificing its cultural and architectural heritage.

FROM THE BEGINNING

Although the origins of the Japanese race remain unclear, anthropologists believe humans first arrived on the islands via the land bridges that once connected Japan to Siberia and Korea, and by sea from the islands of the South Pacific. The first recorded evidence of civilisation in Japan is pottery fragments with cord marks (jōmon) produced in the Neolithic period, about 10,000 BC. During this Jōmon period, people lived a primitive existence as independent fishers, hunters and food-gatherers.

This Stone Age period was gradually superseded by the Yayoi era, dating roughly from 300 BC. The Yayoi people are considered to have had a strong connection with Korea and their most important developments were the wet cultivation of rice and the use of bronze and iron implements. The Yayoi period witnessed the progressive development of communities represented in more than 100 independent family clusters dotting the archipelago.

As more and more of these settlements banded together to defend their land, regional groups became larger and by AD 300 the Yamato kingdom had emerged in the region of present-day Nara. Forces were loosely united around the imperial clan of the Yamato court, whose leaders claimed descent from the sun goddess, Amaterasu, and who introduced the title of emperor (tennō). The Yamato kingdom established Japan's first fixed capital in Nara,

TIMELINE

Early 7th century	784
Kyoto basin first settled	Japan's capital is moved from Nara to Nagaoka (a suburb of Kyoto)

eventually unifying the regional groups into a single state. By the end of the 4th century, official relations with the Korean peninsula were initiated and Japan steadily began to introduce arts and industries such as shipbuilding, leather-tanning, weaving and metalwork.

The Yamato period is also referred to as the Kofun period by archaeologists, who discovered thousands of ancient burial mounds *(kofun)*, mainly in western Japan. These massive tombs contained various artefacts, including tools, weapons and *haniwa* (clay figurines of people and animals that had been ceremonially buried with people of nobility). With the arrival of Buddhism, this labour-intensive custom was abandoned in favour of cremation.

BUDDHISM & THE NARA PERIOD

When Buddhism drifted on to the shores of Japan, Kyoto was barely more than a vast, fertile valley. First introduced from China in 538 via the Korean kingdom of Paekche, Buddhism was pivotal in the evolution of the Japanese nation. It brought with it a flood of culture – in literature, arts and architecture – and *kanji* (a distinctive system of writing in Chinese characters). Buddhism eventually received the endorsement of the nobility and emperors, who authorised widespread temple construction, and in 588, as recorded in the 8th-century *Chronicle of Japan* (Nihon Shoki), Japan's first great temple complex, Asuka-dera, was completed.

Gradually, the wealth and power of the temples began to pose a threat to the governing Yamato court, prompting reforms from Prince Shōtoku (574–622), regent for first Empress Suiko. He set up the Constitution of 17 Articles and laid the guidelines for a centralised state headed by a single ruler. He also instituted Buddhism as a state religion and ordered the construction of more temples, including Nara's eminent Hōryū-ji, the world's oldest surviving wooden structure.

Despite family feuds and coups d'état, subsequent rulers continued to reform the country's administration and laws. Previously, it had been the custom to avoid the pollution of imperial death by changing the site of the capital for each successive emperor, but in 710 this custom was altered and the capital, known as Heijō-kyō, was shifted to Nara, where it remained for 75 years.

ESTABLISHMENT OF HEIAN-KYŌ

The Kyoto basin was first settled in the 7th century when the region was known as Yamashiro-no-kuni. The original inhabitants were immigrants from Korea, the Hata clan, who established Koryū-ji in 603 as their family temple in what is today the Uzumasa district.

By the end of the 8th century the Buddhist clergy in Nara had become so meddlesome that Emperor Kammu decided to insulate the court from their influence by moving the capital. The first move occurred in 784, to Nagaoka (a suburb of Kyoto), and a decade later the capital was shifted to present-day Kyoto, where it was to remain until 1868.

The new capital was given the name Heian-kyō; literally, the capital of peace *(hei)* and tranquillity *(an)*. As with the previous capital in Nara, the city was laid out in accordance with Chinese geomancy in a grid pattern adopted from the Tang dynasty (618–907) capital, Chang'an (present-day Xi'an). The rectangle-shaped precincts were established west of where the Kamo-gawa flows today. Originally measuring 4.5km east to west and 5.3km north to south, the city was about one-third the size of its Chinese prototype. Running through the centre was Suzaku-ōji, an 85m-wide, willow-lined thoroughfare dividing the eastern part of the city (Sakyō-ku) from the west (Ukyō-ku). The northern tip of the promenade was the site of the ornate Imperial Palace (p66) and to the far south stood the 23m-high, two-storey Rajō-mon, over 35m wide and 10m deep.

The ensuing Heian period (794–1185) effectively lived up to its name. Over four centuries, the city went beyond its role as a political hub to become the country's commercial and cultural centre. Towards the end of the 9th century, contact with China became increasingly sporadic, providing an opportunity for Japan to develop its native culture. This produced a

1192	1281
Japan's political capital is moved to Kamakura	Mongol invasion force is destroyed by a typhoon (kamikaze)

Detail at Heian-jingū (p44)

great flowering in literature, the arts and religious thinking, as the Japanese adapted ideas and institutions imported from China.

The development of *hiragana* (Japanese native characters) led to a popular literary trend best recalled by Murasaki Shikibu's legendary saga, *Genji Monogatari* (The Tale of Genji). This period in Kyoto's history conjures up romantic visions of riverside moon-gazing parties where literati drew calligraphy and composed poetry, while the aristocracy frolicked in their self-imposed seclusion.

Rivalry between Buddhism and Shintō, the traditional religion of Japan, was reduced by presenting Shintō deities as manifestations of Buddha. Religion was separated from politics, and Japanese monks returning from China established two new sects, Tendai and Shingon, which became the mainstays of Japanese Buddhism. Soon other sects were springing up and temples were being enthusiastically built.

The Heian period is considered the apogee of Japanese courtly elegance, but in the provinces a new power was on the rise – the samurai warrior class, which built up its armed forces to defend its autonomy. Samurai families moved into Kyoto, where they muscled in on the court, and subsequent conflicts between rival military clans led to civil wars and strife. This was the start of a long period of feudal rule by successive samurai families (shōgunates). This feudal system lingered on for seven centuries, until imperial power was restored in 1868.

FROM ARISTOCRACY TO MILITARY RULE

Although Kyoto served as home to the Japanese imperial family from 794 to 1868, it was not always the focus of Japanese political power. During the Kamakura period (1185–1333), Kamakura (near present-day Tokyo) was the national capital, and during the Edo period (1600–1867) the Tokugawa Shōgunate ruled Japan from Edo (present-day Tokyo). Still, despite the decline in influence of the imperial court, the city flourished commercially as townspeople continued their age-old manufacturing traditions.

By the 12th century the imperial family had become increasingly isolated from the mechanics of political power. By the time the corrupt Fujiwara Shōgunate was eclipsed by the Taira clan, who ruled briefly before being ousted by the Minamoto family (also known

1333	1467
Japan's political capital returns to Kyoto	The Ōnin War, Kyoto's most devastating war, breaks out

as the Genji) in the epic battle of Dannoura (Shimonoseki) in 1185, the name 'Kyoto' had emerged as the common title of the city.

Minamoto Yoritomo set up his headquarters in Kamakura in 1192, while the emperor remained nominal ruler in Kyoto. Yoritomo purged members of his own family who stood in his way, but after his death in 1199 his wife's family, the Hōjō, eliminated all of his potential successors and in 1213 became the true wielders of power behind the figureheads of shōguns and warrior lords.

During this era, the popularity of Buddhism spread to all levels of society. From the late 12th century, Japanese monks returning from China introduced a new sect, Zen, the austerity of which appealed particularly to the samurai class. Meanwhile, as the spiritual fervour grew, Japanese merchants prospered in increased trade dealings with China.

Forces beyond the sea undermined the stability of the Kamakura regime. The Mongols, under Kublai Khan, reached Korea in 1259 and sent envoys to Japan seeking Japanese submission. The envoys were expelled and the Mongols sent an invasion fleet that arrived near present-day Fukuoka in 1274. This first attack was only barely repulsed, with the aid of a typhoon, and further envoys were beheaded as a sign that the government of Japan was not interested in paying homage to the Mongols.

In 1281 the Mongols dispatched an army of over 100,000 soldiers to Japan. After an initial success, the Mongol fleet was almost completely destroyed by yet another typhoon. Ever since, this lucky typhoon has been known to the Japanese as kamikaze (divine wind) – a name later given to the suicide pilots of WWII.

Although the Kamakura government emerged victorious, it was unable to pay its soldiers and lost the support of the warrior class. Emperor Go-Daigo led an unsuccessful rebellion against the government and was exiled to the Oki Islands, near Matsue. A year later he toppled the government, ushering in a return of political authority to Kyoto.

A COUNTRY AT WAR

After completing his takeover, Emperor Go-Daigo had refused to reward his warriors, favouring the aristocracy and priesthood instead. In the early 14th century this led to a revolt by the warrior Ashikaga Takauji, who had previously supported Go-Daigo. Ashikaga defeated the emperor in Kyoto, then installed a new emperor and appointed himself shōgun, initiating the Muromachi period (1333–1576). Go-Daigo escaped to set up a rival court at Yoshino in a mountainous region near Nara. Rivalry between the two courts continued for 60 years until Ashikaga made a promise (which was not kept) that the imperial lines would alternate.

Kyoto gradually recovered its position of political significance and within the sanctuary of the art-loving Ashikaga enjoyed an epoch of cultural and artistic fruition. Talents now considered typically Japanese flourished, including arts such as landscape painting, classical nō drama, ikebana (flower arranging) and *chanoyu* (tea ceremony). Many of Kyoto's famous gardens date from this period, as do such monuments as Kinkaku-ji (Golden Temple; p77) and Ginkaku-ji (Silver Temple; p64). Eventually, formal trade relations were reopened with Ming China and Korea, although Japanese piracy remained a bone of contention with both.

The Ashikaga ruled, however, with diminishing effectiveness in a land slipping steadily into civil war and chaos. By the 15th century Kyoto had become increasingly divided as *daimyō* (domain lords) and local barons fought for power in bitter territorial disputes that were to last for a century. In 1467 the matter of succession to the shōgun between two feudal lords, Yamana and Hosokawa, ignited the most devastating battle in Kyoto's history. With Yamana's army of 90,000 camped in the southwest and Hosokawa's force of 100,000 quartered in the north of the city, Kyoto became a battlefield. The resulting Ōnin War (Ōnin-no-ran; 1467–77) wreaked untold havoc on the city; the Imperial Palace and most of the city was destroyed in fighting and subsequent fires, and the populace left in ruin.

The war marked the rapid decline of the Ashikaga family and the beginning of the Warring States period (Sengoku-jidai), which lasted until the start of the Momoyama period in 1576.

1600	1646
Tokugawa Ieyasu establishes Tokugawa Shōgunate government in Edo (present-day Tokyo)	Omotesenke tea-ceremony school is founded

RETURN TO UNITY

In 1568 Oda Nobunaga, the son of a *daimyō*, seized power from the imperial court in Kyoto and used his military genius to initiate a process of pacification and unification in central Japan. This manoeuvre marked the start of the short-lived Momoyama period (1576–1600). In 1582 Nobunaga's efforts were cut short when he was betrayed by his own general, Akechi Mitsuhide. Under attack from Mitsuhide and seeing all was lost, Nobunaga disembowelled himself in Kyoto's Honnō-ji.

Nobunaga was succeeded by his ablest commander, Toyotomi Hideyoshi, who was reputedly the son of a farmer, although his origins are not clear. His diminutive size and pop-eyed features earned him the nickname Saru-san (Mr Monkey). Hideyoshi worked on extending unification so that by 1590 the whole country was under his rule and he developed grandiose schemes to invade China and Korea. The first invasion was repulsed in 1593 and the second was aborted on Hideyoshi's death in 1598.

By the late 16th century, Kyoto's population had swelled to 500,000 and Hideyoshi was fascinated with redesigning and rebuilding the city. He transformed Kyoto into a castle town and greatly altered the cityscape by ordering major construction projects, including bridges, gates and the Odoi, a phenomenal earthen rampart designed to isolate and fortify the perimeter of the city, and to provide a measure of flood control.

The rebuilding of Kyoto is usually credited to the influence of the city's merchant class, which led a citizens' revival that gradually shifted power back into the hands of the towns-people. Centred in Shimogyō, the commercial and industrial district, these enterprising people founded a self-governing body *(machi-shū)*, which contributed greatly to temple reconstruction. Over time, temples of different sects were consolidated in one quarter of the city, creating the miniature 'city of temples' *(tera-machi)*, a part of Kyoto that still exists.

The Momoyama period has been referred to as the 'Japanese Renaissance' as the arts flourished further. Artisans of the era are noted for their boisterous use of colour and gold-leaf embellishment, while the Zen-influenced tea ceremony was developed to perfection under Master Sen no Rikyū. The performing arts also matured, along with skill in ceramics, lacquerware and fabric-dyeing. There was also a vogue for building castles and palaces on a flamboyant scale; the most impressive examples were Osaka-jō, which reputedly required three years of labour by up to 100,000 men, and the extraordinary Ninomaru palace (p78) in Kyoto's Nijō-jō.

PEACE & SECLUSION

The supporters of Hideyoshi's young heir, Toyotomi Hideyori, were defeated in 1600 by his former ally, Tokugawa Ieyasu, at the battle of Sekigahara. Ieyasu set up his field head-quarters *(bakufu)* in Edo, marking the start of the Edo (Tokugawa) period (1600–1868). Meanwhile the emperor and court exercised purely nominal authority in Kyoto.

The Tokugawa family retained large estates and took control of major cities, ports and mines; the remainder of the country was allocated to autonomous *daimyō*. Tokugawa society was strictly hierarchical. In descending order of importance were the nobility, who had nom-inal power; the *daimyō* and their samurai; farmers; and, at the bottom, artisans and merchants. Mobility from one class to another was blocked; social standing was determined by birth.

To ensure political security, the *daimyō* were required to make ceremonial visits to Edo every alternate year, and their wives and children were kept in permanent residence in Edo as virtual hostages of the government. At the lower end of society, farmers were subject to a severe system of rules that dictated in minutest detail their food, clothing and housing.

There emerged a pressing fear of religious intrusion (seen as a siphoning of loyalty to the shōgun) and Ieyasu set out to stabilise society and the national economy. Japan entered a period of national seclusion *(sakoku)* during which Japanese were forbidden on pain of death to travel to (or return from) overseas, or to trade abroad. As efforts to 'expel the

1853	1867
American Commodore Matthew Perry's 'black ships' arrive in Japan	End of Tokugawa Shōgunate, restoration of imperial rule

barbarians and protect the throne' spread, only Dutch, Chinese and Koreans were allowed to remain and they were placed under strict supervision.

One effect of this strict rule was to create an atmosphere of relative peace and isolation in which the native arts were able to excel. There were great advances in haiku poetry, *bunraku* puppet plays and kabuki theatre. Crafts such as weaving, wood-block printing, pottery, ceramics and lacquerware became famous for their refined quality. Furthermore, the rigid emphasis during these times on submitting unquestioningly to rules of obedience and loyalty has lasted up to the present day.

By the turn of the 19th century the Tokugawa government was facing stagnation and corruption. Famines and poverty among the peasants and samurai further weakened the system. Foreign ships started to probe Japan's isolation with increasing insistence and the Japanese soon realised that their outmoded defences were ineffectual. Russian contacts in the north were followed by British and American visits. In 1853 Commodore Matthew Perry of the US Navy arrived with a squadron of 'black ships' to demand the opening of Japan to trade. Other countries also moved in with similar demands.

Meiji-period aqueduct, Nanzen-ji (p58)

Despite being far inland, Kyoto felt the foreign pressure, which helped bring to a head the growing power struggle between the shōgun and emperor, eventually pushing Japan back into a state of internal conflict. A surge of antigovernment feeling among the Japanese followed, and Kyoto became a hotbed of controversy. The Tokugawa government was accused of failing to defend Japan against foreigners, and of neglecting the national reconstruction necessary for Japan to meet the West on equal terms. In 1867 the ruling shōgun, Keiki, resigned and Emperor Meiji resumed control of state affairs.

EMERGENCE FROM ISOLATION

Prior to the Meiji era (1868–1912) Kyoto was under the jurisdiction of the prefectural government. With the Meiji Restoration in 1868, political power was again restored in Kyoto, but the following year the capital was transferred to Edo along with the imperial court. Many great merchants and scholars of the era followed the emperor. After more than a millennium as capital, the sudden changes came as a major blow to Kyoto as the population dropped dramatically and the city entered a state of bitter depression.

Kyoto quickly set its sights on revival, taking steps to secure self-autonomy and rebuild its infrastructure. It again flourished as a cultural, religious and economic centre, with progressive industrial development. By the late 1800s Kyoto led the country in education reforms by establishing Japan's first kindergarten, elementary and junior high schools and public library. In the same period the city introduced Japan's first electricity system, water system and fully functioning transportation network. In 1885 work began on the monumental Lake Biwa Canal, which in just five years made Kyoto the first Japanese city to harness hydroelectric power.

1869	1871
Japan's capital is moved to Edo	Japan's first exposition is held in Kyoto

A city-government system was finally formed in 1889, a factor which further strengthened Kyoto's industries. As traditional industry pushed on, research developed in the sciences, in particular physics and chemistry. Modern industries such as precision machinery also grew, as did the introduction of foreign technologies such as the automated weaving loom; Western architectural techniques are reflected in many of the city's Meiji-era brick and stonework buildings. In 1895, to celebrate the 1100th anniversary of the city's founding, Kyoto hosted the fourth National Industrial Exhibition Fair and established the country's first streetcar system (fuelled by the Keage Hydroelectric Plant). The same year saw the construction of Heian-jingū (a five-to-eight scale replica of Daigokuden, the emperor's Great Hall of State; p59), and the birth of the Jidai Matsuri (Festival of the Ages; p11).

The initial stages of this restoration were resisted in a state of virtual civil war. The abolition of the shōgunate was followed by the surrender of the *daimyō*, whose lands were divided into the prefectures that exist today. With the transfer of the capital to Edo, now renamed Tokyo (Eastern Capital), the government was recentralised and Western-style ministries were appointed for specific tasks. A series of revolts by the samurai against the erosion of their status culminated in the Saigō Uprising, when they were finally beaten and stripped of their power.

Despite nationalist support for the emperor under the slogan of *sonnō-jōi* (revere the emperor, repel the barbarians), the new government soon realised it would have to meet the West on its own terms. Promising *fukoku kyōhei* (rich country, strong military), the economy underwent a crash course in Westernisation and industrialisation. An influx of Western experts was encouraged to provide assistance, and Japanese students were sent abroad to acquire expertise in modern technologies. In 1889 Japan created a Western-style constitution.

By the 1890s government leaders were concerned by the spread of liberal Western ideas and encouraged a swing back to nationalism and traditional values. Japan's growing confidence was demonstrated by the abolition of foreign treaty rights and by the ease with which it trounced China in the Sino-Japanese War (1894–95). The subsequent treaty nominally recognised Korean independence from China's sphere of influence and ceded Taiwan to Japan. Friction with Russia led to the Russo-Japanese War (1904–05), in which the Japanese navy stunned the Russians by inflicting a crushing defeat on their Baltic fleet at the battle of Tsu-shima. For the first time, the Japanese commanded the respect of Western powers.

THE PURSUIT OF EMPIRE

On his death in 1912, Emperor Meiji was succeeded by his son, Yoshihito, whose period of rule was named the Taishō era. When WWI broke out, Japan sided against Germany but did not become deeply involved in the conflict. While the Allies were occupied with war, the Japanese took the opportunity to expand their economy at top speed.

The Shōwa period commenced when Emperor Hirohito ascended to the throne in 1926. A rising tide of nationalism was quickened by the world economic depression that began in 1930. Popular unrest was marked by political assassinations and plots to overthrow the government. This led to a significant increase in the power of the militarists, who approved the invasion of Manchuria in 1931 and the installation of a Japanese puppet regime, Manchukuo. In 1933 Japan withdrew from the League of Nations and in 1937 entered into full-scale hostilities against China.

As the leader of a new order for Asia, Japan signed a tripartite pact with Germany and Italy in 1940. Japanese military leaders saw their main opponents as the USA. When diplomatic attempts to gain US neutrality failed, the Japanese drew the USA into WWII with a surprise attack on Pearl Harbor on 7 December 1941.

At first, Japan scored rapid successes, pushing its battle fronts across to India, down to the fringes of Australia and out into the mid-Pacific. But eventually the Battle of Midway turned the tide of the war against Japan. Exhausted by submarine blockades and aerial bombing,

1915	1941
First streetlamps installed on Shijō-dōri	Japan attacks Pearl Harbor

What Really Saved Kyoto?

Kyoto's good fortune in escaping US bombing during WWII is a well-publicised fact. Still, while it may provide patriotic colour for some Americans to hear that the city was consciously spared out of US goodwill and reverence for Kyoto's cultural heritage, not everyone agrees with the prevailing story.

The common belief is that Kyoto was rescued through the efforts of American scholar Langdon Warner (1881–1955). Warner sat on a committee during the latter half of the war, which endeavoured to save artistic and historical treasures in war-torn regions. Now, more than a half-century later, Warner is a household name in Japan and is still alluded to in discussions on the future preservation of Kyoto. He is said to have gotten a desperate plea through to top US military authorities to spare the cities of Kyoto, Nara, Kamakura and Kanazawa.

Despite this popular account, other theories have surfaced, along with documentation pointing to an elaborate *X Files*–style conspiracy aimed at quelling anti-American sentiment in occupied Japan. The evidence has fuelled a debate as to whether or not it was in fact a well-planned public relations stunt scripted by US intelligence officials to gain the trust of a nation that had been taught to fear and hate the American enemy.

Some historians have suggested that both Kyoto and Nara were on a list of some 180 cities earmarked for air raids. Kyoto, with a population of over one million people, was a prime target (along with Hiroshima and Nagasaki) for atomic annihilation, and many avow the choice could easily have been Kyoto. Nara, it has been suggested, escaped merely due to having a population under 60,000, which kept it far down enough on the list not to be reached before the unconditional surrender of Japan in September 1945.

Whether the preservation of Kyoto was an act of philanthropy or a simple twist of fate, the efforts of Warner and his intellectual contemporaries are etched into the pages of history and even taught in Japanese schools. Disbelievers avow that the 'rumour' was sealed as fact for good after Warner was posthumously honoured by the Japanese government, who bestowed upon him the esteemed Order of the Sacred Treasure in recognition of his invaluable contribution to the Japanese nation. There is a symbolic tombstone placed as a memorial to Warner in the precincts of Nara's Hōryū-ji.

by 1945 Japan had been driven back on all fronts. In August the declaration of war by the Soviet Union and the atomic bombs dropped by the USA on Hiroshima and Nagasaki were the final straws: Emperor Hirohito announced unconditional surrender.

Despite avoiding air raids (see the boxed text above), Kyoto suffered a great drain of people and resources during the war. To prevent the spread of fires, hundreds of magnificent wooden shops and houses were torn down, and even great temple bells and statues were melted down into artillery, but thankfully most of Kyoto's cultural treasures survived.

POSTWAR RECONSTRUCTION & REVIVAL

Japan was occupied by Allied forces until 1952 under the command of General Douglas MacArthur. The chief aim was a major reform of Japanese government through demilitarisation, the trial of war criminals and the weeding out of militarists and ultranationalists from the government. A new constitution was introduced, which dismantled the political power of the emperor, who completely stunned his subjects by publicly renouncing any claim to divine origins. This left him with the status of mere figurehead.

At the end of the war the Japanese economy was in ruins and inflation was running rampant. A programme of recovery provided loans, restricted imports and encouraged capital investment and personal saving. In 1945 the Kyoto Revival Plan was drafted and again, as had happened repeatedly in its history, Kyoto was set for rebuilding. By 1949 Kyoto University had produced its first in a long line of Nobel Prize winners and the city went on to become a primary educational centre.

By the late 1950s, trade was flourishing and the Japanese economy continued to experience rapid growth. From textiles and the manufacture of labour-intensive goods such as cameras, the Japanese 'economic miracle' had branched out into virtually every sector of society and Kyoto increasingly became an international hub of business and culture.

1966	1981
Kyoto International Conference Hall opens	Karasuma subway line starts service

In 1956 Japan's first public orchestra was founded in Kyoto and two years later the city established its first sister-city relationship, with Paris. Japan was now looking seriously towards tourism as a source of income and foreign visitors were steadily arriving on tours for both business and pleasure. By this time Kyoto had further developed as a major university centre, and during the 'Woodstock era' of the late 1960s anti-war movements and Japanese flower power mirrored that of the West and brought student activism out into the streets.

In the 1970s Japan faced recession. Inflation surfaced in 1974 and again in 1980, mostly as a result of steep price hikes for imported oil, on which Japan is still gravely dependent. By the early '80s, however, Japan had fully emerged as an economic superpower and Kyoto's high-tech companies were among those dominating fields such as electronics, robotics and computer technology. The notorious 'bubble economy' that followed led to an unprecedented era of free spending by Japan's nouveau riche. Shortly after the 1989 death of Emperor Shōwa and the start of the Heisei period (with the accession of the current emperor, Akihito), the miracle bubble burst, launching Japan into a critical economic downfall from which many contend it may never fully recover.

1994	1997
Kyoto celebrates the 1200th anniversary of its founding	New Kyoto Station building opens

Neighbourhoods

Neighbourhoods

Exploring Kyoto is a fascinating and potentially endless pursuit. Along with the wealth of beautiful temples and shrines that dot the city and its outskirts, there are the Imperial Palace and Imperial Villas, the gardens and parks, the traditional geisha quarters and teahouses of the Gion district, the bustling department stores and markets downtown, and plenty of museums to keep the visitor occupied.

Add to this the myriad of hikes that can be done in the hills surrounding the city, and the excellent opportunities to view and learn Kyoto's famous crafts (p182), and you will find that Kyoto can keep you happily occupied not only for days, but for weeks and even months.

Fortunately for the traveller, many of Kyoto's most important sights are grouped together in distinct clusters throughout the city. These areas are usually extremely easy to navigate on foot or bicycle. And getting to these places is far easier than you might imagine, as Kyoto has an excellent public transportation system that is easy to use, relatively inexpensive and highly efficient.

This chapter is organised to reflect the natural groupings of Kyoto's sights into particular neighbourhoods. We start with the Kyoto Station area (p138), which is where most travellers enter the city. From there, we move on to Downtown Kyoto (p139), which is primarily a shopping, dining and entertainment district but also contains a few interesting sights. Next is Higashiyama, the principal sightseeing area of Kyoto, which is covered in the Southeast Kyoto (p140) and Northeast Kyoto (p142) sections.

What's Free in Kyoto

A quick glance through the pages of this chapter might convince you that sightseeing in Kyoto is going to require taking out a second mortgage on your home. Luckily there are plenty of free things you can do. Indeed, you could fill at least a week with activities that are absolutely free. Here are just a few:

Temples There is no charge to enter the grounds of many of Kyoto's temples, including Nanzen-ji (p58), Chion-in (p60), Hōnen-in (p64) and Tōfuku-ji (p63).

Shrines Almost all shrines in Kyoto can be entered free of charge. A few good ones include Fushimi-Inari-taisha (p86), Heian-jingū (p59), Shimogamo-jinja (p64) and Yasaka-jinja (p61).

Kyoto Imperial Palace Park (p75) Kyoto's Central Park is a treasure that many visitors overlook.

Kamo-gawa Like the Imperial Palace Park, this is a great place to spend a relaxing afternoon strolling and picnicking. In the summer you'll be treated to free fireworks shows as local youths hold impromptu *hanabi-taikai* (fireworks festivals).

Nishiki Market (p57) It costs nothing to wander through this wonderful market. Of course, you might find something that you just *have* to buy...

Department stores (p128) Have a look at the fabulous variety of goods for sale in Kyoto's department stores. While you're there, stop by the food floor and snag some free food samples.

Kyoto Station (p54) Kyoto's station building is pretty impressive, and the view from the roof-top observatory is the best you'll get – short of paying to ascend Kyoto Tower or expending the energy to climb Daimonji-yama.

Festivals (p8) There's nothing like a colourful Kyoto festival, and they're always free. If you're lucky, you might even be asked to participate.

Hikes It doesn't cost anything to enjoy Kyoto's natural beauty. There are myriad hikes in the mountains that surround the city.

Imperial Properties The Kyoto Imperial Palace (p66), Shūgaku-in Rikyū Imperial Villa (p65) and Katsura Rikyū Imperial Villa (p85) can all be toured free of charge.

Private Tours of Kyoto

A private tour is a great way to see the sights and learn about the city without having to worry about transport and logistics. There are a variety of private tours on offer in Kyoto, including the following:

All Japan Private Tours & Speciality Services (www.kyotoguide.com/yjpt) This company offers exclusive unique tours of Kyoto, Nara and Tokyo, as well as business coordination and related services.

Chris Rowthorn's Walks and Tours of Kyoto and Japan (www.chrisrowthorn.com) Lonely Planet *Kyoto* author Chris Rowthorn offers private tours of Kyoto, Nara, Osaka and the rest of Kansai.

Johnnie's Kyoto Walking (http://web.kyoto-inet.or.jp/people/h-s-love/) Hirooka Hajime, aka Johnnie Hillwalker, offers an interesting guided walking tour of the area around Kyoto Station and Higashiyama.

Naoki Doi (☎ 090 9596 5546; http://www3.ocn.ne.jp/~doitaxi/) This English-speaking taxi driver offers private taxi tours of Kyoto and Nara.

Peter MacIntosh (☎ 090 5169 1654; www.kyotosightsandnights.com) Canadian Peter MacIntosh offers guided walks through Kyoto's geisha districts. He can also arrange geisha entertainment in Kyoto teahouses and restaurants.

The Northwest Kyoto (p142) and Southwest Kyoto (p143) sections cover the main attractions in the central and western areas of the city. Kyoto's far western sightseeing area is covered under Arashiyama & Sagano Area (p80). Finally, areas on the outskirts of Kyoto are covered in the Kyoto Outskirts section (p82).

Note that the directions we give to most sights assume you're starting out from Kyoto Station. Of course, it's usually possible to access these sights from other parts of the city as well. We recommend that you arm yourself with a bus map (p187) and a sense of adventure.

Children's admission prices vary for some attractions in Kyoto. In this chapter, where a range is given, the admission price differs depending on the child's age.

ITINERARIES

Kyoto is so rich with things to see and do that it really makes sense to plan your visit carefully, especially if you have only a few days in the city. Whatever your time limit, try not to overdo the number of sights you visit. Instead, choose a few venues that really appeal to your interests and take your time to savour them. And if you don't find temples to your liking, don't visit them; there are plenty of other things to do, including shopping (p128), people-watching, strolling through the backstreets (p94) and picnicking in the parks or by the Kamo-gawa.

One Day

If you have only one day in Kyoto you should make a beeline to the **Higashiyama area**, covered in the Southeast Kyoto section of this chapter (p57). This area runs roughly from Nanzen-ji in the north down to Sanjūsangen-dō in the south, and contains many of Kyoto's must-see sights – it should be given the highest priority on any visit to the city. Furthermore, this area provides the perfect introduction to what Kyoto is all about.

Three Days

If you've got three days in the city, we recommend that you spend your first day exploring the **Higashiyama area** (p57). Your second day could be spent closer to the city centre, hitting such important sights as the **Kyoto Imperial Palace Park** (p75), the Central Park of Kyoto; **Nijō-jō** (p78), a splendid castle with wonderful gardens; and then checking out the shopping attractions of downtown, including **Nishiki Market** (p57), the city's best.

Your third day should be planned according to what you've enjoyed on your first two days in the city. If you're in the mood for more temples, head west to **Arashiyama** and **Sagano** (p80) and visit the temples and bamboo groves there, or head northwest to visit another trio of fine temples: **Kinkaku-ji** (p77), **Ryōan-ji** (p83) and **Ninna-ji** (p84). If you're in the mood for something else, we recommend heading up to the lovely rural villages of **Kurama** and **Kibune** (p91) for a hike (you will see more temples here, too, but you'll also get a chance to see a bit of rural Japan, bathe in a hot spring and escape from the confines of central Kyoto).

One Week

If you've got a week in the city, then you've got the latitude to combine some of Kyoto's main sights with some of its lesser-known attractions, and perhaps even go back and savour the areas you really enjoyed on your first day or two.

Your first three or four days could be spent as described in the previous Three Days itinerary. The following days could be spent hitting some of the city's less-popular sights, such as the temples in the north around **Manshu-in** (p64); or heading southwest to **Katsura Rikyū Imperial Villa** (p85), the finest piece of Japanese architecture in the whole country; or heading southeast to **Tōfuku-ji** (p63) and **Fushimi-Inari-taisha** (p86), a temple and shrine combo that make a fine half-day trip. You might also make a thorough exploration of the city's gardens (see the boxed text 'My Favourite Gardens' on p59).

If you have a whole week to spend, then you should strongly consider a day trip south to **Nara** (p149), which is probably the most rewarding destination outside of Kyoto. Or, if you'd like a glimpse of what modern Japan is all about, then a day trip to the urban madness of **Osaka** (p157) is highly recommended.

KYOTO STATION AREA

Eating p103; Sleeping pp138–9

The area around Kyoto Station, south of the city centre, is a fairly drab part of town. The main sights are a pair of giant temples, Higashi Hongan-ji and Nishi Hongan-ji. And, of course, there's always Kyoto Station itself!

In this section, we list places in the order that you are most likely to visit them. In this case, we start at Kyoto Station and work north.

KYOTO STATION Map pp230-1
Karasuma-dōri-Shiokōji

The Kyoto Station building is a striking steel-and-glass structure – a kind of futuristic cathedral for the transportation age. Unveiled in September 1997, the building has met with some decidedly mixed reviews. Some critics assail the building as not keeping with the traditional architecture of Kyoto; others love its wide-open spaces and dramatic lines.

Whatever the case, you're sure to be impressed by the tremendous space that arches above you as you enter the main concourse. Moreover, you'll probably enjoy a brief exploration of the many levels of the station, all the way up to the 15th-floor observation level. And be sure to take the escalator from the 7th floor on the east side of the building up to the 11th-floor glass corridor that runs high above the main concourse – not a good spot for those with a fear of heights!

In the station building you'll find several food courts (p103), Isetan department store, the Kyoto Prefectural International Center, the Kyoto Tourism Federation, a Joypolis game centre and an outdoor performance space.

KYOTO TOWER Map pp230-1
☎ 361 3215; Karasuma-dōri-Higashi Shiokōji; adult ¥770, child ¥150-620; ⏰ 9am-8.40pm; 3min walk from Kyoto Station, central exit

Directly north of the station is one of the city's greatest architectural blunders – the 131m-high Kyoto Tower. The tower is said to represent a 'forever-burning candle', but it looks more like a misguided space rocket. Many cite the construction of the tower in 1964 as the beginning of the end of Kyoto's once-graceful skyline.

The tower's observation deck offers a panoramic 360° view of the city (on a clear day you can see all the way to Osaka). If you don't feel like shelling out the admission fee, you might opt for a slightly less dramatic but free vista from the top of the Kyoto Station building.

NISHI HONGAN-JI Map pp230-1
☎ 371 5181; Horikawa-dōri-Hanaya-chō; admission free; ⏰ 5.30am-5.30pm, closes later in summer; 15min walk from Kyoto Station, central exit

Nishi Hongan-ji was originally built in 1272 in the Higashiyama Mountains by the priestess Kakushin, daughter of Shinran, who was

Kyoto Station (opposite)

founder of the Buddhist Jōdo Shin-shū (True Pure Land) school. The temple complex was relocated to its present site in 1591, on to land provided by Toyotomi Hideyoshi. By then, the Jōdo Shin-shū had accumulated immense power and the temple became its headquarters. Tokugawa Ieyasu sought to weaken the power of Jōdo Shin-shū by encouraging a breakaway faction to found Higashi Hongan-ji (right) in 1602. The original Hongan-ji then became known as Nishi Hongan-ji. It is now the headquarters of the Hongan-ji branch of Jōdo Shin-shū, which has over 10,000 temples and 12 million followers worldwide.

The temple contains five buildings featuring some of the finest examples of the architectural and artistic achievements of the Momoyama period. Unfortunately, the main hall (Goe-dō) is presently being restored and will be under wraps until 2010. The Daisho-in hall has sumptuous paintings, carvings and metal ornamentation. A small garden and Japan's oldest nō stages are connected with the hall. The dazzling Chinese-style Kara-mon gate displays intricate ornamental carvings and metalwork. The gate has been dubbed Higurashi-mon (Sunset Gate), purporting that its beauty can distract one from noticing the setting sun. Both Daisho-in and Kara-mon were transported here from Fushimi-jō castle in the south of the city.

The Goe-dō dates from 1636 and contains a seated statue of Shinran. The *hondō* (main hall), last reconstructed in 1760, houses a priceless collection of painted sliding screens with images of the phoenix and peacock.

HIGASHI HONGAN-JI Map pp230-1
☎ 371 9181; Karasuma-dōri-Shichijō; admission free; ☽ 5.50am-5.30pm, 5.50am-4.30pm in winter; 5min walk from Kyoto Station, central exit

In 1602, when Tokugawa Ieyasu engineered the rift in the Jōdo Shin-shū school, he founded this temple as a competitor to Nishi Hongan-ji (opposite). Rebuilt in 1895 after a series of fires destroyed all of the original structures, it is certainly monumental but less impressive artistically than its rival. The temple is now the headquarters of the Ōtani branch of Jōdo Shin-shū.

The Taishidō-mon gate stands 27m high and features giant doors made out of a single slab of wood. Wade through the sea of pigeons to the *hondō* – place your shoes in one of the plastic bags and carry them with you so you can exit from the neighbouring building. This hall enshrines a 13th-century statue of Amida Nyorai (Buddha of the Western Paradise).

In the corridor between the two main buildings you'll find a curious item encased in glass: a tremendous coil of rope made from human hair. Following the destruction of the temple in the 1880s, an eager group of female temple devotees donated their locks to make the ropes that hauled the massive timbers used for reconstruction.

55

In Hot Water

After a day spent marching from temple to temple, nothing feels better than a good hot bath. Kyoto is full of *sentō* (public baths), ranging from small neighbourhood baths with one or two tubs to massive complexes offering saunas, mineral baths and even electric baths. The following baths are worth a visit and could even double as an evening's entertainment. It's best to bring your own bath supplies (soap, shampoo, a towel to dry yourself and another small one for washing); if you've forgotten, you can buy toiletries and rent towels at the front desk. Washing buckets are available for free inside the bathing area.

Funaoka Onsen (Map pp216–18; ☎ 441 3735; 82-1 Minami-Funaoka-chō, Kuramaguchi-dōri, Murasakino, Kita-ku; adult ¥350, child ¥60-140; ☽ 3pm-1am Mon-Sat, 8am-1am Sun & public holidays; 5min walk from Senbon-Kuramaguchi bus stop, bus 206 from Kyoto Station) is our favourite *sentō* in Kyoto. This old bath boasts an outdoor bath and sauna, as well as some museum-quality woodcarvings in the changing room (apparently carved during Japan's invasion of Manchuria). To find it, head west from Horikawa-dōri on Kuramaguchi-dōri. It's on the left not far past the Lawson convenience store. Look for the large rocks out the front.

Gokō-yu (Map pp222–4; ☎ 841 7321; 590-1 Kakinomoto-chō, Gojō agaru, Kuromon-dōri; adult ¥350, child ¥60-140; ☽ 2.30pm-12.30am Tue-Sat, 7am-midnight Sun, closed Mon & 3rd Tue of each month; 3min walk from Ōmiya-Gojō bus stop, bus 43 or 206 from Kyoto Station), a popular bath, is another great spot to sample the joys of the *sentō*. It's a large two-storey bath with a wide variety of tubs. There's also a giant sauna with two rooms; one is merely hot, the other is incendiary! We also like the TV-fish tank in the entrance (you'll see what we mean). Note that Gokō-yu is a little hard to find – turn north of Gojō-dōri at the store that sells charcoal and gas burners.

Shōmen-yu (Map pp230-1; ☎ 561 3232; 310 Shōmen-chō, Shōmen agaru, Sayamachi-dōri, Higashiyama-ku; adult ¥350, child ¥60-140; ☽ 1pm-1am Mon & Wed-Sat, 9am-1am Sun; 5min walk from Keihan Shichijō Station, 20min walk from JR Kyoto Station) is perhaps the mother of all *sentō*. Three storeys high, with an outdoor bath on the roof, this is your chance to try riding an elevator naked (if you haven't already had the pleasure). Everything is on a grand scale here, including the sauna, which boasts a TV and room for 20. Men, don't be surprised if you spot some *yakuza* (gangsters) among the bathers (recognisable by their tattoos).

The enormous *taishi-dō* (founder's hall) is one of the world's largest wooden structures, standing 38m high, 76m long and 58m wide. The centrepiece is a self-carved likeness of Jōdo Shin-shū founder Shinran.

It only takes a few minutes to wander through the buildings and you can ask at the information office just inside the main gate for an English leaflet.

About five minutes' walk east of the temple, the garden **Shōsei-en** (☎ 371 9181; admission free; ☽ 9am-3.30pm) is worth a look. The lovely grounds, incorporating the Kikoku-tei villa, were completed in 1657. Bring a picnic (and some bread to feed the carp) or simply stroll around the beautiful Ingetsu-ike pond. Just when you're

caught up in the 'old-Kyoto' moment, note the two love hotels looming in the background outside the wall (modern 'borrowed scenery').

PERIOD COSTUME MUSEUM
Map pp230-1

Fūzoku Hakubutsukan; ☎ 342 5345; 5F Izutsu Bldg Shinhanayachō-dōri-Horikawa higashi iru; adult ¥400, child ¥200-300; ☽ 9am-5pm, closed Sun & public holidays; 15min walk from Kyoto Station, central exit

This is a museum of wax figures wearing costumes representing different periods in Japanese history; they include samurai warriors, merchants and fire fighters. The museum is not a must-see but worth a peek on a rainy day.

DOWNTOWN KYOTO

Eating pp104-9; Sleeping pp139–40

Kyoto's downtown area is mostly a shopping, dining and entertainment district, but there are three sites that are well worth visiting: the Museum of Kyoto, which provides a reasonable introduction to Kyoto history, Nishiki Market, which is the finest food market in the whole city, and Pontochō, which is easily one of the city's most entrancing districts (as long as you go there by night).

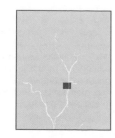

MUSEUM OF KYOTO Map pp228-9

☎ 222 0888; Sanjō-dōri-Takakura; adult/child ¥500/free, adults extra for special exhibits; ☯ 10am-7.30pm, closed Mon; 3min walk from Karasuma subway line, Karasuma-Oike Station

Housed in and behind the former Bank of Japan, a classic brick Meiji-period building, this museum is worth a visit for those with an interest in Kyoto's long history. The regular exhibits consist of models of ancient Kyoto, audiovisual presentations and a small gallery dedicated to Kyoto's film industry. On the 1st floor, the Roji Tempō is a reconstructed Edo-period merchant area showing 10 types of exterior lattice work (this section can be entered for free; some of the shops sell souvenirs and serve local dishes).

NISHIKI MARKET Map pp228-9

Nishiki-kōji; ☯ most stores 9am-5pm; 5min walk from Karasuma subway line, Shijō Station

If you want to see all the weird and wonderful foods required for cooking in Kyoto, wander through Nishiki Market. It's in the centre of town, one block north of Shijō-dōri. This is a great place to visit on a rainy day or as a break from temple-hopping. The variety of foods on display is staggering and the frequent cries of *'irasshaimase'* ('Welcome!') are heartwarming.

PONTOCHŌ Map pp228-9

2min walk from Hankyū Kawaramachi Station

Once the city's red-light district, Pontochō is a traditional centre for dining and night-time entertainment in a narrow street running between the Kamo-gawa and Kiyamachi-dōri. It's a pleasant place to take a stroll if you want to observe Japanese nightlife. Many of the restaurants and teahouses can be difficult to enter, but a number of reasonably priced, accessible places can be found (p104). The **geisha teahouses** (*ocha-ya*) usually control the admittance of foreigners, with a policy of introductions from Japanese persons only, and astronomical charges.

Pontochō is a great place to spot geisha and *maiko* (apprentice geisha) making their way between appointments, especially on weekend evenings at the Shijō-dōri end of the street.

SOUTHEAST KYOTO

Eating pp109–12; Sleeping pp140–2; Walking Tour pp94–5

The area at the base of the Higashiyama (Eastern) Mountains is Kyoto's main sightseeing area. It is packed with temples, shrines, museums, traditional neighbourhoods and shops. This should be your first sightseeing stop in Kyoto and it has ample scope for several days of relaxed exploration if you have the time.

We start our coverage of the area at its northern end and work south, but it is possible, of course, to cover this area from south to north, or any direction you please. Also, the more northern of the Higashiyama attractions, such as Ginkaku-ji and the Tetsugaku-no-Michi (Path of Philosophy) are covered in the Northeast Kyoto section (p63).

One of the best ways to see the sights in this area is to take the Southern (p94) and Northern Higashiyama walking tours (p96).

Addresses in Japan

In Japan, finding a place from its address can be difficult, even for locals. The problem is twofold: first, the address is given by an area rather than a street; and second, the numbers are not necessarily consecutive, as prior to the mid-1950s numbers were assigned by date of construction.

To find an address, the usual process is to ask directions. The numerous local police boxes are there largely for this purpose. Businesses often include a small map in their advertisements or on their business cards to show their location.

In this guide, we use a simplified system for addresses. We either give the area (eg Higashiyama-ku, Nanzen-ji) or we give the street on which the place is located, followed by the nearest cross street (eg Karasuma-dōri-Imadegawa). In some cases, we also give additional information to show where the place lies in relation to the intersection of the two streets mentioned. In Kyoto, the land usually slopes gently to the south; thus, an address might indicate whether a place lies above or north of (*agaru*) or below or south of (*sagaru* or *kudaru*) a particular east–west road. Thus, Karasuma-dōri-Imadegawa simply means the place is near the intersection of Karasuma-dōri and Imadegawa-dōri; Karasuma-dōri-Imadegawa-sagaru indicates that it's south of that intersection. An address might also indicate whether a place lies east (*higashi*) or west (*nishi*) of the north–south road.

EIKAN-DŌ Map pp225-7

Zenrin-ji; ☎ 761 0007; Sakyō-ku, Eikan-dō; adult/child ¥600/400; ✆ 9am-5pm; 3min walk from Nanzen-ji Eikandō-michi bus stop, bus 5 from Kyoto Station

This temple is made interesting by its varied architecture, its gardens and works of art. One of Kyoto's best spots for viewing the autumn colours, the temple was founded in 855 by the priest Shinshō, but the name was changed to Eikan-dō in the 11th century to honour the philanthropic priest Eikan.

In the Amida-dō hall at the southern end of the complex is a famous statue of Mikaeri Amida Buddha glancing backwards.

The best approach is to follow the arrows and wander slowly along the covered walkways connecting the halls and gardens.

From Amida-dō, head north to the end of the curving covered *garyūrō* (walkway). Change into the sandals provided, then climb the steep steps up the mountainside to the **Tahō-tō pagoda**, from where there's a fine view across the city.

NANZEN-JI Map pp225-7

☎ 771 0365; Nanzen-ji, Fukuchi-chō; admission to grounds free, adult to inner buildings & garden ¥1000, child ¥300-400; ✆ 8.40am-5pm; 10min walk from Tōzai subway line, Keage Station or 20min walk from Keihan Sanjō Station

This temple is one of the most pleasant in Kyoto, with its expansive grounds and numerous subtemples. It began as a retirement villa for Emperor Kameyama but was dedicated as a Zen temple on his death in 1291. Civil war in the 15th century destroyed most of the temple; the present buildings date from the 17th century. It operates now as the headquarters of the Rinzai school.

At the entrance to the temple stands the San-mon gate (1628), its ceiling adorned with Tosa and Kanō school murals of birds and angels. Steps lead up to the 2nd storey (admission ¥300), which has a fine view over the city. Beyond the gate is the *hōjō* (abbot's) hall, which has impressive screens painted with a vivid depiction of tigers.

Within the precincts of the same building, the **Leaping Tiger Garden** is a classic Zen garden well worth a look. While you're in the *hōjō*, you can enjoy a cup of tea (¥400) while sitting on tatami mats gazing at a small waterfall; ask at the reception desk.

Perhaps the best part of Nanzen-ji is overlooked by most visitors: **Nanzen-ji Oku-no-in**, a small shrine hidden in a forested hollow behind the main precinct. To get here, walk up to the red-brick aqueduct in front of Nanzen-in. Follow the road that runs parallel to the aqueduct up into the hills, past **Kōtoku-an** (admission free; ✆ dawn-dusk) on your left; be sure to stop in here on your way. Continue into the woods, past several brightly coloured torii (shrine gate) until you reach a waterfall in a beautiful mountain glen. Here, pilgrims pray while standing under the waterfall, sometimes in the dead of winter. Hiking trails lead off in all directions from this point; by going due north you'll eventually arrive at the top of Daimonji-yama, go east and you'll get to the town of Yamashina (also about two hours).

Dotted around the grounds of Nanzen-ji are several subtemples, such as Nanzen-in (below) and Tenju-an (below), which are often skipped by the crowds and consequently easier to enjoy.

NANZEN-IN Map pp225-7

☎ 771 0365; Nanzen-ji, Fukuchi-chō; adult ¥300, child ¥150-250; ✆ 8.40am-5pm; 10min walk from Tōzai subway line, Keage Station

This subtemple is on your right when facing the *hōjō* – follow the path under the aqueduct. It has an attractive garden designed around a heart-shaped pond. This garden is best seen in the morning or around noon, when sunlight shines directly into the pond and illuminates the colourful carp.

TENJU-AN Map pp225-7

☎ 771 0365; Nanzen-ji, Fukuchi-chō; adult ¥300, child ¥100-200; ✆ 8.40am-5pm; 10min walk from Tōzai subway line, Keage Station

This temple stands at the side of San-mon, a four-minute walk west of Nanzen-in. Constructed in 1337, Tenju-an has a splendid garden and a great collection of carp in its pond.

KONCHI-IN Map pp225-7

☎ 771 3511; Nanzen-ji, Fukuchi-chō; adult/child ¥400/200; ✆ 8.30am-5pm; 5min walk from Tōzai subway line, Keage Station

When leaving Tenju-an (above), turn left and continue for 100m – Konchi-in is down a small side street on the left. The stylish gardens fashioned by Kobori Enshū are the main attraction.

NOMURA MUSEUM Map pp225-7

☎ 751 0374; Nanzen-ji, Shimokawahara; admission ¥700; ✆ 10am-4.30pm, closed Mon; 10min walk from Tōzai subway line, Keage Station

This museum is a 10-minute walk north of Nanzen-ji. Exhibits include scrolls, paintings,

My Favourite Gardens *Marc Peter Keane*

What is it about Kyoto that made it so ripe for gardens? Was it something physical, like the ample rain and mists that get trapped by the surrounding mountains, or the rich soil and fine white river sands? Or was it cultural, a cosmopolitan blend of aristocratic, warrior, merchant and priestly cultures? Or was it all of those ingredients, and more, mixing in one place? However it came to be, Kyoto is one of the world's great garden cities, even despite the great loss from 'development' over the past decades.

A few gardens stand out among the others. **Katsura Rikyū** (p85), which was designed by two imperial princes, father and son, is the epitome of refined detailing. When you're there, don't forget, while gazing around in awe of the scenery, to take a look down, too. If God is in the details at Katsura, she lives in the paths. Another garden for strolling is the one at **Heian-jingū** (p59). With its weeping cherries, flows of irises, babbling brooks and cool expanses of mirrored water, it is sure to delight. While the Heian-jingū garden aims to please, some of the most captivating places in Kyoto are far more restrained, such as the garden at **Renge-ji** (p82), a small temple tucked in against a mountainside on the way to Ōhara. The wonder of Renge-ji lies in how its garden merges seamlessly with the surrounding forest so that the boundary between artifice and nature disappears. You sit. You look. And time slips by, quietly, like water from the pond. If artifice merges with nature at Renge-ji, it is polished into art at **Daisen-in** (p76), where a small cluster of stones and some white sand appear to have been morphed straight out of a Sung-dynasty ink landscape painting.

Marc Peter Keane is the author of Japanese Garden Design, *an introduction to Japanese gardens in their cultural and design context. He lived in Kyoto for 20 years and now teaches garden design at Cornell University, in the USA.*

implements used in tea ceremonies, and ceramics that were bequeathed by business magnate Nomura Tokushiki.

MURIN-AN VILLA Map pp225-7
☎ 771 3909; Nanzen-ji, Kusakawa-chō; admission ¥350; 9am-4.30pm; 7min walk from Tōzai subway line, Keage Station

This elegant villa was the home of prominent statesman Yamagata Aritomo (1838–1922) and the site of a pivotal 1902 political conference as Japan was heading into the Russo-Japanese War.

Built in 1896, the grounds contain well-preserved wooden buildings, including a fine Japanese tearoom. The Western-style annex is characteristic of Meiji-period architecture and the serene garden features small streams that draw water from the Biwa-ko Sosui canal. For ¥300 you can savour a bowl of frothy *matcha* (powdered green tea) while viewing the 'borrowed scenery' backdrop of the Higashiyama Mountains.

HEIAN-JINGŪ Map pp225-7
☎ 761 0221; Okazaki, Nishitenno-chō; admission to shrine precincts free, adult admission to garden ¥600, child ¥300-600; 6am-6pm; 1min walk from Kyoto Kaikan/Bijyutsukan-mae bus stop, bus 5 from Kyoto Station

This shrine was built in 1895 to commemorate the 1100th anniversary of the founding of Kyoto. The shrine buildings are gaudy replicas,

reduced to a two-thirds scale, of the Imperial Court Palace of the Heian period (794–1185).

The spacious garden, with its large pond and Chinese-inspired bridge, is also meant to represent gardens that were popular in the Heian period. It is well known for its wisteria, irises and weeping cherry trees. About 500m in front of the shrine is a massive steel torii. Although it appears to be entirely separate, this is actually considered the main entrance to the shrine itself.

Two major events, Jidai Matsuri (22 October; p11) and Takigi Nō (1 to 2 June; p11), are held here.

OKAZAKI-KŌEN AREA Map pp225-7
Sakyō-ku, Okazaki; Kyoto Kaikan/Bijyutsukan-mae bus stop, bus 206 from Kyoto Station

Okazaki-kōen is an expanse of parks and canals that lies between Niōmon-dōri and Heian-jingū. Two of Kyoto's most important museums can be found here, as well as two smaller museums and a zoo.

The **National Museum of Modern Art** (☎ 761 4111; Okazaki Enshoji-chō; adult ¥420, child free-¥130; 9.30am-5pm, closed Mon) is renowned for its Japanese ceramics and paintings. There is an excellent permanent collection, including many pottery pieces by Kawai Kanjirō.

The **Kyoto Municipal Museum of Art** (☎ 771 4107; Okazaki Enshoji-chō; admission varies by exhibition, child free; 9am-4.30pm, closed Mon) organises several major exhibitions a year.

For a break from temple gazing, pop into the **Fureai-kan Kyoto Museum of Traditional Crafts** (☎ 762 2670; Okazaki Seishoji-chō; admission free; ☷ 9am-5pm). Exhibits include woodblock prints, lacquerware, bamboo goods and gold-leaf work. It's in the basement of Miyako Messe (Kyoto International Exhibition Hall).

A nearby museum of limited interest is the **Lake Biwa Aqueduct Museum** (☎ 752 2530; Nanzenji Kusakawa-chō; admission free; ☷ 9am-4.30pm, closed Mon), dedicated in 1989 to mark the 100th anniversary of the building of the canal.

Those with children might want to stop by the **Kyoto Municipal Zoo** (Kyoto-shi Dōbutsu-en; ☎ 771 0210; Okazaki Houshouji-chō; adult/child ¥500/300; ☷ 9am-5pm Tue-Sun Mar-Nov, 9am-4.30pm Dec-Feb). The zoo is home to about 1000 animals and has some decent gardens and groves of cherry trees.

SHŌREN-IN Map pp225-7

☎ 561 2345; Higashiyama-ku, Sanjō-Awataguchi; adult/child ¥500/400; ☷ 9am-5pm; 3min walk from Tōzai subway line, Higashiyama Station, exit 2

This temple is hard to miss, with its giant camphor trees growing just outside the walls. Shōren-in, commonly called Awata Palace after the road it faces, was originally the residence of the chief abbot of the Tendai school. Founded

in 1150, the present building dates from 1895 and the main hall has sliding screens with paintings from the 16th and 17th centuries. Often overlooked by the crowds, who descend on other Higashiyama area temples, this is a pleasant place to sit and think while gazing out over one of Kyoto's finest landscape gardens.

CHION-IN Map pp225-7

☎ 531 2111; Shinbashi-dōri-Yamatooji Higashi iru; admission to grounds free, adult admission to inner buildings & garden ¥400, child ¥200-400; ☷ 9am-4pm Mar-Nov, 9am-3.40pm Dec-Feb; 10min walk from Tōzai subway line, Higashiyama Station, exit 2

A grand temple, Chion-in was built by the monk Genchi in 1234 on the site where his mentor, Hōnen, had taught and eventually fasted to death. Today it is still the headquarters of the Jōdo school, which was founded by Hōnen, and it's a hive of religious activity. For visitors with a taste for the grand and glorious, this temple is sure to satisfy.

The oldest of the present buildings date from the 17th century. The two-storey Sanmon gate at the main entrance is the largest in Japan, and prepares the visitor for the massive scale of the temple. The immense main hall contains an image of Hōnen and is connected with the Dai Hōjō hall by a nightingale floor.

Chion-in (above)

After visiting the main hall, with its fantastic gold altar, you can walk around the back of the same building to see the temple's gardens. On the way, you'll pass a darkened hall with a small statue of Amida Buddha on display, glowing eerily in the darkness. It makes a nice contrast to the splendour of the main hall.

The Daishōrō belfry houses a bell cast in 1633, measuring 2.7m in diameter and weighing almost 80 tonnes – the largest in Japan. The combined muscle power of 17 monks is required to make the bell budge for a ceremony to ring in the new year.

MARUYAMA-KŌEN Map pp225-7
Higashiyama-ku; 1min walk from Gion bus stop, bus 206

This park is a favourite of locals and visitors alike. It's a place to escape the bustle of the city centre and amble around gardens, ponds, souvenir shops and restaurants. Peaceful paths meander through the trees and carp glide through the waters of a small pond in the centre of the park.

For two weeks in early April, when the park's cherry trees come into bloom, the calm atmosphere of the park is shattered by hordes of drunken revellers having *hanami* (cherry-blossom viewing) parties under the trees. The centrepiece is a massive *shidare-zakura* cherry tree – one of the most beautiful sights in Kyoto, particularly when lit up from below at night. For those who don't mind crowds, this is a good place to observe the Japanese at their most uninhibited. Arrive early and claim a good spot high on the east side of the park, from where you can peer down on the mayhem below.

YASAKA-JINJA Map pp225-7
☎ 561 6155; Higashiyama-ku, Gion; admission free; ☯ 24hr; 5min walk from Keihan Shijō Station

This colourful shrine is down the hill from Maruyama-kōen. It's considered the guardian shrine of Gion. The present buildings, with the exception of the older, two-storey west gate, date from 1654. The granite torii on the south side was erected in 1666 and stands 9.5m high, making it one of the tallest in Japan. The roof of the main shrine is covered with cypress shingles. Among the treasures here are a pair of carved wooden *koma-inu* (mythological animals) attributed to the renowned sculptor Unkei.

This shrine is particularly popular as a spot for *hatsu-mōde* (the first shrine visit of the new year). If you don't mind a stampede, come here around midnight on New Year's Eve or any of

the following days. Surviving the crush is proof that you're blessed by the gods!

Yasaka-jinja sponsors Kyoto's biggest festival, Gion Matsuri (p10).

KŌDAI-JI Map pp225-7
☎ 561 9966; Higashiyama-ku, Kōdai-ji; adult/child ¥500/300; ☯ 9am-5pm; 5min walk from Higashiyama-yasui bus stop, bus 206

This temple was founded in 1605 by Kita-no-Mandokoro in memory of her late husband, Toyotomi Hideyoshi. The extensive grounds include gardens designed by Kobori Enshū, teahouses designed by the renowned master of tea ceremony, Sen no Rikyū, and a lovely little grove of bamboo trees.

ROKUHARAMITSU-JI Map pp225-7
☎ 561 6980; Matsubara-dōri-Yamatooji; adult admission to treasure house ¥500, child ¥300-400; ☯ 8am-5pm; 5min walk from Kiyomizu-michi bus stop, bus 206 from Kyoto Station

An important Buddhist pilgrimage stop, this temple was founded in 963 by Kūya Shōnin, who carved an image of an 11-headed Kannon and installed it in the temple in the hope of stopping a plague that was ravaging Kyoto at the time.

The temple itself is unremarkable but the treasure house at the rear contains a rare collection of 15 fantastic statues; the most intriguing is a standing likeness of Kūya, staff in hand and prayer gong draped around his neck, with a string of tiny figurines parading from his gums. Legend holds that while praying one day, these manifestations of the Buddha suddenly ambled out of his mouth.

KIYOMIZU-DERA Map pp225-7
☎ 551 1234; Higashiyama-ku Kiyomizu; adult ¥300, child ¥200-300; ☯ 6am-6pm; 10min walk from Gojō-zaka bus stop, bus 206 or 100 from Kyoto Station

This temple was first built in 798 and devoted to Jūichi-men, an 11-headed Kannon. The present buildings – built under order of Iemitsu, the third Tokugawa shōgun – are reconstructions dating from 1633. As an affiliate of the Hossō school, which originated in Nara, the temple has survived through the centuries the many intrigues of Kyoto Buddhist schools and is now one of the most famous landmarks of the city. This, unfortunately, makes it a prime target for busloads of Japanese tourists, particularly during cherry-blossom season. Some travellers are also put off by the rather mercantile air of the temple – endless stalls selling

Maiko Costume

If you ever wondered how *you* might look as a *maiko* (apprentice geisha), Kyoto has many outfits in town that offer the chance. **Maika** (Map pp225-7; ☎ 551 1661; Higashiyama-ku, Miyagawa suji; maiko-san from ¥6720, geiko-san from ¥7350; ☯ 9.30am-4.30pm Mon-Fri, 9am-7pm public holidays; 10min walk from Keihan Shijō Station) is in the Gion district. Here you can be dressed up to live out your *maiko* fantasy. Prices begin at ¥6720 for the basic treatment, which includes full make-up and formal kimono (studio photos cost ¥500 per print and you can have stickers made from these). If you don't mind spending some extra yen, it's possible to head out in costume for a stroll through Gion (and be stared at like never before!). The process takes about an hour. Call to reserve at least one day in advance.

good luck charms, fortunes and all manner of souvenirs. If you find this bothersome, head to the quieter temples further north.

The main hall has a huge veranda that juts out over the hillside, supported by 139 15m-high wooden pillars. The terrace commands an excellent view over the city centre.

Just below this hall is **Otowa-no-taki water-fall**, where visitors drink the sacred waters believed to have therapeutic properties (and also thought to improve school test results). South of the main hall is **Koyasu-no-tō**, a three-storey pagoda housing a statue of the goddess responsible for the safe delivery of babies (which explains the frequent visits by pregnant women). At the **Jishu-jinja**, north of the main hall, visitors try to ensure success in love by closing their eyes and walking about 18m between a pair of stones – if you miss the stone, your desire for love won't be fulfilled!

Before you enter the actual temple precincts, we strongly recommend that you take a few minutes to check out one of the oddest 'sights' that we've come across at a Japanese temple: the **Tainai-meguri** (admission ¥100; ☯ 9am-4pm), the entrance to which can be found just to the left (north) of the pagoda that is located in front of the main entrance to the temple (you may have to ask a temple official since there is no English sign).

We don't want to tell you too much about this hall as it will take away from the experience. Suffice it to say, by entering the hall, you are figuratively entering the womb of Daizuigu Bosatsu, a female Bodhisattva who has the power to grant any human wish. Once you get

to the inner sanctum, you are meant to turn the large stone found there in a clockwise direction and make your wish. Be warned, there are several 90° turns in the darkness – walk slowly and keep a hand in front of your face.

GION DISTRICT Map pp225-7
1min walk from Keihan Shijō Station

Gion is the famous entertainment and geisha quarter on the eastern bank of the Kamo-gawa. While Gion's true origins were in teahouses catering to weary visitors to the Yasaka-jinja shrine, by the mid-18th century the area was Kyoto's largest pleasure district. Despite the looming modern architecture, congested traffic and contemporary nightlife establishments that have cut a swathe through its historical beauty, there are still some places left in Gion for an enjoyable walk.

Hanami-kōji runs north to south and bisects Shijō-dōri. The southern section is lined with 17th-century, traditional restaurants and teahouses, many of which are exclusive establishments for geisha entertainment. At the south end you reach **Gion Corner** (p122) and next door **Gion Kōbu Kaburen-jō Theatre** (p123).

If you walk from Shijō-dōri along the northern section of Hanami-kōji, you will reach **Shinbashi-dōri** and its traditional restaurants. A bit further north are **Shinmonzen-dōri** and **Furu-monzen-dōri**, running east to west. Wander in either direction along these streets, which are packed with old houses, art galleries and shops specialising in antiques – but don't expect flea-market prices here.

For more historic buildings in a beautiful waterside setting, wander down **Shirakawa Minami-dōri**, which is roughly parallel with, and one block south of, the western section of Shinmonzen-dōri.

One of the best ways to explore Gion is to take the Night Walk Through the Floating World walking tour (p97).

KAWAI KANJIRŌ MEMORIAL HALL
Map pp225-7

☎ 561 3585; Higashiyama-Gojō-zaka; adult/child ¥900/free; ☯ 10am-4.30pm, closed Mon; 3min walk from Umamachi bus stop, bus 206 from Kyoto Station

This museum was once the self-designed home and workshop of one of Japan's most famous potters, Kawai Kanjirō (1890–1966). The 1937 house is built in rural style and contains examples of Kanjirō's work, his collection of folk art and ceramics, and his workshop and kiln. The museum is near the intersection of Gojō-dōri and Higashioji-dōri.

KYOTO NATIONAL MUSEUM Map pp225-7

☎ 531 7509; Higashiyama-ku, Chaya-machi; adult ¥420 (extra for special exhibitions), child free-¥130; ⏲ 9.30am-5pm, closed Mon; 1min walk from Hakubutsukan/Sanjūsangendō-mae bus stop, bus 206 or 208 from Kyoto Station, or 10min walk from Keihan Shichijō Station

The Kyoto National Museum was founded in 1895 as an imperial repository for art and treasures from local temples and shrines. It is housed in two buildings opposite Sanjūsangen-dō temple. There are 17 rooms with displays of over 1000 artworks, historical artefacts and handicrafts. The fine arts collection is especially highly rated, holding some 230 items that have been classified as National Treasures or Important Cultural Properties.

SANJŪSANGEN-DŌ Map pp225-7

☎ 525 0033; Higashiyama-ku, Chaya-machi; adult ¥600, child ¥300-400; ⏲ 8am-4.30pm in summer, 9am-4pm in winter; 1min walk from Hakubutsukan/Sanjūsangendō-mae bus stop, bus 206 or 208 from Kyoto Station, or 10min walk from Keihan Shichijō Station

The original temple, called Rengeō-in, was built in 1164 at the request of the retired Emperor Go-shirakawa. After it burnt to the ground in 1249 a faithful copy was constructed in 1266.

The temple's name refers to the 33 *sanjūsan* (bays) between the pillars of this long, narrow building. The building houses 1001 wooden statues of Kannon (the Buddhist goddess of mercy); the chief image, the 1000-armed Senjū-Kannon, was carved by the celebrated sculptor Tankei in 1254. It is flanked on either side by 500 smaller Kannon images, neatly lined in rows.

There are an awful lot of arms, but if you are picky and think the 1000-armed statues don't have the required number, you should remember to calculate according to the nifty Buddhist mathematical formula, which holds

that 40 arms are the equivalent of 1000 because each saves 25 worlds.

At the back of the hall are 28 guardian statues in a great variety of expressive poses. The gallery at the western side of the hall is famous for the annual Tōshi-ya festival, held on 15 January, when archers shoot arrows the length of the hall. The ceremony dates from the Edo period, when an annual contest was held to see how many arrows could be shot from the southern to northern end in 24 hours. The all-time record was set in 1686, when an archer successfully landed over 8000 arrows at the northern end.

TŌFUKU-JI Map pp225-7

☎ 561 0087; Higashiyama-ku, Honmachi; admission to main temple/subtemples/grounds ¥400/400/free; ⏲ 9am-4pm Dec-Oct, 8.30am-4.30pm Nov; 1min walk from Tōfuku-ji bus stop, bus 202, 207 or 208 from Kyoto Station, or 15min walk from Keihan Tōfuku-ji Station (local train-only stop)

Founded in 1236 by the priest Enni, Tōfuku-ji belongs to the Rinzai school. Since this temple was intended to compete with Tōdai-ji and Kōfuku-ji in Nara, it was given a name combining characters in each of these.

This impressive temple complex is considered one of the five main Zen temples in Kyoto. The huge San-mon gate is the oldest Zen main gate in Japan. Other ancient structures include the *tōsu* (lavatory) and *yokushitsu* (bathroom), which date from the 14th century. The present complex includes 24 subtemples; at one time there were 53.

The *hōjō* was reconstructed in 1890. The gardens, laid out in 1938, are worth a visit. As you approach the northern gardens, you cross a stream over the Tsūten-kyō (bridge to heaven), which is a pleasant, leafy spot – the foliage is renowned for its autumn colour. The northern garden has stones and moss neatly arranged in a chequerboard pattern. The nearby **Reiun-in** receives few visitors to its attractive garden.

NORTHEAST KYOTO

Eating pp112–15; Sleeping pp142; Walking Tour pp97–9

Northeast Kyoto is second only to Southeast Kyoto in terms of sightseeing attractions. The main sights here include Ginkaku-ji, one of Kyoto's most important temples, and the Tetsugaku-no-Michi, the city's loveliest footpath. The area's other main attractions are Hōnen-in, a quiet little temple that is one of our favourites in Kyoto, and the grand Shūgaku-in Rikyū Imperial Villa.

One of the best ways to see the sights in this area is to take the Northern Higashiyama walking tour (p96).

GINKAKU-JI Map pp219-21

☎ 771 5725; Sakyō-ku, Ginkaku-ji; adult ¥500; ⏱ 8.30am-5pm; 5min walk from Ginkaku-ji-Michi bus stop, bus 5 from Kyoto Station

One of Kyoto's most breathtaking temples, Ginkaku-ji is definitely worth seeing; unfortunately it is usually swamped with busloads of visitors jamming the narrow pathways. Also known as Jishō-ji, the temple belongs to the Shōkokuji school of the Rinzai school.

In 1482 shōgun Ashikaga Yoshimasa constructed a villa here, which he used as a genteel retreat from the turmoil of civil war. Although its name translates as Silver Pavilion, the scheme to completely cover the building in silver leaf was never carried out. After Yoshimasa's death it was converted to a temple.

The approach to the main gate runs between tall hedges before turning sharply into the extensive grounds. Walkways lead through the gardens, which were laid out by painter and garden designer Sōami. The gardens include meticulously raked cones of white sand (*kōgetsudai*) designed to reflect moonlight and enhance the beauty of the garden at night.

In addition to the Buddha image in the main hall, the Tōgudō (residence of Yoshimasa) houses an effigy of Yoshimasa dressed in monk's garb. The tiny tearoom (closed to the public) here is said to be the oldest in Japan.

TETSUGAKU-NO-MICHI Map pp219-21

Sakyō-ku, Ginkaku-ji; 7min walk from Ginkaku-ji-Michi bus stop, bus 5 or 17 from Kyoto Station

The name translates as the 'path of philosophy'. It has been a favourite with contemplative strollers since 20th-century philosopher Nishida Kitarō is said to have meandered along the path 'lost in thought'. Follow the traffic-free route along a canal lined with cherry trees that come into spectacular bloom in April. It only takes 30 minutes to do the walk, which starts at Nyakuōji-bashi, above Eikan-dō, and leads to Ginkaku-ji. During the day you should be prepared for crowds; a night stroll will definitely be quieter.

HŌNEN-IN Map pp219-21

☎ 771 2400; Sakyō-ku, Shishigatani; admission free; ⏱ 6am-4pm; 10min walk from Jyodō-ji bus stop, bus 5 from Kyoto Station

This temple was founded in 1680 to honour the priest Hōnen. It's a lovely, secluded temple with carefully raked gardens set back in the woods. The temple buildings include a small gallery where frequent exhibitions featuring local and international artists are held.

Hōnen-in is a 12-minute walk from Ginkaku-ji, on a side street east of Tetsugaku-no-michi.

SHIMOGAMO-JINJA Map pp219-21

☎ 781 0010; Shimogamo, Izumikawa-chō; admission free; ⏱ 6.30am-5.30pm; 1min walk from Shimogamo-jinja-mae bus stop, bus 205 from Kyoto Station

Shimogamo-jinja dates from the 8th century and is a Unesco World Heritage site. It is nestled in the fork of the Kamo-gawa and Takano-gawa Rivers, and is approached along a shady path through the lovely **Tadasu-no-mori**. This wooded area is said to be a place where lies cannot be concealed and is considered a prime location to sort out disputes.

The shrine is dedicated to the god of harvest. Traditionally, pure water was drawn from the nearby rivers for purification and agricultural ceremonies. The *hondō* dates from 1863 and, like the Haiden hall at its sister shrine, Kamigamo-jinja (p75), is an excellent example of *nagare*-style shrine architecture.

SHISEN-DŌ Map pp219-21

☎ 781 2954; Ichijōji, Monkuchi-chō; adult ¥500, child ¥200-400; ⏱ 9am-5pm; 5min walk from Ichijōji kudari matsu machi bus stop, bus 5 from Kyoto Station

With a name meaning 'house of poet-hermits', Shisen-dō was built in 1641 by Ishikawa Jōzan, a scholar of Chinese classics and a landscape architect who wanted a place to retire to. Formerly a samurai, Jōzan abandoned his warrior status after a rift with Tokugawa Ieyasu and became a recluse here until his death in 1672 at the age of 90.

The hermitage is noted for its display of poems and portraits of 36 ancient Chinese poets, which are found in the Shisen-no-ma room. The *karesansui* (waterless pond) white-sand garden is lined with azaleas, which are said to represent islands in the sea. The garden also reflects Jōzan's distinct taste for Chinese aesthetics. It's a tranquil place to relax.

Water flows from a small waterfall to the *shi-shi-odoshi*, or *sōzu*, a device designed to scare away wild boar and deer. It's made from a bamboo pipe into which water slowly trickles, fills up and swings down to empty. On the upswing to its original position the bamboo strikes a stone with a 'thwack' – just loud enough to interrupt your snooze – before starting to refill.

MANSHU-IN Map pp219-21

☎ 781 5010; Ichijōji, Takenouchi-chō; adult ¥500, child ¥300-400; ⏱ 9am-4.30pm; 20min walk from Eizan Shūgakuin Station

About 30 minutes' walk north of Shisen-dō you'll reach the stately gate of Manshu-in, a popular retreat of former emperors and a great escape from the crowds. The temple was originally founded by Saichō on Hiei-zan, but was re-located here at the beginning of the Edo period by Ryōshōhō, the son of Prince Hachijōnomiya Tomohito (who built Katsura Rikyū).

The graceful temple architecture is often compared with Katsura Rikyū for its detailed woodwork and rare works of art, such as sliding *fusuma-e* doors painted by Kanō Eitoku, a famed artist of the Momoyama era. The *karesansui* garden by Kobori Enshū features a sea of gravel intended to symbolise the flow of a waterfall, and stone islands representing cranes and turtles.

SHŪGAKU-IN RIKYŪ IMPERIAL VILLA
Map pp219-21

☎ 211 1215; Sakyō-ku, Shūgakuin; admission free; 10min walk from Shūgakuinrikyū-michi bus stop, bus 5 from Kyoto Station

Lying at the foot of Hiei-zan, this villa, or detached palace, was begun in the 1650s by Emperor Go-Mizunō following his abdication; work was continued by his daughter Akenomiya after his death in 1680. It was designed as a lavish summer retreat for the imperial family.

The villa grounds are divided into three enormous garden areas on a hillside – lower, middle and upper. Each has superb tea-ceremony houses; the upper, **Kami-no-chaya**, and lower, **Shimo-no-chaya**, were completed in 1659, and the middle teahouse, **Naka-no-chaya**, was completed

in 1682. The gardens' reputation rests on their ponds, pathways and impressive use of 'borrowed scenery' in the form of the surrounding hills. The view from the Rinun-tei teahouse in Kami-no-chaya is particularly impressive.

One-hour tours (in Japanese) start at 9am, 10am, 11am, 1.30pm and 3pm; try to arrive early. A basic leaflet in English is provided and more detailed literature is on sale in the tour waiting room.

You must make reservations through the Imperial Household Agency (p66) – usually several weeks in advance.

TAKARA-GA-IKE-KŌEN Map pp219-21
Sakyō-ku, Matsugasaki; 10min walk from Karasuma subway line, Kokusaikaikan Station, exit 5

This expansive park is an excellent place for a stroll or picnic in natural surroundings. Far from the throngs in the city centre, it is a popular place for bird-watching and has spacious gardens. It runs an 1.8km loop around the main pond, where rowing boats can be hired for ¥1000 per hour.

In the northeast of the park, the **Kyoto International Conference Hall** is an unfortunate attempt at replicating Japan's traditional thatched-roof *gasshō zukuri* style in concrete. Behind the conference hall, the **Hosho-an Teahouse** (designed by Soshitsu Sen, Grand Tea Master XV of the Urasenke school) is worth a look.

Kyoto for Children

Japan is an extremely easy place to travel with children: it's safe, clean and easy to get around. The only problem for parents is that you can't expect your kids to enjoy the same things you do. While you might be content to contemplate a rock garden at a Zen temple for hours at a time, your kids will probably have other ideas. Luckily, Kyoto has plenty of attractions to keep your kids busy, some of which parents are likely to enjoy as well. The following is just a sample of activities and attractions that children will enjoy in Kyoto.

Game centres Kyoto has some great high-tech game centres. And despite the fact that everything is in Japanese, we've found that most kids have no trouble understanding how to play the games. **JJ Club 100** (p126) is downtown and has enough games to keep your kids busy all day.

Iwatayama Monkey Park (p80) Both kids and adults will find the antics of the monkeys here fascinating, and it's easy to combine this with a trip to the sights of Arashiyama.

Kamo-gawa There's a river running through Kyoto and it's a great place to bring the kids for an afternoon picnic. On hot days they can wade in the river while you relax on the banks. The area around Demachiyanagi (Map pp216-18) is one of the most popular spots for parents and children to play.

Kyoto Imperial Palace Park (p75) The Central Park of Kyoto, this sprawling expanse of fields, trails, ponds and woods is a great place for a picnic, walk or bicycle ride with the kids.

Kyoto Municipal Zoo (p60) This small zoo is far from world class, but it is quite convenient to the sights of southeastern Kyoto, so that you can easily combine it with a trip to the temples, shrines and museums nearby.

Umekōji Steam Locomotive Museum (p79) With 18 vintage steam locomotives, one of which you can ride, this museum is a must for train-crazy boys and girls.

NORTHWEST KYOTO

Eating pp115–16; Sleeping pp142–3

This section covers the sights that can be found on the north-west side of the city centre, including Kyoto Imperial Palace and Kyoto Imperial Palace Park, the Nishijin area – Kyoto's famous textile district – and the sprawling Daitoku-ji temple complex. We start with the Kyoto Imperial Palace, work up to Kami-gamo-jinja and then cover the sights that lie to the west of these attractions.

Neighbourhoods – Northwest Kyoto

KYOTO IMPERIAL PALACE Map pp216-18

☎ 211 1215; Kamigyō-ku, Kyoto goen; admission free; 10min walk from Karasuma subway line, Imade-gawa Station

The original Imperial Palace (Kyoto Gosho) was built in 794 and has undergone numerous rebirths after destruction by fires. The present building, on a different site and smaller than the original, was constructed in 1855. Cere-monies related to the enthronement of a new emperor and other state functions are still held here.

The tour guide will elaborate on the de-tails in English while you are led for about one hour past the Shishin-den (ceremonial hall), Ko Gosho (small palace), Tsune Gosho (regu-lar palace) and Oike-niwa (pond garden). Re-grettably, it is forbidden to enter any of these buildings.

The Shinsen-den is an outstanding, single-storey structure thatched with a cypress-bark roof. Covered walkways connect it to the sur-rounding buildings. From outside you can see a *takamikura* (throne) where the emperor sat on formal occasions. It is covered with a silk canopy and on each side are stands to hold treasures such as swords, jewels and other imperial regalia. Just in front of the throne are two wooden *koma-inu* statues. The palace is full of other treasures, including priceless slid-ing screens adorned with Tosa school paint-ings. Though the hall initially was used as living quarters for the emperor, it was later set aside for ceremonial use only.

Foreigners are given preferential access to the palace and can obtain permission to enter in a few hours or days, while Japanese visitors (unless acting as an interpreter to a foreigner) may have to wait months. Twice-yearly, in spring and autumn, the palace grounds are chock-full when the inner sanctum is opened to the public for several days.

Entry is controlled by the **Imperial Household Agency** (Map pp216-18; Kunaichō; ☎ 211 1215; ☺ 8.45am-noon & 1-4pm Mon-Fri), a short walk southeast of the Imadegawa Station on the Karasuma subway line, or the Karasuma-

Imadegawa bus stop. The office is inside the walled park surrounding the palace.

To make a reservation you must fill out an application form in person and show your passport. Children must be accompanied by an adult over 20 years of age. Permission to tour the Imperial Palace is usually granted on the same day. Guided tours in English are given at 10am and 2pm from Monday to Friday and at 10am on the third Saturday of the month (except during April, May, October and No-vember); once permission has been granted, you should arrive at the Seisho-mon gate no later than 20 minutes before the tour time. Allow extra time to find your way.

The agency's office is also the place to make reservations to see Sentō Gosho and the Kat-sura Rikyū and Shūgaku-in Rikyū Imperial Villas. As there is limited space for each tour of these three places, you may need to work around the agency's schedules. To arrange reservations from abroad or from outside of Kyoto, the application forms are available from JNTO offices (p192).

SENTŌ GOSHO Map pp216-18

☎ 211 1215; Kamigyō-ku, Kyoto goen; 10min walk from Karasuma subway line, Imadegawa Station

A few hundred metres southeast of the Imperial Palace is the Sentō Gosho. It was originally con-structed in 1630 during the reign of Emperor Go-Mizunō as a residence for retired emperors. The palace was repeatedly des-troyed by fire and reconstructed but served its purpose until a final blaze in 1854 (it was never rebuilt). Today only two structures, the Seika-tei and Yūshin-tei teahouses, remain. The magnificent gardens, laid out in 1630 by renowned landscape de-signer Kobori Enshū, are the main attraction.

Visitors must obtain advance permission from the Imperial Household Agency (p66) and be over 20 years old. One-hour tours (in Japanese) start daily at 11am and 1.30pm.

(Continued on page 75)

1 Monk, Shijō-Ōhashi Bridge
2 Geisha, downtown Kyoto
3 Worshippers burning incense,
Chion-in (p60) *4* Young people
strolling, downtown Kyoto

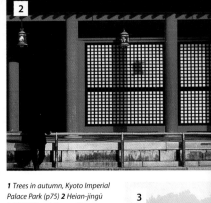

1 Trees in autumn, Kyoto Imperial Palace Park (p75) 2 Heian-jingū (p59) 3 Mountains and fog surrounding Kyoto 4 Traditional roof, southeast Kyoto

1 *Saihō-ji (p86)* 2 *Heian-jingū (p59)* 3 *Rock garden at Ryōan-ji (p83)* 4 *Detail on torii, Fushimi-Inari-taisha (p86)*

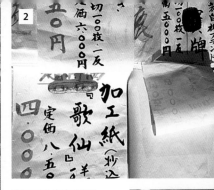

1 Kimono on display (p133)
2 Washi paper (p133) **3** Pottery crafts (p132) **4** Wood-block prints, Kyoto Handicraft Center (p129)

1 Men carrying torches, Kurama Hi Matsuri (p11) 2 Female archer, Jidai Matsuri (p11) 3 Marchers in traditional clothes, Jidai Matsuri (p11) 4 Paper lanterns hanging from a float, Gion Matsuri (p10)

1 *Ippo-dō tea shop (p134)*
2 *Sweets (p34)* 3 *Pontochō kaiseki restaurant* 4 *Fresh sushi at Musashi Sushi (p108)*

1 *Ninen-zaka, Higashiyama (p94)*
2 *Pontochō street at night (p57)*
3 *Cherry trees along Shirakawa Minami-dōri (p62)* 4 *Taxis, downtown Kyoto*

1 *Kyoto Station (p54)* 2 *Window-shoppers* 3 *Kyoto Tower (p54)* 4 *Shoppers outside Kintetsu Department Store*

(Continued from page 66)

KYOTO IMPERIAL PALACE PARK
Map pp216-18

Kamigyō-ku, Kyoto goen; 8min walk from Karasuma subway line, Imadegawa Station

The Imperial Palace is surrounded by a spacious park with a welcome landscape of trees and open lawn. It's perfect for picnics, strolls and just about any sport that doesn't require retrieving balls over walls. Best of all, it's free. Take some time to visit the pond at the park's southern end, with its gaping carp. The park is most beautiful in the plum and cherry-blossom seasons (early March and early April, respectively). It is bounded by Teramachi-dōri and Karasuma-dōri on the east and west, and by Imadegawa-dōri and Marutamachi-dōri on the north and south.

KAMIGAMO-JINJA Map pp216-18

☎ 781 0011; Kamigamo, Motoyama; admission free; 🕑 8am-5.30pm; 5min walk from Kamigamomisono-bashi bus stop, bus 9 from Kyoto Station

Kamigamo-jinja is one of Japan's oldest shrines and predates the founding of Kyoto. Established in 679, it is dedicated to Raijin, the god of thunder, and is one of Kyoto's 17 Unesco World Heritage sites. The present buildings (over 40 in all), including the impressive Haiden hall, are exact reproductions of the origin-als, dating from the 17th to 19th centuries. The shrine is entered from a long approach through two torii. The two large conical white-sand mounds in front of Hosodono hall are said to represent mountains sculpted for gods to descend upon.

KAMIGAMO-YAMABATA-SEN
Map pp216-18

This street, which runs along a canal from Kamigamo-jinja to Ōta-jinja, is one of Kyoto's most picturesque. It's lined with traditional Japanese homes, each of which has its own private bridge over the canal. You can do this walk after visiting Kamigamo-jinja, finishing with lunch at the charming Azekura restaurant (p115).

KYOTO BOTANICAL GARDENS
Map pp216-18

☎ 701 0141; Sakyō-ku, Shimogamo; adult ¥200, greenhouse extra ¥200, child ¥80-150; 🕑 9am-5pm; 2min walk from Karasuma subway line, Kitayama Station

This vast garden, opened in 1914, occupies 240,000 sq m and features 12,000 plants, flowers and trees. It is pleasant to stroll through the rose, cherry and herb gardens or see the rows of camphor trees and the large tropical greenhouse.

NISHIJIN TEXTILE CENTER
Map pp216-18

☎ 451 9231; Horikawa-dōri-Imadegawa; admission free; 🕑 9am-5pm; 7min walk from Karasuma subway line, Imadegawa Station

In the heart of the Nishijin textile district, this centre is a good place to observe the weaving of fabrics used in kimono and their ornamental *obi* (belts). There are also displays of completed fabrics and kimono.

Neighbourhoods – Northwest Kyoto

Kyoto Botanical Gardens (above)

ORINASU-KAN Map pp216-18

☎ 431 0020; Kamigyō-ku, Daikoku-chō; adult/child ¥500/350; 🕙 10am-4pm, closed Mon; 15min walk from Karasuma subway line, Imadegawa Station

This museum is housed in a Nishijin weaving factory. It has impressive exhibits of Nishijin textiles. The **Susamei-sha** building (recently restored) next door is also open to the public and worth a look. With advance reservations, traditional weaving workshops can be attended (p183).

URASENKE CHADŌ RESEARCH CENTER Map pp216-18

☎ 431 6474; Horikawa-dōri-Teranouchi; admission ¥500; 🕙 9.30am-4.30pm; 15min walk from Karasuma subway line, Kuramaguchi Station

Anyone interested in tea ceremony should make their first stop at the Urasenke Chadō Research Center. Urasenke is Japan's largest tea school, and hosts hundreds of students annually who come from branch schools worldwide to further their studies in 'the way of tea'.

The **gallery** (admission ¥800; 🕙 9.30am-4.30pm, closed Mon) on the 1st and 2nd floors holds quarterly exhibitions on tea-related arts; call to see if there is a show being held during your stay. The entrance fee entitles you to a bowl of *matcha* and a sweet.

The **Konnichi-an library** (☎ 431 6474; admission free; 🕙 10am-4pm Mon-Fri, 10am-3pm Sat, closed Sun & public holidays) has more than 50,000 books (about 100 in English), plus videos on tea, which can be viewed.

For more information, contact Urasenke's **Office of International Affairs** (Kokusai Kyoku; ☎ 431 3111).

KITANO TENMAN-GŪ Map pp216-18

☎ 461 0005; Kamigyō-ku, Bakuro-chō; admission free; 🕙 5am-dusk; 1min walk from Kitano Tenmangū-mae bus stop, bus 50 or 101 from Kyoto Station

Commonly known as Kitano Tenjin, this shrine was established in 947 to honour Sugawara Michizane (845–903), a noted Heian-era statesman and scholar.

It is said that having been defied by his political adversary Fujiwara Tokihira, Sugawara was exiled to Kyūshū for the rest of his life. Following his death in 903, earthquakes and storms struck Kyoto, and the Imperial Palace was repeatedly struck by lightening. Fearing that Sugawara, reincarnated as Raijin, had returned from beyond to avenge his rivals, locals erected and dedicated this shrine to him.

The present buildings were built in 1607 by Toyotomi Hideyori, and the grounds contain an extensive grove of plum and apricot trees *(baika)*, said to have been Sugawara's favourite fruits.

Unless you are trying to avoid crowds, the best time to visit is during the Tenjin-san market fair, held here on the 25th of each month. Those held in December and January are particularly colourful.

SHŌKOKU-JI Map pp216-18

☎ 231 0301; Imadegawa-dōri-Karasuma; admission free; 🕙 10am-4pm; 7min walk from Karasuma subway line, Imadegawa Station

Shōkoku-ji, the headquarters of the Rinzai Shōkoku-ji school, sits in an ancient pine grove north of Dōshisha University. It was established in 1392 by the third Ashikaga shōgun, Yoshimitsu. The original buildings were almost totally destroyed during the civil wars in the 15th century. Inside the vast compound, the **Jōtenkaku Museum** (☎ 231 0301; Imadegawa-dōri-Karasuma, East; admission ¥800; 🕙 10am-4pm; 5min walk from Imadegawa Station) houses treasures from Kinkaku-ji and Ginkaku-ji.

DAITOKU-JI Map pp216-18

☎ 491 0019; Kita-ku, Murasakino, Daitokuji-chō; admission free; 🕙 dawn to dusk; 15min from Karasuma subway line, Kitaōji Station, exit 2

The precincts of this temple, headquarters of the Rinzai Daitoku-ji school, contain an extensive complex of 24 subtemples – including Daisen-in, Kōtō-in and Zuihō-in – but only eight are open to the public. If you want an intensive look at Zen culture, this is the place to visit.

The eponymous Daitoku-ji is on the eastern side of the grounds. It was founded in 1319, burnt down in the next century and rebuilt in the 16th century. The San-mon gate (1589) has a self-carved statue of its erector, the famous tea master Sen no Rikyū, on the 2nd storey.

Some sources say that Toyotomi Hideyoshi was so angry when he discovered he'd been demeaning himself by walking under Rikyū's effigy that he forced the master to commit *seppuku* (ritual suicide) in 1591.

DAISEN-IN Map pp216-18

☎ 491 8346; Kita-ku, Murasakino, Daitokuji-chō; adult/child ¥400/free; 🕙 9am-5pm Mar-Nov, 9am-4.30pm Dec-Feb; 15min from Karasuma subway line, Kitaōji Station, exit 2

The Zen garden masterpiece in this subtemple is an elegant example of 17th-century *kare-*

sansui style, and ranks with the revered rock garden at Ryōan-ji. Here the trees, rocks and sand are said to represent and express various spectacles of nature, from waterfalls and valleys to mountain lakes.

KŌTŌ-IN Map pp216-18

☎ 492 0068; Kita-ku, Murasakino, Daitokuji-chō; admission ¥400; ⏰ 9am-4.30pm; 20min from Karasuma subway line, Kitaōji Station, exit 2

This subtemple in the western part of the grounds swarms with slightly fewer visitors than Daisen-in. Surrounded by lovely maples and bamboo, the moss garden viewed from the temple veranda is superb.

ZUIHŌ-IN Map pp216-18

☎ 491 1454; Kita-ku, Murasakino, Daitokuji-chō; adult ¥400, child ¥300-400; ⏰ 9am-5pm; 20min from Karasuma subway line, Kitaōji Station, exit 2

Zuihō-in enshrines the 16th-century Christian *daimyō* (domain lord), Ōtomo Sōrin. In the early 1960s, a landscape architect named Shigemori Misuzu rearranged the stones in its rock garden into the shape of a crucifix!

KINKAKU-JI Map pp216-18

☎ 461 0013; Kita-ku, Kinkaku-ji-chō; adult ¥400, child ¥300-400; ⏰ 9am-5pm; 2min walk from Kinkakuji-michi bus stop, bus 205 from Kyoto Station

Kinkaku-ji, the famed 'Golden Temple', is one of Japan's best-known sights. Also known as Rokuon-ji, it belongs to the Shōkokuji school. The original building was constructed in 1397 as a retirement villa for shōgun Ashikaga Yoshimitsu. His son, complying with his father's wishes, converted it into a temple.

The three-storey pavilion is covered in bright gold leaf and features a bronze phoenix on top of the roof. The mirror-like reflection of the temple in the Kyō-ko pond is extremely photogenic, especially when the maples are ablaze in autumn. In 1950 a young monk consummated his obsession with the temple by burning it to the ground. The monk's story is fictionalised in Mishima Yukio's *The Temple of the Golden Pavilion*.

In 1955 a full reconstruction was completed, which followed the original design exactly, but the gold-foil covering was extended to the lower floors. The temple may not exactly be to everyone's taste, but it is still an impressive feat.

KŌETSU-JI Map pp216-18

☎ 491 1399; Kita-ku, Takagamine Kōetsu-chō; admission ¥300; ⏰ 8am-5pm; 3min walk from Takagamine Genko-an-mae bus stop, bus 1 from Karasuma subway line, Kitaōji Station

This temple dates from 1651 and was once the hermitage of Honami Kōetsu, a celebrated Edo-period artisan. After his death the villa was reconstructed as a temple and dedicated to him. The grounds contain seven tea-ceremony houses and a notable fence called Kōtsu-gaki, made with slats of interwoven bamboo.

A short walk northeast of Kōetsu-ji, two other small temples worth a visit are **Genkō-an** (☎ 492 1858; admission ¥300; ⏰ 8am-5pm) and **Jōshō-ji** (☎ 492 6775; admission ¥300; ⏰ 8.30am-5pm).

SHŌDEN-JI Map pp216-18

☎ 491 3259; Kita-ku, Nishigamo Kita Chinjuan-chō; admission ¥300; ⏰ 9am-5pm; 15min walk from Jinko-in-mae bus stop, bus 9 from Kyoto Station

This temple is approached up a long flight of stone steps and through a thick grove of trees. Shōden-ji was founded south of its current location in 1268, but shortly after was destroyed in a fire and was rebuilt in 1282 on the present site. Of interest here are the wooden ceiling boards of the Chi Tenjō (blood ceiling), which were once used as flooring for a corridor of Fushimi-jō, where 1200 people committed ritual suicide following the surrender of the castle in 1600.

SOUTHWEST KYOTO

Eating pp116–17; Sleeping pp143–5

The Southwest Kyoto section covers attractions to the southwest of the city centre, including Nijō-jō, the splendid castle of Tokugawa Ieyasu, Tō-ji, one of the city's most important temples, and Umekōji Steam Locomotive Museum, a must-see for travellers who have kids in tow. We start with places that are close to the city centre and then work our way south and west to the more outlying destinations.

NIJŌ-JŌ Map pp222-4

☎ 841 0096; Nijō-dōri-Horikawa; adult ¥600, child ¥190-500; 🕒 8.45am-4pm (gates close 5pm), closed Tue in Dec, Jan, Jul & Aug; 1min walk from Tōzai subway line, Nijōjō-mae Station

This castle was built in 1603 as the official residence of Tokugawa Ieyasu. The ostentatious style was intended as a demonstration of Ieyasu's prestige and to signal the demise of the emperor's power. To safeguard against treachery, Ieyasu had the interior fitted with 'nightingale' floors (intruders were detected by the squeaking boards) and concealed chambers where bodyguards could keep watch and spring out at a moment's notice. Fans of ninja movies will recognise the features immediately.

The Momoyama-era (1576–1600) Kara-mon gate, originally part of Hideyoshi's Fushimi-jō castle, features lavish, masterful woodcarving and metalwork. After passing through the gate, you enter the **Ninomaru palace,** which is divided into five buildings with numerous chambers. Access to the buildings used to depend on rank – only those of highest rank were permitted into the inner buildings.

The Ōhiroma Yon-no-Ma (fourth chamber) has spectacular screen paintings. Also, don't miss **Seiryu-en garden**, designed by Kobori Enshū. The vast garden is composed of three separate islets spanned by stone bridges, and is meticulously kept. The Ninomaru palace and garden take about an hour to walk through. A detailed fact sheet in English is provided.

The neighbouring **Honmaru palace** dates from the mid-19th century. After the Meiji Restoration in 1868, the castle became a detached palace of the imperial household and in 1939 was given to Kyoto City. It's only open for a special autumn viewing.

While you're in the neighbourhood, you might want to take a look at **Shinsen-en** (admission free), just south of the castle outside the walls. This forlorn garden, with its small shrines and pond, is all that remains of the original 8th-century Imperial Palace, abandoned in 1227.

NIJŌ JINYA Map pp222-4

☎ 841 0972; Ōmiya-dōri-Oike; adult/child ¥1000/800; 🕒 tours 10am, 11am, 2pm, 3pm, closed Wed; 10min walk from Tōzai subway line, Nijōjō-mae Station

A few minutes' walk south of Nijō-jō, Nijō Jinya is one of Kyoto's hidden gems. Seldom seen by short-term visitors, this former merchant's home was built in the mid-1600s and served as an inn for provincial feudal lords visiting the capital. What appears to be an average Edo-period mansion, however, is no ordinary dwelling.

The house contains fire-resistant earthen walls and a warren of 24 rooms, and was ingeniously designed to protect the *daimyō* against possible surprise attacks. Here you'll find hidden staircases, secret passageways and an array of counterespionage devices. The ceiling skylight of the main room is fitted with a trap door from where samurai could pounce on intruders, and sliding doors feature alternate panels of translucent paper to expose the shadows of eavesdroppers.

One-hour tours are conducted (in Japanese) several times daily. Reservations are necessary. An English leaflet is provided, but you might consider arranging a volunteer guide through the Tourist Information Centre (TIC; p192).

HORINO MEMORIAL MUSEUM
Map pp222-4

Horino Kinenkan; ☎ 223 2072; Sakaimachi-dōri, Nijō agaru; adult/child ¥300/200; 🕒 11am-9pm, closed Mon; 10min walk from Karasuma subway line, Marutamachi Station

A few minutes' walk south of the Imperial Palace Park is the Horino Memorial Museum, an 18th-century sake brewery housed in a vintage *kyō-machiya* (wooden townhouse). Though the original Kinshi Masamune brewery moved south to Fushimi in the 1880s, spring water (a key ingredient in sake brewing) continues to flow from the Momo-no-I well in the courtyard, where it has been since 1781.

Much of the old architecture remains well preserved, including a fine *kura* (warehouse) open for viewing. There are interesting displays on traditional sake-brewing methods. Don't miss the cosy café that serves tasters of the house sake, micro-brewed beer and light meals. For a unique souvenir, you can pick up a bottle of sake and put your own artistic touch on the label.

MIBU-DERA Map pp222-4

☎ 841 3381; Boujou-Bukkō-ji; admission free; 🕒 8.30am-5.30pm; 10min walk from Hankyū Ōmiya Station

Mibu-dera was founded in 991 and belongs to the Risshū school. In the late Edo period, it became a training centre for samurai. Mibu-dera houses tombs of pro-shōgunate Shinsen-gumi members, who fought bloody street battles resisting the forces that succeeded in restoring the emperor in 1868. Except for an unusual stupa covered in Jizō statues, visually the temple is of limited interest. It is, however, definitely worth visiting during Mibu kyōgen performances in late April, or the Setsubun celebrations in early February.

KODAI YŪZEN-EN GALLERY Map pp222-4

☎ 823 0500; Takatsuji-dōri-Inokuma kado; adult ¥500, child ¥250-400; ☺ 9am-5pm; 10min walk from Horikawa-Matsubara bus stop, bus 9 or 28 from Kyoto Station

This building is devoted to Kyoto's traditional Yūzen fabric-dyeing, created in the 17th century by painter Miyazaki Yūzen. It houses the Yūzen Art Museum, displaying an impressive collection of antique kimono, paintings, scrolls, dyeing patterns and tools. There is a film shown in English about the Yūzen-dyeing process and, of course, a shop selling Yūzen-dyed goods. On the top floor you can catch a glimpse of fabric artists at work and even stencil-dye your own handkerchief (p184).

From Kyoto Station take bus 9 or 28 to the Horikawa-Matsubara stop and walk for two minutes west on Takatsuji-dōri; or walk southeast for eight minutes from Ōmiya Station on the Hankyū Kyoto line.

A similar facility, the **Yūzen Cultural Hall** (Map pp214-15; Kyoto Yūzen Bunka Kaikan; ☎ 311 0025; admission ¥400; ☺ 9am-4pm, closed Sun) has a museum dedicated to the craft.

SUMIYA PLEASURE HOUSE Map pp222-4

☎ 351 0024; Nishishinyashikiageya-chō; adult ¥1000, child ¥500-800; ☺ 10am-4pm, closed Mon; 7min walk from JR Tanbaguchi Station, 10min walk from Umekōji-kōen-mae bus stop, bus 205 from Kyoto Station

Shimabara, a district northwest of Kyoto Station, was Kyoto's original pleasure quarters. At its peak during the Edo period (1600–1867) the area flourished, with over 20 enormous ageya – magnificent banquet halls where artists, writers and statesmen gathered in a 'floating world' ambience of conversation, art and fornication. Geisha were often sent from their okiya (living quarters) to entertain patrons at these restaurant-cum-brothels. By the start of the Meiji period, however, such activities had drifted north to the Gion district and Shimabara had lost its prominence.

Though the traditional air of the district has dissipated, a few old structures remain. The tremendous **Shimabara-no-Ō-mon** gate, which marked the passage into the quarter, still stands, as does the Sumiya Pleasure House, the last remaining ageya, which is now designated a National Cultural Asset. Built in 1641, this stately two-storey, 20-room structure allows a rare glimpse into Edo-era nirvana. With a delicate lattice-work exterior, Sumiya has a huge open kitchen and an extensive series of rooms (including one extravagantly decorated with mother-of-pearl inlay).

Special tours in Japanese (requiring advance reservations in Japanese, booked through Sumiya Pleasure House) allow access to the 2nd storey and are conducted daily. An English pamphlet is provided, but you might want to consider arranging a volunteer guide through the TIC (p192).

TŌ-JI Map pp222-4

☎ 691 3325; Minami-ku, Kujō-dōri; adult ¥500, child ¥300-400; ☺ 9am-4.30pm; 15min walk from Kyoto Station

This temple was established in 794 by imperial decree to protect the city. In 823 the emperor handed it over to Kūkai (known posthumously as Kōbō Daishi), the founder of the Shingon school. Many of the temple buildings were destroyed by fire or fighting during the 15th century, and most of the remaining buildings were destroyed in the Momoyama period (1576–1600).

The main gate (Nandai-mon) was moved here in 1894 from Sanjūsangen-dō in the southern Higashiyama area. The kōdō (lecture hall) dates from the 1600s and contains 21 images representing a Mikkyō (esoteric Buddhist) mandala. The kondō (main hall), rebuilt in 1606, combines Chinese, Indian and Japanese architectural styles and contains statues depicting the Yakushi (Healing Buddha) trinity. In the southern part of the garden stands the gojū-no-tō (five-storey) pagoda which, despite having burnt down five times, was doggedly rebuilt in 1643. Standing at 57m, it is now the highest pagoda in Japan.

The **Kōbō-san market fair** is held here on the 21st of each month. There is also a regular market on the first Sunday of each month.

UMEKŌJI STEAM LOCOMOTIVE MUSEUM Map pp222-4

☎ 314 2996; Shimogyō-ku, Kannon-ji-chō; museum adult/child ¥400/100, train ride adult/child ¥200/100; ☺ 9.30am-5pm, closed Mon; 15min walk from Kyoto Station

A hit with steam-train buffs and kids, this museum features 18 vintage steam locomotives (dating from 1914 to 1948) and related displays. It is in the former JR Nijō Station building, which was recently relocated here and thoughtfully reconstructed. You can take a 10-minute ride on one of the smoke-spewing choo-choos (departures at 11am, 1.30pm and 3.30pm).

ARASHIYAMA & SAGANO AREA

Eating pp117–18; Sleeping p145; Walking Tour pp99–100

Tucked into the western hills of Kyoto, Arashiyama and Sagano are both worth visiting if you feel like strolling in pleasant natural surroundings and visiting temples tucked inside bamboo groves. The area makes a nice full-day excursion from central Kyoto.

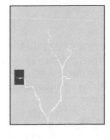

Note that this area is wildly popular with Japanese tourists and can be packed, particularly in the cherry-blossom and maple-leaf seasons. To avoid the crowds, go early on a weekday or head to some of the more offbeat spots. Upon arrival here, you may wonder why the Japanese make such a fuss about this place; it's not very beautiful around the stations, particularly with all the tacky shops and vending machines nearby. The best advice is to head north immediately to the quieter regions of Sagano.

One of the best ways to explore this area is to take the Arashiyama & Sagano walking tour (p99).

IWATAYAMA MONKEY PARK Map p232

☎ 861 1616; Arashiyama, Togetsu-kyō; adult/child ¥500/150; ⏰ 9am-5pm 15 Mar-15 Nov, 9am-4pm winter; 10min walk from Keifuku Arashiyama line, Keifuku Arashiyama Station

Home to some 200 monkeys, this nature park is a joy. Though it is common to spot wild monkeys in the nearby mountains, here you can encounter them at a close distance and enjoy watching the playful creatures frolic about. It makes for an excellent photo opportunity, not only for the monkeys but for the panoramic view over Kyoto. Refreshingly, it is the animals who are free to roam while the humans who observe them are caged in a box!

You enter the park near the south side of Togetsu-kyō (below), through the orange torii of Ichitani-jinja. Reaching the monkeys involves a moderate hike uphill.

HŌRIN-JI Map p232

☎ 862 0069; Arashiyama Kokuzouyama-chō; admission free; ⏰ 9am-5pm; 10min walk from Keifuku Arashiyama line, Keifuku Arashiyama Station

This temple was originally founded in 713 by the priest Gyōki. There are 80 steps up the *hondō*, where in 829 Dōshō, a disciple of maverick monk Kūkai, installed a large Jizō statue and named the temple Hōrin-ji. Hōrin-ji is renowned for the *jūsan-mairi* ceremony. The temple is close to the southern end of Togetsu-kyō bridge.

TOGETSU-KYŌ Map p232

Saga Tenryū-ji; 5min walk from Keifuku Arashiyama line, Keifuku Arashiyama Station

This bridge is the dominant landmark in Arashiyama and is just a few minutes on foot from either the Keifuku line or Hankyū line Arashiyama Stations. The original crossing,

constructed in 1606, was about 100m upriver from the present bridge.

On 13 April *jūsan-mairi*, an important rite of passage for local children aged 13, takes place here. Boys and girls (many in kimono), after paying respects at Hōrin-ji and receiving a blessing for wisdom, cross the bridge under strict parental order not to look back towards the temple until they've reached the northern side of the bridge. Not heeding this instruction is believed to bring bad luck for life!

From July to mid-September, this is a good spot to watch *ukai* (cormorant fishing) in the evening. If you want to get close to the action, you can pay ¥1700 to join a passenger boat. The TIC (p192) can provide more details.

TENRYŪ-JI Map p232

☎ 881 1235; Saga Tenryū-ji; adult ¥600, child ¥300-500; ⏰ 8.30am-5.30pm Mar-Oct, 8.30am-5pm Nov-Feb; 5min walk from Keifuku Arashiyama line, Keifuku Arashiyama Station

This is a major temple of the Rinzai school. It was built in 1339 on the old site of Go-Daigo's villa after a priest dreamt of a dragon rising from the nearby river. The dream was seen as a sign that the emperor's spirit was uneasy, and the temple was built as appeasement – hence the name *tenryū* (heavenly dragon). The present buildings date from 1900, but the main attraction is the 14th-century Zen garden.

Tenryū-ji is a popular place to sample Zen vegetarian cuisine *(shōjin ryōri)*.

KAMEYAMA-KŌEN Map p232

Just upstream from Togetsu-kyō and behind Tenryū-ji, this park is a nice place to escape the crowds of Arashiyama. It's laced with trails, the best of which leads up to a lookout over Katsura-gawa and up into the Arashiyama mountains. It's particularly nice here during cherry-blossom and autumn-foliage seasons.

ŌKŌCHI-SANSŌ VILLA Map p232

☎ 872 2233; Saga Ōgura-yama; admission with tea & cake adult ¥1000, child ¥500-900; ☼ 9am-5pm; 15min walk from Keifuku Arashiyama line, Keifuku Arashiyama Station

This is the lavish home of Ōkōchi Denjirō, a famous actor in samurai films. The gardens allow fine views over the city and are open to visitors. If you've got the extra cash, it's worth visiting this spot, particularly during the early morning before the crowds arrive.

JŌJAKKŌ-JI Map p232

☎ 861 0435; Saga Ōgura-yama; adult ¥300, child ¥150-200; ☼ 9am-5pm; 20min walk from Keifuku Arashiyama line, Keifuku Arashiyama Station

This temple sits atop a mossy knoll, and is famed for its brilliant maples and thatched-roof Niō-mon gate. The *hondō* was constructed in the 16th century from wood from Fushimi-jō.

RAKUSHISHA Map p232

☎ 881 1953; Saga Ōgura-yama; admission ¥150; ☼ 9am-5pm; 20min walk from Saga Arashiyama Station

This building was the hut of Mukai Kyorai, the best-known disciple of illustrious haiku poet Bashō. Literally 'House of the Fallen Persimmons', legend holds that Kyorai dubbed the house Rakushisha after waking one morning after a storm to find the persimmons he had planned to sell from the garden's trees scattered on the ground.

NISON-IN Map p232

☎ 861 0687; Saga Nison-in, Monzen-chō; admission ¥500; ☼ 9am-4.30pm; 20min walk from Keifuku Arashiyama line, Keifuku Arashiyama Station

This is a popular spot with maple-watchers. Nison-in was originally built in the 9th century by Emperor Saga. It houses two important Kamakura-era Buddha statues side by side (Shaka on the right and Amida on the left). The temple features lacquered nightingale floors.

TAKIGUCHI-DERA Map p232

☎ 871 3929; Saga Kameyama-chō; adult/child ¥300/200; ☼ 9am-5pm; 35min walk from Keifuku Arashiyama line, Keifuku Arashiyama Station

The history of this temple reads like the romance of Romeo and Juliet. Takiguchi-dera was founded by Heian-era nobleman Takiguchi Nyūdō, who entered the priesthood after being forbidden by his father to marry his peasant consort Yokobue. One day, Yokobue came to the temple with her flute to serenade Takiguchi, but was again refused by him; she wrote a farewell love sonnet on a stone (in her own blood) before throwing herself into the river to perish. The stone remains at the temple.

Hozu-gawa River Trip

The **Hozu-gawa River Trip** (☎ 0771-22 5846; Kameoka-shi, Hozu-chō; adult/child ¥3900/2500; ☼ 9am-3.30pm, closed 29 Dec-4 Jan; 10min walk from JR Kameoka Station) is a great way to enjoy the beauty of Kyoto's western mountains without any strain on the legs. With long bamboo poles, boatmen steer flat-bottom boats down the Hozu-gawa from Kameoka, 30km west of Kyoto Station, through steep forested mountain canyons, before arriving at Arashiyama.

Between 10 March and 30 November there are seven trips daily (from 9am to 3.30pm). During winter the number of trips is reduced to four a day and the boats are heated.

The ride lasts two hours and covers 16km through occasional sections of choppy water – a scenic jaunt with minimal danger. The scenery is especially breathtaking during cherry-blossom season in April and maple-foliage season *(momiji)* in autumn.

The boats depart from a dock that is eight minutes' walk from Kameoka Station. Kameoka is accessible by rail from Kyoto Station or Nijō Station on the Sagano line (San-in main line). The TIC (p192) provides an English leaflet and timetable for rail connections. The fare from Kyoto to Kameoka is ¥400 one way by regular train (don't spend the extra for the express, as it makes little difference in travel time).

GIŌ-JI Map p232

☎ 861 3574; Saga Nisonin, Monzen-chō; admission ¥300; 🕙 9am-5pm; 15min walk from Saga Shakado-mae bus stop

This quiet temple was named for the Heian-era *shirabyōshi* (traditional dancer) Giō. Giō, aged 21, committed herself here as a nun after her romance with Taira-no-Kiyomori, the mighty commander of the Heike clan. She was usurped by a fellow entertainer, Hotoke Gozen (who later deserted Kiyomori to join Giō at the temple). Enshrined in the main hall are five wooden statues: these are Giō, Hotoke Gozen, Kiyomori and Giō's mother and sister (who were also nuns at the temple).

ADASHINO NEMBUTSU-JI Map p232

☎ 861 2221; Sagatorii Moto Adashino-chō; adult/child ¥500/400; 🕙 9am-4.30pm; 4min walk from Toriimoto bus stop

This rather unusual temple is where the abandoned bones of paupers and destitutes without kin were gathered. More than 8000 stone images are crammed into the temple grounds, dedicated to the repose of their spirits. The abandoned souls are remembered with candles each year in the Sentō Kuyō ceremony held here on the evenings of 23 and 24 August.

DAIKAKU-JI Map p232

☎ 871 0071; Saga Osawa-chō; adult/child ¥500/300; 🕙 9am-4.30pm; 15min walk from Saga Arashiyama Station

Just a 25-minute walk northeast of Nison-in you will find Daikaku-ji. It was built in the 9th century as a palace for Emperor Saga, who then converted it into a temple. The present buildings date from the 16th century and are palatial in style; they also contain some impressive paintings. The large Osawa-no-ike pond was once used by the emperor for boating and is a popular spot for viewing the harvest moon.

KYOTO OUTSKIRTS

Eating pp118–20; Sleeping pp145–6

The listings in this section are located on the fringes of Kyoto City proper. We cover these areas in an anti-clockwise direction, starting with the northeast outskirts and working to the southeast outskirts. At the end of this section, we cover three rural hamlets that lie to the north of the city: Ōhara, Kurama and Kibune, all three of which make wonderful day- or half-day trips out of the city.

NORTHEAST OUTSKIRTS

The area at the far northern end of the Higashiyama (eastern) Mountains has several important sights, including Manshu-in, one of the city's loveliest temples, and the mountain-top temple complex of Enryaku-ji, which sits atop Hiei-zan, the imposing mountain that marks the northern end of the Higashiyama Mountains.

RENGE-JI Map pp214-15

☎ 781 3494; Kamitakano, Hachiman-chō; admission ¥400; 🕙 9am-5pm; 5min walk from Mitake-Hachiman bus stop, bus 17 or 18 from Kyoto Station

Renge-ji is a charming temple that belongs to the Tendai sect of Buddhism. It's famed for its peaceful garden, which is set against a background of maple foliage (best in autumn). The main hall was once located in central Kyoto, but was moved here in 1663 by Imaeda Chikayoshi, an official of the Kaga Daimyō.

ENTSŪ-JI Map pp214-15

☎ 781 1875; Sakyō-ku, Iwakura Hataeda-chō; admission ¥500; 🕙 10am-4pm; 5min walk from Karasuma subway line, Matsugasaki Station, exit 2

Emperor Reigen built this remote temple in 1678 on the ruins of Emperor Go-Mizunō's villa. The picturesque garden, with some 40 carefully arranged rocks, is bordered by a manicured hedge of sananqua trees; there are fantastic views of Hiei-zan from here. In an effort to keep the place quiet, no photography, children or tour guides are permitted.

HIEI-ZAN & ENRYAKU-JI Map pp212-13

☎ 077-578 0001; Sakamoto Honmachi, Ōtsu city; adult/child ¥550/350; 🕙 8.30am-4.30pm, earlier in winter; 2min walk from Enryaku-ji bus terminal, Sanjō Keihan or Kyoto Stations

A visit to 848m-high Hiei-zan and the vast Enryaku-ji complex is a good way to spend half a day hiking, poking around temples and enjoying the atmosphere of a key site in Japanese history.

Enryaku-ji was founded in 788 by Saichō, also known as Dengyō-daishi, the priest who established the Tenzai school. This school did not receive imperial recognition until 1823, after Saichō's death. But from the 8th century the temple grew in power; at its height it possessed some 3000 buildings and an army of thousands of *sōhei* (warrior monks). In 1571 Oda Nobunaga saw the temple's power as a threat to his aims to unify the nation and he destroyed most of the buildings, along with the monks inside. Today only three pagodas and 120 minor temples remain.

The complex is divided into three sections: Tōtō, Saitō and Yokawa. The **Tōtō** (eastern pagoda section) contains the Kompon Chū-dō (primary central hall), which is the most important building in the complex. The flames on the three Dharma (wheel of the law, in Sanskrit) lamps in front of the altar have been kept lit for over 1200 years. The Daikō-dō (great lecture hall) displays life-size wooden statues of the founders of various Buddhist schools. This part of the temple is heavily geared to group access, with large expanses of asphalt for parking.

The **Saitō** (western pagoda section) contains the Shaka-dō, which dates from 1595 and houses a rare Buddha sculpture of the Shaka Nyorai (Historical Buddha). The Saitō, with its stone paths winding through forests of tall trees, temples shrouded in mist and the sound of distant gongs, is the most atmospheric part of the temple. Hold on to your ticket from the Tōtō section, as you may need to show it here.

The **Yokawa** is of minimal interest and a 4km bus ride away from the Saitō area. The Chū-dō here was originally built in 848. It was destroyed by fire several times and has undergone repeated reconstruction (the most recent in 1971). If you plan to visit this area as well as Tōtō and Saitō, allow a full day for in-depth exploration.

NORTHWEST OUTSKIRTS

The far northwestern part of Kyoto is predominantly residential, but there are a number of superb temples with tranquil gardens. For Zen fans, a visit to Ryōan-ji is a must. Closer to the city centre, the Nishijin area still retains a feeling of old Kyoto and is home to two traditional weaving museums.

Hiei-zan & Enryaku-ji Transport Details

You can reach Hiei-zan and Enryaku-ji by train or bus. The most interesting way is the train/cable-car/ropeway route described below. If you're in a hurry or would like to save money, the best way is a direct bus from Sanjō Keihan or Kyoto Stations.

By train, take the Keihan line north to the last stop, Demachiyanagi, and change to the Yaseyūen/Hiei-bound Eizan line train (be careful not to board the Kurama-bound train that sometimes leaves from the same platform). At the last stop, Yaseyūen (¥260), board the cable car (¥530, nine minutes) and then the ropeway (¥310, three minutes) to the peak, from which you can walk down to the temples.

By bus, take Kyoto bus (not Kyoto city bus) 17 or 18, which run from Kyoto Station to the Yaseyūen stop (¥390, about 50 minutes). From there it's a short walk to the cable-car station.

Alternately, if you want to save money (by avoiding the cable car and ropeway), there are direct Kyoto buses from Kyoto and Keihan Sanjō Stations to Enryaku-ji, which take about 70 and 50 minutes, respectively (both cost ¥800).

RYŌAN-JI Map pp214-15

☎ 463 2216; Ukyō-ku, Ryōan-ji; adult ¥500, child ¥300-500; ☼ 8am-5pm Mar-Nov, 8.30am-4.30pm Dec-Feb; 1min walk from Ryōan-ji-mae bus stop, bus 59 from Hankyū Kawaramachi Station

This temple belongs to the Rinzai school and was founded in 1450.

The main attraction is the garden arranged in the *karesansui* style. An oblong of sand with an austere collection of 15 carefully placed rocks, apparently adrift in a sea of sand, is enclosed by an earthen wall. The designer, who remains unknown, provided no explanation.

Although many historians believe it was arranged by Sōami during the Muromachi period (1333–1576), some contend that it is a much later product of the Edo period. It is Japan's most famous *hira-niwa* (a flat garden void of hills or ponds) and reveals the stunning simplicity and harmony of the principles of Zen meditation.

The viewing platform for the garden can become packed solid, but the other parts of the temple grounds are also interesting and less of a target for the crowds. Among these, Kyoyo-chi pond is perhaps the most beautiful, particularly in autumn.

Ryōan-ji (p83)

NINNA-JI Map pp214-15

☎ 461 1155; Ukyō-ku, Omuro oouchi; adult ¥500, child ¥300-500; ⏱ 9.30am-4.30pm; 1min walk from Omuro Ninna-ji bus stop, bus 26 from Kyoto Station

Ninna-ji was built in 888 and is the head temple of the Omuro branch of the Shingon school. Originally there were more than 60 structures; the present temple buildings, including a five-storey pagoda, date from the 17th century. On the extensive grounds you'll find a peculiar grove of short-trunked, multi-petal cherry trees called Omuro-no-Sakura, which draw large crowds in April.

Separate admission fees (¥500) are charged for the *kondō* and *reihōkan* (treasure house), which are only open for the first two weeks of October.

MYŌSHIN-JI Map pp214-15

☎ 461 5226; Ukyō-ku, Hanazono Myōshin-ji-chō; adult ¥400, child ¥250-400; ⏱ 9.10am-3.40pm, closed 1hr at lunch; 10min walk from JR Hanazono Station

Myōshin-ji, a vast complex dating back to 1342, belongs to the Rinzai school. There are 47 sub-temples, but only a few are open to the public.

From the north gate, follow the broad stone avenue flanked by rows of temples to the southern part of the complex. The ceiling of the *hattō* (lecture hall) features Tanyū Kanō's unnerving painting *Unryūzu* (meaning 'dragon glaring in eight directions').

TAIZŌ-IN Map pp214-15

☎ 463 2855; Ukyo-ku, Hanazono Myōshin-ji-chō; adult/child ¥400/300; ⏱ 9am-5pm; 10min walk from JR Hanazono Station

This subtemple is in the southwestern corner of the grounds of Myōshin-ji. The *karesansui* garden depicting a waterfall and islands is well worth a visit.

TŌEI UZUMASA MOVIE VILLAGE
Map pp214-15

Tōei Uzumasa Eiga Mura; ☎ 864 7716; Ukyo-ku, Uzumasa Higashi Hachioka-chō; adult/child 6 to 18/under 6 ¥2200/1300/1100; ⏱ 9am-5pm 1 Mar-30 Nov, 9.30am-4pm 1 Dec-Feb; 13min walk from Sagano line, Uzumasa Station

In the Uzumasa area, Tōei Uzumasa Movie Village is one of Kyoto's most notorious tourist traps. However, it does have some recreations of Edo-period street scenes that give a decent idea of what Kyoto must have looked like before the advent of concrete.

The main conceit of the park is that real movies are actually filmed here. While this may occasionally be the case, more often than not this entails a bunch of bored flunkies being ordered around by an ersatz movie 'director' complete with megaphone and a vintage 1930s-era movie camera. This delights some tourists but left us a little less than convinced.

Aside from this, there are displays relating to various aspects of Japanese movies and regular performances involving Japanese TV and movie characters such as the Power Rangers. This should entertain the kids – adults will probably be a little bored.

KŌRYŪ-JI Map pp214-15

☎ 861 1461; Ukyō-ku, Uzumasa Hachioka-chō; adult ¥700, child ¥300-350; ☯ 9am-5pm Mar-Nov, until 4.30pm Dec-Feb; 2min walk from Keifuku line, Uzumasa Station

Kōryū-ji, one of the oldest temples in Japan, was founded in 622 to honour Prince Shōtoku, who was an enthusiastic promoter of Buddhism.

The *hattō* to the right of the main gate houses a magnificent trio of 9th-century statues: Buddha, flanked by manifestations of Kannon. The *reihōkan* contains numerous fine Buddhist statues, including the Naki Miroku (Crying Miroku) and the renowned Miroku Bosatsu, which is extraordinarily expressive. A national upset occurred in 1960 when an enraptured university student embraced the statue in a fit of passion and inadvertently snapped off its little finger.

Takao Area

The Takao area (Map pp212–13) is tucked far away in the northwestern part of Kyoto. It is famed for autumn foliage and a trio of temples: Jingo-ji, Saimyō-ji and Kōzan-ji.

Jingo-ji (☎ 861 1769; Ukyo-ku Takao-chō; admission ¥400; ☯ 9am-4pm; 20min walk from Yamashiro Takao bus stop) is the best of the three temples. This mountain temple sits at the top of a long flight of stairs that stretch from the Kiyotaki-gawa to the temple's main gate. The Kondō (Gold Hall) is the most impressive of the temple's structures, located roughly in the middle of the grounds at the top of another flight of stairs.

After visiting the Kondō, head in the opposite direction along a wooded path to

Transport

To reach Takao, take bus 8 from Nijō Station to the last stop, Takao (¥500, 40 minutes). From Kyoto Station, take the hourly JR bus to the Yamashiro Takao stop (¥500, 50 minutes). To get to Jingo-ji, walk down to the river and climb the steps on the other side.

an open area overlooking the valley. Here you'll see people tossing small disks over the railing into the chasm below. These are *kawarakenage*, light clay disks that people throw in order to rid themselves of their bad karma. Be careful, it's addictive and at ¥100 for two it can get expensive (you can buy the disks at a nearby stall). The trick is to flick the disks very gently, convex side up, like a Frisbee. When you get it right, they sail all the way down the valley – taking all that bad karma with them (try not to think about the hikers down below).

If you have time after visiting Jingo-ji, you can walk north from the base of the steps (follow the river upstream) for around five minutes to reach **Saimyō-ji** (admission free; ☯ 9am-5pm); walk up on to the main road and in another 10 minutes you'll reach **Kōzan-ji** (admission to grounds/main hall free/¥600; ☯ 8.30am-5pm). Lovely Saimyō-ji is the better of the two, but if you've got the energy, it's also worth exploring the grounds of Kōzan-ji (but don't waste the money to enter the main hall – it's just not worth the steep admission fee).

SOUTHWEST OUTSKIRTS

The southwestern outskirts of Kyoto are predominantly residential and are pretty drab, but there are several important sights scattered about, including Katsura Rikyū Imperial Villa and Saihō-ji, Kyoto's beguiling moss temple.

KATSURA RIKYŪ IMPERIAL VILLA

Map pp214-15

☎ 211 1215; Nishikyō-ku, Katsura misono; admission free; 7min walk from Katsura Rikyū-mae bus stop, bus 33 from Kyoto Station

This villa, considered one of the finest examples of Japanese architecture, was built in 1624 for the emperor's brother, Prince Toshihito. Every conceivable detail of the villa – the teahouses, the large pond with islets and the surrounding garden – has been given meticulous attention.

Tours (in Japanese) start at 10am, 11am, 2pm and 3pm, and last about 40 minutes. You should be there 20 minutes before the start time. An explanatory video is shown in the waiting room and a leaflet is provided in English. You must make reservations through the Imperial Household Agency (p66), often several weeks in advance. Visitors must be over 20 years of age.

MATSUO-TAISHA Map pp214-15

☎ 871 5016; Nishikyō-ku, Arashiyama Miyamachi; admission to grounds free, to garden & treasure house ¥500; ☺ grounds dawn to dusk, garden & treasure house 9am-4pm; 5min walk from Matsuo-taisha-mae bus stop, bus 28 from Kyoto Station

Founded in 701, Matsuo-taisha is one of Kyoto's oldest shrines. It enshrines the deity of water, which sake-brewing families have worshipped since the Muromachi period (hence the large stacks of sake barrels). Pure spring water, designated 'one of the 100 best in Japan', spews from the mouth of the *kame-no-ido* (turtle well) statue here.

SAIHŌ-JI Map pp214-15

☎ 391 3631; Nishikyō-ku, Matsuo Jingatani-chō; admission ¥3000; 5min walk from Kokedera bus stop, Kyoto bus 28 from Hankyū Arashiyama Station

The main attraction at this temple is the heart-shaped garden, designed in 1339 by Musō Kokushi. The garden is famous for its luxuriant mossy growth – hence the temple's other name, Koke-dera (Moss Temple). Visiting the temple is recommended only if you have time and patience to follow the reservation rules. If you don't, visit nearby Jizō-in (above right) to get a taste of the atmosphere of Saihō-ji without the expense or fuss.

Reservations are the only way you can visit. This is to prevent the overwhelming crowds that used to swamp the place (and consequently pulverise the moss) in the days when reservations were not required.

Send a postcard (to the address listed) at least one week before the date you require and include details of your name, number of visitors, address in Japan, occupation, age (you must be over 18) and desired date (a choice of alternative dates is preferred). Enclose a pre-stamped postcard for a reply to your Japanese address. You might find it convenient to buy an *ōfuku-hagaki* (send-and-return postcard set) at any post office.

You should arrive at the time and on the date supplied by the temple office. After paying your 'donation', you spend up to 90 minutes chanting sutras or doing Zen meditation before finally being guided around the garden for 90 minutes.

Take city bus 28 from Kyoto Station to the Matsuo-taisha-mae stop (¥240, 35 minutes) and walk 15 minutes southwest; or from Keihan Sanjō Station, take Kyoto bus 63 to Kokedera, the last stop (¥270, 50 minutes), and walk two minutes.

JIZŌ-IN Map pp214-15

☎ 381 3417; Nishikyō-ku, Yamadakitano-chō; adult/child ¥500/200; ☺ 9am-4.30pm; 5min walk from Koke-dera bus stop, Kyoto bus 78 from Hankyū Arashiyama Station

This delightful little temple could be called the 'poor man's Saihō-ji'. It's only a few minutes' walk south of Saihō-ji (left) in the same atmospheric bamboo groves. While the temple does not boast any spectacular buildings or treasures, it has a nice moss garden and is almost completely ignored by tourists, making it a great place to sit and contemplate.

From the parking lot near Saihō-ji, there is a small stone staircase that climbs to the road that leads to Jizō-in (it helps to ask someone to point the way as it's not entirely clear).

SOUTHEAST OUTSKIRTS

The district to the south of Kyoto is a rather unprepossessing industrial suburb, lacking the greenery that makes the more northerly parts of Kyoto so attractive. However, there are some attractions in the area that warrant a visit for those with time. Tōfuku-ji and Fushimi-Inari-taisha are quite close to downtown Kyoto and rate highly, as does Byōdō-in, further south in the city of Uji. To the southeast, Daigo-ji is in semi-rural surroundings and offers scope for some strenuous hiking to complement the area's architectural splendours.

FUSHIMI-INARI-TAISHA Map pp214-15

☎ 641 7331; Fushimi-ku, Fukakusa Yabunouchi-chō; admission free; ☺ dawn to dusk; 1min walk from JR Nara line, Inari Station, or 1min walk from Keihan Fushimi-Inari Station

This intriguing shrine was dedicated to the gods of rice and sake by the Hata family in the 8th century. As the role of agriculture diminished, deities were enrolled to ensure prosperity in business. Nowadays, the shrine is one of Japan's most popular, and is the head shrine for some 40,000 Inari shrines scattered the length and breadth of the country.

The entire complex, consisting of five shrines, sprawls across the wooded slopes of Inari-san. A pathway wanders 4km up the mountain and is lined with hundreds of red torii. There are also dozens of stone foxes. The fox is considered the messenger of Inari, the god of cereals, and the stone foxes, too, are often referred to as Inari. The key often seen in the fox's mouth is for the rice granary. On an incidental note, the Japanese traditionally see the fox as a sacred, somewhat mysterious figure capable of 'possessing' humans – the favoured point of entry is under the fingernails.

The walk around the upper precincts of the shrine is a pleasant day hike. It also makes for a very eerie stroll in the late afternoon and early evening, when the various graveyards and miniature shrines along the path take on a mysterious air. It's best to go with a friend at this time.

On 8 April there's a Sangyō-sai festival with offerings and dances to ensure prosperity for national industry. During the first few days in January, thousands of believers visit this shrine as their *hatsu-mōde* to pray for good fortune.

Delicacies sold on the approach streets include barbecued sparrow and *inari-sushi* (fried tofu wrapped around sweet sushi) – believed to be the favourite food of the fox.

DAIGO-JI Map pp212-13

☎ 571 0002; Fushimi-ku Daigo Garan-chō; admission to grounds free, during cherry-blossom & autumn-foliage seasons ¥600; ☽ 9am-5pm; 10min walk from Tōzai subway line, Daigo Station, exit 2

Daigo-ji was founded in 874 by Shobo, who gave it the name Daigo (meaning the ultimate essence of milk). This refers to the five periods of Buddha's teaching, which were compared to the five forms of milk prepared in India – the highest form is called 'daigo' in Japanese.

The temple was expanded into a vast complex on two levels, Shimo Daigo (lower) and Kami Daigo (upper). During the 15th century those buildings on the lower level were destroyed, with the sole exception of the five-storey pagoda. Built in 951, this pagoda is treasured as the oldest of its kind in Japan and is the oldest existing building in Kyoto.

In the late 16th century, Hideyoshi took a fancy to Daigo-ji and ordered extensive rebuilding. It is now one of the Shingon school's main temples. To explore Daigo-ji thoroughly and at a leisurely pace, mixing hiking with temple-viewing, you will need at least half a day.

From Sampō-in it's a steep and tiring 50-minute climb up to Kami Daigo. To get here, walk up the large avenue of cherry trees, through the Niō-mon gate, out the back gate of the lower temple, up a concrete incline and into the forest, past the pagoda.

SAMPŌ-IN

☎ 571 0002; Fushimi-ku, Daigo Higashioji-chō; adult ¥600, child ¥250-500; ☽ 9am-5pm; 10min walk from Tōzai subway line, Daigo Station, exit 2

Sampō-in was founded as a subtemple of Daigo-ji in 1115, but received a total revamp

under Hideyoshi's orders in 1598. It is now a fine example of the amazing opulence of that period. The Kanō paintings and the garden are special features.

The garden is jam-packed with about 800 stones – the Japanese mania for stones goes back a long way. The most famous stone here is Fujito-no-ishi, which is linked to deception, death and a fabulous price that was turned down; it's even the subject of a nō play, *Fujito*.

HŌJU-IN TREASURE HOUSE

☎ 571 0002; Fushimi-ku, Daigo Higashioji-chō; adult ¥600, child ¥200-500; ☽ 9am-5pm; 15min walk from Tōzai subway line, Daigo Station, exit 2

This subtemple of Daigo-ji is close to Sampō-in. Despite the steep admission fee, it should not be missed if you're a fan of traditional Japanese art. The display of sculptures, scrolls, screens, miniature shrines and calligraphy is superb.

DAIGO-YAMA Map pp212-13

From Sampō-in, walk up the avenue of cherry trees, through Niō-mon gate and past the pagoda. From there you can continue for a steep climb through the upper part of Daigo-yama, browsing through temples on the way. Allow at least 50 minutes to reach the top.

Fushimi

Fushimi, home to 37 sake breweries, is one of Japan's most famous sake-producing regions. Its location on the Uji-gawa made it a perfect location for sake production, as fresh, high-quality rice was readily available from the fields of neighbouring Shiga-ken, and the final product could be easily loaded on to boats for export downriver to Osaka.

Despite its fame as a sake-producing region, Fushimi is one of Kyoto's least attractive areas. It's also a hard area to navigate due to a lack of English signage. It's probably only worth a visit if you've got a real interest in sake and sake production.

Transport

To get to Fushimi, take a local or express (not a limited express) on the Keihan line to Chūshojima Station (¥260, 20 minutes). Alternatively, you can take the Kintetsu Kyoto line from Kyoto Station to Momoyama-Goryōmae Station (¥250, 11 minutes). There is a useful map on a pillar outside Chūshojima Station that you can use to orient yourself.

GEKKEIKAN SAKE ŌKURA MUSEUM

Map pp214-15

☎ 623 2056; Fushimi-ku, Minamihama-chō; admission ¥300; ⏰ 9.30am-4.30pm, closed Mon; 10min walk from Keihan Chūshojima Station

The largest of Fushimi's sake breweries is Gekkeikan, the world's leading producer of sake. Although most of the sake is now made in a modern facility in Osaka, a limited amount of handmade sake is still made in a Meiji-era *kura* here in Fushimi.

The Gekkeikan Sake Ōkura Museum houses a collection of artefacts and memorabilia tracing the 350-year history of Gekkeikan and the sake-brewing process. Giant murals depicting traditional methods of brewing adorn the walls and there is the chance to taste (and of course buy) some of the local brew.

If you are travelling with a tour group that is larger than 20 people and if you call two weeks in advance (☎ 623 2001), you can arrange a guided English tour of the brewery. Otherwise, ask at the TIC (p192) about joining a tour given in Japanese.

The museum is a 10-minute walk northeast of Chūshojima Station. To get here from the station, go right at the main exit, take a right a right down an unpaved road, a left at the playground, cross the bridge over the canal and follow the road around to the left; the museum is on the left.

KIZAKURA KAPPA COUNTRY

Map pp214-15

☎ 611 9919; Fushimi-ku, Shioya machi; admission free; ⏰ 11.30am-2pm & 5-9.30pm Mon-Fri, 11am-10pm Sat & Sun; 6min walk from Keihan Chūshojima Station

A short walk from its competitor, Gekkeikan, Kizakura is another sake brewery worth a look while you're in the neighbourhood. The vast complex houses both sake and beer breweries, courtyard gardens and a small gallery dedicated to the mythical (and sneaky) creature, Kappa. The restaurant-bar is an appealing option for a bite to eat or a freshly brewed ale (p119).

It's a short walk north of the Ōkura Museum.

TERADAYA MUSEUM Map pp214-15

☎ 611 1223; Fushimi-ku, Minamihama-chō; adult ¥400, child ¥200-300; ⏰ 10am-3pm; 10min walk from Keihan Chūshojima Station

Famed as the inn of choice for rebel samurai Sakamoto Ryōma (1834–67), today Teradaya operates as a museum. Fans of Ryōma faithfully make the pilgrimage here to see the room where he slept.

You might have to ask a passer-by for directions as the way is poorly marked. There is a sign in English that reads: 'The site of the Teradaya Feud' out front.

FUSHIMI MOMOYAMA-JŌ Map pp214-15

☎ 611 5121; Fushimi-ku, Momoyama-chō Ōkura; admission ¥800; ⏰ 9.30am-5pm; 15min walk from Kintetsu Kyoto line, Tanbabashi Station

Toyotomi Hideyoshi's Fushimi-jō was completely destroyed during the Sekigahara war in 1600, then reconstructed by Tokugawa Ieyasu, but by 1623 it was abandoned. The present buildings are unfortunate modern replicas from the 1960s. Unless you are travelling with kids and fancy visiting the on-site Castle Land (Kasuru-rando) amusement park, you can safely give this place a miss. If you want to visit a proper castle, make the day trip to Himeji (p168).

Uji

Uji (Map pp214–15) is a small city south of Kyoto. Historically rich in Heian-period culture, its main claims to fame are Byōdō-in and Ujigami-jinja (both Unesco World Heritage sites) and tea cultivation. The Uji-bashi Bridge, originally all wood and the oldest of its kind in Japan (it is now constructed of concrete and wood), has been the scene of many bitter clashes in previous centuries, though traffic jams seem to predominate nowadays.

Between 17 June and 31 August, *ukai* trips are organised in the evening around 7pm on the river near Byōdō-in. Prices start at ¥1800 per person. The TIC (p192) has a leaflet with up-to-date information on booking.

Transport

Uji can be easily reached by rail from Kyoto on the Keihan Uji line (¥460, 30 minutes from Keihan Sanjō Station; change at Chūshojima) or JR Nara line (¥210, 20 minutes from Kyoto Station). To get to Byōdō-in from the Keihan Uji Station, cross the river on the bridge right outside the station; immediately after crossing the bridge, take a left past a public toilet (don't take the street with the large stone torii), and continue straight through the park.

BYŌDŌ-IN

☎ 0774-21 2861; Uji-shi, Uji renge; admission ¥600;
🕑 8.30am-5.30pm Mar-Nov, 9am-4pm Dec-Feb;
10min walk from JR Nara line, Uji Station

This temple was converted from a Fujiwara villa into a Buddhist temple in 1052.

The **Phoenix hall** (Hōō-dō), more properly known as the Amida-dō, was built in 1053 and is the only original building remaining. The phoenix was a popular mythical bird in China and was revered by the Japanese as a protector of Buddha. The architecture of the building resembles the shape of the bird, and there are two bronze phoenixes perched opposite each other on the roof. The building was originally intended to represent Amida's heavenly palace in the Pure Land. This building is one of the few extant examples of Heian-period architecture, and its graceful lines make you wish that far more had survived the wars and fires that have plagued Kyoto's past. Inside the hall is the famous statue of Amida and 52 Bosatsu (Bodhisattvas) dating from the 11th century and attributed to the priest-sculptor, Jōchō.

The temple, complete with its reflection in a pond, is a major attraction in Japan and draws huge crowds. For a preview without the masses, take a look at the 10 yen coin.

Nearby, the **Hōmotsukan Treasure House** (admission ¥300; 🕑 9am-4pm 1 Apr–31 May & 15 Sep–23 Nov) contains the original temple bell and door paintings, and the original phoenix roof adornments. Allow about an hour to wander through the grounds.

The approach street to the complex is lined with souvenir shops, many of which roast local tea outside. A small packet of the tea is popular as a souvenir or gift.

MAMPUKU-JI

☎ 0774-32 3900; Uji-shi, Gokashou; admission ¥500;
🕑 9am-4pm; 5min walk from JR Nara line, Oubaku Station

Mampuku-ji was established as a Zen temple in 1661 by the Chinese priest Ingen. It is a rare example in Japan of a Zen temple built in the pure Chinese style of the Ming dynasty. The temple follows the Ōbaku school, which is linked to the mainstream Rinzai school but incorporates a wide range of esoteric Buddhist practices.

UJIGAMI-JINJA

☎ 0774-21 4634; Uji-shi, Uji Yamada; admission free;
🕑 9am-4.30pm; 5min walk from Keihan Uji line, Uji Station

Ujigami-jinja holds the distinction of being Japan's oldest shrine (and the least visited of

---

Uji Tea

On the river bank behind Byōdō-in, is the delightful **Taihō-an** (☎ 0774-23 3334; info@kyoto-uji-kankou.or.jp; Uji-shi Uji Araragi gawa; admission ¥500; 🕑 10am-4pm; 10min walk from Keihan Uji line, Uji Station). The friendly staff conduct a 30-minute tea ceremony (unless you've got knee trouble, ask for the tatami room). Casual dress is fine here and no reservations are necessary. Buy your tickets at the Uji-shi Kanko centre next door.

Another stop for a taste of Uji's famed green tea is **Tsūen-jaya** (☎ 0774-21 2243; www.tsuentea.com/engindex.htm; Uji-shi Uji Higashiuchi; 🕑 9.30am-5.30pm; across from Keihan Uji line, Uji Station). Japan's oldest-surviving tea shop, it has been in the Tsūen family for more than 830 years. The present building, near Uji-bashi, dates from 1672 and is full of interesting antiques. You can try fresh *matcha*, including a sweet, for ¥680.

Kyoto's 17 Unesco World Heritage sites). According to ancient records, Uji-no-waki-Iratsuko, a 5th-century prince, tragically sacrificed his own life to conclude the matter of whether he or his brother would succeed the imperial throne; needless to say his brother, Emperor Nintoku, won the dispute. The main building was dedicated to the twosome and their father Emperor Ōjin, and enshrines the tombs of the trio.

The shrine is across the river from Byōdō-in and a short walk uphill; take the orange bridge across the river.

On the way, you'll pass through **Uji-jinja** (admission free; 🕑 dawn-dusk), which is actually better looking than its more famous neighbour.

FAR NORTHERN OUTSKIRTS

The Kitayama (northern) Mountains that lie to the north of Kyoto contain some wonderful little villages that make nice day trips out of the city. The best of these are Ōhara, which contains several beautiful temples, and Kurama and Kibune, a pair of villages that can easily be visited as part of a day trip by hiking over the ridge that separates them. All told, we rate Kurama and Kibune as the most rewarding short trip out of Kyoto, so if you want a break from the crowds and congestion of downtown, head from Demachiyanagi Station and hop on the first train to Kurama!

Ōhara

Since ancient times Ōhara, a quiet farming town about 10km north of Kyoto, has been regarded as a holy site by followers of the Jōdo school. The region provides a charming glimpse of rural Japan, along with the picturesque Sanzen-in, Jakkō-in and several other fine temples. It's most popular in autumn, when the maple leaves change colour and the mountain views are spectacular. During the peak foliage season (late October to mid-November) avoid this area on weekends as it will be packed.

SANZEN-IN Map p233
☎ 744 2531; Ōhara Raikoin-chō; adult/child ¥600/300; 8.30am-4.30pm Feb-Dec, 8.30am-4pm Jan; 10min walk from Ōhara bus stop, Kyoto bus 17 or 18 from Kyoto Station

Founded in 784 by the priest Saichō, Sanzen-in belongs to the Tendai school. Saichō, considered one of the great patriarchs of Buddhism in Japan, also founded Enryaku-ji.

The temple's garden, **Yūsei-en**, is one of the most-photographed sights in Japan, and rightly so. Take some time to sit on the steps of the Shin-den hall and admire the garden's beauty. Then head off to Ōjō-gokuraku-in hall (Temple of Rebirth in Paradise) to see the impressive Amitabha trinity, which is a large Amida image flanked by attendants Kannon and Seishi (god of wisdom). After this, walk up to the hydrangea garden at the back of the temple where, in late spring and summer, you can walk among hectares of blooming hydrangea.

The approach to Sanzen-in is opposite the main bus stop; there is no English sign but you can usually just follow the Japanese tourists. The temple is located about 600m up this walk on your left as you crest the hill. On the way up, pop into **Shibakyū**, a venerable *tsukemono* (Japanese-pickle) store. It's located inside an atmospheric old Japanese country house and free samples are available.

A short walk uphill from Sanzen-in, **Raigō-in** (☎ 744 2161; admission ¥300; 9am-5pm) is where Shōmyō Buddhist chanting originated. These chants are said to have had a profound influence on *minyō* (traditional Japanese folk music). Each Sunday from 1pm you can come and see the monks chanting here.

If you feel like a short hike after leaving the temple, continue up the hill to see the rather oddly named **Soundless Waterfall** (Oto-nashi-no-taki). Though in fact it sounds like any other waterfall, its resonance is believed to have inspired Shōmyō Buddhist chanting.

JIKKŌ-IN Map p233
☎ 744 2537; Ōhara Shorinin-chō; adult/child incl green tea & sweets ¥600/500; 9am-5pm; 10min walk from Ōhara bus stop, Kyoto Bus 17 or 18 from Kyoto Station

Only about 50m north of Sanzen-in, this small temple is often praised for its lovely garden and *fudan-zakura* cherry tree, which blossoms between October and March.

SHŌRIN-IN Map p233
☎ 744 2409; Ōhara Shorinin-chō; adult ¥300, child ¥200-300; 9am-5pm; 15min walk from Ōhara bus stop, Kyoto Bus 17 or 18 from Kyoto Station

This temple is worth a look, if only through its admission gate, to admire the thatched roof of the main hall.

HŌSEN-IN Map p233
☎ 744 2409; Ōhara Shorinin-chō; adult/child ¥600/ free; 9am-5pm; 10min walk from Ōhara bus stop, Kyoto bus 17 or 18 from Kyoto Station

This temple is just down the path west of Shōrin-in's entry gate. The main tatami room offers a view of a bamboo garden and the surrounding mountains, framed like a painting by the beams and posts of the building. There is also a fantastic 700-year-old pine tree in the garden. The blood-stained Chi Tenjō ceiling boards came from Fushimi-jō castle.

JAKKŌ-IN Map p233
☎ 744 2545; Ōhara Kusao-chō; adult ¥500, child free-¥500; 9am-5pm; 10min walk from Ōhara bus stop, Kyoto bus 17 or 18 from Kyoto Station

The history of Jakkō-in is exceedingly tragic. The actual founding date of the temple is subject to some debate (somewhere between the 6th and 11th centuries), but it acquired fame as the temple that harboured Kenrei Mon-in, a lady of the Taira clan. In 1185 the Taira were soundly defeated in a sea battle with the Minamoto clan at Dan-no-ura. With the entire Taira clan slaughtered or drowned, Kenrei Mon-in threw herself into the waves with her son Antoku, the infant emperor; she was fished out – the only member of the clan to survive.

She was returned to Kyoto, where she became a nun and lived in a bare hut until it collapsed during an earthquake. Kenrei Mon-in was accepted into Jakkō-in and stayed there, immersed in prayer and sorrowful memories, until her death 27 years later. Her tomb is located high on the hill behind the temple.

The main building of the temple burned down in May 2000 and the newly reconstructed main hall lacks some of the charm of the original. Nonetheless, it's a nice spot.

Jakkō-in is west of Ōhara. Walk out of the bus station up the road to the traffic lights, then follow the small road to the left. Since it's easy to get lost on the way, we recommend familiarising yourself with the kanji for Jakkō-in (see the map key) and following the Japanese signs.

Kurama & Kibune

Only 30 minutes north of Kyoto, Kurama and Kibune are a pair of tranquil valleys long favoured as places to escape the crowds and stresses of the city. Kurama's main attractions are its mountain temple and *onsen* (mineral hot spring). Kibune, over the ridge, is a cluster of ryokan (traditional inns) overlooking a mountain river. Kibune is best in summer, when the ryokan serve dinner on platforms built over the rushing waters of Kibune-gawa, providing welcome relief from the summer heat.

Transport

To get to Kurama and Kibune, take the Eizan line from Kyoto's Demachiyanagi Station. For Kibune, get off at the second-to-last stop, Kibune-guchi, take a right out of the station and walk about 20 minutes up the hill. For Kurama, go to the last stop, Kurama, and walk straight out of the station. Both destinations are ¥410 and take about 30 minutes to reach.

The two valleys lend themselves to being explored together. In winter, you can start from Kibune, walk 30 minutes over the ridge, visit Kurama-dera, then soak in the *onsen* before heading back to Kyoto. In summer, the reverse route is best: start from Kurama, walk up to the temple, then down the other side to Kibune to enjoy a meal suspended above the cool river. If you happen to be in Kyoto on the night of 22 October, be sure not to miss the Kurama Hi Matsuri fire festival. It's one of the most exciting festivals in the Kyoto area.

KURAMA-DERA Map p233
☎ 741 2003; Sakyō-ku, Kurama Honmachi; admission ¥200; ◷ 9am-4.30pm; 3min walk from Eizan Kurama Station

In 770 the monk Gantei left Nara's Toshōdai-ji in search of a wilderness sanctuary in which to meditate. Wandering in the hills north of Kyoto,

Kurama-dera (above)

he came across a white horse that led him to the valley known today as Kurama. After seeing a vision of the deity Bishamon-ten, guardian of the northern quarter of the Buddhist heaven, he established Kurama-dera just below the peak of Kurama-yama. Originally belonging to the Tendai school of Buddhism, since 1949 Kurama has been independent, describing its own brand of Buddhism as Kurama-kyō.

The entrance to the temple is just up the hill from Kurama Station. A tram goes to the top for ¥100, or you can hike up in about 30 minutes (follow the main path past the tram station). The trail is worth taking if it's not too hot, as it winds through a forest of towering old-growth cryptomeria trees, passing **Yuki-jinja** on the way. Near the peak, there is a courtyard dominated by the *honden* (main hall). Behind the *honden* a trail leads off to the mountain's peak.

At the top, you can take a brief detour across the ridge to **Ōsugi-gongen**, a quiet shrine in a grove of trees. Those who want to continue to Kibune can take the trail down the other side. It's a 1.2km, 30-minute hike from the *honden* to the valley floor of Kibune. On the way down are two mountain shrines, **Sōjō-ga-dani Fudō-dō** and **Okuno-in Maō-den**, which make pleasant rest stops.

KURAMA ONSEN Map p233

☎ 741 2131; Sakyō-ku, Kurama Honmachi; adult/child from ¥1100/700; 🕙 10am-9pm; 10min walk from Eizan Kurama Station

This hot-spring resort, one of the few *onsen* within easy reach of Kyoto, is a great place to relax after a hike. The outdoor bath, with its fine view of Kurama-yama, costs ¥1100/700 (adult/child). For ¥2300/1600, you get use of the indoor bath as well, but even with a sauna and locker thrown in, it's difficult to imagine why you would opt for the indoor bath. For both baths, buy a ticket from the machine outside the door of the main building (instructions are in Japanese and English).

To get to Kurama Onsen, walk straight out of Kurama Station and continue up the main street, passing the entrance to Kurama-dera on your left. The *onsen* is about 10 minutes' walk on the right. There's also a free shuttle bus between the station and the *onsen*, which meets incoming trains.

KIBUNE Map p233

Kibune's main attractions are its river-dining platforms, which are open from 1 June to the end of September. In addition to these, all the ryokan in the valley are open year-round and are a romantic escape for travellers willing to pay mid-range to top-end ryokan prices (p146).

Halfway up the valley, **Kifune-jinja** is worth a quick look, particularly if you can ignore the unfortunate plastic horse statue at its entrance. The shrine predates the 8th century founding of Kyoto. It was established to worship the god of water and has been long revered by farmers and sake brewers.

From Kibune you can hike over the mountain to Kurama-dera (p91); the trail starts halfway up the valley on the east side.

Walking Tours

Walking Tours

Kyoto is a city that begs to be explored on foot. Indeed, walking is just about the only way to get into some of its narrower alleys and lanes. More importantly, for those who don't fancy long urban slogs, Kyoto's major sights tend to be grouped together into distinct areas, which lend themselves to half-day walking excursions.

Even the briefest walking excursion in Kyoto will be full of wonderful little discoveries that remind you of why you travel in the first place: from ancient art treasures displayed in shop windows to quirky street characters, with shrines, temples and traditional houses thrown in for good measure. And because the Japanese love convenience, you'll never be far from a vending machine for a hot or cool drink, or a sit-down meal in a restaurant.

In this chapter we present four walks that take you through some of Kyoto's most picturesque sightseeing areas. These should provide a good introduction to the beauty of Kyoto, and hopefully will inspire you to do some more exploring on your own.

HILLS, TEMPLES & LANES OF SOUTHERN HIGASHIYAMA

If you have only one day in Kyoto, this walk is the best way to sample several of Kyoto's most important sights and neighbourhoods. It's pretty much a must-see route, heading right through the heart of Kyoto's premier sightseeing district. Be warned, though, that almost every visitor to Kyoto, both Japanese and foreign, eventually makes their way here, so you'll have to hit it very early in the day to avoid the crush.

The walk begins at Gojō-zaka bus stop on Higashiōji-dōri. From here, walk south for a few metres and turn up Gojō-zaka slope (there is an old noodle shop and pharmacy at the bottom of this street). Head uphill until you reach the first fork in the road; bear right and continue up Chawan-zaka (Teapot Lane). This street is lined with pottery shops selling

Sannen-zaka

Kiyomizu-yaki (a distinctive type of local pottery), much of it for use in the tea ceremony. At the top of the hill, you'll come to **Kiyomizu-dera 1** (p61), with its unmistakeable pagoda rising against the skyline. Before you enter the main complex of Kiyomizu-dera, we recommend that you pay ¥100 to descend into the **Tainai-meguri 2**, the entrance to which is just to the left of the main temple entrance (for an explanation of this, see p61).

After touring Kiyomizu-dera, exit down Kiyomizu-michi, the busy approach to the temple. This is the classic Japanese temple-front arcade, with shops selling all the usual suspects: tacky souvenirs, snacks, *tsukemono* (Japanese pickles) and rice crackers, along with several more pottery shops. About 100m down this street, you'll come to **Hōtoku-ji 3**, a small temple that contains a figure of the Yakuyōke Amida Buddha, which is believed to ward off evil. This small Buddha, almost hidden in the dark of this tiny temple is a nice contrast to its gaudy neighbour up the hill. Another

100m further along brings you to another small temple, **Dainichi-dō 4**, which contains a lovely seated Buddha image. The ceiling and walls of this temple are festooned with stickers that Japanese pilgrims use to mark their visit to a particular temple – this is a unique form of socially acceptable 'graffiti' in Japan.

After Dainichi-dō, continue down the hill for a short while until you reach a four-way intersection; take a right here down the stone-paved steps. This is Sannen-zaka, a charming street lined with old wooden houses, traditional shops and restaurants. If you fancy a break, there are many teahouses and cafés along this stretch; the most atmospheric is tiny **Kasagi-ya 5** (p112), which has been serving tea and Japanese-style sweets for as long as anyone can remember. Its *uji-kintoki* (green tea–flavoured shaved ice over sweet beans and *mochi*) is pure refreshment on a hot day. It's on the left, immediately after starting down Sannen-zaka, just below a vending machine.

Further along Sannen-zaka, the road curves to the left. Follow it a short distance, then go right down a flight of steps into Ninen-zaka, another quaint street lined with historic houses, shops and teahouses. At the end of Ninen-zaka zigzag left (at the vending machines) then right (just past the car park), and continue north. Very soon, on your left, you'll come to the entrance to **Ishibei-kōji 6**, perhaps the most beautiful street in Kyoto, although it's actually a cobbled alley lined on both sides with elegant, traditional Japanese inns and restaurants. Take a detour to explore this, then retrace your steps and continue north on Nene-no-Michi, passing almost immediately the entrance to **Kōdai-ji 7** (p61) on the right up a long flight of stairs.

Walk Facts

Start Gojō-zaka bus stop on Higashiōji-dōri (bus 18, 100, 206, 207)

End Jingū-michi bus stop on Sanjō-dōri (bus 5, 100 to Kyoto Station); Higashiyama-Sanjō Station on the Tōzai subway line

Distance About 5km

Duration Four hours

Fuel stop Kasagi-ya (p112)

After Kōdai-ji continue north to the T-junction and turn right. Here, just to your left you'll see the verdigris-coloured tower of the small temple **Taiu-in 8**. Take a quick left after Taiu-in and, heading north, on your right you'll cross the wide pedestrian arcade that leads to **Ōtani cemetery 9** (☸dawn-dusk). Descend into **Maruyama-kōen 10** (p61), a pleasant park in which to take a rest. In the centre of the park, you'll see the giant Gion *shidare-zakura*, Kyoto's most famous cherry tree. Opposite the tree there's a bridge that leads across a carp pond to the lovely upper reaches of the park. This is a good place for a picnic; it's best to bring something to eat with you, since the offerings in the park are limited to junk food.

From the park, head west into the grounds of **Yasaka-jinja 11** (p61). Return east back through the park and head north to tour the grounds of the impressive **Chion-in 12** (p60). From here it's a quick walk to **Shōren-in 13** (p60), which is famous for its enormous camphor trees out front. From Shōren-in descend to Sanjō-dōri (you'll see the giant shrine gate of Heian-jingū in the distance). Turning left on Sanjō-dōri, you'll soon come to the Jingū-michi bus stop, or continue a little further and you'll soon come to the Higashiyama Station.

A PHILOSOPHICAL MEANDER THROUGH NORTHERN HIGASHIYAMA

The walk described here is a great way to see some of the most important temples in Kyoto, along with some wonderful natural scenery. Start at Keage Station, walk downhill, cross the pedestrian overpass, head back uphill and go through the tunnel under the old funicular tracks. This leads to a narrow street that winds towards **Konchi-in 1** (p58), famous for its rock garden, and passes by maple trees that are stunning in autumn.

Just past Konchi-in, take a right on the main road and walk up through the gate into **Nanzen-ji 2** (p58). Walking up through the grounds of Nanzen-ji, you'll first see the impressive **San-mon gate 3** on your left. From here, continue east, up the slope. You'll soon see the brick **Sōsui aqueduct 4** (p58) on your right, cross under this, take a quick left and walk up the hill towards the mountains. You'll come first to the lovely **Kōtoku-an 5** (p58) subtemple. Beyond this, the trail enters the woods. Follow it up to the secluded **Nanzen-ji Oku-no-in 6**, a tiny shrine built around a waterfall. It's one of Kyoto's most entrancing spots. After walking through the vast grounds of Nanzen-ji, return the way you came in, exiting on the north side of Nanzen-ji, following the road through the gate. The road bears right and passes the **Nomura Museum 7** (p57).

Walk Facts

Start Keage Station on the Tōzai subway line
End Ginkaku-ji-Michi bus stop, near the intersection of Shirakawa-dōri and Imadegawa-dōri (bus 5, 56, 100, 203, 204)
Distance About 6km
Duration Four hours
Fuel stop Hinode (p112), Kanō Shōju-an (p110)

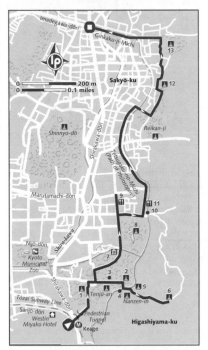

You'll soon come to **Eikan-dō 8** (p58), a large temple famous for its artworks and pagoda. At the corner just beyond Eikan-dō, there's a sign in English and Japanese pointing up the hill (right) to the Tetsu-gaku-no-michi (Path of Philosophy). If you are hungry at this point, take a short detour north to **Hinode 9** (p112), a fine noodle restaurant with an English menu (there's no English sign, however, it's about 100m north of the corner before a bank of vending machines). Otherwise, head east up the hill and check out **Kumanonyakuōji-jinja 10** (☼ dawn-dusk), before starting up the Tetsugaku-no-michi, which is the pedestrian path that heads north along the canal.

About 50m up the path you'll see a wooden bridge on your right. This leads to **Kanō Shōju-an 11** (p110), which offers a very simplified tea ceremony for ¥1050. From here, it's a straight shot up the tree-lined canal for about 800m until you reach a small sign in English and Japanese pointing up the hill to **Hōnen-in 12** (p64). Follow the sign up the hill, take a left at the top, walk past a small park and you'll see the entrance to the temple on your right. You'll soon reach the picturesque thatched gate of Hōnen-in, which is one of Kyoto's loveliest sights, particularly when framed by blazing maple leaves in autumn. After checking out the temple (admission free), exit via the thatched gate and take a quick right downhill.

From here, follow the side streets north to **Ginkaku-ji 13** (p64). Then head down the souvenir arcade and follow Ginkaku-ji-Michi, along the canal, down to Shirakawa-dōri and the Ginkaku-ji-Michi bus stop, from where you can catch buses to most parts of Kyoto.

NIGHT WALK THROUGH THE FLOATING WORLD

Kyoto's traditional entertainment areas of Gion and Pontochō have been the scene of Kyoto's floating world for centuries. Each night a legion of kimono-clad *mama-sans*, gaudy hostesses, slick suit-wearing businessmen and shady characters descend on these areas to transact the business of this world of illusion. Whether you intend to participate fully or just peer in from the outside, this walk is a fantastic way to acquaint yourself with Kyoto's main nightlife districts. Along the way, there are plenty of spots for a quick drink or a full meal.

This walk starts on the steps of the main gate into **Yasaka-jinja 1** (p61). Take a quick walk round the grounds of the shrine, which is beautifully illuminated at night. You might even want to say a quick prayer for a successful evening – like many Japanese who visit the shrine before heading into the fray of Gion. Leaving Yasaka-jinja, cross west to the south side of Shijō-dōri and just after passing Gion Hotel turn left. Walk about 80m and take the second right. Another 80m brings you to Hanami-kōji, a picturesque street of *ryōtei* (traditional-style, high-class restaurants) and teahouses. This is where many visiting dignitaries and businesspeople are entertained. Head a little south down this street before making your way back up to Shijō-dōri.

Turn left and walk for about 20m before turning right into Kiri-dōshi. You are now plunging into the heart of Gion. As you continue along Kiri-dōshi, you'll cross Tominagachō-dōri, lined with buildings containing hundreds of hostess bars – every one of those signs represents an individual bar (and – dare we say it? – another small nightly drama of longing and despair).

Walk Facts

Start Yasaka-jinja (at the intersection of Shijō-dōri and Higashiōji-dōri), a 10-minute walk from Keihan Shijō or Hankyū Kawaramachi Stations
End Hankyū Kawaramachi Station, at the intersection of Shijō-dōri and Kiyamachi-dōri
Distance About 3km
Duration Two hours
Fuel stop Ōzawa (p106) or Issen Yōshoku (p108) for food; bars along Pontochō and Kiyamachi-dōri for drinks

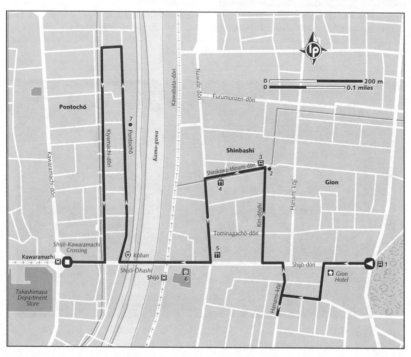

Continue north on Kiri-dōshi. It crosses another street and then narrows to a tiny alley. You are now about to enter Gion's most lovely area, which lies just across **Tatsumi-bashi bridge 2**. This is the Shinbashi district, which features some of Kyoto's finest traditional architecture, mostly upscale restaurants and exclusive hostess bars. If you're lucky enough to be here in cherry-blossom season, you will find the cherry trees heavy with pink and white blossoms (and, you guessed it, mobs of people).

At the fork in the road you will find small the **Tatsumi shrine 3**. This is a favourite shrine of those engaged in arts and entertainment and you will often see geisha and *maiko* (apprentice geisha) here praying for luck in their artistic endeavours. At the shrine, take a left and walk west along the canal on Shirakawa-Minami-dōri. Gaze across the river into the interiors of some of the restaurants and bars that line the canal – you'll be peering right into the elite heart of the floating world. Just before you come to the end of the street, on your left, across a bridge, you'll find **Ōzawa 4** (p106), a fine tempura restaurant at home with foreign guests (look for the sign reading 'Tempura Dinner'). This is a great spot for a proper sit-down meal along the route.

At the end Shirakawa-Minami-dōri, take a left on to gaudy Nawate-dōri (note the gangster-types in black Mercedes with dark-tinted windows). Just before you reach Shijō-dōri, you'll pass **Issen Yōshoku 5** (p108), a popular *okonomiyaki* (Japanese pizza or pancake) restaurant. There's only one thing on the menu here – a simple type of *okonomiyaki* that costs ¥630 per serving (just hold up your fingers to indicate how many you want).

From here, head west on Shijō-dōri, passing **Minami-za 6** (p122), Kyoto's main kabuki theatre, on your left. Cross the Kamo-gawa on the north side of Shijō-Ōhashi and walk to the *kōban* (police box), which you'll find on your right. You are now standing at the intersection of Shijō and Pontochō streets. If you cross Shijō and walk south on Pontochō here, you'll find yourself in one of Kyoto's seedier districts – the businesses here are mostly massage parlours that go under various pseudonyms like 'fashion health clubs' and 'pink salons'.

Heading north on **Pontochō 7** (p57) brings you into an entirely different world of upscale restaurants, bars, clubs and cafés. This pedestrian-only alley is truly one of Kyoto's most atmospheric lanes, and it really should be visited in the evening to understand its special charms. This is also one of the best spots in Kyoto to spot a geisha or *maiko*, many of whom entertain clients in exclusive establishments here. While most places along Pontochō are difficult for foreigners to enter, there are some who welcome foreign visitors and we list several of these in the Eating (p104) and Entertainment (p123) chapters.

Pontochō (p57)

When you reach the north end of Pontochō, take a left and another left and you will find yourself on Kiyamachi-dōri. This is a much more casual and inexpensive entertainment district from the ones you've just passed through. Here is where Kyoto's mere mortals drink and the place is usually chock-a-block with packs of young people, half-drunk salarymen and wide-eyed foreigners. We expect you'll be ready for a few drinks by the time you reach Kiyamachi, and we list several good bars in this area in the Entertainment chapter of this book (p123). Or, if you'd just like to head back to your digs, continue south along Kiyamachi, turn right on to Shijō-dōri, and you'll soon come to Hankyū Kawaramachi Station.

AMBLING THROUGH THE BAMBOO GROVES & TEMPLES OF ARASHIYAMA & SAGANO

This walk takes in almost all of the Arashiyama-Sagano area's most important sights, including some fine temples, an atmospheric bamboo forest and a lavish hillside villa. It begins at **Tenryū-ji 1** (p80), which is justifiably famous for its garden. If you'd like to skip the temple, you can bypass it by walking 200m north on the main road and taking a left (turn at the sign that reads 'Nonomiya Shrine'). After checking out the temple, exit via the north gate, take a right and walk down the hill for a few metres to see humble **Nonomiya-jinja 2** (☪ dawn-dusk), which was mentioned in the *Tale of the Genji*.

From Nonomiya-jinja, continue back up the hill, passing through Arashiyama's famous bamboo forest. It's one of the city's most photographed spots, but you'll be hard

Walk Facts

Start Arashiyama bus stop (bus 11, 28, 61, 62, 71, 72, 93); Keifuku Arashiyama Station or Torokko Arashiyama Station
End Torii-moto bus stop (bus 62, 72)
Distance About 4km
Duration Four hours
Fuel stop Ayu Chaya Hiranoya (p117)

Walking Tours – Ambling Through the Bamboo Groves & Temples of Arashiyama & Sagano

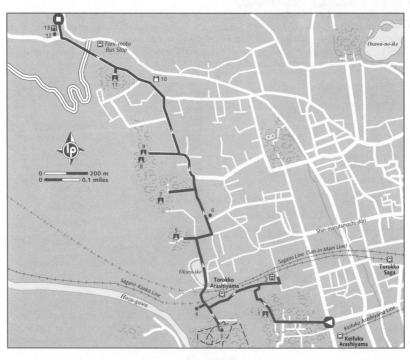

pressed to capture its beauty on film. At the top of the hill, you can take a quick detour south to sample **Kameyama-kōen 3** (p81), a good spot for a picnic lunch, or else enter **Ōkōchi-sansō villa 4** (p81), the entrance to which is almost directly in front of you. This villa, formerly the home of actor Ōkōchi Denjirō, is well worth a visit and fans of Japanese architecture and garden design will find plenty to inspire them here. All in all, this is the ultimate Japanese dream home – alas, we mortals can only dream.

Continuing north from Ōkōchi-sansō, head downhill and past Okura-ike pond. From this point on, you'll pass several smaller temples; since it would be costly and time consuming to enter all of them, it's best to choose one and savour it (our vote goes to Giō-ji, the second-to-last temple on this route). Soon after passing the pond, you'll see the gate of **Jōjakkō-ji 5** (p81). After Jōjakkō-ji, walk east straight away from the temple gate, avoiding the temptation to take a left out of the gate and go north – this is a dead end. About 150m east of Jōjakkō-ji gate, take a left (just before a cornfield) and you'll soon come to **Raku-shisha 6** (p81), a charming poet's hut. This quaint hut is a pleasant contrast to the grandeur of Ōkōchi-sansō. After Rakushisha, continue north. You'll soon pass a public toilet on your right. About 150m further on brings you to the gate of **Nison-in 7** (p81), a small temple in an attractive setting on the wooded hillside.

Return to the main road from Nison-in and follow it gradually northwest for a few minutes. This will bring you to the turn-off for **Takiguchi-dera 8** (p81) and **Giō-ji 9** (p82), two wonderfully atmospheric little hillside temples (there is no English sign here; look for the four stone way markers). After visiting one or both of these temples, return to the main road and continue walking northwest. You'll pass many souvenir shops here, including **Iwai 10** (☎ 871 3198; Sagatorimoto Rokutan-chō; ⌚ 10am-5pm), which is our favourite souvenir shop in all Kyoto – look for the old *machiya* (traditional Japanese townhouse) with the open front. About 100m past Iwai, you'll see the stone steps that lead up to **Adashino Nembutsu-ji 11** (p82) on your left. From here, it's a short walk onward to the huge orange **Atago Torii 12** and some lovely old thatch-roofed houses. A nice place to refresh yourself after all the walking you've done is **Ayu Chaya Hiranoya 13** (p117), just north of the torii. You can enjoy a cup of *matcha* tea (green powdered tea) and a sweet here for ¥840.

From here you can backtrack to the Torii-moto bus stop and catch bus 62 or 72 back to Arashiyama or onward to Kyoto Station (the bus stop is up the stone steps on the left just before the highway overpass). Note that there are few departures on the route, and if you've got the energy, it's not a bad idea to simply walk all the way back to Arashiyama, where you'll find frequent transport connections to all parts of Kyoto.

Eating

Eating

Thoug h it may not have the variety of New York or the reputation of Paris, Kyoto can hold its own with the world's great culinary capitals. The city's long imperial history, artistic traditions and sophisticated populace all combine to endow Kyoto with a rich and varied culinary scene that is out of proportion with its relatively small size.

Fans of Japanese food will, of course, find Kyoto a paradise – every type of Japanese cooking is well represented here and it's the perfect city in which to make a thorough exploration of the gastronomy of Japan. Of course, it's not just food we're talking about, it's the full experience of dining in a Japanese restaurant: attentive service, pleasant surroundings, careful preparation and exquisite presentation.

And if you want a break from Japanese food, you'll have plenty to choose from, for Kyoto boasts a wide array of international restaurants, including lots of great Indian, Korean, Taiwanese, Italian and French restaurants. Because of the quality of ingredients and the abundance of good chefs in the city, it often seems that ethnic food tastes better here than on its own turf.

In addition to relatively formal traditional restaurants, Kyoto has a huge array of casual places that are easy to enter, even for the non-Japanese speaker. These include a growing number of hip cafés that are popping up in almost every neighbourhood across town; for more on some of these cafés, see the boxed text 'Cool Cafés' on p104. Quick casual meals can also be had at one of Kyoto's many excellent noodle houses, where you can enjoy tasty *rāmen* (noodles in a meat broth, served with toppings), *soba* (thin, brown buckwheat noodles) and *udon* (thick, white wheat noodles); for more on *rāmen* restaurants, see the boxed text 'Rāmen Meguri' (p109). And, needless to say, Kyoto also has its share of fast-food eateries, both the well-known international chains and some home-grown favourites.

One of the most exciting trends in Kyoto is the so-called '*machiya* boom', in which many of the city's old *machiya* (traditional Kyoto townhouses) are being converted into Japanese and international restaurants and cafés. These places offer you a chance to enjoy a variety of cuisines in a lovely 'old Kyoto' setting; for more on these places, see the boxed text 'Machiya Magic' (p111).

How Much?

Kyoto has restaurants that cover the entire price spectrum, from dirt-cheap noodle houses where you can fill up for as little as ¥400, to top-of-the-line *kaiseki* (Japanese *haute cuisine*) places where you can drop ¥50,000 per person for a single meal. However, if you stick to the sorts of places where Japanese do most of their eating, you can expect to pay between ¥800 and ¥1500 for lunch and between ¥1000 and ¥3500 for dinner. Since tipping is not required and only first-class places add a service charge to your bill, this is the total price of the meal. Most of the restaurants listed in this chapter fall into these price ranges. In the Cheap Eats sections, we also list a wide variety of economical places, where you can get a meal for less than ¥1000.

Self-Catering

If you want a break from eating out, there are plenty of options in Kyoto for self-catering. You'll find supermarkets in every neighbourhood in town. The city also has a wide selection of fruit-and-vegetable shops *(yaō-ya)*, fish shops *(sakana-ya)* and bakeries *(pan-ya)*.

To do all of your food shopping under one roof, try one of Kyoto's many *shōtengai* (market streets). The best of these is **Demachiyanagi Shōtengai** (Map pp219-21), a humble shopping street in the northern part of town. **Nishiki Market** (p57), in the centre of town, is a much more upscale version that caters primarily to Kyoto restaurateurs. All of Kyoto's department stores also have food floors where you can buy just about any food item, domestic or imported, but you'll certainly have to pay for the convenience.

If you're looking specifically for imported foods, see p134.

KYOTO STATION AREA

Kyoto Station is chock-a-block with restaurants, and if you find yourself anywhere near the station around meal time, this is probably your best bet in terms of variety and price.

For a quick cuppa while waiting for a train try Café du Monde on the 2nd floor overlooking the central atrium. Or you might want to snag a few pieces of sushi off the conveyor belt at Kaiten-zushi Iwamaru, on the ground floor at the east end of the station building.

For more substantial meals there are several food courts scattered about. The best of these can be found on the 11th floor on the west side of the building: the Cube food court and Isetan department store's Eat Paradise food court. In the Cube, we like Katsu Kura, a popular *tonkatsu* (breaded pork cutlet) specialist that usually has a tasty lunch special. In Eat Paradise, we highly recommend Tenichi for sublime tempura, and Wakuden for approachable *kaiseki* fare. To get to these food courts, take the west escalators from the main concourse all the way up to the 11th floor and look for the Cube on your left and Eat Paradise straight in front of you.

Other options in the station include Kyoto Rāmen Koji, a collection of seven *rāmen* restaurants on the 10th floor (underneath the Cube), and Italia Ichiba Bar, a casual Italian place with excellent views north over Kyoto, which is also on the 10th floor (take the escalator, exit to the right and walk past Nova English school).

If you're departing by train or bus from Kyoto Station and want to pick up some nibblies for the ride, head downstairs to the B1 floor Porta underground shopping arcade. Here, you can purchase excellent sushi *bentō* (lunch boxes) at Kyōtaru and good bread and pastries at Shinshindō. Both are near the *kita* (north) entrance/exit of the Karasuma subway line.

AMAZON Map pp230-1 *Café*
☎ 561 8875; Shichijō-dōri-Kawabata; ⏰ 7.30am-6pm, closed Wed; coffee from ¥400; 2min walk from Keihan Shichijō Station

This typical Japanese coffee shop, near Sanjūsangen-dō, turns out some surprisingly good sandwiches and coffee; it's one of the few decent options in this area.

A RI SHAN
Map pp230-1 *Taiwanese*
☎ 344 1555; Shiokōji-dōri-Karasuma; ⏰ 5-11pm; dinner from ¥2500; 1min walk from Kyoto Station

This Taiwanese place is a favourite and serves a range of tasty little Chinese dishes, such as fried rice and dumplings.

DAI-ICHI ASAHI RĀMEN
Map pp230-1 *Rāmen*
☎ 351 6321; Takakura-dōri-Shiokōji; ⏰ 5am-2am, closed Thu; rāmen from ¥500; 5min walk from Kyoto Station

The *rāmen* is delicious at this unprepossessing place that brings to mind the film *Tampopo*.

IIMURA Map pp230-1 *Japanese*
☎ 351 8023; Shichijō-dōri-Higashinotōin; ⏰ 11.30am-2pm; set lunch ¥650; 5min walk from Kyoto Station

Try this classic little restaurant for its ever-changing set lunch, usually simple Japanese home-style cooking. It's in a traditional Japanese house set back a bit from the street, alongside a new five-storey building (look for the black-and-white sign).

SECOND HOUSE Map pp230-1 *Café*
☎ 342 2555; Shichijō-dōri-Nishinotōin; ⏰ 10am-11pm; coffee from ¥400; 10min walk from Kyoto Station

For a quick drink or a light meal near Nishi Hongan-ji, pop into this unusual coffee shop located in an old bank building.

SHINPUKU SAIKAN HONTEN
Map pp230-1 *Rāmen*
☎ 371 7648; Takakura-dōri-Shiokōji; ⏰ 7.30am-11pm, closed Wed; rāmen from ¥600; 5min walk from Kyoto Station

A similar joint to Dai-Ichi that is famous for its chicken-flavoured broth. Shinpuku is the first one of these that you come to when walking from Kyoto Station.

SUISHIN Map pp230-1 *Izakaya*
☎ 365 0271; Karasuma-dōri-Shiokōji; ⏰ 5pm-midnight; dinner from ¥2000; 1min walk from Kyoto Station

For a wide range of *izakaya* favourites, try this giant underground *izakaya* that's located in front of Kyoto Station. It's not as good as some of the other *izakaya* in town, but it's fun, cheap and easy.

Eating – Kyoto Station Area

DOWNTOWN KYOTO

The area between Oike-dōri and Shijō-dōri (north and south) and Kiyamachi-dōri and Karasuma-dōri (east and west) has the highest concentration of restaurants in the city. There's a wide range of both international and Japanese eateries in all price ranges. This is definitely the best place for a meal out in Kyoto.

844 STORE CAFÉ

Map pp228-9   *Japanese Vegetarian*

☎ 241 2120; Nishikiyamachi-dōri; 🕙 5.30-11pm, closed Tue; dishes from ¥700; 5min walk from Keihan Shijō Station

Kyoto vegetarians like this offbeat café for specialities such as vegie *gyōza* (Chinese dumplings). It's a colourful place down a tiny alley beneath A-Bar (below); look for the large glass windows.

A-BAR Map pp228-9   *Izakaya*

☎ 213 2129; Nishikiyamachi-dōri; 🕙 5pm-midnight; dishes from ¥500; 10min walk from Keihan Sanjō Station

This student *izakaya* with a log-cabin interior is popular with ex-pats and Japanese students for a raucous night out. The food is fairly typical *izakaya* fare, with plenty of fried items and some decent salads. It's a little tough to find – look for the small black-and-white sign at the top of a flight of steps near a place called Reims.

BIOTEI

Map pp228-9   *Japanese Vegetarian*

☎ 255 0086; Sanjō-dōri-Higashinotōin; 🕙 11.30am-2pm & 5-8.30pm, closed dinner Sun, Mon & Thu, lunch Sat & public holidays; lunch/dinner ¥840/1050; 5min walk from Karasuma subway line, Karasuma-Oike Station

Diagonally across from the Nakagyō post office, Biotei is the best vegetarian restaurant in the city. It serves daily lunch and dinner sets of well-prepared Japanese vegetarian food (the occasional bit of meat is offered as an option, but you'll be asked your preference). It's at the top of a spiral metal staircase.

CAPRICCIOSA Map pp228-9   *Italian*

☎ 221 7496; Kawaramachi-dōri-Sanjō kudaru; 🕙 11.30am-11pm; dinner from ¥1500; 5min walk from Keihan Sanjō Station

For heaped portions of pasta at rock-bottom prices you won't do much better than this long-time student favourite. It's near the Sanjō-Kawaramachi crossing.

DANIEL'S Map pp228-9   *Italian*

☎ 212 3268; Nishikikōji-dōri-Takakura; 🕙 11.30am-3pm, 5.30-11pm; mains from ¥750; 2min walk from Karasuma subway line, Shijō Station

For simple Italian fare while in the neighbourhood of Daimaru Department Store, head to Daniel's, where the offerings include simple pasta dishes and fish and meat entrées. It's located just outside the entrance to Nishiki Market, on the 2nd floor.

Cool Cafés

Kyoto is known the world over for its elegant traditional Japanese restaurants. What few travellers realise, however, is that it's also home to a great number of hip, cool cafés, which are easy to enter, fun to hang out in, and surprisingly inexpensive. Some of these cafés have art galleries or small libraries on the premises, others hold art events and live music shows, and most serve light meals throughout the day and drinks in the evening. So, if you need a cuppa and a break from temple-hopping, pop into one of the cafés listed here.

Bazaar Café (p116) A garden café near Dōshisha University.

Bon Bon Café (p113) An open café with riverside seating, near Demachiyanagi Station.

Café Bibliotec Hello! (p117) A literary café a short walk from the centre of town.

Café Carinho/Asian Diner (p114) Our favourite lunch spot in the Ginkaku-ji area.

Café Doji (p116) A cool, dimly lit space way up near the Kyoto Botanical Gardens.

Café Independants (p107) A subterranean slice of the bohemian life in the centre of town.

Café Peace (p114) A laid-back vegetarian enclave near Kyoto University.

Tranq Room (p115) A mod space not far from Ginkaku-ji.

Womb (p113) A gallery, bookshop and garden space in the northeast of town.

FUJINO-YA Map pp228-9 *Japanese*
☎ 221 2446; Pontochō-Shijō; 🕑 5-8pm, closed Wed; tempura set ¥2500; 3min walk from Hankyū Kawaramachi Station

This is one of the easiest places to enter on Pontochō, a street where many of the other restaurants turn down even unfamiliar Japanese diners. Here you can feast on tempura, *okonomiyaki* (Japanese pizza or pancake), *yakisoba* (fried noodles) and *kushikatsu* (deep-fried skewers of meat, seafood and vegetables) in tatami rooms overlooking the Kamo-gawa.

GANKO ZUSHI Map pp228-9 *Japanese*
☎ 255 1128; Sanjō-dōri-Kawaramachi; 🕑 11.30am-10.30pm; lunch ¥1000, dinner ¥3000; 3min walk from Keihan Sanjō Station

This place may have the most plastic-looking food models in the window out of any restaurant in Kyoto. It serves just about anything Japanese and the picture menu makes ordering a breeze. The speciality is sushi, but you can also get *yakitori* (skewers of grilled chicken and vegetables), *kushikatsu* and tempura. It's near Sanjō-Ōhashi bridge.

HATI HATI Map pp228-9 *Indonesian*
☎ 212 2228; B1 Kyoto Kankō Bldg, Nishikiyamachi-dōri-Takoyakushi; 🕑 6pm-2am Sun-Thu, 6pm-3am Fri & Sat; dishes from ¥600; 5min walk from Hankyū Kawaramachi Station

Hati Hati offers some of the best Indonesian food in Kyoto, including all of the standard favourites, such as *nasi goreng* (fried rice) and *mee goreng* (fried noodles). It's on the basement floor of the Kankō building; look for the green stairwell.

ICHI-BAN Map pp228-9 *Yakitori*
☎ 751 1459; Sanjō-dōri Ōhashi East; 🕑 5.30pm-midnight, closed Sun & public holidays; dinner from ¥3000; 3min walk from Keihan Sanjō Station

This popular *yakitori* joint has an English menu and a friendly owner to help with ordering. Best of all, it has that classic old *yakitori-ya* (*yakitori* restaurant) ambience – smoking charcoal grills, old beer posters on the walls and *oden* (winter stew) bubbling away on the counter. Look for the yellow-and-red sign and the big lantern.

KAGIZEN YOSHIFUSA
Map pp228-9 *Sweets & Tea*
☎ 525 0011; Higashiyama-ku Gion-chō; 🕑 9.30am-6pm, closed Mon; tea from ¥400; 5min walk from Keihan Shijō Station

This Gion institution is one of Kyoto's oldest and best-known *okashi-ya* (sweet shops). It sells a variety of traditional sweets and has a cosy tearoom upstairs where you can sample cold *kuzukiri* (transparent arrowroot noodles) served with a *kuro-mitsu* (sweet black sugar) dipping sauce. Look for the sweets in the window, the wide front and the *noren* (curtains).

KANE-YO Map pp228-9 *Unagi*
☎ 221 0669; Shinkyōgoku-dōri-Rokkaku; 🕑 11.30am-9pm; unagi over rice ¥890; 10min walk from Keihan Sanjō Station

This is a good place to try *unagi* (eel), that most sublime of Japanese dishes. You can sit downstairs with a nice view of the waterfall, or upstairs on the tatami. The *kane-yo donburi* (eel over rice) set is great value. Look for the barrels of live eels outside and the wooden façade.

KATSU KURA Map pp228-9 *Tonkatsu*
☎ 212 3581; Teramachi-dōri-Sanjō; 🕑 11am-9.30pm; tonkatsu from ¥819; 10min walk from Keihan Sanjō Station

This restaurant in the Sanjō covered arcade is a good place to sample *tonkatsu*. It's not the best in Kyoto, but it's relatively cheap and casual.

KERALA Map pp228-9 *Indian*
☎ 251 0141; Kawaramachi-dōri-Sanjō; 🕑 11.30am-2pm & 5-9pm; lunch from ¥850, dinner from ¥3000; 3min walk from Tōzai subway line, Kyoto-Shiyakusho-mae Station

We highly recommend the lunch sets at this reliable Indian specialist, arguably the best in Kyoto. Dinners are a little overpriced, but the quality is high. It's on the 2nd floor; look for the display of food on street level.

MERRY ISLAND CAFÉ
Map pp228-9 *International*
☎ 213 0214; Kiyamachi-dōri-Oike; 🕑 11.30am-11pm, closed Mon; lunch/dinner ¥800/3000; 2min walk from Tōzai subway line, Kyoto-Shiyakusho-mae Station

Behind the Kyoto Hotel, Merry Island is a good place for coffee or a light lunch. In warm weather the front doors are opened and the place takes on the air of a sidewalk café. For a few moments, you might actually believe that you've been transported to Europe.

MISHIMA-TEI Map pp228-9 *Sukiyaki*
☎ 221 0003; Teramachi-dōri-Sanjō kudaru; 🕑 11.30am-10pm, closed Wed; sukiyaki sets from ¥4400; 5min walk from Keihan Sanjō Station

In the Sanjō covered arcade, this is an inexpensive place to sample sukiyaki. There is an English menu and a discount for foreign travellers.

MISOKA-AN KAWAMICHI-YA

Map pp228-9 *Soba*

☎ 221 2525; Fuyachō-dōri-Sanjō; ☺ 11am-8pm, closed Thu; dishes ¥700-3800; 3min walk from Tōzai subway line, Kyoto-Shiyakusho-mae Station

For a taste of some of Kyoto's best *soba* noodles in traditional surroundings, head to this place, where they've been hand-making noodles for 300 years. Try a simple bowl of *nishin* (fish-topped) *soba*, or the more elaborate *nabe* dishes (cooked in a special cast-iron pot). There is a small English sign.

MORITA-YA Map pp228-9 *Sukiyaki*

☎ 231 5118; Kiyamachi-dōri-Sanjō agaru; ☺ noon-11pm; dishes ¥8000; 3min walk from Keihan Sanjō Station

This is Kyoto's most famous beef restaurant. It serves excellent sukiyaki and *shabu-shabu* (thin slices of beef and vegetables cooked in broth) in tatami rooms, some overlooking the Kamo-gawa. It's on Kiyamachi-dōri, down an ally between a sweet shop and a gallery.

ŌZAWA Map pp228-9 *Tempura*

☎ 561 2052; Gion Shirakawa Nawate Higashi iru, South; ☺ 11.30am-10pm (last orders 9pm), closed Thu; lunch ¥2500, dinner from ¥3800; 5min walk from Keihan Shijō Station

Located on one of the most beautiful streets in Gion, this charming little restaurant offers excellent tempura in refined Japanese surroundings. Unless you choose a private tatami room, you'll sit at the counter and watch as the chef prepares each piece of tempura individually right before your eyes. Considering the location and the quality of the food, this place is great value.

PONTO-CHŌ UAN Map pp228-9 *Kaiseki*

☎ 221 2358/2269; Pontochō-Sanjō kudaru; ☺ 5-10pm, closed Wed; dinner from ¥5000; 8min walk from Hankyū Kawaramachi Station

Ponto-chō Uan (formerly Uzuki) is an elegant *kaiseki* restaurant with a great platform for riverside dining in the summer. We recommend that you have a Japanese speaker call to reserve and choose your meal. Look for the rabbit on the sign.

SARACCA Map pp228-9 *Café*

☎ 231 8797; Tominokoji-dōri-Sanjō; ☺ noon-10pm, closed Wed; coffee from ¥400, light meals from ¥700; 5min walk from Karasuma subway line, Shijō Station

You'll have to look long and hard to find a coffee shop more relaxing than this one. It serves a variety of international food, some of it vegetarian. It's above a bike shop.

SHIRUKŌ Map pp228-9 *Obanzai*

☎ 221 3250; Nishikiyamachi-dōri-Shijō; ☺ 11.30am-9pm, closed Wed; lunch & dinner from ¥2600; 2min walk from Hankyū Kawaramachi Station

For a light meal, Shirukō has been serving simple Kyoto *obanzai-ryōri* (Kyoto home-style cooking) since 1932. The restaurant features more than 10 varieties of miso soup, and the *rikyū bentō* (¥2600) is a bona fide work of art. It's down a somewhat seedy pedestrian alley near Shijō-Kawaramachi crossing; look for the bamboo out front.

TOMI-ZUSHI Map pp228-9 *Sushi*

☎ 231 3628; Shinkyōgoku-dōri-Shijō; ☺ 5pm-midnight, closed Thu; dinner ¥3000; 5min walk from Hankyū Kawaramachi Station

For good sushi in lively surroundings try Tomi-zushi, where you rub elbows with your neighbour, sit at a long marble counter and watch as some of the fastest sushi chefs in the land do their thing. Go early or wait in line. It's near the Shijō-Kawaramachi crossing; look for the lantern and the black-and-white signs.

TŌSAI

Map pp228-9 *Japanese Vegetarian*

☎ 213 2900; Takoyakushi-dōri-Sakaimachi East; ☺ 5-10pm, closed Mon & 1st Sun of the month; dinner from ¥4000; 5min walk from Karasuma subway line, Shijō Station

For creative Japanese vegetarian fare (the name means 'vegetables and beans') we recommend Tōsai. It's just in from a corner, next to a tiny automatic parking lot – look for the traditional wooden front.

UMEZONO Map pp228-9 *Sweets*

☎ 221 5017; Kawaramachi-dōri-Rokkaku; ☺ 10.30am-7.30pm; mitarashi dango set ¥500; 10min walk from Keihan Sanjō Station

Locals line up at this Kyoto institution for *mitarashi dangō* (sweet, rice gluten balls), a peculiarly Japanese sweet.

UONTANA Map pp228-9 *Izakaya*

☎ 221 2579; Rokkaku-dōri-Shinkyōgoku; ☺ noon-3pm & 5-10pm, closed Wed; dinner from ¥3000; 7min walk from Keihan Sanjō Station

This upscale *izakaya* is a good spot to try a range of sake and elegantly presented Japanese fare (sashimi, fried dishes, salads). There is an English menu and a tiny lantern with English writing out front.

YAGURA Map pp228-9 *Soba*

☎ 561 1035; Shijō-dōri-Kawabata; ⏱ 11am-9.30pm, closed Thu; nishin soba ¥1000; 1min walk from Keihan Shijō Station

Across from Minami-za kabuki theatre, this old noodle specialist somehow reminds us of an American diner, with a row of wooden booths and tough old mamas running the show. We recommend the *nishin soba*. It's located between a *rāmen* joint and a Japanese gift shop – look for the bowls of noodles in the window.

YAK & YETI Map pp228-9 *Nepalese*

☎ 213 7919; Gokomachi-dōri-Nishikikōji; ⏱ 11.30am-4.30pm, 5-9.30pm, closed Mon; curry lunch sets from ¥600; 5min walk from Karasuma subway line, Shijō Station

This tiny Nepalese joint serves more than just the *dal bhaat* (rice and lentil curry) that most associate with Nepalese cuisine. In fact, the fare is probably closer to Indian, including good curries and tasty nan bread. There is counter seating but we like to sit on the comfortable cushions here.

YAMATOMI Map pp228-9 *Japanese*

☎ 221 3268; Pontochō-Shijō; ⏱ noon-2pm, 4-10.30pm, closed irregularly; dishes ¥150-2800; 3min walk from Hankyū Kawaramachi Station

This is a fun spot where you can try your hand at the house special, *teppin-age*, frying up tasty tempura on skewers in a cast-iron pot (per person ¥2800). Look for the small figure of a Japanese woman bowing in the window.

YOSHIKAWA Map pp228-9 *Tempura*

☎ 221 5544; Tominokoji-dōri-Oike kudaru; lunch ¥2000-6000, dinner ¥6000-12,000; ⏱ 11am-2pm & 5-8pm, closed Sun; 5min walk from Tōzai subway line, Kyoto-Shiyakusho-mae Station

For superb tempura head for Yoshikawa. It offers fancy table seating (lunch/dinner ¥6000/12,000), but it's much more interesting to sit and eat around the small counter (¥2000/6000) and observe the chefs at work. Look for the English sign reading 'Yoshikawa Inn'; the restaurant entrance is next door.

ZU ZU Map pp228-9 *Izakaya*

☎ 231 0736; Pontochō-Takoyakushi; ⏱ 6pm-2am; dinner from ¥3000; 5min walk from Hankyū Kawaramachi Station

This Pontochō *izakaya* is a fun place to eat. The best bet is to ask the waiter for a recommendation. The fare is sort of nouveau-Japanese –

things like shrimp and tofu or chicken and plum sauce. Look for the white stucco exterior and black bars on the windows.

CHEAP EATS

ASK A GIRAFFE Map pp228-9 *Café*

☎ 257 8028; Karasuma-dōri-Aneyakōji, 1F Shin-Puh-Kan; ⏱ 11am-11pm, closed irregularly; coffee from ¥400, cakes from ¥430, lunch set ¥900; 2min walk from Karasuma subway line, Karasuma-Oike Station

This casual café is our favourite of the six restaurants in the Shin-Puh-Kan shopping complex. It offers light meals (sandwiches, pastas, salads) and all the standard drinks, which make a nice pick-me-up while shopping here. Like you, we're totally puzzled by the name.

CAFÉ INDEPENDANTS Map pp228-9 *Café*

☎ 255 4312; Sanjō-dōri-Gokomachi; ⏱ 11.45am-midnight; coffee drinks from ¥300, salads & sandwiches from ¥400; 10min walk from Keihan Sanjō Station

Located beneath a gallery, this cool subterranean café offers a range of light meals and café drinks in a bohemian atmosphere. A lot of the food offerings are laid out on display for you to choose from – with the emphasis on healthy sandwiches and salads. Take the stairs on your left before the gallery.

DOUTOR COFFEE Map pp228-9 *Café*

☎ 213 4041; Shijō-dōri-Fuya-chō nishi iru; ⏱ 7.30am-10pm Mon-Sat, 8am-10pm Sun & public holidays; coffee ¥180; 10min walk from Hankyū Kyoto line, Kawaramachi Station

For a cheap coffee fix you can't beat Doutor Coffee. There are branches all over Kyoto, including this one on Shijō-dōri.

GONBEI Map pp228-9 *Soba*

☎ 561 3350; Higashiyama-Gion-chō; ⏱ noon-9.30pm, closed Thu; noodle dishes from ¥630; 5min walk from Keihan Shijō Station

For *soba* or *udon* while exploring Gion or Higashiyama, this casual noodle house is a great choice. The English menu makes ordering a breeze. Look for the lantern and wooden sign.

INODA COFFEE Map pp228-9 *Café*

☎ 221 0507; Sakaimachi-dōri-Sanjō; ⏱ 7am-8pm; coffee from ¥500; 5min walk from Karasuma subway line, Karasuma-Oike Station

This chain is a Kyoto institution and has branches throughout the city. Though slightly overrated for the price, the old-Japan atmosphere at this, Inoda's main shop, is worth a try.

ISSEN YŌSHOKU

Map pp228-9   *Okonomiyaki*

☎ 533 0001; Nawate-dōri-Shijō; ⏰ 11am-3am Mon-Sat, 10.30am-10pm Sun & public holidays; okonomiyaki ¥630; 5min walk from Keihan Shijō Station

Heaped with red ginger and green scallions, the *okonomiyaki* at this Gion institution is a garish snack – which somehow seems fitting considering the surrounding neighbourhood.

KOBEYA DINING Map pp228-9   *Café*

☎ 253 3751; Kawaramachi-dōri-Shijō; ⏰ 10am-9.30pm; lunch & dinner from ¥700; 1min walk from Hankyū Kawaramachi Station

This casual bakery/café makes the perfect refreshment stop while shopping in the Shijō-Kawaramachi area – it's very easy to enter and ordering is a breeze since most items are laid out for your perusal. You'll find the usual coffee/tea suspects and some decent salads and sandwiches.

KŌSENDŌ-SUMI Map pp228-9   *Japanese*

☎ 241 7377; Aneyakōji-dōri-Sakaimachi; ⏰ 11am-4pm, closed Sun & public holidays; lunch from ¥870; 5min walk from Karasuma subway line, Karasuma-Oike Station

For a pleasant lunch downtown, try this unpretentious little restaurant located in an old

Japanese house. The daily lunch special, which is usually simple and healthy Japanese fare, is always displayed out front for your inspection. It's near the Museum of Kyoto, next to a small parking lot.

MUSASHI SUSHI Map pp228-9   *Sushi*

☎ 222 0634; Kawaramachi-dōri-Sanjō; ⏰ 11am-10pm; dishes ¥100; 5min walk from Keihan Sanjō Station

If you've never tried *kaiten-zushi* (conveyor-belt sushi), don't miss this place, where all the dishes are a mere ¥100. It's just outside the entrance to the Sanjō covered arcade; look for the mini sushi conveyor belt in the window.

MUSE Map pp228-9   *Café*

☎ 221 4965; Nishikiyamachi-dōri-Shijō agaru; ⏰ noon-10.30pm; coffee ¥400; 3min walk from Hankyū Kawaramachi Station

Muse is an elegant little café that plays excellent classical music (this sort of place used to be common in Japan, but they're now being crowded out by modern chains). It's a very relaxing place for a civilised cup of tea (and you'll soon forget that you're only a stone's throw from one of Kyoto's seedier streets).

QU'IL FAIT BON Map pp228-9   *Café*

☎ 254 8580; Kiyamachi-dōri-Sanjō; ⏰ 11am-8pm; cakes from ¥500; 5min walk from Keihan Sanjō Station

For a quick cuppa or some tasty cakes, try this canal-side restaurant on Kiyamachi-dōri. It's a pretty good date spot – at least that's how the locals see it.

SANTŌKA Map pp228-9   *Rāmen*

☎ 532 1335; Sanjō-dōri-Kawabata; ⏰ 11am-2am; rāmen from ¥750; 1min walk from Keihan Sanjō Station

The young chefs at this sleek new restaurant dish out some seriously good Hokkaidō-style *rāmen*. You will be given a choice of three kinds of soup when you order: *shio* (salt), *shōyu* (soy sauce) or miso – we highly recommend you go for the miso soup. For something totally decadent, try the *tokusen toroniku rāmen*, which is made from pork cheeks, of which only 200 grams can be obtained from one animal (this will come on a separate plate from the *rāmen* – just shovel it all into your bowl). The restaurant is located on the east side and ground floor of the new Kyōen restaurant and shopping complex.

Musashi Sushi (right)

Eating – Downtown Kyoto

Rāmen Meguri

The *meguri* (pilgrimage) is an essential part of Japanese life. It's possible to make a pilgrimage to temples, shrines, natural sites, *onsen* (hot springs), and, yes – you guessed it – *rāmen* restaurants. Although Kyoto is known in Japan as the capital of *kaiseki* (Japanese *haute cuisine*), it has a surprising number of excellent *rāmen* restaurants. If you're a fan of these magical noodles, we highly recommend performing a little *rāmen meguri* of your own.

Karako (p112) This place elevates *rāmen* to *haute cuisine*, with rich soup and sublime pork slices.

Santōka (opposite) A bit of Hokkaidō-*rāmen* heaven right here in Kyoto.

Shin-Shin-Tei (p117) An offbeat bowl of noodles in white miso soup.

Tenka-Ippin Honten (p114) The main store of Kyoto's most popular *rāmen* chain – a fatty indulgence.

Tsuruhashi (p115) The only duck-flavoured soup that we've ever come across – unique and very tasty.

TAGOTO HONTEN Map pp228-9 *Soba*
☎ 221 3030; Sanjō-dōri-Teramachi; 🕐 11am-9pm; noodle dishes from ¥997; 10min walk from Karasuma subway line, Shijō Station
This is one of Kyoto's oldest and most revered *soba* restaurants. The prices are higher than many comparable restaurants downtown, but you're paying for history here. It's in the Sanjō covered arcade.

ZAPPA Map pp228-9 *Indonesian*
☎ 255 4437; Takoyakushi-dōri-Kawaramachi; 🕐 6pm-midnight, closed Sun; dishes from ¥850; 10min walk from Keihan Sanjō Station
Zappa is a cosy little place that once played host to David Bowie (he's said to have happened on the place randomly). The friendly owner, Hiroko-san, serves up savoury Southeast Asian fare. Prices are reasonable and the music is groovy (but no Frank Zappa?). It's down an alley between Kiyamachi-dōri and Kawaramachi-dōri; go south at the wooden torii (shrine gate).

SOUTHEAST KYOTO
Southeast Kyoto is second only to the downtown area in terms of variety and number of restaurants. You'll find the largest concentration of eateries in Gion, with others scattered around the main sightseeing spots at the base of the Higashiyama Mountains. This area contains many of Kyoto's fanciest and most elite restaurants. There are, of course, humble places as well.

ASUKA Map pp225-7 *Shokudō*
☎ 751 9809; Sanjō-dōri-Higashiyama nishi iru; 🕐 11am-11pm; meals from ¥1000; 3min walk from Tōzai subway line, Higashiyama Station
With an English menu and a staff of *mama-sans* at home with foreign customers, this is a

great place for a cheap lunch or dinner while sightseeing in Higashiyama. The *tempura moriawase* (assorted tempura set) is a big pile of tempura for ¥1000. Look for the red lantern.

AUNBO Map pp225-7 *Japanese*
☎ 525 2900; Higashiyama-Yasaka Torii mae; 🕐 noon-2pm, 5.30-10pm, closed Wed; lunch ¥2500, dinner ¥6000-10,000; 10min walk from Keihan Shijō Station
Aunbo serves elegant, creative Japanese cooking in traditional Gion surroundings – the last time we were here we started with sublime sashimi, went on to fried *yuba* (tofu skimming) pockets and went from there. We recommend asking for the set and leaving the difficult decisions to the master. Aunbo takes reservations in the evening. There is no English sign; look for the traditional Japanese façade.

DAIKICHI Map pp225-7 *Yakitori*
☎ 771 3126; Sanjō-dōri Ōhashi East; 🕐 5pm-1am; dishes ¥3000; 3min walk from Keihan Sanjō Station
The *yakitori* is good and the owner is friendly at this brightly lit *yakitori* place. Look for the red lanterns outside.

EL LATINO Map pp225-7 *Mexican*
☎ 751 0647; Shogoin-Sanno-chō; 🕐 6pm-1am; dinner from ¥2000; 10min walk from Keihan Marutamachi Station
El Latino is a fun Mexican joint that serves good tacos, *taqitos* (rolled tacos), guacamole and chips, and tasty frozen margaritas. It's located near the Higashiōji-Marutamachi crossing.

GANKO NIJŌ-EN Map pp225-7 *Japanese*
☎ 223 3456; Kiyamachi-dōri-Nijō; 🕐 11.30am-10pm; lunch from ¥1500, dinner from ¥2500; 3min walk from Tōzai subway line, Kyoto-Shiyakusho-mae Station
This is an upscale branch of Ganko Zushi that serves sushi and *kaiseki* sets. There's a picture

Eating – Southeast Kyoto

menu and you can stroll in the stunning garden before or after your meal. It is near the Nijō-Kiyamachi crossing.

GION MORIKŌ

Map pp225-7   *Cantonese*

☎ 531 8000; Shirakawa-tsuji Chion-in-bashi agaru nishi-gawa; ☷ 11.30am-2pm & 5-9.30pm, closed Wed; lunch set ¥800, dinner sets from ¥3000, à la carte dishes from ¥900; 3min walk from Tōzai subway line, Higashiyama Station

All the usual Cantonese favourites in a fairly casual Japanese setting are the draw at this friendly little place. It's located along the picturesque Shira-kawa canal on the northern edge of Gion. The master speaks some English and can help with ordering (and an English menu is apparently in the works).

HYŌTEI Map pp225-7   *Kaiseki*

☎ 771 4116; Nanzen-ji; ☷ 11am-8pm; meals from ¥3500; 10min walk from Tōzai subway line, Keage Station

The Hyōtei is considered to be one of Kyoto's oldest and most picturesque traditional restaurants. In the main building you can sample exquisite *kaiseki* courses in private tearooms (¥18,000).

IKKYŪ-AN KIKYOU

Map pp225-7   *Buddhist Vegetarian*

☎ 531 0210; Higashiyama-dōri-Shichijō, Chishaku-in; ☷ 11am-6.30pm; lunch ¥1500; 1min walk from Higashiyama Shichijō bus stop, bus 206

This may be the cheapest place in town to sample *shōjin-ryōri* (Buddhist vegetarian cooking). It specialises in dishes made from *konyaku* (arum root). It's in the grounds of Chishaku-in, a few minutes' walk east of the Kyoto National Museum.

IMOBŌ HIRANOYA HONTEN

Map pp225-7   *Imobō*

☎ 561 1603; Maruyama-kōen-Chion in north gate; ☷ 10.30am-8pm; set meal from ¥2400; 10min walk from Keihan Shijō Station

Tucked inside the north gate of Maruyama-kōen, this traditional restaurant specialises in *imobō*, a dish consisting of a local type of sweet potato and dried fish, which was the only seafood most Kyotoites could get before the advent of refrigeration. All meals are served in restful, private tatami rooms. There is an English menu.

KANŌ SHŌJU-AN

Map pp225-7   *Teahouse*

☎ 751 1077; Sakyō-ku, Nyakuoji-chō; ☷ 10am-4.30pm, closed Wed; matcha tea & sweet ¥1050; 10min walk from Nanzenji Eikando michi bus stop, bus 5

A full tea ceremony can be both hard to arrange and rather formal, but you can sample a simplified version here. It's an excellent way to refresh yourself as you make your way along the Path of Philosophy. Just ask for *matcha* (powdered green tea) and the staff will do the rest. On crowded days you may have to wait to be seated. Look for the bridge across the canal.

MANZARA HONTEN

Map pp225-7   *Modern Japanese*

☎ 253 1559; Kawaramachi-dōri agaru; ☷ 5pm-midnight (last orders 11.30pm); set dinner from ¥4000, à la carte dishes from ¥500; 10min walk from Karasuma subway line, Marutamachi Station

Like Shuhari (opposite), Manzara is located in a converted *machiya*. The fare here is creative modern Japanese and the surroundings are decidedly stylish. The *omakase* (chef's recommendation) course is good value, with eight dishes for ¥4000.

MINOKŌ Map pp225-7   *Kaiseki*

☎ 561 0328; Gion-Shimokawara; ☷ 11.30am-2.30pm & 5-8pm; lunch box ¥4500, lunch from ¥10,000, dinner from ¥13,000; 12min walk from Keihan Shijō Station

This classic Gion restaurant serves a lunch *bentō* and *cha-kaiseki* (tea-ceremony *kaiseki*) dinner. There is no English sign; it's across from a parking lot – look for the metal lantern out front.

OKARIBA Map pp225-7   *Wild Game*

☎ 751 7790; Okazaki-Higashitenno-chō; ☷ 5-10.30pm, closed Sun; dinner ¥4000; 1min walk from Higashitenno-chō bus stop, bus 203

For an experience you won't soon forget, try Okariba, near Hotel Heian no Mori Kyoto. If it crawls, walks or swims, it's probably on the menu. The *inoshishi* (wild boar) barbecue is a good start. Non-meateaters can try the fresh *ayu* (Japanese trout).

OKUTAN Map pp225-7   *Tofu*

☎ 771 8709; Nanzen-ji; ☷ 10.30am-5pm, closed Thu; set meal ¥3000; 10min walk from Tōzai subway line, Keage Station

Just outside the precincts of Nanzen-ji you'll find Okutan, a restaurant inside the luxurious garden of Chōshō-in. This is a popular place

Machiya Magic

Machiya (Kyoto's traditional wooden townhouses) are wonderful examples of the best in Japanese design and carpentry. Unfortunately they are being torn down at an alarming rate to make room for modern concrete structures that appeal to more modern sensibilities. Luckily, a few of Kyoto's most lovely *machiya* have been purchased by forward-thinking restaurateurs and converted into atmospheric eateries where you can enjoy excellent cuisine and true old-Kyoto ambience.

Café Sua (p115) This tiny café in the northwest of town is hard to find but easy to like.

Manzara Honten (opposite) Kyoto connoisseurs flock to this slick *machiya* restaurant for creative Japanese fare.

Mukade-ya (p117) A downtown temple of *kaiseki* cuisine in a fine *machiya*.

Shuhari (below) Casual French food in a fine old *machiya* makes this one of our favourite downtown lunch spots.

that has specialised in vegetarian temple food for hundreds of years. Try a course of *yudōfu* (bean curd cooked in a pot) together with vegetable side dishes (¥3000).

SENMONTEN Map pp225-7   *Chinese*
☎ 531 2733; Hanami-kōji-dōri-Shinbashi; ☷ 6pm-2am, closed Sun & public holidays; 10 dumplings for ¥460; 5min walk from Keihan Shijō Station
This place serves only one thing: crisp fried *gyōza* (Chinese dumplings), which come in pallets of ten, washed down with beer or Chinese *raoshu* (rice wine). If you can break the record for the most *gyōza* eaten in one sitting, your meal will be free and you'll receive – guess what? – more *gyōza* to take home. The last time we were here, the men's record was approaching 150 *gyōza*. Look for the red-and-white sign and glass door.

SHUHARI Map pp219-21   *French*
☎ 222 6815; Kawaramachi-dōri-Marutamachi agaru; ☷ noon-11pm Mon-Thu, noon-2am Fri-Sun; lunch course from ¥850, dinner around ¥2500; 10min walk from Karasuma subway line, Marutamachi Station
Shuhari is a great example of Kyoto's newest dining trend – fine restaurants in renovated *machiya*. In this case, the food is casual French, with an emphasis on light fish dishes and healthy salads. Look for the red stove pipe with the name of the restaurant written on it out front.

TŌKAN-SŌ Map pp225-7   *Kaiseki*
☎ 561 0581; Yasaka Torii mae, Higashiyama-ku; ☷ 11am-2pm & 5-10pm, closed irregularly; lunch from ¥3000, dinner from ¥8000; 15min walk from Keihan Shijō Station
For reasonable *kaiseki* fare in private tatami rooms overlooking a simple garden, this restaurant, located above Maruyama-kōen, is a

good bet. We recommend having the folks at your lodgings call to reserve and place your order. It's up a flight of stone steps with trees on either side.

CHEAP EATS

CHABANA Map pp225-7   *Okonomiyaki*
☎ 751 8691; Kawabata-dōri-Nijō; ☷ 5pm-4am; okonomiyaki from ¥600; 10min walk from Keihan Sanjō Station
This classic *okonomiyaki* joint is good for a late-night snack after prowling the bars of Kiyamachi-dōri. If you don't have a favourite just ask for the mixed *okonomiyaki* (¥750). Look for the rotating light outside.

COCOHANA Map pp225-7   *Korean*
☎ 525 5587; Honmachi-dōri-Kujo; ☷ 11am-11pm Thu-Mon, 11am-5.30pm Tue, closed Wed; coffee drinks from ¥300, lunch from ¥680; 2min walk from Keihan Tōfukuji Station
This place is one of a kind: a Korean café in a converted old Japanese house. Dishes here include *bibimbap* (a Korean rice dish) and *kimchi* (Korean pickles). A full range of coffee and tea is also available. It's a woody rustic place with both table and tatami seating. There is no English menu but the friendly young staff will help with ordering. This makes a great stop while exploring southeastern Kyoto (Tōfuku-ji etc).

EARTH KITCHEN COMPANY
Map pp225-7   *Bentō*
☎ 771 1897; Marutamachi-dōri-Kawabata; ☷ 10.30am-6.30pm Mon-Fri, 10.30am-3.30pm Sat, closed Sun & public holidays; lunch ¥700; 1min walk from Keihan Marutamachi Station
Near the Kamo-gawa, this tiny place seats just two people but does a bustling business serving tasty takeaway lunch *bentō*.

GION KOISHI Map pp225-7 *Tea Shop*
☎ 531 0301; Higashiyama Gion North; ☻ 11am-7pm, closed 2nd & 4th Wed of the month; tea from ¥500; 10min walk from Hankyū Shijō Station

If it's a hot summer day and you need a cooling break, try this tea shop for some typical Japanese summer treats. The speciality here is *uji kintoki* (¥700), a mountain of shaved ice flavoured with green tea, sweetened milk and sweet beans (it tastes a lot better than it sounds, trust us). It's the fifth shop in from the corner, between two souvenir/craft shops.

HINODE Map pp225-7 *Udon & Soba*
☎ 751 9251; Nanzenji-Kitanobou-chō; ☻ 11am-6pm, closed Sun; noodle dishes from ¥400; 5min walk from Higashitenno-chō bus stop

Hinode serves filling noodle-and-rice dishes in a pleasant little shop with an English menu. Plain *udon* here is only ¥400, but we recommend the *nabeyaki udon* (pot-baked *udon* in broth) for ¥750.

KARAKO Map pp225-7 *Rāmen*
☎ 752 8234; Okazaki Tokusei-chō; ☻ 11.30am-3pm & 6pm-midnight, closed Tue; rāmen from ¥650; 15min walk from Keihan Sanjō Station

Karako is our favourite *rāmen* restaurant in Kyoto. While it's not much on atmosphere, the *rāmen* here is excellent – the soup is thick and rich and the *chashū* (pork slices) melt in your mouth. We recommend that you ask for the *kotteri* (thick soup) *rāmen*. Look for the lantern outside.

KASAGI-YA Map pp225-7 *Sweets*
☎ 561 9562; Higashiyama-ku Kodaiji Masuya chō; ☻ 11am-6pm, closed Tue; sweets from ¥600; 7min walk from Kiyomizumichi bus stop, bus 206

At Kasagi-ya, on Sannen-zaka near Kiyomizu-dera, you can try *o-hagi* cakes made from *adzuki* (sweet red beans). This funky old wooden shop has atmosphere to boot and friendly staff – which makes it worth the wait if there's a queue.

MIKŌ-AN
Map pp225-7 *Japanese Vegetarian*
☎ 751 5045; Kawabata-dōri-Ebisugawa; ☻ 11am-11pm; lunch ¥800, dinner ¥1000; 8min walk from Keihan Marutamachi Station

Kyoto vegetarians like this place for its daily set lunch and dinner sets of mostly organic Japanese vegetarian fare. Look for the white front and small English sign on street level.

MOMIJI-AN Map pp225-7 *Tea Shop*
☎ 561 2933; Higashiyama-ku-Maruyama-chō; ☻ 9am-5pm, closed Thu; tea & sweet beans ¥600; 10min walk from Keihan Shijō Station

Located in a rustic old Kyoto house overlooking Maruyama-kōen, this is a great spot for a rest while touring the Higashiyama area. Ask for the *usucha* (thin green tea) and the staff will do the rest. It's just to the right of a traffic mirror up a flight of steps.

ZAC BARAN Map pp225-7 *International*
☎ 751 9748; Higashiōji-dōri-Marutamachi; ☻ noon-3am; dishes from ¥500; 5min walk from Kumanojinja-mae bus stop

Near the Kyoto Handicraft Center, this place used to be the main hangout for Kyoto's ex-pat crew. Now, most of the ex-pats have moved on, but the food is still good and the atmosphere is laid back and relaxing. There are daily specials, lots of pasta dishes and other things such as quiche and curry.

NORTHEAST KYOTO

Northeast Kyoto has an excellent variety of restaurants and cafés, both Japanese and international. For those on a tight budget, the area around Kyoto University is crammed with cheap student eateries, many of a higher quality than that designation might suggest.

DIDI Map pp219-21 *Indian*
☎ 791 8226; Higashiōji-dōri, Tanaka-Okubo-chō; ☻ 11am-9.30pm, closed Wed; lunch from ¥750, dinner from ¥900; 1min walk from Eizan Mototanaka Station

This friendly little smoke-free restaurant serves passable Indian lunch and dinner sets. There are plenty of vegetarian choices on the menu.

HONYARADŌ Map pp216-18 *Japanese*
☎ 222 1574; Imadegawa-dōri-Teramachi; ☻ 10am-10pm; lunch ¥700; 1min walk from Kawaramachi Imadegawa bus stop, bus 205

This woodsy place overlooking the Kyoto Imperial Palace Park is an institution, and has one of the best lunch deals in town (a daily stew set). It's a good place to relax over coffee.

KUSHI HACHI Map pp219-21 *Kushikatsu*
☎ 751 6789; Shirakawa-dōri-Imadegawa; ☻ 5-11.30pm, closed Mon; dinner from ¥2000; 5min walk from Ginkaku-ji-Michi bus stop, bus 5

Kushi Hachi, part of a popular Kyoto chain, is a fun spot to sample *kushikatsu*, a fried dish that is well suited to Western palates. We like to sit at the counter and watch as the frenetic chefs work the grills and deep-fryers. With a picture menu, ordering is a snap.

MAGO'S Map pp219-21 *International*
☎ 721 3443; Matsugazaki-Kowaki-chō; ☼ 11.30am-midnight, closed Mon; lunch & dinner from ¥750; 7min walk from Karasuma subway line, Matsugasaki Station

Mago's is a Western-style bistro that serves good sandwiches on fresh French bread or croissants.

OMEN Map pp219-21 *Udon*
☎ 771 8994; Shirakawa-dōri-Imadegawa; ☼ 11am-10pm, closed Thu; noodle dishes ¥1000; 1min walk from Ginkaku-ji-mae bus stop

About five minutes' walk from Ginkaku-ji, Omen is a noodle shop that is named after the thick, white noodles served in a hot broth with a selection of seven vegetables. Just say 'omen' and you'll be given your choice of hot or cold noodles, a bowl of soup to dip them in and a plate of vegetables (you put these into the soup along with some sesame seeds). There is an English menu. It's in a traditional Japanese house with a lantern outside.

PRINZ Map pp219-21 *Café*
☎ 712 3900; Higashikurama-dōri-Shirakawa; ☼ 8am-2am (last orders 11.30pm); coffee drinks from ¥300, lunch set from ¥1200; 2min walk from Eizan Chayama Station

Behind the blank white façade of Prinz, you'll find a café/restaurant, gallery, bookshop, garden and library – a chic island of coolness in an otherwise bland residential neighbourhood. You can sit at the counter and request music from the CDs that line the walls. The lunch set usually includes a light assortment of Western and Japanese dishes, generally on the healthy side of things. All in all, this is a very interesting stop while you're in the northeast part of town.

SPEAKEASY Map pp219-21 *American*
☎ 781 2110; Higashiōji-dōri-Kitayama; ☼ 9am-2am; meals from ¥500; 5min walk from Eizan Shūgakuin Station

Speakeasy is a foreigner's hangout in Shūga-kuin, famous as the only place in town for a 'real' Western breakfast. It also serves good tuna melts, tacos and burgers. Look for the US flag outside.

WOMB Map pp219-21 *Café*
☎ 721 1357; Ichijōji Hinokuchi-chō; ☼ 11.30am-11pm (last orders 10pm), closed Wed & 3-6pm Mon-Fri; drinks from ¥400, lunch set from ¥1300; 2min walk from Eizan Chayama Station

Womb appears to be an experiment in stark Spartan design – it's all open spaces, blank walls and simple furniture. Following the Spartan ethic, the menu is limited to only a few dishes such as creative sushi and healthy noodles. This place often holds evening art events.

YATAI Map pp219-21 *Yatai*
Imadegawa-dōri; ☼ dusk to midnight; dishes from ¥300; 10min walk from Keihan Demachiyanagi Station

This *yatai* (tent) pops up along Imadegawa-dōri every evening and serves a variety of food to go, along with beer and sake. It's fun but don't expect English to be spoken (pointing at what you want is the easiest way to go).

CHEAP EATS

BAR CAFÉ ZINHO Map pp219-21 *Brazilian*
☎ 712 5477; Kitaōji-dōri-Shimogamohon South; ☼ 9am-midnight Mon-Sat, 10am-11pm Sun & public holidays; Brazilian coffee ¥200, fejoada & rice ¥750; 10min walk from Karasuma subway line, Kitaōji Station

This tiny Brazilian-style restaurant is a good spot for a light meal or perhaps an evening drink when in northeast Kyoto.

BON BON CAFÉ Map pp219-21 *Café*
☎ 213 8686; Imadegawa-dōri higashi iru-Kawaramachi; ☼ 10am-midnight; coffee drinks from ¥300, sandwiches from ¥500; 3min walk from Keihan Demachiyanagi Station

If you find yourself in need of a light meal or drink while you're in the Demachiyanagi area, this casual open café is an excellent choice. There are a variety of cakes and light meals on offer. While there is no English menu, much of the ordering can be done by pointing, and the young staff can help you figure out what's not on display. It's on the west bank of the Kamo-gawa and outdoor seats here are very pleasant on warm evenings.

BUTTERCUPS Map pp219-21 *Café*
☎ 751 7837; Shirakawa-dōri; coffee from ¥300, meals from ¥580; ☼ noon-11pm, closed Tue; 5min walk from Kinrinshako-mae bus stop, bus 5

Buttercups is a favourite of the local ex-pat community and a great place for lunch, dinner or a cup of coffee. The menu is international. Look for the plants and whiteboard menu outside.

CAFÉ CARINHO/ASIAN DINER

Map pp219-21   *Indonesian*

☎ 752 3636; Imadegawa-dōri-Shirakawa; 🕑 11am-10pm Tue-Thu, 11am-11pm Fri-Sun; coffee from ¥400, lunch from ¥750; 5min walk from Ginkaku-ji-Michi bus stop, bus 5

This excellent little café near Ginkaku-ji is one of the only places in town for proper bagel sandwiches. It also serves specials that change daily, light meals and excellent coffee/tea drinks. In the evening it morphs into an Indonesian restaurant with a Java-born chef turning out some delicious Indonesian dishes that go far beyond the usual *nasi goreng* and *mee goreng*. All told, this is one of the best spots in the neighbourhood for a drink or meal.

CAFÉ PEACE Map pp219-21   *Vegetarian*

☎ 707 6856; Higashiōji-dōri-Imadegawa, Hyakumanben; 🕑 11.30am-10.30pm Mon-Sat, 11.30am-9.30pm Sun & public holidays; drinks from ¥550, dishes from ¥600; 10min walk from Keihan Demachiyanagi Station

Café Peace is a welcome addition to Kyoto's vegetarian line-up. You can order à la carte or go for a good-value set meal, which always includes healthy brown rice and miso soup. It's on the 3rd floor; there's a small English sign on street level.

EATING HOUSE HI-LITE

Map pp219-21   *Shokudō*

☎ 721 1997; Sakyō-ku-Hyakumanben; 🕑 11am-11pm, closed Sun, 2nd Sat each month & public holidays; set meals from ¥540; 5min walk from Keihan Demachiyanagi Station

Kyoto University students cram into this popular shokudō (Japanese-style cafeteria) for filling set-course meals. Try the *cheezu chicken katsu teishoku* (fried chicken with cheese set meal). The name is written in English on the sign outside.

HIRAGANA-KAN Map pp219-21   *Shokudō*

☎ 701 4164; Higashiōji-dōri-Mikage; lunch & dinner from ¥800; 🕑 11.30am-4pm & 6-10pm, closed Tue; 8min walk from Eizan Mototanaka Station

This place, popular with Kyoto University students, dishes up creative variations on chicken, fish and meat. Most entrées come with rice, salad and miso soup. The menu is only in Japanese, but if you're at a loss for what to order try the tasty *roll chicken katsu*, a delectable and filling creation of chicken and vegetables. Look for the words 'Casual Restaurant' on the white awning.

KAGIYA MASAAKI

Map pp219-21   *Sweets*

☎ 761 5311; Higashiōji-dōri-Imadegawa; 🕑 9am-6pm, closed Sun; sweets from ¥700; 10min walk from Keihan Demachiyanagi Station

Since 1682 Kagiya Masaaki has been preparing a delightful Kyoto confection called *tokiwagi*. It's near Kyoto University.

KUISHINBŌ-NO-MISE

Map pp219-21   *Shokudō*

☎ 712 0656; Kitashirakawa-Kubota-chō, Hyakumanben East; 🕑 11.30am-2pm & 6-11pm, closed Wed; set meals from ¥500; 5min walk from Keihan Demachiyanagi Station

Bring a large appetite to this cheap and filling shokudō near Ginkaku-ji. The daily lunch and dinner specials are great value; ask for the *sabisu-teishoku* (set meat). Look for the photos of the food out front.

KYOTO UNIVERSITY STUDENT CAFETERIA

Map pp219-21   *Japanese Dining Hall*

Imadegawa-dōri-Higashiōji, Hyakumanben; 🕑 8.20am-8pm Mon-Fri, 10am-2pm Sat, closed Sun, public holidays & end of Apr–end of Aug; meals from ¥500; 5min walk from Hyakumanben bus stop, bus 206

If you're on a tight budget, you can fill up at this student cafeteria (*kyōdai* shokudō) for a pittance. Technically it's for students only, but you won't be hassled. You might have to ask a student to point the way.

SHINSHINDŌ NOTRE PAIN QUOTIDIEN Map pp219-21   *Café*

☎ 701 4121; Kitashirakawa Oiwake-chō; 🕑 8am-6pm, closed Tue; coffee from ¥340; 2min walk from Hyakumanben bus stop, bus 206

This atmospheric old Kyoto coffee shop is a favourite of Kyoto University students for its curry and bread lunch set (¥780), which is kind of an acquired taste. It's located near Kyoto University.

TENKA-IPPIN HONTEN

Map pp219-21   *Rāmen*

☎ 722 0955; Shirakawa-dōri-Kitaōji; 🕑 11am-3pm, closed Thu; rāmen from ¥600; 1min walk from Ichijōji Kinomoto-chō bus stop, bus 5

This is the original store of Kyoto's most famous *rāmen* chain. We love the thick soup (*kotteri*) *rāmen* served here (but we didn't say it was healthy).

TRANQ ROOM Map pp219-21 *Café*
☎ 762 4888; Shirakawa-dōri-Jyodoji Shinnyo-chō; ⏰ noon-2am Mon-Fri, noon-midnight Sat, Sun & public holidays; coffee drinks from ¥400, meals from ¥600; 1min walk from Shinnyodo-mae bus stop

Tranq Room (which gets its name from the word 'tranquil') is a mod café/bar/restaurant that is popular with many of the ex-pats who live nearby. It has a very open feeling and is a good place to hang in the evening. It's on the west side of the street, just north of a pedestrian overpass.

TSURUHASHI Map pp219-21 *Rāmen*
☎ 722 3434; Ichijōji nishi Suginomiya-chō; ⏰ 11am-2pm & 5-11pm, closed Thu; rāmen from ¥600; 5min walk from Eizan Ichijōji Station

Kyoto *rāmen* fans make the trek to this unprepossessing little joint for its unique duck-flavoured soup, a serious rarity in Japan. For lunch, big eaters will enjoy the B set, which includes duck-soup *rāmen*, rice and *karaage* (pieces of deep-fried chicken). Look for the yellow awning and the red and yellow sign.

NORTHWEST KYOTO

There are a lot of good restaurants scattered across this largely residential area of Kyoto. Since they are so spread out, it's best to plan ahead and find one that is located near the sights that you want to see in the area.

A RI SHAN Map pp216-18 *Taiwanese*
☎ 465 7771; Nishiōji-dōri-Imadegawa; ⏰ 5-11pm Mon-Sat, noon-3.30pm & 4.30-10.30pm Sun & public holidays; meals from ¥2000; 3min walk from Keifuku line, Kitano Hakubaichō Station

This is a fun Taiwanese *izakaya* that serves a variety of small and tasty dishes. A picture menu is available. It's near the Imadegawa-Nishiōji crossing; look for the three circular openings on the front of the building (you'll see what we mean when you get there).

AZEKURA Map pp216-18 *Soba*
☎ 701 0161; Kamigamo-Okamoto-chō; ⏰ 9am-5pm, closed Mon; noodle dishes from ¥800; 15min walk from Karasuma subway line, Kitayama Station

Not far from Kamigamo-jinja, this place is an intriguing noodle shop and gallery in a converted Edo-period sake warehouse. The building features huge pine and cypress beams, earthen floors and an open hearth. Handmade *soba* noodles are the speciality.

CAFÉ SUA Map pp216-18 *Southeast Asian*
☎ 415 9039; Kuromon-dōri-Imadegawa kudaru; ⏰ 11am-3pm & 6-10pm, closed Tue; dinner from ¥2000; 5min walk from Imadegawa-Ōmiya bus stop, bus 9

This intimate place serves Southeast Asian (mostly Vietnamese) food in a *machiya*. Dishes include *pho* (Vietnamese noodles), raw spring rolls and fried rice. It's very casual and the food is quite good. There's no English menu, but the young owners will help you figure out what's on offer. It's hidden down a tiny alley and located on the east side of Mizuho Bank.

DA MAEDA Map pp216-18 *Italian*
☎ 465 5258; Senbon-dōri-Nakatachiuri; ⏰ 11.30am-2.30pm & 5.30-10pm, closed Thu; dishes from ¥1000; 2min walk from Senbon Nakatachiuri bus stop, bus 201

We're not sure how an Italian restaurant wound up in this otherwise traditional part of northwestern Kyoto, but we're sure glad it did. The food is reliably good and the casual atmosphere is very pleasant. We particularly like the gnocchi. Look for the Italian flag and the English writing on the sign.

DEN SHICHI Map pp216-18 *Sushi*
☎ 463 9991; Nishiōji-dōri-Imadegawa; ⏰ 11.30am-2pm & 5-10.30pm, closed Mon; lunch/dinner from ¥480/3000; 3min walk from Keifuku line, Kitano Hakubaichō Station

Like its sister restaurant of the same name in Saiin (p117), this is a good-value place that has cheap lunch specials, including *tekkadon* (raw tuna over rice) for ¥480. In terms of price and quality, Den Shichi is always a good bet. Look for the black-and-white sign and the pictures of the lunch specials in the window.

IZUSEN Map pp216-18 *Buddhist Vegetarian*
☎ 491 6665; Murasakino-Daitokuji-chō; ⏰ 11am-4pm; lunch ¥3000; 3min walk from Daitoku-ji-mae bus stop, bus 1, 12, 92 or 204

Izusen, in the Daiji-in subtemple at Daitoku-ji, offers Zen vegetarian *(shōjin ryōri)* lunch. There are seven selections served in vermilion-coloured lacquered bowls *(tepastu)*, fashioned after monks' alms bowls.

KAZARIYA Map pp216-18 *Sweets*
☎ 491 9402; Kita-ku Murasakino Imamiya-chō; ⏰ 10am-5pm, closed Wed; sweets ¥500; 1min walk from Imamiya-jinja bus stop, bus 46

For more than 300 years, Kazariya has been specialising in *aburi-mochi* (grilled rice cakes coated with soybean flower) and served with *miso-dare* (sweet-bean paste).

SARACA NISHIJIN Map pp216-18 *Café*
☎ 432 5075; Kuramaguchi-dōri-Ōmiya; ☾ noon-10pm, closed Wed; coffee from ¥400, lunch from ¥900; 7min walk from Daitoku-ji-mae bus stop, bus 1, 12, 92 or 204
This is one of Kyoto's most interesting cafés – it's built inside an old *sentō* (public bathhouse) and the original tiles have been preserved. Light meals and the usual coffee drinks are the staples here. It's near Funaoka Onsen.

SUNNY PLACE
Map pp216-18 *Japanese Vegetarian*
☎ 722 1738; Kita-ku, Kamigamo Iwagakiuchi chō; ☾ noon-9pm, closed Mon; set meal from ¥1200; 5min walk from Karasuma subway line, Kitayama Station
Sunny Place is a fine little vegetarian eatery not far from the Kyoto Botanical Gardens. The one plate set (¥1200) includes brown rice, miso soup, a main dish, salad and two very small side dishes. Fresh juices are also available. Look for the English sign out front.

CHEAP EATS
BAZAAR CAFÉ Map pp216-18 *Café*
☎ 411 2379; Karasuma-dōri-Imadegawa; ☾ 11.30am-8pm Thu-Sat; coffee from ¥400; 5min walk from Karasuma subway line, Imadegawa Station
This simple café/restaurant with outdoor garden seating is a great place for a relaxing cuppa while in the neighbourhood of Dōshisha University. In addition to coffee and tea, a variety of simple light meals are available. The only drawback is the limited opening hours.

CAFÉ DOJI Map pp216-18 *Café*
☎ 491 3422; Kitayama-dōri, Kita-ku Koyamamoto-chō; ☾ noon-11pm, closed Thu; coffee from ¥500; 10min walk from Karasuma subway line, Kitayama Station
This café is an excellent place for a drink after exploring the Kyoto Botanical Gardens or Kamigamo-jinja. It's a cool, dark space where you can sample a variety of coffee and tea drinks and mango smoothies in season. Sandwiches and set meals are available from ¥1000. There is a simple English menu.

LE PETIT MEC Map pp216-18 *French Bakery*
☎ 432 1444; Imadegawa-dōri-Ōmiya nishi iru; ☾ 8am-8pm (last orders 7pm), closed Tue; bread from ¥120, sandwiches & coffee from ¥400; 1min walk from Imadegawa-Ōmiya bus stop, bus 201
This little French bakery offers a decent range of breads and pastries and has a few seats where you can enjoy a sandwich and coffee

while pretending that you're in Paris. Look for the red awning.

PAPA JON'S Map pp216-18 *Café*
☎ 415 2655; Karasuma-dōri-Kamitachiuri; ☾ 11am-10.30pm, closed Tue; coffee ¥400, cheesecake ¥550; 7min walk from Karasuma subway line, Imadegawa Station
Papa Jon's is known for good coffee, cappuccino and cheesecake. There are two others: on **Kitayama-dōri** (Map pp219–21); and downtown in the **Shinkyōgoku covered arcade** (Map pp228–9).

TACO TORA Map pp216-18 *Tako Yaki*
☎ 461 9292; Imadegawa-dōri-Nanahonmatsu; ☾ 5pm-2am, closed Tue; 9 octopus balls ¥600; 5min walk from Kitanotenmangū-mae bus stop
Try this spot for Kyoto's best *tako yaki* (fried octopus balls – no, not those balls). It's near Kitano Tenman-gū.

TOYOUKE-JAYA Map pp216-18 *Tofu*
☎ 462 3662; Imadegawa-dōri-Onmae; ☾ 11am-3pm, closed Thu; meals from ¥650; 1min walk from Kitanotenmangū-mae bus stop
Locals line up for the tofu lunch sets at this famous restaurant across from Kitano Tenman-gū. If you can get here when there's no line, pop in for a healthy meal.

TSURUYA YOSHINOBU
Map pp216-18 *Sweets*
☎ 441 0105; Imadegawa-dōri-Horikawa; ☾ 9am-6pm; sweets from ¥600; 5min walk from Karasuma subway line, Imadegawa Station
This is one of Kyoto's most esteemed sweet makers and a good spot to sample traditional Japanese sweets.

SOUTHWEST KYOTO
Southwest Kyoto is not high on most tourist itineraries, but if you do find yourself in this neck of the woods, there are plenty of good eating options, including Den Shichi in Saiin, which is one of our favourite sushi restaurants.

BISTRO DE PARIS Map pp222-4 *French*
☎ 256 1825; Shinmachi-dōri-Shijō; ☾ 11.30am-1.30pm & 5.30-9.30pm, closed Mon; lunch/dinner from ¥1600/2500; 5min walk from Karasuma subway line, Shijō Station
We like this cramped little French spot for its authentic and carefully prepared fare, especially the daily fish dish.

DEN SHICHI Map pp222-4   *Sushi*

☎ 323 0700; Shijō-dōri-Sai; ⏰ 11.30am-2pm &
5-10.30pm; lunch/dinner from ¥500/4000; 3min walk
from Hankyū Saiin Station

This is our favourite sushi restaurant in Kyoto.
It's a classic – long counter, bellowing sushi
chefs and great fresh fish. The lunch sets are
unbelievable value and the glass sushi cases
make ordering a little easier than at some
other places.

JŪNIDAN-YA Map pp222-4   *Sweets*

☎ 211 5884; Marutamachi-dōri-Karasuma;
⏰ 11.30am-2.30pm & 5-8pm, closed Wed; lunch &
dinner from ¥1000; 5min walk from Karasuma subway
line, Marutamachi Station

This stylish restaurant is famous for its *ochazuke*
(rice with Japanese tea poured over it). It tastes
better than it sounds.

LE BOUCHON Map pp222-4   *French*

☎ 211 5220; Teramachi-dōri-Nijō; ⏰ 11.30am-
2.30pm, 5.30-9.30pm, closed Thu; set dinner ¥2500;
3min walk from Tōzai subway line, Kyoto-Shiyakusho-
mae Station

We really like this unpretentious little place for
reliable and honest French standards such as
steak and *frites* and *salade Nicoise*. The ¥2500
dinner course, which includes an appetizer,
main and dessert is great value.

MUKADE-YA Map pp222-4   *Japanese*

☎ 256 7039; Shinmachi-dōri-Nishikikōji; ⏰ 11am-
2pm & 5-9pm, closed Wed; meals from ¥3000; 5min
walk from Karasuma subway line, Shijō Station

Mukade-ya is an atmospheric restaurant located in an exquisite *machiya* west of Karasuma-dōri. For lunch try the special *bentō*: two
rounds (five small dishes each) of delectable
obanzai (Kyoto-style home cooking) fare. *Kaiseki* courses start at ¥5000.

CHEAP EATS
CAFÉ BIBLIOTEC HELLO!
Map pp222-4   *Café*

☎ 231 8625; Nijō-dōri-Yanaginobanba higashi iru;
⏰ noon-11pm, closed irregularly; coffee ¥400, dishes
from ¥700; 10min walk from Karasuma subway line,
Karasuma-Oike Station

Like its name suggests, books line the walls of
this cool café located in a converted *machiya*.
You can get the usual range of coffee and tea
drinks here, as well as light café lunches. It's
popular with young ladies who work nearby

and it's a great place to relax with a book or
magazine. Look for the plants out front.

SHIN-SHIN-TEI Map pp222-4   *Rāmen*

☎ 221 6202; Nijō-dōri-Fuyachō; ⏰ 10.30am-4pm,
closed Sun, Mon & public holidays; rāmen from ¥600;
4min walk from Tōzai subway line, Kyoto-Shiyakusho-
mae Station

This place is famous for its *shiro* (white) miso
rāmen, which has a distinctive thick soup and
good chewy noodles. Look for the yellow-and-
black sign.

SHIZENHA RESTAURANT OBANZAI
Map pp222-4   *Obanzai*

☎ 223 6623; Koromodana-dōri-Oike; ⏰ 11am-9pm,
closed Wed dinner; lunch ¥840, dinner ¥2100; 5min
walk from Karasuma subway line, Karasuma-Oike
Station

A little out of the way, but good value, this
place serves a decent buffet-style lunch and
dinner of mostly organic Japanese vegetarian food. It's northwest of the Karasuma-Oike
crossing, set back a bit from the street.

ARASHIYAMA &
SAGANO AREA

The area to the far west of Kyoto is a hugely
popular destination with both foreign and
Japanese travellers and it's packed with eateries, many of which serve the speciality
of the area: *yudōfu* (chunks of tofu served
in an iron pot). Simpler meals can be had
in the shokudō that line the street outside
Arashiyama Station.

AYU CHAYA HIRANOYA
Map p232   *Tea & Kaiseki*

☎ 861 0359; Saga Toriimoro Senno-chō; ⏰ 11.30am-
9pm; tea ¥840, dinner from ¥15,000; 5min walk from
Otaginenbutsu-ji-mae bus stop

Located next to the famous Atago Torii (Shintō
shrine gate) this thatched-roof restaurant is
about as atmospheric as they get. While you
can sample full-course *kaiseki* meals here from
¥15,000 (by telephone reservation in Japanese
only), we prefer to soak up the atmosphere
over a simple cup of *matcha* tea for a relatively modest ¥840 (it comes with a traditional
sweet). It's the perfect way to cool off after a
long slog around the temples of Arashiyama
and Sagano. Just ask for '*ocha*' and you're
away.

GYĀTEI Map p232 *Japanese*

☎ 862 2411; Saga Tenryū-ji; 🕐 11am-2.30pm & 5-9.50pm, closed Mon; lunch ¥1580, dinner ¥3000; 1min walk from Keifuku Arashiyama line, Keifuku Arashiyama Station

Just beside the station, this place offers an all-you-can-eat lunch buffet of Japanese fare (there are over 30 dishes). In the evening, Gyātei turns into an *izakaya*, with à la carte choices (¥500) or a full-course tasting menu (¥3000). The food may not be very special, but how can you complain when it's all-you-can-eat? Look for the ochre building.

KUSHI-TEI Map p232 *Kushikatsu*

☎ 861 0098; Saga Tenryū-ji; 🕐 noon-10pm; lunch from ¥2500, dinner from ¥3000; 1min walk from Keifuku Arashiyama line, Keifuku Arashiyama Station

Kushi-tei offers tasty *kushikatsu* in casual surroundings. Sit at the counter and watch the chef do his thing. Look for the *noren* hanging in the entrance.

RANKYŌ-KAN RYOKAN

Map p232 *Kaiseki*

☎ 871 0001; Arashiyama Togetsukyō South; 🕐 11am-3pm; lunch from ¥4000; 3min walk from Hankyū Arashiyama line, Arashiyama Station

Upriver from Togetsu-tei, Rankyō-kan has a fine lunchtime *bentō* (¥4000), and mini-*kaiseki* courses (¥5000). It even offers a soothing Japanese bath (¥300) to lunch guests, with a small towel supplied.

SEIZANSŌ-DŌ Map p232 *Tofu*

☎ 861 1609; Saga Tenryū-ji; 🕐 11.30am-5pm, closed Wed; courses from ¥3000; 1min walk from Keifuku Arashiyama line, Keifuku Arashiyama Station

For a sample of the area's acclaimed tofu, try this place, where the *yudōfu teishoku* is good value (¥3000). The seven-course meal includes a pot of fresh *yudōfu* and an array of tofu-based dishes displaying the creative possibilities of the soya bean. If you come at lunchtime during the tourist season, you'll have to take a number and wait to be seated. Look for the wooden gate set back just slightly from the street.

SHIGETSU Map p232 *Buddhist Vegetarian*

☎ 882 9725; Saga Tenryū-ji; 🕐 11am-2pm; lunch from ¥3000; 1min walk from Keifuku Arashiyama line, Keifuku Arashiyama Station

To sample *shōjin ryōri* try Shigetsu in the precinct of Tenryū-ji (the fare is similar to Seizansō-dō, above). It has beautiful garden views.

SUNDAY'S SUN Map p232 *American*

☎ 861 8836; Saga Tenryū-ji; 🕐 7am-2am; lunch/dinner from ¥900/1500; 10min walk from Keifuku Arashiyama line, Keifuku Arashiyama Station

If you fancy some Western food, then head into this casual 'family restaurant' for options such as steak and chicken.

TOGETSU-TEI Map p232 *Japanese*

☎ 871 1310; Arashiyama Togetsukyō South; 🕐 11am-7pm, closed irregularly; lunch & dinner from ¥2700; 3min walk from Hankyū Arashiyama line, Arashiyama Station

On the south side of Togetsu-kyō Bridge, Togetsu-tei has great riverside views. Try the delightful *take-kago bentō* basket with locally grown bamboo shoots (¥2700) or tofu courses (¥3500).

YOSHIDA-YA Map p232 *Noodles*

☎ 861 0213; Saga Tenryū-ji Tsukurimichi-chō; 🕐 10am-6pm, closed Tue; lunch from ¥800; 10min walk from Sagano line, Saga Arashiyama Station

This quaint and friendly little *teishoku-ya* (set-meal restaurant) is the perfect place to grab a simple lunch while in Arashiyama. All the standard *teishoku* favourites are on offer, including things such as *oyakodon* (egg and chicken over a bowl of rice) for ¥1000. You can also cool off here with a refreshing *uji kintoki* for ¥600. There is no English sign; the restaurant is the first place south of the station and it has a rustic front.

YUDŌFU SAGANO Map p232 *Tofu*

☎ 871 6946; Sagano, Tenryū-ji; 🕐 11am-7pm; lunch & dinner from ¥3800; 15min walk from Sagano line, Saga Arashiyama Station

This is another popular place to sample *yudōfu* (the fare is similar to Seizansō-dō, left) and it's usually possible to enter here without waiting. There is both indoor and outdoor seating. Look for the old cart wheels outside.

KYOTO OUTSKIRTS

Some of Kyoto's best sights are located in the small villages and suburbs that surround the city. All of these places have plenty of good dining options, so it's never necessary to wait until you return to the city centre to eat. Kibune, in particular, is packed with good restaurants and many Kyotoites make the trip there in the summer to eat elegant meals on platforms suspended over the Kibune-gawa.

FUSHIMI

KIZAKURA KAPPA COUNTRY

Map pp214-15   *Japanese*

☎ 611 9919; Fushimiku Shioya-chō; ⏲ 11.30am-2pm & 5-9.30pm; meals from ¥800; 6min walk from Keihan Chūshojima Station

This sake brewery restaurant/bar has a full-course barbecue dinner (¥2000), an all-you-can-eat lunch buffet (¥800; Monday to Friday), and three shades of delicious microbrew beer on tap. To get here, walk north from the Gekkeikan Sake Ōkura Museum (p88), take the first left (west) and look for the English sign on the right (the main entrance is actually one block north of the sign). Alternatively, walk straight, north from Chūshojima Station (orient yourself with the map located outside the station).

ŌRYŪ-KAKU   *Buddhist Vegetarian*

☎ 0774-32 3900; Gokasho Sanbanwari; ⏲ 11.30am-1pm, closed irregularly; veg course ¥5000; 5min walk from Nara line, Obaku Station

This lovely spot at Mampuku-ji (p89) serves vegetarian *fucha-ryōri* (a type of temple cuisine). It also has a lunch *bentō* (¥3150) and full courses (¥5000). Bookings are necessary. There is a temple entry fee of ¥500.

SANCHO Map pp214-15   *Salad*

☎ 622 1458; Fushimi-Kyomachi-dōri; ⏲ 11.30am-9pm, closed irregularly; meals from ¥700; 3min walk from Keihan Fushimi-Momoyama Station

This restaurant is known for its salads and fried dishes, most of which come together as set meals. The *shiso fumi chicken katsu* (chicken cutlet) lunch is an excellent choice. To get here, exit Fushimi-Momoyama Station to the west and take your first left out of the shopping arcade; walk one block south and you'll see it on the corner on the right.

UOSABURŌ Map pp214-15   *Kaiseki*

☎ 601 0061; Fushimi-Kyomachi-dōri; ⏲ 11am-7.30pm; dinner ¥10,000; 5min walk from Keihan Fushimi-Momoyama Station

Another Fushimi treat is the exquisite *kaiseki* haunt Uosaburō, based since 1764 in a magnificent *machiya*. It serves a lovely *hanakago bentō* lunch of seasonal dishes brilliantly presented in flower-shaped baskets (¥4000). To get here, exit Fushimi-Momoyama Station to the east and take your first right; look for it on the right, just past an automatic parking lot.

Cheap Eats

GENYA Map pp214-15   *Rāmen*

☎ 602 1492; Higashikumi-chō; ⏲ 11.30am-7.30pm, closed Thu; rāmen from ¥600; 5min walk from Keihan Fushimi-Momoyama Station

For a great body-warmer, try the *sake-kasu rāmen* noodles (¥650) at this quaint *rāmen* joint; the central ingredient in the soup is the *kasu* (sediment) left behind in the sake-brewing process. To get here, exit Fushimi-Momoyama Station and walk west in the shopping arcade for about 200m; take the fourth right off the arcade and Genya is on the right. There's a yellow-and-black sign and sake casks out front.

TEUCHIUDON KENDONYA

Map pp214-15   *Udon*

☎ 641 1330; Fushimi Fukakusa; ⏲ 11am-3pm & 5-9pm, closed Wed; daily lunch set ¥680; 1min walk from Keihan Fushimi-Inari Station

For a quick lunch before or after visiting Fushimi-Inari-taisha, pop into this shop that specialises in handmade *udon* noodles. To get here from Fushimi-Inari Station, exit the station and turn right, cross the street at the lights and look for it next to a *yakitori* restaurant with red lanterns.

UJI

If you're hungry while in Uji there are plenty of places for a quick lunch, most of which are located along the road leading to Byōdō-in.

Cheap Eats

KAWABUN   *Shokudo*

☎ 0774-21 2556; Uji-shi; ⏲ 10am-4pm; donburi from ¥750; 10min walk from Keihan Uji line, Uji Station

Try this shokudō for Uji sweets, tea and simple meals. On a hot day, the *uji kintoki* is a refreshing treat. For something more filling, try the tempura *udon* for ¥650. It's the last restaurant on the street that leads to Byōdō-in temple; look for the food models and green-and-white sign.

TSŪEN-JAYA ANNEX   *Japanese*

☎ 0774-24 3523; Uji-shi; ⏲ 11am-5pm, closed Thu; light meals from ¥700; 5min walk from Keihan Uji line, Uji Station

Tsūen-jaya, the modern annex of the old Tsūen tea shop, is on the road up to Ujigami-jinja. It serves tasty *soba* and *sansai* (mountain vegetables), as well as tempting desserts made with fresh green tea (try the *matcha* parfait).

ŌHARA

KUMOI-JAYA Map p233 _Nabe_
☎ 744 2240; Ōhara Sanzenin hotori; ⏲ 9am-5pm; meals from ¥800; 12min walk from Ōhara bus stop
Near Jakkō-in, Kumoi-jaya serves a delectable miso-based _nabe_ (chicken stew; ¥2000) and has cheaper _udon_ noodles (¥800). It's just off the main road in a new white building.

SERYŌ-JAYA Map p233 _Japanese_
☎ 744 2301; Ōhara Sanzenin hotori; ⏲ 11am-5pm; lunch sets from ¥2756; 10min walk from Ōhara bus stop
Just by the entry gate to Sanzen-in, Seryō-jaya serves wholesome _sansai ryōri_ (mountain-vegetable cooking), fresh river fish and _soba_ noodles topped with grated yam. There is outdoor seating in warmer months. Look for the food models.

TAMBA-JAYA Map p233 _Japanese_
☎ 744 2527; Ōhara Sanzenin hotori; ⏲ 9am-5pm; lunch from ¥1000; 5min walk from Ōhara bus stop
Also near Jakkō-in, this place dishes up great homemade _udon_ – you can fill up on the _inaka-teishoku_ (country-cooking set; ¥1000).

KURAMA

ABURAYA-SHOKUDŌ
Map p233 _Shokudō_
☎ 741 2009; Kurama honmachi; ⏲ 9.30am-5.30pm, closed last 3 days of each month; meals from ¥800; 5min walk from Eizan Kurama Station
Just down the steps from the main gate of Kurama-dera, this classic old-style shokudō reminds us of what Japan was like before it got rich. The _sansai teishoku_ (¥1700) is a delightful selection of vegetables, rice and _soba_ topped with grated yam.

YŌSHŪJI Map p233 _Japanese_
☎ 741 2848; Kurama honmachi; ⏲ 10am-6pm, closed Tue; meals from ¥1050; 5min walk from Eizan Kurama Station
Yōshūji serves superb _shōjin ryōri_ in a delightful old Japanese farmhouse with an _irori_ (open hearth). The house special, a sumptuous selection of vegetarian dishes served in red lacquered bowls, is called _kurama-yama shōjin zen_ (¥2500). If you just feel like a quick bite, try the _uzu-soba_ (_soba_ topped with mountain vegetables; ¥1050). It's halfway up the steps leading to the main gate of Kurama-dera; look for the orange lanterns out front.

KIBUNE

Visitors to Kibune from June to September should not miss the chance to dine at one of the picturesque restaurants beside the Kibune-gawa. Known as _kawa-doko_, meals are served on platforms suspended over the river as cool water flows underneath. Most of the restaurants offer a lunch special for around ¥3000. For a _kaiseki_ spread (¥5000 to ¥10,000) have a Japanese person call to reserve in advance. In the cold months you can dine indoors overlooking the river.

BENIYA Map p233 _Kaiseki_
☎ 741 2041; Kurama Kibune-chō; ⏲ 11.30am-7.30pm; meals from ¥3000; 5min taxi ride from Eizan Kibune-guchi Station
This elegant riverside restaurant serves _kaiseki_ sets for ¥6000, ¥8000 or ¥10,000, depending on size. There is a wooden sign with white lettering out the front.

HIROBUN Map p233 _Japanese_
☎ 741 2147; Kurama Kibune-chō; ⏲ 11am-10pm; noodle dishes ¥1200, kaiseki courses from ¥7000; 5min taxi ride from Eizan Kibune-guchi Station
Here you can try _nagashi-somen_ (¥1200; served until 5pm), which are thin noodles that flow to you in globs down a split-bamboo gutter; just pluck them out and slurp away. Look for the black-and-white sign and the lantern.

NAKAYOSHI Map p233 _Kaiseki_
☎ 741 2000; Kurama Kibune-chō; ⏲ 11am-7pm; lunch from ¥3500, kaiseki dinner from ¥8500; 5min taxi ride from Eizan Kibune-guchi Station
One of the more reasonably priced restaurants is Nakayoshi, which serves a lunch _bentō_ for ¥3500. It has some lovely dining platforms over the river and the food is well prepared.

TOCHIGIKU Map p233 _Kaiseki_
☎ 741 5555; Kurama Kibune-chō; ⏲ 11.30am-9pm (last orders 7.30pm), closed irregularly; sukiyaki from ¥8000; 5min taxi ride from Eizan Kibune-guchi Station
Try this lovely riverside restaurant for sukiyaki and _kaiseki_ sets. There is a small English sign.

Cheap Eats

KIBUNE CLUB Map p233 _Café_
☎ 741 2146; Kurama Kibune-chō; ⏲ 11.30am-6pm; coffee from ¥450; 5min taxi ride from Eizan Kibune-guchi Station
The exposed wooden beams and open, airy feel of this rustic café make it a great spot for a cuppa while exploring Kibune.

Eating – Kyoto Outskirts

Entertainment

Entertainment

If you've still got some energy left after a day of temple-hopping, there's plenty to do in Kyoto when night falls. Indeed, the area around Kawaramachi-dōri and Kiyamachi-dōri fairly pulses with activity almost any night of the week. You can choose from *izakaya* (Japanese pubs/eateries), bars, clubs and karaoke boxes, many of which stay open almost until dawn. The fact is, Kyoto knows how to party – it's just a matter of whether you can keep up.

As for traditional Japanese culture, you will have to work a little harder. Most of Kyoto's cultural entertainment is of an occasional nature, and you'll need to check with the Tourist Information Centre (TIC; p192), *Kansai Time Out* or the *Kyoto Visitor's Guide* to find whether anything interesting is going on while you're in town. Regular events are generally geared towards the tourist market and tend to be expensive and, naturally, somewhat touristy.

THEATRE

Kyoto is the best city in Japan in which to see traditional forms of Japanese theatre. The easiest way to find out what's on while you're in town is to check *Kansai Time Out* or to ask at the TIC (p192).

GION CORNER Map pp225-7

☎ 561 1119; Gion-Hanami-kōji-dōri; admission ¥2800; ☾ performances at 7.40pm & 8.40pm 1 Mar–29 Nov, closed 16 Aug; 5min walk from Keihan Shijō Station

You should think carefully about whether tourist-oriented events of this kind are your cup of tea before forking out the entry charge. While you get a chance to see snippets of the tea ceremony, Koto (Japanese zither) music, ikebana (flower arrangement), *gagaku* (court music), *kyōgen* (ancient comic plays), Kyōmai (Kyoto-style dance) and *bunraku* (puppet plays), you will be doing so with a couple of camera-and-video-toting tour groups, and the presentation is a little on the tacky side. On top of this, 50 minutes of entertainment for ¥2800 is a little steep by anyone's standards.

Kabuki

MINAMI-ZA Map pp228-9

☎ 561 0160; Shijō-Ōhashi; admission ¥4200-12,600; ☾ irregular; 1min walk from Keihan Shijō Station

The oldest kabuki theatre in Japan is in Gion. The major event of the year is the *kaomise* festival (1 to 26 December), which features Japan's finest kabuki actors. Other performances take place on an irregular basis. Those interested should check with the TIC (p192). The most likely months for performances are May, June and September.

Nō

For nō performances, the main theatre is **Kanze Kaikan Nō Theatre** (Map pp225-7; ☎ 771 6114; Sakyō-ku-Okazaki; admission free-¥8000; ☾ 9am-5pm, closed Mon; 10min walk from Tōzai subway line, Higashiyama Station). Takigi Nō is an especially picturesque form of nō performed in the light of blazing fires. This takes place on the evenings of 1 and 2 June at Heian-jingū (p59). Tickets cost ¥2000 if you pay in advance (ask at the TIC for the location of ticket agencies) or ¥3300 at the entrance gate.

Minami-za (right)

DANCE
Geisha Dances

Annually in spring and fall, geisha and their *maiko* (apprentices) from Kyoto's five schools dress elaborately to perform traditional dances in praise of the seasons. The cheapest tickets cost about ¥1650 (unreserved on tatami mats), better seats cost ¥3000 to ¥3800, and spending an extra ¥500 includes participation in a quick tea ceremony. The dances are similar from place to place and are repeated several times a day. Dates and times vary, so check with the TIC (p192).

Gion Kaikan Theatre (Map pp225-7; ☎ 561 0160; Higashiyama-ku Gion; admission/with tea ¥3300/3800; 🕙 1.30pm & 3.30pm; 10min walk from Keihan Shijō Station) The Gion Odori takes place from 1 to 10 November.

Gion Kōbu Kaburen-jō Theatre (Map pp225-7; ☎ 561 1115; Higashiyama-ku, Gion-chō, South; nonreserved seat/reserved seat/reserved seat with tea ¥1900/3800/4300; 🕙 12.30pm, 2pm, 3.30pm & 4.50pm; 5min walk from Keihan Shijō Station, near Gion Corner) Miyako Odori takes place here throughout April.

Kamishichiken Kaburen-jō Theatre (Map pp216-18; ☎ 461 0148; Imadegawa-dōri-Nishihonmatsu nishi iru; admission/with tea ¥3800/4300; 🕙 1pm & 3pm; 500m from Kamishichiken bus stop, east of Kitano Tenman-gū) Kitano Odori happens here between 15 and 25 April.

Miyagawa-chō Kaburen-jō Theatre (Map pp225-7; ☎ 561 1151; Kawabata-dōri-Shijō kudaru; admission/with tea ¥3800/4300; 🕙 12.30pm, 2.30pm & 4.30pm; 400m from Keihan Shijō Station, btwn Shijō-dōri & Gojō-dōri) Kyō Odori is held here on the 1st to 3rd Sun in April.

Pontochō Kaburen-jō Theatre (Map pp228-9; ☎ 221 2025; Pontochō, Sanjō kudaru; admission ¥2000; 🕙 12.30pm, 2.20pm & 4.10pm; 5min walk from Keihan Sanjō Station) The Kamogawa Odori takes place here from 1 to 24 May and 15 October to 7 November.

CINEMAS

You'll find a large number of movie theatres in Kyoto's downtown area around Kawaramachi-dōri and Kiyamachi-dōri. Like elsewhere, these theatres are dominated by Hollywood films, which arrive in Japan up to six months after their original release. Foreign films are screened in their original language, with Japanese subtitles. Tickets average around ¥1800. The exception to this is the first Tuesday of each month (*Eiga-no-Hi*, or 'Movie Day'), when tickets cost only ¥1000.

Who Goes There?

Kyoto has an incredibly wide range of bars, from three-seat establishments that cater to the same three drunken salarymen every night to sprawling venues that draw hundreds of patrons on a weekend night. Some cater strictly to Japanese folk, others are as international as the UN. If you'd like to choose your drinking spot by the types of people you'll rub shoulders with, here is a general guide:

Japanese university students A-bar (p124)

Younger ex-pat English teachers Hub (p124)

Older ex-pat English teachers Tadg's Irish Pub (p125)

Fashionable young Japanese things Marble Room (p124)

International backpackers Pig & Whistle (p124)

Groovy international hipsters Boogie Lounge (p124)

Japanese Rastafarian wannabes Rub-a-Dub (p125)

Sozzled Japanese sake lovers Shizuka (p125)

All of the above (and then some) Ing (p124)

KYOTO MINAMI KAIKAN Map pp222-4

☎ 661 3993; Nishi-Kujō-dōri, Higashihienjo-chō, Minami-ku; admission ¥1800; 🕙 varies; 2min walk from Kintetsu Kyoto line, Tōji Station

Try this theatre for lesser-known imports and eclectic Japanese films, including Japanese *anime* (animation). It's on Kujō-dōri.

SUKARA-ZA THEATRE Map pp228-9

☎ 221 5151; 5F Kyōhō Bldg, Sanjō kudaru, Kawaramachi-Rokkaku; admission ¥1800; 🕙 varies; 5min walk from Keihan Sanjō Station

Sukara-za usually shows first-run Hollywood films with their original English soundtrack and Japanese subtitles. It's also a good place to check out Japanese *anime*. The theatre is comfortable and centrally located.

DRINKING

Kyoto has an astounding variety of bars, from exclusive Gion clubs, where it's possible to spend ¥100,000 in a single evening, to grungy *gaijin* (foreigner) bars. Most bars are concentrated downtown, around Kawaramachi-dōri and Kiyamachi-dōri. During the warmer months, rooftop beer gardens spring up throughout town and offer tempting all-you-can-eat-or-drink deals and great views of the surrounding mountains. For something a little more upscale than the bars and pubs listed in this section, try one of the bars in any of Kyoto's upmarket hotels; both the Hotel Fujita Kyoto (p140) and the Hotel Granvia Kyoto (p138) have excellent bars.

A-BAR Map pp228-9

☎ 213 2129; Nishikiyamachi-dōri; drinks from ¥350; 5pm-midnight; 10min walk from Keihan Sanjō Station

This is perhaps the best place to start a Kyoto evening. A raucous student *izakaya* with a log-cabin interior in the Kiyamachi area. There's a big menu to choose from and everything's cheap (see p104). The best part is when they add up the bill – you'll swear they've under-charged you by half. It's a little tough to find – look for the small black-and-white sign at the top of a flight of concrete steps above a place called Reims.

ATLANTIS Map pp228-9

☎ 241 1621; Shijō-Pontochō agaru; drinks around ¥1000; 6pm-2am; 5min walk from Keihan Shijō Station

This is one of the few bars on Pontochō that foreigners can walk into without a Japanese friend. It's a slick, trendy place that draws a fair smattering of Kyoto's beautiful people and wannabe beautiful people. In summer you can sit outside on a platform looking over the Kamo-gawa.

BOOGIE LOUNGE Map pp228-9

☎ 212 2200; ABC Museum 2F, Kawaramachi-dōri-Sanjō kudaru; drinks from ¥700; 7pm-5am, closed irregularly; 5min walk from Keihan Sanjō Station

This place brings back the '70s in a big way, complete with a disco ball and a groovy funk and soul soundtrack. There are plush seats scattered about, but unless you're early, you'll have no choice but to stand and/or dance. We feel strangely at home here, but maybe that's because the owner seems to have stolen our record collection.

HILL OF TARA Map pp228-9

☎ 213 3330; Oike-dōri-Kawaramachi; drinks from ¥500; 5pm-midnight Sun-Thu, 5pm-1am Fri & Sat; 1min walk from Tōzai subway line, Kyoto-Shiyakusho-mae Station

This is an Irish-style pub that tends to draw a more Japanese crowd than Tadg's (opposite). There is a good selection of beer on tap and plenty of room to spread out. Live music is sometimes featured.

HUB Map pp228-9

☎ 212 9026; Kawaramachi-dōri-Sanjō kudaru; drinks ¥350-1000; 5pm-midnight Sun-Thu, 5pm-3am Fri & Sat, happy hour 5-7pm; 5min walk from Keihan Sanjō Station

We think of this place as the Kyoto English teachers' lounge – it's the main watering hole of ex-pats teaching in area *eikaiwa* (private English schools). It's a spacious, two-level bar with plenty of room to spread out and relax. If you're after info about teaching English in Kyoto, this is an obvious choice.

ING Map pp228-9

☎ 255 5087; Nishikiyamachi-dōri-Takoyakushi; drinks from ¥580; 6pm-2am Mon-Thu, 6pm-5am Fri & Sat; 8min walk from Keihan Sanjō Station

This bar/*izakaya* on Kiyamachi is one of our fa-vourite spots for a drink in Kyoto. It's got cheap bar snacks and drinks, good music and friendly staff. It's in the Royal building on the 2nd floor; you'll know you're getting close when you see all the hostesses out trawling for customers on the streets nearby.

LOOP Map pp228-9

☎ 257 6009; Kawaramachi-dōri-Sanjō kudaru; drinks from ¥800; 8pm-7am, closed irregularly; 5min walk from Keihan Sanjō Station

This place is an experiment in stark minimalism, just a few tables and stools in a setting that looks like something out of a sci-fi movie or a fashion spread. It draws a mixed crowd, but only models manage to look at home in this setting.

MARBLE ROOM Map pp228-9

☎ 213 0753; Pontochō Sanjō kudaru; drinks from ¥700; 5.30pm-3am Sun-Thu, 3pm-3am Fri & Sat; 5min walk from Keihan Sanjō Station

The Marble Room is what a lot of people in the 1950s imagined the year 2000 would look like. It's a mod space that draws Kyoto's fashion-able young set for decent drinks and snacks. If you're over 30 here, you'll probably feel like an antique. It's on the 4th floor of the Ponto-chō Building, which has a white front.

PIG & WHISTLE Map pp228-9

☎ 761 6022; Kawabata-dōri-Sanjō; drinks from ¥500; 5pm-midnight Sun-Thu, 5pm-1am Fri & Sat; 1min walk from Keihan Sanjō Station

The Pig is a British-style pub with darts, pint glasses and fish and chips. While many of the Pig's patrons have moved on to other venues, we still like this place for its relaxed layout and homey interior. The pub's two main drawcards are Guinness on tap and its friendly bilingual staff. It's on the 2nd floor of the Shobi building near the Sanjō-Kawabata crossing.

PUB AFRICA Map pp228-9

☎ 221 6049; Rokkaku Shijō-Kawaramachi higashi iru; drinks from ¥500; 🕒 6pm-3am Sun-Thu, 6pm-4am Fri & Sat; 5min walk from Keihan Sanjō Station

This long-time *gaijin* bar is pretty much your standard-issue dimly lit bar. It's not a good place to meet people because the video screens tend to dominate everyone's attention, but it still manages to draw a regular crowd of ex-pats and their Japanese associates.

REFUEL Map pp228-9

☎ 211 8862; Kawaramachi-dōri-Sanjō kudaru; drinks from ¥600; 🕒 5pm-5am, closed irregularly; 5min walk from Keihan Sanjō Station

Refuel is a nice modern place with a twist. The bartenders pride themselves on being able to make perfect drinks and are always accommodating to special requests or stronger drinks. It has a bar that will seat about 10 and table seating for about 12.

RUB-A-DUB Map pp228-9

☎ 256 3122; Kiyamachi-dōri-Sanjō; drinks from ¥600; 🕒 7pm-2am Sun-Thu, 7pm-4am Fri & Sat; 5min walk from Keihan Sanjō Station

At the northern end of Kiyamachi-dōri, Rub-a-Dub is a funky little reggae bar with a shabby tropical look. It's a good place for a quiet drink on weekdays, but on Friday and Saturday nights you'll have no choice but to bop along with the crowd. Look for the stairs heading down to the basement beside the popular (and delightfully 'fragrant') Nagahama Rāmen shop.

SHIZUKA Map pp228-9

☎ 221 5148; Nakagyō-ku-Shinkyōgoku-dōri; drinks from ¥350; 🕒 5.30-11pm, closed Mon; 5min walk from Hankyū Kyoto line, Kawaramachi Station

Tucked down a tiny little alley near the Shinkyōgoku covered arcade, this *izakaya* has a classic, traditional Japanese atmosphere and cheap beer and sake. Food is also served here, but we advise you to eat before you come, since it's memorably unpalatable.

TADG'S IRISH PUB Map pp228-9

☎ 525 0680; Yamatooji-dōri-Shijō agaru; drinks from ¥600; 🕒 5pm-midnight, later on weekends; 5min walk from Keihan Shijō Station

Tadg's is our favourite bar in Kyoto. It's a delightfully convivial spot that plays host to a

good crowd of ex-pats and Japanese every night of the week. This is an easy spot for solo travellers to enter – you'll soon be drawn into the conversation. Tadg's serves a variety of pub favourites, including tasty fish and chips, and Irish stew. Some evenings there are open-mic nights and live Irish music. Tadg's serves a roast dinner every Sunday, and Christmas and Thanksgiving dinners. It's on the 2nd floor of the Kamo Higashi building; take the steps on your right just after you enter.

CLUBBING

Yes, you can dance the night away in the cultural heart of Japan and give the temples and shrines a miss the next day while you sleep off your hangover. Most clubs charge an admission fee of ¥2000, which usually includes a drink or two.

METRO Map pp225-7

☎ 752 4765; Kawabata-dōri-Marutamachi kudaru; average admission ¥1000-2000 (varies by event/band); 🕒 10pm-3am Sun-Thu, 10pm-5am Fri-Sat; Keihan Marutamachi Station

Metro is part disco, part 'live house' (small concert hall) and it even hosts the occasional art exhibition. It attracts an eclectic mix of creative types and has a different theme every night, so check ahead in *Kansai Time Out* to see what's going on. Some of the best gigs are Latin night and the popular Non-Hetero-at-the-Metro night, which draws gays, lesbians and everyone in between. Metro is inside exit 2 of the Marutamachi Station.

WORLD Map pp228-9

☎ 213 4119; Nishikiyamachi-dōri-Shijō agaru; admission from ¥1500, drinks from ¥500; 🕒 10pm-5am; 1min walk from Hankyū Kawaramachi Station

World is Kyoto's largest club and it naturally hosts some of the biggest events. It has two floors, a dance floor and lockers where you can leave your stuff while you dance the night away. Events include everything from deep soul to reggae and techno to salsa.

MUSIC
Rock, Folk & Acoustic

There are several options for live music. Most venues vary the type of music they feature from night to night. Check *Kansai Time Out* to see what's happening at the following 'live houses'.

HONKY TONK Map pp219-21

☎ 701 8015; Takaragaike-dōri; admission varies; ☺ 1-11pm, closed Wed; 12min walk from Karasuma subway line, Kokusaikaikan Station

For the best in live country music it's well worth the trip to Honky Tonk. This place is a gas: an authentic Western saloon full of Japanese cowboys dressed in full garb – hats, boots and, occasionally, spurs. Call to confirm that there's a show on before making the haul out.

JUTTOKU Map pp216-18

☎ 841 1691; Ōmiya-dōri-Shimotachiuri; admission ¥1000; ☺ 5.30pm-midnight, live music 7-9pm; 10min walk from Tōzai subway line, Nijōjō-mae Station

Juttoku is located in an atmospheric saka-gura (old sake warehouse). It plays host to a variety of shows – check Kansai Time Out to see what's on.

TAKU-TAKU Map pp222-4

☎ 351 1321; Tominokōji-dōri-Bukkōji; admission ¥1500-3500; ☺ 7-9pm, closed irregularly; 10min walk from Hankyū Kyoto line, Shijō Station

This is one of Kyoto's most atmospheric clubs, located in an old saka-gura. It's central and tends to present major acts (the Neville Brothers, Los Lobos and Dr John have all performed here).

Jazz

Live jazz takes place irregularly at several clubs in Kyoto. The best is **Rag** (Map pp228-9; ☎ 241 0446; 5th fl, Empire Bldg, Kiyamachi-dōri-Sanjō; admission ¥1500-4000; ☺ varies; 5min walk from Keihan Sanjō Station).

Classical Music

The **Kyoto Concert Hall** (Map pp216-18; ☎ 361 6629; Kitayama-dōri Sakyō-ku; admission varies; ☺ performance times vary, office 10am-5pm, closed 1st & 3rd Mon of each month; 3min walk from Karasuma subway line, Kitayama Station) and **ALTI** (Kyoto Fumin Hall; Map pp216-18; ☎ 441 1414; Karasuma-dōri-Ichijō kudaru; cost varies; ☺ 9am-9.30pm, office closes at 6pm, closed 1st & 3rd Mon of each month; 5min walk from Karasuma subway line, Imadegawa Station) both hold regular performances of classical music and dance (traditional and contemporary). Ticket prices average between ¥3000 and ¥5000. Check with the usual sources for current schedules.

Traditional Performances

Performances featuring the koto, shamisen (three-stringed Japanese instrument) and shakuhachi (bamboo flute) are held irregularly in Kyoto. Performances of bugaku (court music and dance) are held at shrines during festivals. Occasionally, contemporary butō dance is performed in Kyoto. Check with the TIC (p192) to see if any performances are scheduled while you are in town.

GAME CENTRES

Japanese kids are wild about video games and the city is full of game centres, ranging from the ultra-high-tech to simpler spots with only a few machines. If you or your kids love these sorts of games, you've come to the right place!

JJ CLUB 100 Map pp228-9

☎ 241 0510; Kawaramachi-dōri-Sanjō kudaru; games per 15min ¥105; ☺ 24hr; 3min walk from Hankyū Kyoto line, Kawaramachi Station

This is a multistorey game centre that offers everything from table tennis and pool to karaoke, with, of course, all the latest electronic games. You're charged by the hour and you pay as you leave. You have to join the club on first entry, which is a little complicated for non-Japanese speakers – ask a staff member to help you with the procedure.

KARAOKE

It would be crazy to come all the way to Japan and not sing karaoke! If you shy away from karaoke back home, where singing on stage is the norm, you'll feel much more comfortable here, where the 'karaoke box' is king. Here, you and your friends get a small room and karaoke system to yourselves.

JUMBO KARAOKE HIROBA Map pp228-9

☎ 761 3939; Kawabata-dōri-Sanjō, Sanjō-Ōhashi East; per person per hr before 7pm/after 7pm ¥280/640; ☺ 11am-6am; 1min walk from Keihan Sanjō Station

Ex-pats love this place as it's in the same building as the Pig & Whistle (p124) – and more than one drunken evening has started at the Pig and moved on to this place! There's a decent selection of English songs and the price includes all drinks. There's also a **Sanjō Kawaramachi branch** (Map pp228-9; ☎ 231 6777; Kawaramachi-dōri-Sanjō, northwest; 3min walk from Keihan Sanjō Station).

Shopping

Shopping

Kyoto has always been Japan's artistic and cultural workshop, the place where the country's finest artisans worked to produce the goods used in tea ceremonies, calligraphy, flower arrangement and religious ceremonies, as well as in kimono fabrics and other textiles. Despite the fact that the city's traditional industries are now suffering from Japan's economic downturn, and a lessening demand for their wares, Kyoto is still the best place to find traditional arts and crafts. Hidden in the streets and alleys of downtown Kyoto, the determined shopper will find scores of shops selling traditional items of the highest quality, from wood-block prints to pottery and Japanese fans.

Of course, Kyoto has far more to offer than just traditional items. You will also find the latest fashions in the Shijō-Kawaramachi shopping district, the latest electronics on Teramachi-dōri, and a wondrous assortment of food products in markets such as Nishiki Market (p57). And if you're lucky enough to be in town on the 21st or the 25th of the month, you should make every effort to visit one of the city's excellent flea markets (p131). Even if you have no intention of buying anything, it's a lot of fun to wander the stalls, checking out all the weird and wonderful things for sale (and the eccentric characters selling them).

Shopping Areas

The heart of Kyoto's shopping district is the intersection of Shijō-dōri and Kawaramachi-dōri. The blocks running north and west of here are packed with all sorts of stores selling both traditional and modern goods. Several of Kyoto's largest department stores are here as well, including Hankyū, Daimaru, Fujii Daimaru and Takashimaya.

While you're in these department stores, be sure to check their basement food floors. It's difficult to believe the variety of food on display, as well as some of the prices (check out the ¥10,000 melons, for example). Better still, head to Nishiki Market (p57) for a look at all the wondrous things that go into Japanese cuisine.

Top Five Shopping Streets

Shopping neighbourhoods in Kyoto tend to be organised by specialities, which certainly makes things easier if you're after specific items. The following is a list of some of Kyoto's most important shopping streets and what you'll find there.

- **Teramachi-dōri, north of Oike-dōri** (Map pp222-4) Traditional Japanese crafts, tea-ceremony goods, green tea and antiques.
- **Teramachi-dōri, south of Shijō-dōri** (Map pp222-4) Electronics and computers.
- **Shijō-dōri, between Kawaramachi-dōri and Karasuma-dōri** (Map pp228-9) Department stores, fashion boutiques and traditional arts and crafts.
- **Shinmonzen-dōri** (Map pp225-7) Antiques.
- **Gojō-zaka** (Map pp225-7) Pottery.

Teramachi-dōri, just south of Shijō-dōri, is Kyoto's electronics district and has the full range of the latest in computers, stereos and home appliances. The same street, north of Oike-dōri, is the place to look for a wide variety of traditional Japanese items. A stroll up this street to the Kyoto Imperial Palace Park is a great way to spend an afternoon, even if you don't plan on making any purchases.

The fashion-conscious should explore Kyoto's department stores or the chic boutiques on Kitayama-dōri. Unfortunately, you'll be hard-pressed to find much of a selection of larger ('*gaijin*-sized') clothes and shoes. If you're living in Kyoto, we suggest doing your clothes shopping by mail order from back home.

Antiques hunters should head straight for Shinmonzen-dōri in Gion, the aforementioned Teramachi-dōri, or one of the city's lively monthly markets (p131). To supplement the information in this chapter, pick up a copy of *Old Kyoto: A Guide to Traditional Shops, Restaurants & Inns* by Diane Durston, available at Maruzen bookshop (p134). It's good for finding traditional items that are sold (and often produced) by ancient Kyoto shops. *Kyoto Visitors Guide* has a listing of traditional shops and markets in town, while the TIC (p192) can also help locate unusual or hard-to-find items.

Bargaining

With the exception of antique shops and flea markets, bargaining in Japan is just not done. Possible exceptions are camera and electronic stores (in particular those dealing in used goods). The word 'discount' is usually understood by store clerks. If they are willing to drop the price, their first offer is usually all you'll get – don't haggle further as it will make things very awkward for the clerk.

SOUVENIR EMPORIUMS

If you want to do all of your shopping under one roof, the following places offer a wide selection of Kyoto arts and crafts at reasonable prices.

KYOTO CRAFT CENTER Map pp225-7

☎ 561 9660; Shijō-dōri-Higashiōji; ⊙ 11am-7pm, closed Wed; 5min walk from Keihan Shijō Station

This centre, near Maruyama-kōen, exhibits and sells a decent selection of handicrafts. Look for the very odd metal sculpture out front (we suspect it may be an abstract rendering of Mick Jagger's tongue).

KYOTO HANDICRAFT CENTER

Map pp225-7

☎ 761 5080; Marutamachi-dōri-Kumano-jinja, east; ⊙ 10am-6pm, closed 1-3 Jan; 10min walk from Keihan Marutamachi Station

The Kyoto Handicraft Center is a huge co-operative that exhibits and sells a wide range of Japanese arts and crafts. It also has two in-house wood-block print makers and a corner where you can try your hand at making some of your own prints.

All in all, this is the best one-stop emporium in the whole of Kyoto. It's located near Heian-jingū.

Craftsman, Kyoto Handicraft Center (above)

KYŪKYO-DŌ Map pp228-9

☎ 231 0510; Teramachi-dōri-Aneyakōji agaru; ⏰ 10am-6pm, closed Sun & 1-3 Jan; 1min walk from Tōzai subway line, Kyoto-Shiyakusho-mae Station

This old shop in the Teramachi covered arcade sells a selection of incense, *shodō* (calligraphy) goods, tea-ceremony supplies and *washi* (Japanese paper). Prices are on the high side but the quality is good.

SHOPPING CENTRES & ARCADES

If you want to see where the Kyoto kids are hanging out try one of the following shopping centres and arcades. In addition to these, you might take a stroll through **Teramachi** and **Shinkyōgoku covered arcades** (Map pp228–9). Lined with restaurants, cinemas, a mix of tacky souvenir shops and more traditional, upmarket stores, the arcades are usually swarming with Japanese students on school excursions.

AVANTI Map pp230-1

☎ 671 8761; south side of Kyoto Station; ⏰ shops 10am-9pm, restaurants 11am-10pm; 1min walk from Kyoto Station, Hachijoguchi exit

This shopping centre has a decent bookshop and supermarket, among other things. Take the underground passage from the station.

OPA Map pp228-9

☎ 255 8111; Kawaramachi-dōri-Shijō; ⏰ 11am-9pm, closed irregularly; 1min walk from Hankyū Kawaramachi Station

This new youth shopping centre is the place to go to see swarms of *ko-gyaru* (brightly clad Japanese girls) and their mates. It's also a decent spot for those who want to check out a wide variety of fashion boutiques and other trendy shops.

QANAT RAKUHOKU Map pp219-21

☎ 707 0700; Takano Nishibiraki-chō; ⏰ 10am-9pm; 15min walk from Keihan Demachiyanagi Station

This huge new complex in Takano (northern Kyoto) has stores selling just about everything. There's also a big food court with a Starbucks and a place that sells decent pizza (something of a rarity here).

SHIN-PUH-KAN Map pp228-9

☎ 213 6688; 586-2 Aneyakōji kudaru, Karasuma-dōri; ⏰ shops 11am-8pm Sun-Thu, 11am-9pm Fri & Sat, restaurants 11am-11pm, closed irregularly; 1min walk from Karasuma subway line, Karasuma-Ōike Station

This new downtown shopping complex has a variety of boutiques and restaurants clustered around a huge open-air atrium. The offerings here run to the trendy and ephemeral, which seems to appeal to all the young folks who congregate here. Occasional art and music performances are held in the atrium.

ZEST UNDERGROUND SHOPPING ARCADE Map pp228-9

☎ 253 3100; Oike-dōri-Kawaramachi; ⏰ shops 10.30am-8.30pm, restaurants 11am-10pm, closed irregularly; 1min walk from Tōzai subway line, Kyoto-Shiyakusho-mae Station

This new mall under Oike-dōri in front of Kyoto City Hall has a variety of boutiques, restaurants and a small branch of Kinokuniya bookshop.

Our Favourite Kyoto Shops

With literally thousands of shops to choose from, it's hard to know where to begin your hunt for that perfect Kyoto souvenir. To help you get started, we offer here a completely subjective list of Kyoto shops. These are the first places we head to when we're after something special for the folks back home.

Ippō-dō (p134) This place is a veritable temple to the wonders of Japanese tea. If you can't decide what you want, the staff will brew up a sample.

Kyoto Handicraft Center (p129) For one-stop souvenir shopping, this place can't be beat. We particularly like its wood-block prints.

Maruzen (p134) This is Kyoto's best bookshop, hands down. You can happily spend a few hours browsing the titles here. If you're after a picture book about Kyoto as a memento, look no further!

Morita Washi (p133) The selection of *washi* (Japanese paper) is just mind-boggling here. If you want something special to wrap your souvenirs, this is the place.

Takashimaya Department Store (Map pp228-9) This immaculate Shijō-dōri department store is the perfect example of a Japanese department store, and the food floor is a marvel to behold.

MARKETS

A visit to one of the monthly markets may very well be a highlight of your trip to Kyoto. It's also a good chance to pick up souvenirs at reasonable prices. Scores of dealers set up stalls to display and sell their wares – this is one of the few occasions where bargaining is the norm. Wares on offer include antiques, pottery, food, second-hand clothing, bric-a-brac and antique kimono. Most vendors can manage a bit of English but a smile will often go as far as fluent Japanese. If you're looking for antiques, arrive early and prepare to bargain. There is a better selection in the morning, but vendors loosen up with prices as the market winds down.

If you aren't in Kyoto on the 21st or the 25th of each month, there is also a regular antiques fair at Tō-ji (p79) on the first Sunday of each month.

Flea Markets

KŌBŌ-SAN MARKET Map pp222-4
☎ 691 3325; Tō-ji, Kujō-dōri-Ōmiya, Minami-ku; ☿ dawn to dusk, 21st of each month; 10min walk from Kyoto Station
This market is at Tō-ji on the 21st of each month to commemorate the death of Kōbō Taishi, who in 823 was appointed abbot of the temple.

KYOTO INTERNATIONAL COMMUNITY HOUSE Map pp225-7
☎ 752 3010; Sakyō-ku, Awataguchi; ☿ 11am-4pm; 5min walk from Tōzai subway line, Keage Station
Twice a year, in spring and fall, recycled items, clothes and household goods are sold here. Call for dates as they vary each year.

TENJIN-SAN MARKET Map pp216-18
☎ 461 0005; Kitano Tenman-gū, Kamigyō-ku, Bakuro-chō; ☿ dawn to dusk, 25th of each month; 1min walk from Kitano Tenmangū-mae bus stop, bus 50 or 101 from Kyoto Station
This market is held on the 25th of each month at Kitano Tenman-gū and marks the day of birth (and coincidentally the death) of the Heian-era statesman Sugawara Michizane (845–903).

YWCA'S THRIFT SHOP Map pp216-18
☎ 431 0351; Muromachi-dōri-Demizu agaru; ☿ 11am-2pm 1st & 3rd Sat of each month; 15min walk from Karasuma subway line, Marutamachi Station
On the first and third Saturday of each month there is a flea market and general get-together of foreigners here.

Other Markets

Other markets are held monthly at various temples around town, and feature household goods and handmade wares, among other things.

CHION-JI
Map pp219-21   *Handmade Craft Market*
☎ 781 9171; Higashiōji-dōri-Imadegawa; ☿ dawn to dusk, 15th of each month; 1min walk from Hyakuman-ben bus stop, bus 206 from Kyoto Station
The Tezukuri-ichi (handmade market) is held at Chion-ji on the 15th of each month. Wares include food and handmade clothes. This is a good chance to see Kyoto's alternative community out in full force.

MYŌREN-JI Map pp216-18   *Bazaar*
☎ 451 3527; Teranouchi-dōri-Ōmiya higashi iru; ☿ 10am-4pm 12th of each month; 10min walk from Karasuma subway line, Kuramaguchi Station
On the 12th of each month there is a bazaar at Myōren-ji, northwest of Imadegawa-Horikawa. Goods on offer include such items as Japanese textiles and bric-a-brac.

ANTIQUE & CRAFT FAIRS

The Antique Grand Fair is a major event, with over 100 dealers selling a wide range of Japanese and foreign curios. It is held thrice-yearly at **Pulse Plaza** (Map pp214–15) in Fushimi (southern Kyoto). Ask at the TIC for more details as times vary each year.

There are also several annual pottery events that are great opportunities for finding deals on both local wares and ceramics from around Japan.

TOKI-ICHI Map pp216-18
☎ 461 5973; Imadegawa-Kamishichiken; ☿ 10am-8pm 9-12 Jul; 1min walk from Kamishichiken bus stop
This is a large pottery fair held at Senbon Shaka-dō, with around 30 vendors selling various wares.

ARTS & HANDICRAFTS
Bamboo Crafts

KAGOSHIN Map pp225-7
☎ 771 0209; Sanjō-dōri-Ōhashi higashi iru; ☿ 9am-6pm; 3min walk from Keihan Sanjō Station
This small shop sells a wide variety of inexpensive bamboo products, such as flower holders and baskets.

Bamboo crafts

ONOUECHIKUZAITEN Map pp225-7

☎ 751 2444; Sanjō-dōri-Ōhashi higashi iru; ⏰ 10am-7pm; 3min walk from Keihan Sanjō Station

Just a few doors from Kagoshin, it's almost a carbon copy.

Ceramics

In eastern Kyoto, Ninen-zaka and Sannen-zaka slopes, close to Kiyomizu-dera, are famed for ceramics, in particular a distinctive type of pottery known as Kiyomizu-yaki. You'll find more pottery to the north of Gojō-dōri between Higashiōji-dōri and Kawabata-dōri. Of course, you'll get far better deals at the Tō-ji and Kitano markets (p131).

Combs & Hair Clips

NIJŪSAN-YA Map pp228-9

☎ 221 2371; Shijō-dōri-Kawaramachi east; ⏰ 10am-8pm, closed third Wed of the month; 1min walk from Hankyū Kawaramachi Station

Boxwood combs and hair clips are one of Kyoto's most famous traditional crafts, and are still used in the elaborate hairstyles of the city's geisha and *maiko* (apprentice geisha). This tiny hole-in-the-wall shop has a fine selection for you to choose from (and if you don't

like what's on view, you can ask if it has other choices in stock – it usually does).

Dolls

MATSUYA Map pp228-9

☎ 221 5902; Kawaramachi-dōri-Shijō agaru; ⏰ 10.30am-6.30pm, closed Wed; 1min walk from Hankyū Kawaramachi Station

Just north of Shijō-dōri, on the eastern side of Kawaramachi-dōri, Matsuya sells an impressive assortment of delicately painted *kyō-ningyō* (Kyoto dolls).

TANAKAYA Map pp228-9

☎ 221 1959; Shijō-dōri-Yanaginobanba higashi iru; ⏰ 10am-6pm, closed Wed; 5min walk from Karasuma subway line, Shijō Station

Tanakaya is another good option for traditional Japanese dolls.

Fans

KYŌSEN-DŌ Map pp230-1

☎ 371 4151; Higashinotōin-dōri-Shomen agaru; ⏰ 9am-5pm Mon-Sat, 10am-6pm Sun & public holidays; 10min walk from Kyoto Station

Kyōsen-dō sells a colourful variety of paper fans; here you can see the process of assembling the fans and even paint your own.

YAMANI Map pp222-4

☎ 351 2622; Karasuma-dōri-Gojō kudaru; ⏰ 9am-5pm, closes 4pm Sat, closed Sun & 2nd & 3rd Sat of each month; 2min walk from Karasuma subway line, Gojō Station

A short walk south of Gojō-dōri, Yamani boasts a wide selection of fans.

Japanese Paper
KAKIMOTO WASHI Map pp222-4

☎ 211 3481; Teramachi-dōri-Nijō agaru; ⏰ 9am-6pm, closed Sun & public holidays; 5min walk from Tōzai subway line, Kyoto-Shiyakusho-mae Station

This shop is a close second to Morita Washi for exquisite *washi*. It even has some for use in computer printers!

MORITA WASHI Map pp222-4

☎ 341 1419; Higashinotōin-dōri-Bukkōji agaru; ⏰ 9.30am-5.30pm, closes 4.30pm Sat; 3min walk from Karasuma subway line, Shijō Station

A short walk from the Shijō-Karasuma crossing, this place sells a fabulous variety of handmade *washi* for reasonable prices. It's one of our favourite shops in Kyoto for souvenirs.

RAKUSHI-KAN Map pp228-9

☎ 251 0078; Sanjō-dōri-Takakura; ⏰ 10am-7pm, closed Mon; 5min walk from Karasuma subway line, Karasuma Oike Station

On the 1st floor of the Museum of Kyoto, this shop sells a decent variety of *washi* goods.

Metalwork
AMITA-HONTEN Map pp225-7

☎ 761 7000; Okazaki Heian-jingū kita; ⏰ 10am-6pm; 3min walk from Kumanojinja-mae bus stop, bus 206 from Kyoto Station

You'll find a small selection of traditional Japanese metalwork at this souvenir emporium.

Noren
TANAKAYA Map pp228-9

☎ 221 3076; Takakura-dōri-Nishikikōji agaru; ⏰ 9.30am-7pm, closed 3rd Wed of the month; 10min walk from Karasuma subway line, Shijō Station

This shop sells *noren* (curtains that hang in the entry of Japanese restaurants) and a wide variety of other fabric goods such as placemats, *tenugui* (small hand towels), handkerchiefs and bedding. It's near Daimaru department store.

Textiles & Kimono

There are several central kimono shops worth stopping at for a peek at the elegant fabrics and kimono.

ERIZEN Map pp228-9

☎ 221 1618; Shijō-dōri-Kawaramachi; ⏰ 10am-7pm, closed Mon; 1min walk from Hankyū Kawaramachi Station

For *kyō-yūzen* (Kyoto-style dyed fabrics) head for Erizen, an elegant shop that has the best selection in town.

KYOTO-KIMONO PLAZA Map pp222-4

☎ 352 2323; Karasuma-dōri-Takatsuji; ⏰ 10am-5pm, closed Tue; 2min walk from Karasuma subway line, Shijō Station

This is another possibility for kimono; it's one of the more approachable kimono shops in town.

NISHIJIN TEXTILE CENTER Map pp216-18

☎ 451 9231; Horikawa-dōri-Imadegawa, south; ⏰ 9am-5pm; 7min walk from Karasuma subway line, Imadegawa Station

If you're looking for Nishijin-ori fabrics, some of which are used in kimono, try the shop here.

SHIKUNSHI Map pp222-4

☎ 221 0456; Shijō-dōri-Nishinotōin higashi iru; ⏰ 10.30am-7pm; 5min walk from Karasuma subway line, Shijō Station

In a wonderful old *machiya* on Shijō-dōri, east of Nishinotōin-dōri, this shop sells a variety of kimono. Have a look at the small shop in the restored warehouse at the back.

Wood-Block Prints

We suggest the Kyoto Handicraft Center (p129) for high-quality and inexpensive wood-block prints *(han-ga or moku-han)*. Two other possibilities are the following.

NISHIHARU Map pp228-9

☎ 211 2849; Sanjō-dōri-Teramachi; ⏰ 2-7pm; 10min walk from Keihan Sanjō Station

This is an attractive shop dealing in wood-block prints. All the prints are accompanied by English explanations and the owner is happy to take the time to find something you really like.

TESSAI-DŌ Map pp225-7

☎ 531 9566; Shimogawara-dōri-Kōdaiji; ⏰ 10am-5pm; 7min walk from Higashiyamayasui bus stop, bus 206 from Kyoto Station

This small shop deals in original wood-block prints. Prices average ¥10,000 per piece.

OTHER ITEMS

ARITSUGU

Map pp228-9   *Knives & Kitchenware*

☎ 221 1091; Nishikikōji-dōri-Gokomachi nishi iru; ⏲ 9am-5.30pm; 10min walk from Hankyū Kawara-machi Station

While you're in the Nishiki Market have a look at this store where you can find some of the best kitchen knives in the world. It also carries a selection of excellent and unique Japanese kitchenware.

CAMERA NO NANIWA

Map pp228-9   *Cameras*

☎ 222 0728; Shijō-dōri-Fuyachō; ⏲ 10am-8pm; 1min walk from Hankyū Kawaramachi Station

This vast camera/film/electronics emporium is part of a huge low-cost Osaka chain. You can find some great bargains here, but don't expect much in terms of personal service.

DEMACHI YUNYŪ SHOKUHIN

Map pp219-21   *Imported Foods*

☎ 231 1110; Kawaramachi-dōri-Imadegawa kudaru; ⏲ 10am-7pm; 5min walk from Keihan Demachiyanagi Station

Near the Kawaramachi-Imadegawa crossing, this shop has good deals on coffee, cookies and chocolate.

IPPO-DŌ

Map pp222-4   *Japanese Tea*

☎ 211 3421; Teramachi-dōri-Nijō; ⏲ 9am-7pm, closed Sun; 8min walk from Tōzai subway line, Kyoto-Shiyakusho-mae Station

This old-style tea shop sells the best Japanese tea in Kyoto. Its *matcha* (powdered green tea used in tea ceremonies) makes an excellent and lightweight souvenir. Try a 40g container of *wa-no-mukashi* (meaning 'old-time Japan') for ¥1600, which makes 25 cups of excellent green tea. The tea shop is north of the city hall, near Teramachi-dōri.

KŌJITSU

Map pp228-9   *Outdoor Sporting Goods*

☎ 257 7050; Kawaramachi-dōri-Sanjō agaru; ⏲ 10am-8pm; 5min walk from Keihan Sanjō Station

If you plan to do some hiking or camping while in Japan, you can stock up on equipment at this excellent little shop on Kawaramachi-dōri. You'll find that Japanese outdoor sporting equipment is very high quality (with prices to match).

KUNGYOKU-DŌ Map pp230-1   *Incense*

☎ 371 0162; Horikawa-dōri-Nishihonganji-mae ⏲ 9am-5.30pm, closed 1st & 3rd Sun of each month; 15min walk from Kyoto Station

A haven for the olfactory sense, this place has sold incense and aromatic woods (for burning like incense) for four centuries. It's opposite the gate of Nishi Hongan-ji.

MARUZEN Map pp228-9   *Books*

☎ 241 2161; Kawaramachi-dōri, Shijō agaru; ⏲ 10am-8pm, closed third Wed of the month; 10min walk from Hankyū Kawaramachi Station

This is the best bookshop in Kyoto. On the 8th floor is a large selection of English-language books, magazines and maps, a limited range of French, German and Spanish-language books, and lots of books about Kyoto and Japan.

MEIDI-YA Map pp228-9   *Imported Foods*

☎ 221 7661; Sanjō-dōri-Kawaramachi higashi iru; ⏲ 10am-8pm; 5min walk from Keihan Sanjō Station

This famous Sanjō-dōri gourmet supermarket has Kyoto's best selection of imported food and an excellent selection of wine. Prices are high.

TSUJIKURA Map pp228-9   *Umbrellas*

☎ 221 4396; Kawaramachi-dōri-Shijō agaru; ⏲ 11am-8.30pm, closed Wed; 2min walk from Hankyū Kawaramachi Station

A short walk north of the Shijō-Kawaramachi crossing, Tsujikura has a good selection of waxed-paper umbrellas and paper lanterns with traditional and modern designs.

Sleeping

Sleeping

Kyoto has a wide range of accommodation to suit all budgets, from the finest ryokan (traditional inns) to youth hostels, guesthouses and *shukubō* (temple lodgings). Needless to say, there are also plenty of hotels, from cheap 'business hotels' to first-class luxury hotels, with a smattering of love hotels and capsule hotels thrown in for good measure.

Bear in mind that much of Kyoto's accommodation can be booked out during the high season (the early April cherry-blossom season and the late October to late November fall foliage season). Whatever you do, try to reserve as early as possible if you plan to be in town during these times.

Credit cards are accepted at most hotels, but don't expect to pay with plastic at budget places. At ryokan, the higher the price, the better the chance of being able to use a credit card.

In this guide, cheap sleeps are rooms that cost ¥6000 or less; mid-range rooms cost between ¥6000 and ¥15,000; and high-end rooms cost more than ¥15,000.

Accommodation Types

The following are the most common accommodation types you will encounter in this book and on your travels. A child, for the purposes of hotels and other accommodation options, is under 15. Unless stated otherwise, rooms at the places listed in this chapter have air-conditioning.

BUSINESS HOTELS

A very common form of mid-range accommodation is the so-called 'business hotel'. Generally these are economical and functional places geared to the lone traveller on business, although most in Kyoto also take couples. In Kyoto, a room in a business hotel will have pay TV and a tiny bathroom, and cost between ¥6000 and ¥12,000. Like ryokan, some business hotels accept credit cards, but you should always ask when you check in. There is no room service, and you will usually be required to check out at 10am or 11am and check in after 3pm or 4pm. At some of the nicer business hotels, there are large shared baths and saunas in addition to the private ones in the guest rooms.

Business hotels are identifiable by their small size (usually three to five floors); their simple, often concrete, exteriors; and a sign, usually in both English and Japanese, out the front. Although you can't expect much English from the front-desk clerk, if you smile and speak slowly you should be OK.

LUXURY HOTELS

Once you leave the budget and mid-range category and enter the top-end bracket, you can expect to find all the amenities of top hotels anywhere in the world. The staff speak English, the rooms are spotless and the service is impeccable. In addition, most luxury hotels in Kyoto have several good restaurants and bars on their premises, many of which offer outstanding views over the city.

RYOKAN

For those who crave a really traditional Japanese experience with tatami (mat-floor) rooms and futons instead of beds, nothing beats a night in a ryokan. Although the more exclusive establishments can charge ¥25,000 (and often much more), there are a number of relatively inexpensive ryokan in Kyoto. These places are generally more accustomed to foreigners than their counterparts in more remote parts of Japan and the rules tend to be a bit more relaxed as a result.

Although some ryokan will allow you to pay by credit card, you should always ask at check-in if you hope to do so. The ryokan listed in this book are generally budget; those wishing to stay in mid-range and top-end ryokan should inquire at the **Kyoto Tourist Information**

Center (TIC; Map pp230-1; ☎ 344 3300; 9th fl, Kyoto Station; ☺ 10am-6pm, closed 2nd & 4th Tue of the month & 29 Dec–3 Jan), which has a branch of the **Welcome Inn Reservation Center** (☺ 9am-noon Mon-Fri), an outfit that handles reservations for foreigner-friendly ryokan.

YOUTH HOSTELS

Kyoto's youth hostels are much like youth hostels elsewhere: not much atmosphere and a mixture of dorms and private rooms. They can also be noisy. On the plus side, they are used to foreigners and are cleaner than many of their overseas counterparts. A room in a typical youth hostel is about ¥3200, cash only. Membership might not be necessary.

GUESTHOUSES

Guesthouses are a lot like youth hostels, without the regimented atmosphere and without any need for membership. With a long history of hosting foreign travellers, Kyoto has far more guesthouses than most Japanese cities, including Tokyo. Some are notorious fleapits that should have been closed down long ago, but others, especially the new ones, are excellent places to stay, with spotless facilities and helpful owners. Guesthouses usually have dorms, which average ¥2500 per person, and a variety of private rooms, which average ¥3500 per person.

SHUKUBŌ

Shukubō are usually in peaceful surroundings with spartan tatami rooms, optional attendance at early morning prayer sessions and an early evening curfew. Nightly rates are around ¥4000 per person (most include breakfast), and guests usually use public baths.

> ## The Best of Kyoto
>
> In terms of accommodation in Kyoto, you're really spoiled for choice: there are good places to stay in every category and price range. However, some places really do stand out. These are our picks for the best accommodation in each category.
>
> **Guesthouse** Tour Club (p139) and Budget Inn (p139) – a tie.
>
> **Youth hostel** Utano Youth Hostel (p143)
>
> **Small ryokan** Ryokan Uemura (p141)
>
> **Large ryokan** Yachiyo Ryokan (p141)
>
> **Business hotel** Sun Hotel Kyoto (p140)
>
> **Mid-range hotel** Hotel Gimmond (p140)
>
> **Luxury hotel** Westin Miyako Hotel (p141)

A number of *shukubō* in Kyoto are hesitant to take foreigners who cannot speak Japanese, though those listed in this chapter have English-speakers on hand and are used to having non-Japanese guests. At the TIC you can pick up a copy of a hand-out entitled *Shukubōs in Kyoto*, which has a comprehensive list of local temple lodgings.

LONG-TERM ACCOMMODATION

If you're planning on setting up shop in Kyoto, you can count on spending at least a month finding an acceptable place to live. We suggest booking a room in a place like the I.S.E. Dorm (p142) or Greenpeace Inn Kyoto (p142) while you look.

Once you're established in a decent guesthouse or '*gaijin* house' (foreigner house), you can start your search in earnest. The best places to look for houses and apartments are the message board of the **Kyoto International Community House** (KICH; Map pp225-7; ☎ 752 3512; Sakyō-ku, Awataguchi; 5min walk from Tōzai subway line, Keage Station) and the listings section of *Kansai Time Out*. Word of mouth is also a great way to find a place, and any of the '*gaijin* bars' listed in the Entertainment chapter (p123) would be a good place to ask around.

Kyoto rents average ¥40,000 per month for a room in a *gaijin* house or around ¥65,000 for a whole house. Of course, as elsewhere in Japan, there are hidden fees, such as 'key money' and a damage deposit that may equal up to four month's rent. Some landlords do not require that you pay these fees (houses owned by these landlords are often passed down through the *gaijin* community by word of mouth).

Reservations & Information

Kyoto Tourist Information Center (TIC; Map pp230-1; ☎ 344 3300; 9th fl, Kyoto Station; ☺ 10am-6pm, closed 2nd & 4th Tue of the month & 29 Dec–3 Jan) offers advice, accommodation lists and can help with reservations at its **Welcome Inn Reservation Center** (☺ 9am-noon Mon-Fri).

KYOTO STATION AREA

The area immediately north of Kyoto Station is thick with hotels, ryokan and guesthouses. Staying in this area is convenient not only in terms of transport, but also in terms of shopping and dining.

APA HOTEL Map pp230-1 *Business Hotel*
☎ 365 4111; ahkyoto@apa.co.jp; Nishinotōin-dōri-Shiokōji kudaru; s/tw from ¥8000/15,000; 5min walk from Kyoto Station

This relatively new business hotel is located very close to Kyoto Station, which is useful for those morning departures. Rooms are standard issue for a business hotel – on the small side, but neat and clean.

HOTEL GRANVIA KYOTO
Map pp230-1 *Hotel*
☎ 344 8888; www.granvia-kyoto.co.jp/e/; Shiokōji Sagaru Karasuma-dōri; s/d/tw ¥14,000/18,000/20,000; above Kyoto Station

Located directly above Kyoto Station, this is one of the finest hotels in Kyoto, with a wide range of excellent on-site restaurants and bars. Rooms are relatively large and some have good views over the city.

HOTEL HOKKE CLUB KYOTO
Map pp230-1 *Business Hotel*
☎ 361 1251; fax 361 1255; Karasuma-Central gate of Kyoto Station; s/tw from ¥8400/13,650; 1min walk from Kyoto Station

Just across from Kyoto Station and recently refurbished, this business hotel is a good choice for those who want to be close to transport. Ask about its Welcome Plan, which enables two people to stay for ¥9000.

KYOTO DAI-SAN TOWER HOTEL
Map pp230-1 *Hotel*
☎ 343 3111; fax 343 2054; Shinmachi-dōri-Shichijō kudaru; s/tw/d from ¥6500/12,500/17,000; 5min walk from Kyoto Station

This hotel is worth a try if other places are full. It's a little older than some in the area, but it's still decent value.

KYOTO NEW HANKYŪ HOTEL
Map pp230-1 *Hotel*
☎ 343 5300; hotel.newhankyu.co.jp/kyoto-e/index.html; Shiokōji-dōri; s/tw/d from ¥13,860/25,410/27,720; 1min walk from Kyoto Station

A good range of on-site choices make this hotel another decent option within this price bracket. Rooms are clean and services are of a high standard.

RIHGA ROYAL HOTEL KYOTO
Map pp230-1 *Hotel*
☎ 341 1121; www.rihga.com/kyoto/; Horikawa-dōri-Shiokōji; s/tw/d from ¥13,000/16,000/21,000; 10min walk from Kyoto Station

Famous for its rooftop restaurant, this large hotel has a swimming pool and several good restaurants.

RIVERSIDE TAKASE Map pp230-1 *Ryokan*
☎ 351 7925; www.upwell.jp/kyoto/takase.html; Kiyamachi-dōri-Kaminokuchi agaru; s/d/tr ¥3300/6400/9600; 15min walk from Kyoto Station, or bus 17 or 205 to Kawaramachi-Shōmen bus stop

There are five comfortable rooms in this long-time favourite of foreign travellers. It's conveniently located near the downtown shopping, dining and entertainment areas.

RYOKAN HIRAIWA Map pp230-1 *Ryokan*
☎ 351 6748; www2.odn.ne.jp/hiraiwa/Index_e.htm; Kaminokuchi agaru-Ninomiyacho-dōri; per person ¥4240-5250; 15min walk from Kyoto Station, or bus 17 or 205 to Kawaramachi-Shōmen bus stop

This ryokan is used to foreigners and offers basic tatami rooms. It is close to both central and eastern Kyoto.

RYOKAN KYŌKA Map pp230-1 *Ryokan*
☎ 371 2709; web.kyoto-inet.or.jp/people/kyoka/kyoka.html; Shimojuzuyamachi-dōri-Higashinotōin; per person without bath ¥4200; 10min walk from Kyoto Station

Getting a little long in the tooth, this ryokan has 10 fairly spacious rooms. It's quite close to Kyoto Station and also within walking distance of downtown.

RYOKAN MURAKAMIYA
Map pp230-1 *Ryokan*
☎ 371 1260; www2.odn.ne.jp/ryokanmurakamiya/etop.html; Shichijō-agaru, Higashinotōin-dōri; per person ¥4700; 10min walk from Kyoto Station

This homey little ryokan is conveniently located close to the station. Like other ryokan in this price range, it's simple and clean.

RYOKAN ŌTŌ Map pp230-1 *Ryokan*
☎ 541 7803; fax 541 7804; Shichijō-dōri-Kamogawa higashi; s/d/tr from ¥4000/7600/11,000; 15min walk from Kyoto Station

A member of the Japanese Inn Group, the Ōtō is a decent choice but lacks the atmosphere of some of Kyoto's other ryokan. The location is pretty good for exploring the southern Higashiyama area.

YUHARA RYOKAN Map pp230-1 _Ryokan_
☎ 371 9583; fax 371 9583; Shōmen agaru-Kiyamachi-dōri; per person ¥4200; 15min walk from Kyoto Station, or bus 17 or 205 to Kawaramachi-Shōmen bus stop
With a riverside location and a family atmosphere, Yuhara is popular with foreigners. It's a short walk from the attractions of downtown and eastern Kyoto.

Cheap Sleeps
BUDGET INN Map pp230-1 _Guesthouse_
☎ 344 1510; www.budgetinnjp.com; Aburanokōji, Shichijō sagaru; dm/tr/q ¥2500/9990/11,990; 7min walk from Kyoto Station
This new guesthouse is an excellent choice. It's got two dorm rooms and six private rooms, all of which are clean and well-maintained. All rooms have their own bath and toilet, and there is a spacious quad room that is good for families. The staff here is very helpful and friendly, and Internet access, laundry and bicycle rental are available. All in all, this is a great choice in this price range. From the station, walk west on Shiokōji-dōri and turn north at the Esso station (one street before Horikawa) and look for the English sign out front.

K'S HOUSE KYOTO
Map pp230-1 _Guesthouse_
☎ 342 2444; kshouse.jp/index.html; Shichijō agaru-Dotemachi-dōri; dm ¥2500, s/tw/d per person from ¥3500/2900/2900; 10min walk from Kyoto Station
K's House is a large new guesthouse with both private and dorm rooms. The rooms are simple but adequate and there are spacious common areas. Internet access is available.

KYOTO WHITE HOTEL
Map pp230-1 _Business Hotel_
☎ 351 5511; fax 351 1226; Shiokōji-Higashitōin agaru higashi iru; s/d ¥4600/7200; 5min walk from Kyoto Station
This hotel seems to specialise in housing Japanese businessmen on tight budgets. It is just about the cheapest business hotel in town.

TOUR CLUB Map pp230-1 _Guesthouse_
☎ 353 6968; www.kyotojp.com; 362 Momiji-chō, Shōmen-sagaru, Higashinakasuji; dm ¥2415, tw/tr from ¥7770/9435; 10min walk from Kyoto Station
Run by a charming and informative young couple, this clean and well-maintained guest-

Tour Club (below)

house is a favourite of many foreign visitors. Facilities include Internet access, bicycle rental, laundry, money exchange and free tea and coffee. All private rooms have a private bath and toilet, and there is a spacious quad room for families. This is probably the best choice in this price bracket. To get here, turn north off Shichijō-dōri at the Second House coffee shop (which looks like a bank) and keep an eye out for the Japanese flag.

DOWNTOWN KYOTO
Downtown is the place to be based if you want easy access to shops, restaurants and nightlife options. Since most places in this section are also within easy walking distance to the subway, it's fairly convenient in terms of transport.

HIIRAGIYA RYOKAN
Map pp228-9 _Ryokan_
☎ 221 1136; www.hiiragiya.co.jp/en/; Nakahakusan-chō, Fuyacho Aneyakōji-agaru; per person with 2 meals ¥30,000-60,000; 10min walk from Karasuma subway line, Shijō Station
This elegant ryokan has long been favoured by celebrities from around the world. Facilities and services are impeccable, as you would expect.

HOTEL GIMMOND Map pp228-9   *Hotel*
☎ 221 4111; www.gimmond.co.jp/kyoto/
khome-e.htm; Takakura-dōri-Oike; s/d/tw from
¥9586/16,170/16,747; 5min walk from Karasuma
subway line, Karasuma-Oike Station

This is one of the cheapest hotels (as opposed
to business hotels) in town and has a convenient location and clean rooms. It's good value
and has a loyal following of foreign guests.

KINMATA RYOKAN Map pp228-9   *Ryokan*
☎ 221 1039; fax 231 7632; Shijō agaru-Gokomachi-
dōri; per person with 2 meals ¥40,000-50,000; 5min
walk from Karasuma subway line, Shijō Station

Kinmata commenced operations early in the
19th century and this is reflected in the original décor, interior gardens and *hinoki* (cypress)
bathroom. The exquisite *kaiseki* (Japanese *haute
cuisine*) meals alone are a good reason to stay
here. It's in the centre of town.

KYOTO CENTRAL INN
Map pp228-9   *Business Hotel*
☎ 211 1666; mail@kyoto-centralinn.jp; Shijō-Kawara-
machi-nishi iru; s/tw/d ¥6000/9000/11,000; 1min walk
from Hankyū Kawaramachi Station, exit 6

This nondescript business hotel is right in the
heart of Kyoto's nightlife and shopping district.
It's right above Hankyū Kawaramachi Station,
in case you have business in Osaka.

Tawaraya Ryokan (right)

KYOTO HOTEL ŌKURA
Map pp228-9   *Hotel*
☎ 211 5111; www.kyotohotel.co.jp/oike/
index_e.html; Kawaramachi-dōri-Oike; s/tw/d from
¥16,000/22,000/28,000; 1min walk from Tōzai subway
line, Kyoto-Shiyakusho-mae Station

This vast new hotel is considered by many to
be the best hotel in Kyoto. Without a doubt it
has the widest range of on-site facilities, and is
in a convenient downtown location.

SUN HOTEL KYOTO Map pp228-9   *Hotel*
☎ 241 3351; fax 241 0616; Kawaramachi-dōri-Sanjō
kudaru; s ¥8505, d & tw ¥12,810; 5min walk from
Keihan Sanjō Station

This small but clean hotel is one of the best
in its class. Its central location can't be beaten
and the rooms, while small, are in good condition and are reasonably comfortable.

TAWARAYA RYOKAN
Map pp228-9   *Ryokan*
☎ 211 5566; fax 221 2204; Fuyacho-Oike kudaru; per
person ¥35,000-75,000; 10min walk from Karasuma
subway line, Karasuma-Oike Station

Tawaraya has been operating for over three
centuries and is classed as one of the finest
places to stay in the world. Guests at this ryokan
have included the imperial family and overseas
royalty. It is a classic in every sense. Reservations
are essential, preferably many months ahead.

SOUTHEAST KYOTO

Southeast Kyoto is an excellent place to be
based if you want easy access to Kyoto's
most important sightseeing areas. It's also
quieter and more attractive than downtown
or the station area.

GION FUKUZUMI Map pp225-7   *Ryokan*
☎ 541 5181; www.gion-fukuzumi.com/eng/index
.html; Shinbashi-nishi iru, Higashiōji; per person from
¥8000; 10min walk from Keihan Shijō Station

A group tour–oriented ryokan in a Western-
style building, the Fukuzumi has clean, new
rooms and a good Gion location.

HOTEL FUJITA KYOTO
Map pp225-7   *Hotel*
☎ 222 1511; information@fujita-kyoto.com; Kamogawa
Nijō-Ōhashi Hotori; s/tw/d from ¥10,395/18,480/26,565;
10min walk from Tōzai subway line, Kyoto-Shiyakusho-
mae Station

This hotel is recommended for its riverside location, view of the mountains (ask for a room

on the east side), summertime beer garden and great sunken garden/bar.

HOTEL HEIAN NO MORI KYOTO
Map pp225-7 *Hotel*

☎ 761 9111; fax 761 1333; Okazaki, Higashitenno-chō; d/tw from ¥9900/12,100; 2min walk from Higashi-Tennō-chō bus stop, bus 5

This large, pleasant hotel is located close to the Higashiyama Mountains. It's close to Ginkaku-ji, Nanzen-ji and the Tetsugaku-no-Michi (Path of Philosophy). The rooftop beer garden is perfect for summer drinking.

KYOTO TRAVELLER'S INN
Map pp225-7 *Business Hotel*

☎ 771 0225; traveler@mbox.kyoto-inet.or.jp; Heian-jingū Torii-mae; s/tw ¥6825/12,600; 2min walk from Kyotokaikan/Bijyutsukan-mae bus stop

The Traveller's Inn is a business hotel that's very close to Heian-jingū and offers both Western- and Japanese-style rooms. The restaurant on the 1st floor is open until 10pm. It's good value for the price.

LADY'S HOTEL CHŌRAKUKAN
Map pp225-7 *Women-Only Hotel*

☎ 561 0001; webmaster@chourakukan.co.jp; Gion Maruyama-kōen; per person from ¥4500; 10min walk from Keihan Shijō Station

Housed in a stately, late Meiji-era guesthouse, Lady's Hotel Chōrakukan is central, near Maruyama-kōen. The rooms are clean and the location is perfect for eastern Kyoto sightseeing.

LADY'S INN SAKATA
Map pp225-7 *Women-Only Hotel*

☎ 541 2108; sakata@aurora.ocn.ne.jp; Kōdaiji-Masuya-chō; per person ¥6000; 5min walk from Higashiyama-Yasui bus stop, bus 206

Near the Ninen-zaka slope, this place is good for those who want to hide away from the world. It's small and intimate.

PENSION HIGASHIYAMA

Map pp225-7 *Pension*

☎ 882 1181; www.kid97.co.jp/st-kyoto/ps-higashi yama.html; Shirakawasuji-Sanjō-dōri; s/d/tr from ¥4400/8800/12,000; 2min walk from Chioin-mae bus stop, bus 206

A small pension by the Shira-kawa canal, it's conveniently located for the sights in Higashi-yama. It's a simple, comfortable place and a member of the Japanese Inn Group.

RYOKAN UEMURA
Map pp225-7 *Ryokan*

☎ /fax 561 0377; Ishibei-kōji Shimogawara; per person with breakfast ¥9000; 5min walk from Higashi-yama-Yasui bus stop, bus 206

A beautiful little ryokan, at ease with foreign guests. It's on Ishibei-kōji, a quaint cobblestone alley, just down the hill from Kiyomizu-dera. Book well in advance as there are only three rooms. Note that the manager prefers bookings and cancellations to be made by fax (with only three rooms, no-shows can be pretty damaging). There is a 10pm curfew here.

THREE SISTERS INN ANNEX
Map pp225-7 *Ryokan*

Rakutō-sō Bekkan; ☎ 761 6333; fax 761 6335; Irie-chō Okazaki; s/d without bath ¥5635/11,270, s/d/tr with bath ¥10,810/18,170/23,805; 5min walk from Dōbutsu-en-mae bus stop, bus 5

An annex of the Three Sisters Inn (p142), this ryokan is well run, comfortable and used to foreigners. It has a pleasant breakfast nook that overlooks a wonderful Japanese garden. The bamboo-lined walkway is another highlight.

WESTIN MIYAKO HOTEL
Map pp225-7 *Hotel*

☎ 771 7111; www.westinmiyako-kyoto.com/; Sanjō-dōri-Keage; s & tw from ¥23,000, d from ¥25,000, Japanese-style r from ¥35,000; 1min walk from Tōzai subway line, Keage Station

The Westin Miyako Hotel is a famous Western-style hotel perched on the hills, and is a classic choice for visiting foreign dignitaries. The hotel surroundings stretch over 6.4 hectares of wooded hillside and landscaped gardens.

YACHIYO RYOKAN
Map pp225-7 *Ryokan*

☎ 771 4148; www.biwa.ne.jp/~yachiyo/oideyasu-e .html; Hukuchi-chō; r with 2 meals from ¥18,000; 5min walk from Tōzai subway line, Keage Station

Just down the street from Nanzen-ji, this ryokan is at home with foreigners. Rooms are spacious and clean, and some look out over private gardens. English-speaking staff are available.

Cheap Sleeps

HIGASHIYAMA YOUTH HOSTEL
Map pp225-7 *Youth Hostel*

☎ 761 8135; fax 761 8138; Sanjō-dōri Shirakawa-bashi; dm ¥2650; 3min walk from Higashiyama-Sanjō bus stop, bus 5

This spiffy hostel is an excellent base for the sights in eastern Kyoto. Unfortunately, it's also rather regimented and certainly not a good spot to stay if you want some nightlife (there is a 10.30pm curfew). You can walk here from the Sanjō Keihan area. Bicycle rental is available.

NORTHEAST KYOTO

The northeast is another excellent area in which to be based. It's much quieter than downtown and some of the places listed in this section are still fairly close to the main sightseeing areas. The more northern of the options listed here are a little inconvenient in terms of location, but a good choice if you want proximity to greenery and mountains.

HOLIDAY INN KYOTO Map pp219-21 *Hotel*
☎ 721 3131; onetoone@hi-kyoto.co.jp; Nishihiraki-chō Takano; s/d/tw ¥9,000/12,000/17,000; 5min walk from Takanobashi-Higashizume bus stop, Kyoto bus 17
Although a little far from the city centre, the Holiday Inn gets favourable reviews for its large rooms and swimming pool.

THREE SISTERS INN MAIN BUILDING
Map pp219-21 *Ryokan*
Rakutō-sō; ☎ 761 6336; fax 761 6338; Kasugakita-dōri-Okazaki; s/d/tr from ¥8900/13,000/19,500; 5min walk from Kumanojinja-mae bus stop, bus 206
Perfectly situated for exploration of eastern Kyoto, this long-time favourite of foreign travellers is a good choice for those who want to try a ryokan without any language difficulties.

Cheap Sleeps
CASA CARINHO B&B Map pp219-21 *B&B*
www.gotokandk.com; Jōdō-ji Nishida-chō; B&B per person ¥5000; 10min walk from Ginkakuji-michi bus stop, or bus 5 from Kyoto Station
This is a great B&B. Located close to Ginkaku-ji, this large traditional home has three Japanese-style rooms, and is run by a charming family with a wealth of inside information on Kyoto. Reservation is via email only.

GREENPEACE INN KYOTO
Map pp219-21 *Guesthouse*
☎ /fax 791 9890; Kitayama-dōri-Shimogamohon; dm 3 nights/week/month ¥4800/9800/26,000, s ¥7200/15,000/42,000, d ¥9000/18,000/46,000; 3min walk from Karasuma subway line, Matsugasaki Station
This archetypal *gaijin* house is popular with foreigners setting themselves up to live in Kyoto. It might do for a short stay, after which you'll definitely want something better and quieter. There is a common kitchen and laundry facilities. The minimum stay is three nights.

I.S.E. DORM Map pp219-21 *Guesthouse*
☎ /fax 771 0566; www.niwashi.net/kyotoinfo/ise-dorm/; Higashi-Fukunokawa-chō; r per day ¥2800, per month ¥20,000-56,000; 10min walk from Kumanojinja-mae bus stop, bus 206
Somewhere between a guesthouse and a *gaijin* house, the I.S.E. is an acceptable long-term option and a good place to stay while looking for greener pastures. Rooms can be noisy and run down but there is usually a room available and arrangements for a stay can be made very quickly. Facilities include phone, fridge, shower and washing machine. The office is down a narrow alley, so ask for directions once you get into the general area.

YONBANCHI Map pp219-21 *B&B*
yonbanchi@mac.com; 4, Shinnyō-chō; B&B per person ¥5000; 10min walk from Kinrin Shako-mae, bus 5
Yonbanchi is a charming B&B in a private house with an excellent location for sightseeing in the Ginkaku-ji and Yoshida-yama area. There are two rooms, one of which overlooks a small Japanese garden and can accommodate up to three people. The house is a late Edo–period samurai house just outside the main gate of Shinnyo-dō, a temple famed for its maple leaves and cherry blossoms. There is a private entrance and no curfew. Reservation is via email only.

NORTHWEST KYOTO

There are several accommodation options in northwest Kyoto. It's something of a nondescript area but has some greenery and attractions to recommend it. It's well connected by buses, so it's still within striking distance of downtown and the east side of the city.

RYOKAN RAKUCHŌ Map pp216-18 *Ryokan*
☎ 721 2174; www003.upp.so-net.ne.jp/rakucho-ryokan/indx.html; Higashi hangi chō-Shimogamo; s/tw/tr from ¥5300/8400/12,600; 7min walk from Karasuma subway line, Kitaōji Station
This is a friendly little ryokan in the northern part of the city.

Cheap Sleeps
AOI-SŌ INN Map pp216-18 *Guesthouse*
☎ /fax 431 0788; www5.ocn.ne.jp/~aoisoinn/; Karasuma-Shimei-dōri; per person from ¥2800; 5min walk from Karasuma subway line, Kuramaguchi Station, exit 2
This is a tightly packed warren of rooms built around a small garden. It's cheap and decent

value for the price. The inn is a five-minute walk northwest of Kuramaguchi Station.

KITAYAMA YOUTH HOSTEL
Map pp216-18   *Youth Hostel*

☎ /fax 492 5345; www.jyh.or.jp/english/kinki/kita yama/index.html; Koetsuji-hotori; dm ¥2940; 5min walk from Genkō-an-mae bus stop, bus 6

This hostel is a superb place from which to visit the rural Takagamine area with its fine, secluded temples such as Kōetsu-ji, Jōshō-ji and Shōden-ji. To get here from the bus stop, walk west past a school, turn right and continue up the hill to the hostel (it's a five-minute walk).

MYŌREN-JI Map pp216-18   *Shukubō*

☎ 451 3527; fax 451 3597; Teranouchi Ōmiya Higashi-iru; per person ¥3800; 5min walk from Horikawa-Teranouchi bus stop, bus 9

This pleasant temple is used to dealing with foreign guests. It's right in the heart of the Nishijin area, for those with an interest in Kyoto textiles and *machiya* (traditional townhouses).

TAKAYA Map pp216-18   *Guesthouse*

☎ /fax 431 5213; Muromachi-Ichijō agaru; r per day/month ¥3000/50,000; 5min walk from Karasuma subway line, Imadegawa Station

Near the Imperial Palace, this pleasant little *gaijin* house is usually full with long-termers but you might find a bed when someone's just moved out.

TANI HOUSE Map pp216-18   *Guesthouse*

☎ 492 5489; www.kansaiconnect.com/members/ tani/index.htm; Daitokuji Murasakino; dm ¥1800, d ¥4200-4600; 5min walk from Kenkunjinja-mae bus stop, bus 206

This place is an old favourite for both short-term and long-term visitors on a tight budget. There is a certain charm to this fine old house with its warren of rooms and quiet location next to Daitoku-ji. You might have to ask at the police box near the temple for directions once you get into the area.

UTANO YOUTH HOSTEL
Map pp214-15   *Youth Hostel*

☎ 462 2288; web.kyoto-inet.or.jp/org/utano-yh/; Nakayama-chō; dm ¥2800; 1min walk from Yūsu-Hosuteru-mae bus stop, bus 26

The best hostel in Kyoto, Utano is friendly, well organised and makes a convenient base for the sights of northwestern Kyoto. There's a meeting room with bilingual TV news, but for many travellers, fond memories are reserved for the heated toilet seats! If you want to skip the hostel food, turn left along the main road to find several coffee shops offering cheap *teishoku* (set meals). There is a 10pm curfew.

SOUTHWEST KYOTO
The southwest of the city has lots of reasonable places to stay. It's not Kyoto's most lovely area, but is well serviced by transport connections, so you're never far from the rest of the city.

HIIRAGIYA RYOKAN ANNEXE
Map pp222-4   *Ryokan*

☎ 231 0151; fax 231 0153; Gokomachi-dōri-Nijō kudaru; per person with 2 meals from ¥15,000; 10min walk from Karasuma-Oike Station

Close to the Hiiragiya Ryokan (p139), the annexe also offers top-notch ryokan service and surroundings at slightly more affordable rates.

HIROTA GUEST HOUSE
Map pp222-4   *Guesthouse*

☎ 221 2474; h-hirota@msi.biglobe.ne.jp; Tominokōji nishi-Nijō-dōri; r per person from ¥5500, ste/cottage per person ¥7000/9000; 10min walk from Tōzai subway line, Kyoto-Shiyakusho-mae Station

Unassuming from the outside, the popular Hirota is a pleasant Japanese-style inn in an old sake brewery. Its cheerful English-speaking owner, Hirota-san, is a former tour guide and a valuable source of information.

INTERNATIONAL HOTEL KYOTO
Map pp222-4   *Hotel*

☎ 222 1111; information@kyoto-kokusai.com; Nijōjō-mae-Horikawa-dōri; s/tw/d from ¥8085/16,170/18,480; 3min walk from Tōzai subway line, Nijōjō-mae Station

Directly across from Nijō-jō, this is a slightly less appealing choice than the nearby Kyoto ANA Hotel. It's a large facility that is used to foreign guests.

KARASUMA KYOTO HOTEL
Map pp222-4   *Hotel*

☎ 371 0111; www.kyotohotel.co.jp/karasuma/ index_e.html; Karasuma-dōri-Shijō; s/tw/d ¥8800/16,000/20,000; 5min walk from Karasuma subway line, Shijō Station

The Karasuma Kyoto Hotel is one of the better hotels in this class. The rooms are in good condition, the staff is friendly and the location is convenient to downtown.

Kinmata Ryokan (p140)

KYOTO ANA HOTEL Map pp222-4   *Hotel*
☎ 231 1155; www.anahotels.com/eng/hotels/uky/index.html; Nijōjō-mae-Horikawa-dōri; s/tw/d from ¥13,000/16,000/19,000; 3min walk from Tōzai subway line, Nijōjō-mae Station

Just opposite Nijō-jō, this attractive hotel is a decent choice for its on-site facilities (pool, restaurants, shopping etc).

KYOTO TŌKYŪ HOTEL
Map pp222-4   *Hotel*

☎ 341 2411; www.tokyuhotels.co.jp/en/index.html; Horikawa-dōri-Gojō kudaru; s/d/tw from ¥18,480/28,875/30,030; 15min walk from Kyoto Station

This is a big, modern hotel with large rooms and good facilities. It's on the south side of town, but within walking distance of Kyoto Station. There are several good on-site restaurants for those times when you don't want to eat out.

RYOKAN HINOMOTO
Map pp222-4   *Ryokan*

☎ 351 4563; fax 351 3932; Matsubara agaru-Kawara-machi-dōri; s/d from ¥4000/7500; 1min walk from Kawaramachi-Matsubara bus stop, bus 17 or 205

This small, simple place is a favourite with many frequent visitors to Kyoto. It's located near the centre of the city's nightlife action.

Cheap Sleeps
CROSSROADS INN
Map pp222-4   *Guesthouse*
www.rose.sannet.ne.jp/c-inn/; Ebisu Banba-chō, Shimogyō-ku; per person from ¥4000; 20min walk from Kyoto Station

This is a charming little guesthouse with clean, well-maintained rooms and a friendly owner. It's a little hard to find: turn north off Shichijō-dōri just west of the Umekōji-kōen-mae bus stop across from the Daily Yamazaki convenience store. Reservations are by email only.

J. HOPPERS KYOTO
Map pp222-4   *Guesthouse*
☎ /fax 681 2282; www.j-hoppers.com/index.htm; Nakagoryo-chō, Higashikujō; dm ¥2500, r ¥3000-3500; 8min walk from Kyoto Station

Located on the southern side of Kyoto Station, J. Hoppers is a popular guesthouse with a variety of private rooms and dorms. Internet access is available. It's quite close to southern attractions such as Tōfuku-ji and Fushimi.

SHŌHŌ-IN Map pp222-4   *Shukubō*
☎ /fax 811 7768; Ōmiya Matsubara; per person ¥4725 with breakfast; 5min walk from Ōmiya-Matsubara bus stop, bus 6 or 206

If you want a break from the usual hotel/ryokan experience, try this *shukubō*, which offers clean rooms and a decent location. The temple also offers lessons in Japanese calligraphy. To inquire in English, call Ms Katō (☎ 090-3947 4520).

UNO HOUSE Map pp222-4 *Guesthouse*
☎ 231 7763; fax 256 0140; Shinkarasuma-dōri; dm/r ¥1650/7500, s from ¥2250; 10min walk from Karasuma subway line, Marutamachi Station
Uno House is a long-running guesthouse that has served as many ex-pats' first stop in the city. There's a big dorm room and a cramped warren of private rooms. It's quite basic but it's cheap and there is none of that youth hostel regimentation.

ARASHIYAMA & SAGANO AREA
Nestled at the base of the western mountains, the Arashiyama-Sagano area is one of Kyoto's most important sightseeing areas. It's quite scenic, with lots of bamboo groves and temples. However, it's something of a hike to the rest of town, so we only recommend staying here if you either want to concentrate your sightseeing in the west of town, or if you don't mind spending a fair bit of time on trains or buses.

ARASHIYAMA BENKEI RYOKAN
Map p232   *Ryokan*
☎ 872 3355; www.benkei.biz/english.html; Susuki-nobaba-chō-Tenryūji; per person with 2 meals from ¥20,000; 15min walk from Keifuku Arashiyama line, Keifuku Arashiyama Station
This elegant ryokan has a pleasant riverside location and serves wonderful *kaiseki* cuisine.

HOTEL RAN-TEI Map p232 *Hotel*
☎ 371 1119; hotelrantei@kyoto-centuryhotel.co.jp; Susukinobaba-chō-Tenryūji; per person ¥18,000-24,000; 10min walk from Keifuku Arashiyama line, Keifuku Arashiyama Station
The excellent Ran-tei has spacious gardens and both Japanese- and Western-style rooms.

MINSHUKU ARASHIYAMA
Map p232   *Minshuku*
☎ /fax 861 4398; info@arasiyama.net; Saga Kitahori-chō; per person without/with 2 meals ¥4500/7000; 5min walk from Keifuku Arashiyama line, Sagaeki-mae Station
This little *minshuku* (Japanese B&B) is great for its convenient location and pleasant rooms.

RANKYŌ-KAN RYOKAN
Map p232   *Ryokan*
☎ 871 0001; yoyaku@rankyokan.com; Arashiyama Togetsukyō South; per person with 2 meals from ¥18,000; 7min walk from Keifuku Arashiyama line, Keifuku Arashiyama Station
Sitting in a secluded area on the south bank of the Oi-gawa in Arashiyama, this is a classic Japanese-style inn that boasts manicured gardens, hot-spring baths and river views from most rooms. Walk five minutes up the riverside path or, better still, call ahead and be chauffeured by private boat from the Togetsu-kyō Bridge!

ROKUŌ-IN
Map p232   *Women-Only Shukubō*
☎ /fax 861 1645; Sanjō hitosuji kita; per person with breakfast ¥4500; 3min walk from Keifuku Arashiyama line, Rokuōin Station
Close to Arashiyama, this is one of the few women-only *shukubō* in town.

KYOTO OUTSKIRTS
There are lots of interesting accommodation options spread around the outskirts of Kyoto, including two of the city's youth hostels. If you don't mind a daily commute to the sightseeing areas, you may find these places a good choice.

Ōhara
If you want to experience something of rural Japan yet still be within an hour's bus ride to Kyoto, the quaint little village of Ōhara is an interesting and pleasant choice.

ŌHARA SANSŌ Map p233 *Ryokan*
☎ 744 2227; www.ohara-sansou.com/english/index .htm; Kusao-chō-Ōhara; per person with 2 meals ¥9500; 13min walk from Ōhara bus stop, Kyoto bus 17 or 18
A pleasant inn, Ōhara Sansō has a soothing outdoor bath. It's just before Jakkō-in; look for the large *tanuki* (racoon dog) figure out the front.

RYOSŌ CHADANI Map p233 *Ryokan*
☎ 744 2952; info@r-chatani.com; Kusao-chō-Ōhara; per person with meals ¥6825; 5min walk from Ōhara bus stop, Kyoto bus 17 or 18
Not far from the Ōhara bus stop, Ryosō Chadani is part of the Welcome Inn Group. Look for the large stones out front.

SERYŌ RYOKAN Map p233 *Ryokan*
☎ 744 2301; www.seryo.co.jp/english.htm; Ōhara Sanzen-in hotori; per person with 2 meals ¥13,000-20,000; 10min walk from Ōhara bus stop, Kyoto bus 17 or 18

A stone's throw from Sanzen-in, this would be a good spot to stay for those who really want to linger over the temples of Ōhara. The friendly owner speaks some English.

Kibune

Like Ōhara, Kibune is something of a getaway from Kyoto proper. There are several ryokan located along the banks of the Kibune-gawa, most of which offer dining on platforms suspended above the river in summer.

HIROYA RYOKAN Map p233 *Ryokan*
☎ 741 2401; hiroya-goroh@kyoto.zaq.ne; Kibune jinjya hotori; per person ¥30,000-40,000; 30min walk from Eizan Kibune-guchi Station, free shuttle-bus service

This is a pleasant ryokan famous for its food. In winter it serves either a *kaiseki* or *botan-nabe* (wild boar cooked in an iron pot) dinner, while in summer the fare is *kawa-doko-ryōri* (river-top dining).

KIBUNE FUJIYA Map p233 *Ryokan*
☎ 741 2501; fujiya@kibune.or.jp; Kibune jinjya torii-mae; per person with meals from ¥20,000; 30min walk from Eizan Kibune-guchi Station, free shuttle-bus service

This is another nice ryokan with a lovely riverside location.

RYOKAN UGENTA Map p233 *Ryokan*
☎ 741 2146; www.kyoto.zaq.ne.jp/ugenta_e/index.html; Kibune chō-Kurama; per person with 2 meals from ¥20,000; 30min walk from Eizan Kibune-guchi Station, free shuttle-bus service

The Ugenta is an attractive old inn with a wonderful stone bath tub.

ITAMI AIRPORT
HOTEL CREVETTE *Hotel*
☎ 06-6843 7201; fax 6843 0043; Kuko Ikeda; s/tw/d from ¥6500/12,000/15,000; 10min walk from Itami Airport South Terminal

This is the best deal near Itami. Prices are discounted if you reserve through the main tourist information counter at the airport. The helpful folks at the information counter can also arrange for the hotel's shuttle bus to come and pick you up.

KANSAI INTERNATIONAL AIRPORT
HOTEL NIKKŌ KANSAI AIRPORT *Hotel*
☎ 0724-55 1111; www.nikkokix.com/; Senshu-kuko Kita; s/tw/d from ¥11,550/16,170/17,325; 5min walk from international arrivals hall

The only hotel at the airport is the expensive Hotel Nikkō Kansai Airport. The rooms here are in excellent condition and are comfortable enough for brief stays. You should definitely ask for a discount or promotional rate outside peak travel times.

Excursions

Excursions

While Kyoto has enough wonders to keep you busy for weeks, it's worth heading out of the city at least once to sample some of Kansai's other attractions, most of which are less than an hour's train ride away. Nara – Japan's first permanent capital – boasts a collection of temples to rival Kyoto's, including Tōdai-ji with its enormous Daibutsu (Great Buddha), and Hōryū-ji which houses some of the country's most important Buddhist treasures. Down-to-earth Osaka, Japan's second city, is a great place to see modern Japan without traipsing all the way to Tokyo. Kōbe, the nation's version of San Francisco, is a pleasant city with great cafés and restaurants. Smaller destinations include Himeji, home of Japan's finest surviving castle, and Miyama-chō, northern Kyoto's rustic hinterland filled with quaint villages and thatched-roof houses.

NARA
☎ 0742

As a repository of Japan's cultural legacy, Nara is second only to Kyoto. Japan's capital from 710 to 785, Nara is the number two tourist attraction in Kansai after Kyoto. It's uninspiring at first glance, but careful inspection of Nara will reveal the rich history and hidden beauty of the city. Indeed, the city has eight Unesco World Heritage sites.

NARA-KŌEN AREA

Nara's most important sights are located in Nara-kōen, a sprawling park that covers much of the east side of the city. Created from wasteland in 1880, the park covers a large area at the foot of Wakakusa-yama. The JNTO's leaflet *Walking Tour Courses in Nara* (also available at the Kyoto TIC, see p192) includes a map for this area. Although walking time is estimated at two hours, you'll need at least half a day to see a selection of the sights and a full day to see the lot.

Daibutsu-den (p151)

Excursions – Nara

NARA

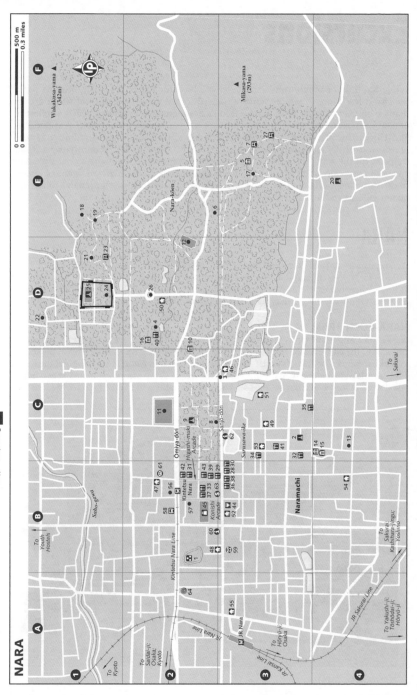

0   500 m
0   0.3 miles

Wakakusa-yama
(342m)

Mikasa-yama
(293m)

Nara-kōen

Sabu-gawa

To
Youth
Hostels

To Kyoto

To
Saidai-ji;
Osaka,
Kyoto

Kintetsu Nara Line

To
Hōryū-ji;
Osaka

JR Nara Line

JR Nara

JR Kansai Line

JR Sakurai Line

To Yakushi-ji;
Tōshōdai-ji;
Hōryū-ji

To
Sakurai;
Kashihara-jingū;
Yoshino

Naramachi

To Sakurai

Ōmiya-dōri

Higashi-muki
Arcade

Kintetsu
Nara

Konishi
Arcade

Sanjō-dōri

Sarusawa-ike

The park is home to about 1200 deer, which in old times were considered to be messengers of the gods and today enjoy the status of national treasures. They roam the park and surrounding areas in search of hand-outs from tourists. You can buy special biscuits (*shika-sembei*, ¥150) from vendors to feed the deer (don't eat them yourself, as we saw one misguided foreign tourist doing).

Nara's main attraction – and a must-see for any visitor to the city – is **Tōdai-ji**, a huge temple complex on the north side of Nara-kōen. On your way to the temple you'll pass through the **Nandai-mon**, which contains two fierce-looking Niō guardians. These recently restored wooden images, carved in the 13th century by the sculptor Unkei, are some of the finest wooden statues in all of Japan, if not the world. These truly dramatic works of art seem ready to spring to life at any moment.

Tōdai-ji's **Daibutsu-den** (Hall of the Great Buddha) is the largest wooden building in the world. Unbelievably, the present structure, rebuilt in 1709, is a mere two-thirds of the size of the original! The *daibutsu* (Great Buddha) contained within is one of the largest bronze figures in the world and was originally cast in 746. The present statue, recast in the Edo period, stands just over 16m high and consists of 437 tonnes of bronze and 130kg of gold.

As you circle the statue towards the back of the Buddha, you'll see a wooden column with a hole through its base. Popular belief maintains that those who can squeeze through the hole, which is exactly the same size as one of the Great Buddha's nostrils, are ensured of enlightenment. It's fun to watch the kids wiggle through nimbly and the adults get wedged in like champagne corks. A hint for determined adults: it's a lot easier to go through with both arms held above your head.

Walk east from the entrance to Daibutsu-den, climb a flight of stone steps, and continue to your left to reach the following two halls. **Nigatsu-dō Hall** is famed for its **Omizutori Festival** (p154) and a splendid view across Nara that makes the climb worthwhile – particularly at dusk. A short walk south of Nigatsu-dō is **Sangatsu-dō Hall**, which is the oldest building in the Tōdai-ji complex. This hall contains a small collection of fine statues from the Nara period.

About 15 minute's walk roughly south of Sangatsu-dō is **Kasuga-taisha**, Nara's most important shrine. It was founded in the 8th century by the Fujiwara family and was completely rebuilt every 20 years according to Shintō tradition, until the end of the 19th century. It lies at the foot of the hill in a pleasant wooded setting with herds of sacred deer awaiting hand-outs.

Transport

Unless you have a Japan Rail Pass, the best option is the Kintetsu line (sometimes written in English as the Kinki Nippon railway), which links Kyoto (Kintetsu Kyoto Station) and Nara (Kintetsu Nara Station). There are direct limited express trains (¥1110, 35 minutes) and ordinary express trains (¥610, 45 minutes; may require a change at Saidai-ji). Kintetsu Kyoto Station is on the southwest corner of the main Kyoto Station building; go to the south side of the station – the *shinkansen* (bullet train) side – and follow the signs.

The JR Nara line also connects Kyoto Station with JR Nara Station. Your best bet is a *kaisoku* (rapid train; ¥690, 46 minutes), but departures are often few and far between.

Most of the area around Nara-kōen is covered by two circular bus routes. Bus 1 runs counter-clockwise and bus 2 runs clockwise. There's a ¥180 flat fare. You can easily see the main sights in the park on foot and use the bus as an option if you are pressed for time or tired.

Bicycles are a good way to get around Nara. **Kintetsu Sunflower Rent-a-Cycle** (☎ 24 3528) is close to the Nara City Tourist Center. Weekday rates are ¥300 per hour and ¥900 per day; weekend rates are ¥350 per hour and ¥1000 per day.

Southwest Temples Transport

Three of Nara's most important temples, Hōryū-ji, Yakushi-ji and Tōshōdai-ji, are located well outside the city centre, and are best visited by bus or train from the city. To get to the Hōryū-ji, take the JR Kansai line from JR Nara Station to Hōryū-ji Station (¥210, 10 minutes). From there, a bus service shuttles the short distance between the station and Hōryū-ji (bus 73, ¥170, five minutes) or you can walk there in 20 minutes. Alternatively, take bus 52, 60, 97 or 98 from either JR Nara Station or Kintetsu Nara Station and get off at the Hōryūji-mae stop (¥760, 50 minutes). From Hōryū-ji you continue by bus 52, 97 or 98 (¥560, 30 minutes) up to Yakushi-ji and Tōshōdai-ji, which are a 10-minute walk apart.

The approaches to the shrine are lined with hundreds of lanterns and there are many more hundreds in the shrine itself. The lantern festivals held twice a year at the shrine are a major attraction as are other festivals held at the nearby Wakamiya-jinja (Map pp150-1).

The Hōmotsu-den (Treasure Hall) is just north of the torii (entrance gate) for the shrine. The hall displays Shintō regalia and equipment used in *bugaku*, nō and *gagaku* performances.

Nara's most splendid garden, Isui-en, is a short walk north of Tōdai-ji. The garden dates from the Meiji era and is beautifully laid out with abundant greenery and a pond filled with ornamental carp. It's without a doubt the best garden in the city and is well worth a visit. For ¥450 you can enjoy a cup of tea on tatami mats overlooking the garden or have lunch in the adjoining Sanshūtei restaurant (p154), which also shares the view. Next to Isui-en is the Neiraku Art Museum, which displays Chinese and Korean ceramics and bronzes.

Walking to or from Nara-kōen, you can't miss the soaring main pagoda of Kōfuku-ji, which was transferred here from Kyoto in 710 as the main temple for the Fujiwara family. Although the original temple complex had 175 buildings, fires and destruction through power struggles have left only a dozen still standing. There are actually two pagodas, a three-storey one and a five-storey one, dating from 1143 and 1426, respectively. The taller of the two pagodas is the second tallest in Japan, outclassed by the one at Kyoto's Tō-ji by only a few centimetres. The National Treasure Hall (Kokuhō-kan) contains a variety of statues and art objects salvaged from previous structures.

Just east of Kōfuku-ji, you'll find the Nara National Museum, which is divided into two main galleries linked by an underground passage. The western gallery exhibits archaeological finds and the eastern gallery has displays of sculptures, paintings and calligraphy. A special exhibition is held in May and the contents of the Shōsō-in hall, which holds the treasures of Tōdai-ji, are displayed here from around 21 October to 8 November (call the tourist centre to check as these dates vary slightly each year). The exhibits include priceless items from the cultures along the Silk Road.

NARAMACHI AREA

South of Sanjō-dōri and Sarusawa-ike pond you will find the pleasant neighbourhood of Naramachi, with many well-preserved *machiya* (traditional townhouses). It's a nice place for a stroll before or after hitting the big sights of Nara-kōen and there are several good restaurants in the area to entice hungry travellers (see p155).

Highlights of Naramachi include the **Naramachi Shiryō-kan Museum**, which has a decent collection of bric-a-brac from the area, including a display of old Japanese coins and bills. A good place to check out a *machiya* is the **Naramachi Koushi-no-le**. Also in Naramachi is the interesting **Naramachi Monogatari-kan**, a small art gallery with changing displays built inside a fine old *machiya*.

TEMPLES SOUTHWEST OF NARA CITY

There are several **temples** located southwest of Nara, the most important of which are Hōryū-ji, Yakushi-ji and Tōshōdai-ji. These three can be visited in one afternoon. For transport details, see opposite.

Hōryū-ji was founded in 607 by Prince Shōtoku, considered by many to be the patron saint of Japanese Buddhism. Hōryū-ji is a veritable shrine to Shōtoku and is renowned not only as the oldest temple in Japan, but also as a repository for some of the country's rarest treasures. Several of the temple's wooden buildings have survived earthquakes and fires to become the oldest of their kind in the world. The layout of the temple is divided into two parts, **Sai-in** (West Temple) and **Tō-in** (East Temple).

The entrance ticket allows admission to the Sai-in, Tō-in and Great Treasure Hall. A detailed map is provided and a guidebook is available in English and several other languages. The JNTO leaflet *Walking Tour Courses in Nara* includes a basic map for the area around Hōryū-ji.

The main approach to the temple proceeds from the south along a tree-lined avenue and continues through the Nandai-mon and Chū-mon, the temple's two main gates, before entering the Sai-in precinct. As you enter the Sai-in, you'll see the **Hondō** (Main Hall) on your right, and a pagoda on your left. On the eastern side of the Sai-in are the two concrete buildings of the **Daihōzō-den** (Great Treasure Hall), containing numerous treasures from Hōryū-ji's long history. If you leave this hall and continue east through the Tōdai-mon you reach the Tō-in. The **Yumedono** (Hall of Dreams) in this temple is where Prince Shōtoku is believed to have meditated and been given help with problem sutras by a kindly, golden apparition.

Yakushi-ji was established by Emperor Tenmu in 680. With the exception of the **East Pagoda**, which dates to 730, the present buildings either date from the 13th century or are very recent reconstructions. The main hall was rebuilt in 1976 and houses several images, including the famous Yakushi Triad (the Buddha Yakushi flanked by the Bodhisattvas of the sun and moon), dating from the 8th century. Behind the East Pagoda is the **Tōin-dō** (East Hall), which houses the famous Shō-Kannon image, dating from the 7th century.

Tōshōdai-ji was established in 759 by the Chinese priest Ganjin (Jian Zhen), who had been recruited by Emperor Shōmu to reform Buddhism in Japan. Ganjin didn't have much luck with his travel arrangements from China to Japan: five attempts were thwarted by shipwreck, storms and bureaucracy. Despite being blinded by eye disease, he finally made it on the sixth attempt and spread his teachings to Japan. The lacquer sculpture in the **Miei-dō** hall is a moving tribute to Ganjin: blind and rock steady. It is shown only once a year on 6 June – the anniversary of Ganjin's death.

If you're not lucky enough to be in Nara on that day, it's still well worth visiting this temple to see the fantastic trinity of Buddhas in the **Hondō** hall of the temple. The centrepiece is a seated image of Rushana Buddha, which is flanked by two standing Buddha images, Yakushi-Nyorai and Senjū-Kannon.

Tōshōdai-ji is a 10-minute walk north of Yakushi-ji's north gate.

Orientation

Nara's two main train stations, JR Nara Station and Kintetsu Nara Station, are roughly in the middle of the city and Nara-kōen, which contains most of the important sights, is on the east side against the bare flank of Wakakusa-yama. Most of the other sights are southwest of the city and are best reached by buses that leave from both train stations (or by train in the case of Hōryū-ji). It's easy to cover the city centre and the major attractions in nearby Nara-kōen on foot, though some may prefer to rent a bicycle (see opposite).

Information

The best source of information is the **Nara City Tourist Center** (☎ 22 3900; Sanjō-dōri; ☯ 9am-9pm). It's only a short walk from JR Nara or Kintetsu Nara Stations.

The tourist centre can put you in touch with volunteer guides who speak English and other languages, but you will have to book in advance. Two of these services are the **YMCA Goodwill Guides** (☎ 45 5920, 22 5595) and **Nara Student Guides** (☎ 26 4753). Remember that the guides are volunteers so you should offer to cover the day's expenses for your guide (although most temple and museum admissions are waived for registered guides).

There are three additional tourist information offices located in Nara:

JR Nara Station office (☎ 22 9821; ☯ 9am-5pm) May be able to help you with ryokan and *minshuku* (inn) reservations.

Kintetsu Nara Station office (☎ 24 4858; ☯ 9am-5pm)

Sarusawa Tourist Information Office (☎ 26 1991; ☯ 9am-5pm; Sanjō-dōri)

While you're at any of the tourist offices, pick up a copy of their useful *Welcome to Nara: Sightseeing Map*.

There is an ATM that accepts international cards on the ground floor of the building opposite Kintetsu Nara Station. In the same building you can purchase tickets for highway buses (to Tokyo etc), airport buses (to Kansai airport) and tour buses (around Nara and surrounding areas).

There is an international telephone located on Sanjō-dōri, in front of the NTT building. For Internet access, try **Hotel Asyl Nara's Suien Tea Lounge** (per 2hrs ¥525; ☯ 7.30am-11pm).

Sights

Hōryū-ji (☎ 75 2555; 1-1 Hōryūji-sannai, Ikaruga-chō; admission ¥1000; ☯ 8am-4.30pm 22 Feb–3 Nov, 8am-4pm 4 Nov–21 Feb)

Isui-en (☎ 22 2173; 74 Suimon-chō; admission incl Neiraku Art Museum ¥600; ☯ 9.30am-4pm, closed Tue)

Kasuga-taisha (☎ 22 7788; 160 Kasugano-chō; admission free; ☯ 6am-6pm)

Kasuga-taisha Hōmotsu-den (Treasure Hall; ☎ 22 7788; 160 Kasugano-chō; admission ¥420; ☯ 9am-4.30pm)

Kōfuku-ji (☎ 22 7755; 48 Noborioji-chō; admission grounds/National Treasure Hall free/¥500; ☯ grounds dawn-dusk, National Treasure Hall 9am-4.30pm)

Nara National Museum (☎ 22 7771; 50 Noborioji-chō; general admission/special exhibits ¥420/830; ☯ 9am-4.30pm)

Naramachi Koushi-no-Ie (☎ 22 4820; 44 Gangōji-chō; admission free; ☯ 9am-5pm, closed Mon)

Naramachi Shiryō-kan Museum (☎ 22 5509; 14 Nishi-shinya-chō; admission free; ☯ 10am-4pm, closed Mon)

Neiraku Art Museum (☎ 22 2173; 74 Suimon-chō; admission incl Isui-en ¥600; ☯ 9.30am-4pm, closed Tue)

Shōsō-in Treasure Repository (☎ 26 2811; 129 Zōshi-chō; admission free; ☯ bldg during special exhibitions, grounds 10am-3pm, closed Sat, Sun & public holidays)

Tōdai-ji (☎ 22 5511; 406-1 Zōshi-chō; Daibutsu-den ¥500, Kaidan-in ¥500, Sangatsu-dō ¥500; ☯ 8am-4.30pm Nov-Feb, 8am-5pm Mar, 7.30am-5.30pm Apr-Sep, 7.30am-5pm Oct)

Tōdai-ji Nigatsu-dō (☎ 22 5511; 406-1 Zōshi-chō; ☯ 8am-4.30pm Nov-Feb, 8am-5pm Mar, 7.30am-5.30pm Apr-Sep, 7.30am-5pm Oct)

Tōshōdai-ji (☎ 33 7900; 13-46 Gojō-chō; admission ¥600; ☯ 8.30am-4.30pm)

Yakushi-ji (☎ 33 6001; 457 Nishinokyō-chō; admission ¥500; ☯ 8.30am-5pm)

Festivals & Events

Nara has plenty of festivals throughout the year. The following is a brief list of the more interesting ones. More extensive information is readily available from Nara tourist offices (see left) or from the TIC in Kyoto (p192).

Yamayaki (Grass Burning Festival; 15 Jan) To commemorate a feud many centuries ago between the monks of Tōdai-ji and Kōfuku-ji, Wakakusa-yama is set alight at 6pm with an accompanying display of fireworks.

Mantōrō (Lantern Festival; 2-4 Feb) Held at Kasuga-taisha at 6pm, this festival is renowned for its illumination with 3000 stone and bronze lanterns.

Omizutori (Water-drawing Ceremony; 1-14 Mar) The monks of Tōdai-ji enter a special period of initiation during these days. On the evening of 12 March, they parade enormous flaming torches around the balcony of Nigatsu-dō (in the temple grounds) and embers rain down on the spectators to purify them. The water-drawing ceremony is performed after midnight.

Mantōrō (Lantern Festival; 14-15 Aug) The same as the February festival.

Eating & Drinking

Ayura Café (☎ 26 5339; 28 Hashimoto-chō) We highly recommend this tiny café for its wonderful (mostly vegie) set lunch or just a quick cuppa.

Beni-e (☎ 22 9493; 1-4 Higashimukiminami-machi; lunch/dinner from ¥1500/2000) One of our favourites in Nara, Beni-e serves good tempura sets for ¥1500/2000/2500 (*hana*, *tsuki* and *yuki* sets, respectively). It's located a little back from the street, behind a shoe shop.

Drink Drank (☎ 27 6206; 8 Hashimoto-chō) For a sandwich, light lunch or just a fruit juice, try this intimate little café.

Fluke Café (☎ 23 8981; 10 Higashimukinaka-machi) One of Nara's newest and hippest cafés.

Harishin (☎ 22 2669; 15 Nakanoshinya-chō) Harishin is one of Nara's most elegant *kaiseki* (Japanese *haute cuisine*) restaurants.

Hiranoya (☎ 26 3918; 1-6 Konishi-chō; *okonomiyaki* from ¥680) A good spot to try *okonomiyaki* (Japanese-style pizza or pancake).

Hirasō (☎ 22 0866; 30-1 Imamikado-chō; lunch & dinner from ¥3000) This Naramachi restaurant does elegant *kaiseki* sets for that special night out.

Kosode (☎ 27 2582) A charming tea room-cum-gallery in Naramachi, which makes the perfect break while strolling the area.

Kyōsho-An (☎ 27 7715; 26-3 Hashimoto-chō) An up-stairs tea shop where you can enjoy green tea and a whole range of Japanese sweets.

Mellow Café (☎ 27 9099; 1-8 Konishi-chō) Located down a narrow alley, this open-plan café usually displays their daily lunch special for all to see.

Miyoshino (☎ 22 5239; 27 Hashimoto-chō; lunch & din-ner from ¥650) A simple place that does good-value sets of typical Japanese fare. Stop by and check the daily lunch specials on display outside.

Okaru (☎ 24 3686; 13-2 Higashimukiminami-machi; *okonomiyaki* from ¥680) A casual spot to enjoy tasty *okonomiyaki*. Look for the food models in the window.

Rumours (☎ 26 4327; 9 Tsunofuri-chō) An English-style pub that's a decent spot for a few evening drinks, and a good spot to meet local residents and other travellers.

Sanshūtei (☎ 22 2173; 74 Suimon-chō; lunch from ¥1200; ⏰ 11.30am-2pm, closed Tue) Located alongside Isui-en, Sanshūtei serves *tororo,* a traditional dish made from grated yam, barley and rice. Guests sit on tatami mats enjoying the food while gazing out over the splendour of the garden. Ordering is simple due to the choice of either the *mugitoro gozen* (without eel) for ¥1200 or the *unatoro gozen* (with eel) for ¥2500.

Tempura Asuka (☎ 26 4308; 11 Shōnami-chō; lunch/dinner from ¥1575/3675; ⏰ closed Mon) Tempura Asuka serves attractive sets of tempura and sashimi in a relatively casual atmosphere. At lunchtime try their nicely presented *yumei-dono bentō* (lunchbox containing assorted tasty tidbits such as sashimi and rice) for ¥1500.

Tsukihi-tei (☎ 23 5470; 6 Higashimukiminami-machi; lunch/dinner from ¥1050/3000) Tsukihi-tei serves simple *kaiseki* sets at reasonable prices. The *tenshin bentō,* a good bet at ¥1500, includes sashimi, rice, vegetables, *chawan-mushi* (egg custard with various fillings) and other yummy things.

Za Don (☎ 27 5314; 13-2 Higashimukiminami-machi; lunch & dinner from ¥500) The name is short for *don-buri* (rice bowl) and this place takes the honours in the cheapest eats category. It's healthy Japanese fast food and there's a picture menu to make ordering easier.

Sleeping

Edo San (☎ 26 2662; Takabatake-chō; per person incl 2 meals ¥18,900) Edo San offers private Japanese-style cottages on the edge of Nara-kōen.

Green Hotel Ashibi (☎ 26 7815; fax 24 2465; 16-1 Hi-gashimukikita-machi; s/d/tw from ¥6400/11,000/12,000) Close to Kintetsu Nara Station, this small, serviceable hotel is one of the better-value hotels in Nara.

Hotel Fujita Nara (☎ 23 8111; 47-1 Shimosanjō-chō; s/tw from ¥7200/12,200) A clean, new hotel with a convenient location. During off-peak times, you might get a reduced rate if you reserve through the Kintetsu Nara Station office (see opposite).

Hotel Sunroute Nara (☎ 22 5151; fax 27 3759; 1110 Takabatake-chō; s/tw from ¥9240/17,850) Basic business hotel near the southwest corner of Nara-kōen.

Kankasō (☎ 26 1128; 10 Kasugano-chō; r incl breakfast & dinner from ¥18,900) This is one of Nara's most elegant ryokan. It's located close to Tōdai-ji.

Nara Hotel (☎ 26 3300; fax 23 5252; 1096 Takabatake-chō; s/d/tw from ¥16,170/26,565/25,410) Built near the turn of the century, Nara Hotel still ranks as the city's premier hotel. Rooms in the old wing have much more character.

Nara Youth Hostel (☎ 22 1334; fax 22 1335; 1716 Hōren-chō; dm ¥3150, breakfast ¥630, dinner ¥1050) This is a nicer hostel than Nara-ken Seishōnen Kaikan, below. From either JR or Kintetsu Nara Station, take bus 108, 109, 111, 115 or 130 and get off at the Shieikyūjō-mae bus stop, from which it's a one-minute walk.

Nara-ken Seishōnen Kaikan Youth Hostel (☎ /fax 22 5540; 72-7 Handahiraki-chō; dm/r per person ¥2650/3350) A nondescript, concrete place with a friendly staff. From JR Nara Station or Kintetsu Nara Station, take bus 12, 13, 131 or 140 and get off at the Ikuei-gakuen bus stop, from which it's a five-minute walk.

Ryokan Hakuhō (☎ 26 7891; fax 26 7893; 4-1 Kamisanjō-chō; per person without bath from ¥6000) In the centre of town, this ryokan is just a five-minute walk from JR Nara Station. It's starting to show its age and has less atmosphere than the Seikan-sō (below).

Ryokan Matsumae (☎ 22 3686; 28-1 Higashiteraba-yashi-chō; per person without bath from ¥5000) It lacks the atmosphere of the Seikan-sō, but this ryokan's got a very convenient location.

Ryokan Seikan-sō (☎ /fax 22 2670; 29 Higashikitsuji-chō; per person without bath from ¥4000) A friendly place with wooden architecture and a pleasant garden. This is probably the best-value ryokan in Nara.

Super Hotel (☎ 20 9000; 500-1 Sanjō-chō; s/d from ¥4980/6980) This 'automated' hotel is both impersonal and cheap, which may appeal to some.

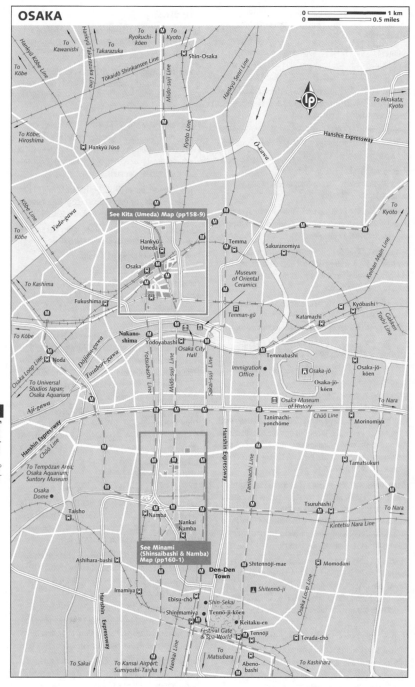

OSAKA

0 — 1 km
0 — 0.5 miles

To Ryokuchi-kōen
To Kyoto
Shin-Osaka
To Kawanishi
Hankyū Kōbe Line
Hankyū Takarazuka Line
To Takarazuka
Tōkaidō Shinkansen Line
Midō-suji Line
Hankyū Senri Line
Kyoto Line

To Hirakata;
Kyoto

Hanshin Expressway

To Kōbe;
Hiroshima

Hankyū Jūsō
Kōbe Line

Ō-kawa

To Kōbe
Yodo-gawa
To Kyoto

Keihan Main Line

See Kita (Umeda) Map (pp158-9)

Hankyū Umeda
Temma
Sakuranomiya

To Kōbe
Osaka
To Kashima
Kyobashi
Gakken Toshi Line
Katamachi

Fukushima
Museum of Oriental Ceramics

Tenman-gū

Nakano-shima
To Kōbe
Dōjima-gawa
Tosabori-gawa
Yodoyabashi
Yotsubashi Line
Midō-suji Line
Sakai-suji Line

Osaka City Hall
Immigration Office
Temmabashi

Osaka-jō
Osaka-jō-kōen

To Nara

Osaka Loop Line
Noda

Osaka Museum of History
Osaka-jō-kōen

To Universal Studios Japan;
Osaka Aquarium
Aji-gawa
Hanshin Expressway
Chūō Line

Tanimachi-yonchōme
Chūō Line
Morinomiya

To Nara

To Tempōzan Area;
Osaka Aquarium;
Suntory Museum

Hanshin Expressway
Tanimachi Line

Tamatsukuri

Osaka Dome
Taishō

Namba
Nankai Namba

Tsuruhashi
To Nara
Kintetsu Nara Line

See Minami
(Shinsaibashi & Namba)
Map (pp160-1)

Ashihara-bashi

Den-Den Town
Shitennō-ji-mae
Momodani

Imamiya
Ebisu-chō
Shin-Sekai
Shitennō-ji
Osaka Loop Line

Shinmamiya
Tennō-ji-kōen
Keitaku-en

Hanshin Expressway
Nankai Line

Festival Gate
& Spa World
Tennōji
Terada-chō

To Sakai
To Kansai Airport;
Sumiyoshi-Taisha
To Matsubara
Abeno-bashi
To Kashihara

OSAKA

☎ 06

The working heart of Kansai, Osaka is famous for its down-to-earth citizens and hearty cuisine. It combines a few historical and cultural attractions with all of the delights of a modern Japanese city. Indeed, Osaka is surpassed only by Tokyo as a showcase of the Japanese urban phenomenon.

This isn't to say that Osaka is an attractive city; almost flattened by bombing during WWII, it appears as an endless expanse of concrete boxes punctuated by *pachinko* parlours and elevated highways. But the city somehow manages to rise above this and exert a peculiar charm. And by night, the city really comes alive when all those drab streets and alleys flash neon, beckoning residents and travellers alike with promises of tasty food and good times.

Osaka's highlights include its famous castle Osaka-jō; Osaka Aquarium, with its resident whale shark; and the sci-fi *Blade Runner* nightscapes of the Dōtombori area.

Umeda Sky Building (below)

KITA

By day, Osaka's centre of gravity is the Kita area. While Kita doesn't have any great attractions to detain the traveller, it does have a few good department stores, lots of good places to eat and the Umeda Sky Building.

Just northwest of Osaka Station, the **Umeda Sky Building** is Osaka's most dramatic piece of architecture. The twin-tower complex looks like a space-age version of Paris' Arc de Triomphe. There are two observation galleries, an open-air one on the roof and an indoor one on the floor below. Getting to the top is half the fun as you take a glassed-in escalator for the final five storeys (definitely not for sufferers of vertigo). Tickets for the observation decks can be purchased on the 3rd floor of the east tower. Below the towers, you'll find **Takimi-kōji Alley**, a recreation of a Showa-era market street crammed with restaurants and *izakaya* (pubs and eateries). The building is reached via an underground passage that starts just north of Osaka or Umeda Stations.

CENTRAL OSAKA

The main attractions of Central Osaka include the Museum of Oriental Ceramics and Osaka-jō.

With more than 1300 exhibits, the **Museum of Oriental Ceramics** has one of the world's finest collections of Chinese and Korean ceramics. To get to the museum, go to Yodoyabashi Station on either the Midō-suji line or the Keihan line (different stations). Walk north to the river and cross to Nakano-shima. Turn right, pass the city hall on your left, bear left with the road and the museum is on the left.

Osaka's most popular attraction, **Osaka-jō** is a 1931 concrete reconstruction of the original castle, which was completed in 1583 as a display of power on the part of Toyotomi Hideyoshi. Refurbished at great cost in 1997, today's castle has a decidedly modern look (for a more authentic castle you should head west to Himeji-jō). The interior of the castle houses a museum of Toyotomi Hideyoshi memorabilia, as well as displays relating the history of the castle.

Ōte-mon, the gate that serves as the main entrance to the park, is a 10-minute walk northeast of Tanimachi-yonchōme Station on the Chūō and Tanimachi subway lines. You

Excursions – Osaka

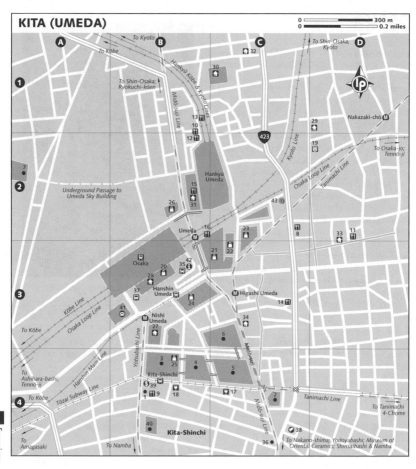

KITA (UMEDA)

can also take the Osaka Loop Line, get off at Osaka-jō-kōen Station and enter through the back of the castle.

MINAMI

A few stops south of Kita on the Midō-suji subway line (get off at either Shinsaibashi or Namba Stations), the Minami area is the place to spend the evening in Osaka. Its highlights include the Dōtombori Arcade, the National Bunraku Theatre, Dōguya-suji Arcade and Amerika-Mura.

Meaning 'America Village', **Amerika-Mura** is a compact enclave of trendy shops and restaurants, with a few discreet love hotels thrown in for good measure. The best reason to come here is to view the hordes of colourful Japanese teens living out the myth of *Amerika*. Amerika-Mura is located one or two blocks west of Midō-suji, bounded on the north by Suomachi-suji and the south by the Dōtombori-gawa.

Dōtombori is Osaka's liveliest nightlife area. It's centred on **Dōtombori-gawa** and **Dōtombori Arcade**. In the evening, head to **Ebisu-bashi**, the main footbridge over the canal, to sample the glittering nightscape, which calls to mind a scene from the sci-fi movie *Blade Runner*.

Only a short walk south of Dōtombori Arcade, you'll find **Hōzen-ji**, a tiny temple hidden down a narrow alley. The temple is built around a moss-covered **Fudō-myōō statue**. This statue is a favourite of people employed in the so-called 'water trade', or *mizu shōbai*. Nearby, you'll find the atmospheric **Hōzen-ji Yokochō**, a tiny alley filled with traditional restaurants and bars.

If you desperately need a *tako-yaki* (octopus ball) fryer, a red lantern to hang outside your shop or plastic food models to lure the customers in, the **Dōguya-suji shopping arcade** is the place to go. You'll also find endless knives, pots and almost anything else that's even remotely related to the preparation and consumption of food.

OTHER AREAS

Founded in 593, **Shitennō-ji** has the distinction of being one of the oldest Buddhist temples in Japan. However, none of the present buildings are originals: most are the usual concrete reproductions, with the exception of the big stone **torii**. The torii dates back to 1294, making it the oldest of its kind in Japan. The temple is most easily reached from Shitennōji-mae Station on the Tanimachi subway line. Take the southern exit, cross to the left side of the road and take the small road that goes off at an angle away from the subway station. The entrance to the temple is on the left.

Osaka's most important shrine, **Sumiyoshi-taisha** is dedicated to Shintō deities associated with the sea and sea travel, in commemoration of a safe passage to Korea by a 3rd-century empress. Having survived the bombing of WWII, Sumiyoshi-taisha actually has a couple of buildings that date back to 1810. The shrine was founded in the early 3rd century and the buildings that can be seen today are faithful replicas of the originals. The shrine is next to both Sumiyoshi-taisha Station on the Nankai line and Sumiyoshi-torii-mae Station on the Nankai line (the tram line that leaves from Tennō-ji Station).

Osaka Aquarium ('Kaiyūkan' in Japanese) is worth a visit, especially for those who have children in tow. The aquarium is centred on the world's largest aquarium tank, which is home to the star attractions, two enormous whale sharks as well as a variety of smaller sharks, rays and other fish. To get there, take the Chūō subway line to the last stop (Osaka-kō), and from here it's about a five-minute walk to the aquarium. Get there for opening time if you want to beat the crowds – on weekends and public holidays long queues are the norm.

Universal Studios Japan is Osaka's answer to Tokyo Disneyland. Although it wasn't open while we were researching this guide, word has it that the park is a faithful reproduction of the American park, complete with all manner of movie-themed rides, stores and shops. To get there, take the JR Loop Line to Nishi-kujō Station, switch to one of the distinctively painted Universal Studio shuttle trains and get off at Universal City Station. From Osaka Station the trip costs ¥170 and takes about 20 minutes. There are also some direct trains from Osaka Station (ask at the tourist office for times; the price is the same).

Excursions – Osaka

MINAMI (SHINSAIBASHI & NAMBA)

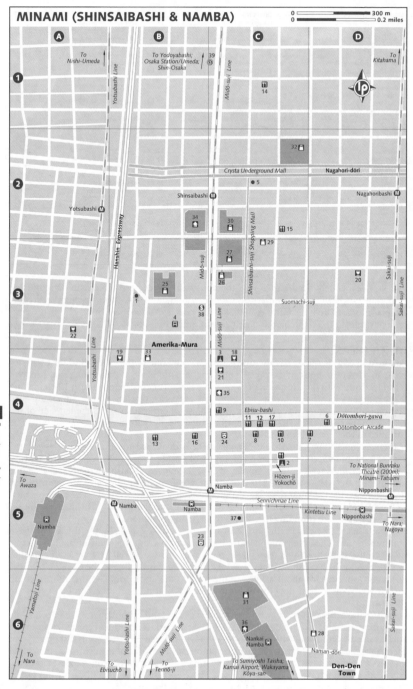

0 — 300 m
0 — 0.2 miles

To Nishi-Umeda

To Yodoyabashi;
Osaka Station/Umeda;
Shin-Osaka

To Kitahama

Yotsubashi Line

Midō-suji Line

14

32

Crysta Underground Mall

Nagahori-dōri

Shinsaibashi

5

Nagahoribashi

Yotsubashi

34

30

15

Hanshin Expressway

Midō-suji

27

29

25

26

20

Shinsaibashi-suji Shopping Mall

Sakai-suji

Sakai-suji Line

1

Suomachi-suji

38

22

4

Midō-suji Line

Amerika-Mura

19

33

3

18

21

35

9

Ebisu-bashi

11 12 17

6

Dōtombori-gawa

Dōtombori Arcade

13

16

24

8

10

7

2

Hōzen-ji
Yokochō

To National Bunraku
Theatre (200m);
Minami-Tatsumi

Namba

Sennichmae Line

Nipponbashi

Yotsubashi Line

Namba

Namba

Kintetsu Line

Nipponbashi

To Nara,
Nagoya

To Awaza

37

23

Yamatoji Line

31

To Nara

36

28

To Ebisuchō

To Tennō-ji

Midō-suji Line

Nankai
Namba

Nansan-dōri

To Sumiyoshi Taisha;
Kansai Airport; Wakayama
Kōya-san

Den-Den
Town

Orientation

Osaka is usually divided into two areas: Kita and Minami. Kita (north) is the city's main business and administrative centre. Minami (south) is the city's entertainment district and contains the bustling shopping and nightlife zones of Namba and Shinsaibashi.

The dividing line between Kita and Minami is formed by the Dōjima-gawa and the Tosabori-gawa, between which you'll find Nakano-shima, a peaceful green island which is home to the Museum of Oriental Ceramics. About one kilometre east of Nakano-shima, you'll find Osaka-jō and its surrounding park, Osaka-jō-kōen.

To the south of the Minami area you'll find another group of sights clustered around Tennōji Station. These include Shitennō-ji, Den-Den Town (the electronics neighbourhood) and the seriously low-rent entertainment district of Shin-Sekai.

Information

The Osaka Tourist Association has offices in Shin-Osaka (☎ 6305 3311), Osaka (☎ 6345 2189), Namba (☎ 6643 2125) and Tennōji (☎ 6774 3077) Stations, the main office being the one in Osaka Station. All are open from 8am to 8pm daily, and closed from 31 December to 3 January. Many travellers have problems finding the tourist office in Osaka Station. To get there from JR trains, go out the Midō-suji exit, take a right and walk about 50 metres; it's just outside the station, beneath a pedestrian overpass, beside the city bus terminal.

The information offices have two excellent maps of the Osaka region, *Your Guide to Osaka* and *Osaka City Map*. Both have subway and transport maps and detailed insets of the city's most important areas. Also worth picking up is *Meet Osaka*, which is a pocket-sized reference guide to upcoming events and festivals, and *Osaka: How to Enjoy It*, which is a pamphlet with details on almost all of Osaka's tourist attractions.

In Kita, there's an international ATM in the Sumitomo Mitsui Bank located on the B1 floor of Hankyū Umeda Station (it's not far from subway exit No 1). Up on street level, you'll find another international ATM down the street from the Hilton Osaka hotel. In Minami, there's an international ATM at the Citibank in Shinsaibashi.

For Internet access in Kita try **Web House** (☎ 6367 9555; per 30min ¥500; 🕙 11am-8.30pm). In Minami try **Kinko's** (☎ 6245 1922; per 30min ¥500; 🕙 24hr).

If you need any outdoor gear for your adventures in Japan, try **IBS Ishii Sports** (☎ 6344 5225; Ekimai Daiichi bldg).

Sights

Kaiyūkan/Osaka Aquarium (☎ 6576 5501; 1-1-10 Kaizandōri, Minato-ku; adult/child ¥2000/900; 🕙 10am-8pm)

Museum of Oriental Ceramics (☎ 6223 0055; 1-1-26 Nakanoshima, Kita-ku; admission ¥500; 🕙 9.30am-5pm, closed Mon)

Osaka-jō (☎ 6941 3044; 1-1 Osaka-jō Chūō-ku; admission to grounds/castle keep free/¥600; 🕙 9am-5pm, 9am-8pm in summer)

Shitennō-ji (☎ 6771 0066; 1-11-18 Shitennō-ji, Tennōji-ku; admission free; 🕙 9am-5pm, closed 28 Dec–1 Jan)

Sumiyoshi-Taisha (☎ 6672 0753; 2-9-89 Sumiyoshi; admission free; 🕙 dawn-dusk)

Umeda Sky Building (☎ 6440 3855; 1-1-88 Ōyodonaka Kita-ku; admission ¥700; 🕙 10am-10.30pm)

Universal Studios Japan (☎ 4790 7000; Universal city; adult/child ¥5500/3700; 🕙 9am-7pm Mon-Fri, 9am-9pm Sat, Sun & public holidays)

Festivals & Events

The major festivals held in Osaka include the following:

Tōka Ebisu (9-11 Jan) Huge crowds of more than a million people flock to the Imamiya Ebisu Shrine to receive bamboo branches hung with auspicious tokens. The shrine is near Imamiya Ebisu Station on the Nankai line.

Doya Doya (14 Jan) Billed as a 'huge naked festival', this event involves a competition between young men, clad in little more than headbands and loincloths, to obtain the 'amulet of the cow god'. This talisman is said to bring a good harvest to farmers. The festival takes place from 2pm at Shitennō-ji.

Tenjin Matsuri (24-25 Jul) This is one of Japan's three biggest festivals. Try to make the second day, when processions of portable shrines and people in traditional attire start at Temman-gū and end up in the O-kawa (in boats). As night falls the festival is marked with a huge fireworks display.

Kishiwada Danjiri Matsuri (14-15 Sep) Osaka's wildest festival, a kind of running of the bulls except with festival *danjiri* (floats), many weighing over 3000kg. The *danjiri* are hauled through the streets by hundreds of people using ropes, and in all the excitement there have been a couple of deaths – take care and stand back. Most of the action takes place on the second day. The best place to see it is west of Kishiwada Station on the Nankai Honsen line (from Nankai Namba Station).

Eating

The restaurants in this section are open during usual business hours (11am to 2pm and 5pm to 10pm) unless otherwise noted.

KITA – JAPANESE

The Kita area is chock-a-block with good restaurants. For a wide selection of different cuisines under one roof, try the Kappa Yokochō Arcade, just north of Hankyū Umeda Station, or the Shin-Umeda Shokudō-Gai, just east of JR Osaka Station (beneath the tracks).

Ganko Umeda Honten (☎ 6376 2001; 1-5-11 Shibata) A giant dining hall serving all the usual Japanese favourites, including sushi.

Gataro (☎ 6373 1484; 1-7-2 Shibata; dinner around ¥3000) This is a cosy little spot that does creative twists on standard *izakaya* themes. Look out for the glass front on the left as you head north in the Kappa Yokochō Arcade.

Isaribi (☎ 6373 2969; 1-5-12 Shibata; dinner from ¥2300) Down a flight of stairs outside Hankyū Umeda Station, this is a slightly less appealing spot to sample *robatayaki* cooking.

Kiji Honten (☎ 6361 5804; 9-20 Kakuda-chō, Shin Umeda Shokudōgai) A hole-in-the-wall *okanamiyaki* specialist.

Maru (☎ 6361 4552; 9-26 Kakuda-chō, Shin Umeda Shokudōgai) Maru serves delicious sashimi sets for lunch and proper fish meals for dinner.

Nawa Zushi Shiten (☎ 6312 9892; 14-1 Sonezaki-chō) One of the area's most popular sushi restaurants.

Oshi Dori (☎ 6375 5818; Hankyū Sanbangai) A reliable *yakitori* (grilled chicken) specialist not far from Kinokunia books.

KITA – INTERNATIONAL

There are several cafés and restaurants in Osaka Station itself. Otherwise, you might try the offerings in the nearby Hilton Osaka (see opposite), which has a wide variety of restaurants on its two basement floors.

Café Org (☎ 6312 0529; 7-7 Dōyama-chō Kita-ku; drinks from ¥250, meals from ¥700) This open, casual café is a good spot for a light meal or a quick pick-me-up while exploring Kita.

Transport

Other than the *shinkansen*, the fastest way between Kyoto Station and Osaka is a JR *shinkaisoku* (special rapid train; ¥540, 29 minutes).

There is also the cheaper private Hankyū line, which runs between Kawaramachi, Karasuma and Ōmiya Stations in Kyoto and Umeda Station in Osaka (Kawaramachi–Umeda limited express ¥390, 40 minutes).

Alternatively, you can take the Keihan line between Demachiyanagi, Marutamachi, Sanjō, Shijō or Shichijō Stations in Kyoto and Yodoyabashi Station in Osaka (Sanjō–Yodoyabashi limited express ¥400, 45 minutes).

Like Tokyo, Osaka has a JR Loop Line (known in Japanese as the JR *kanjō-sen*) that circles the city area. There are also seven subway lines, the most useful of which is the Midō-suji line, which runs north–south stopping at Shin-Osaka, Umeda (next to Osaka Station), Shinsaibashi, Namba and Tennōji Stations.

If you're going to be using the rail system a lot on any day, it might be worth considering a 'one-day free ticket'. For ¥850 (¥650 on Fridays and the 20th of every month) you get unlimited travel on any subway, the New Tram line and all city buses (but not the JR line). Note that you'd really have to be moving around a lot to save any money with this ticket. They are available at the staffed ticket windows in most subway stations.

Court Lodge (☎ 6342 5253; 1-4-7 Sonezakishinchi; curry sets from ¥800) Try this tiny hole-in-the-wall spot for filling sets of Sri Lankan food. Look for the beer signs in the window.

Herradura (☎ 6361 1011; 10-7 Dōyama-chō Kita-ku; dinner ¥2000-5000) An intimate spot with all the usual Mexican favourites, including taco platters and frozen margaritas.

Pina Khana (☎ 6375 5828; 1-7-2 Shibata Kita-ku; lunch/dinner from ¥850/3000) This crowded spot in the Kappa Yokochō Arcade is our favourite Indian restaurant in Kita.

MINAMI – JAPANESE

The place to eat in Minami is the restaurant-packed Dōtombori Arcade. The restaurants in this area win no points for their refined atmosphere, but the prices are low and the portions large.

Chibō (☎ 6212 2211; 1-5-5 Dōtombori Chūō-ku; okonomiyaki from ¥800) A good spot to sample one of Osaka's most popular dishes, *okonomiyaki*. Chibō's *modan yaki* (a kind of *okonomiyaki*) is a good bet at ¥950.

Dōtombori Rāmen Daishokudō (☎ 6213 1014; 1-4-20 Dōtombori Chūō-ku; rāmen ¥650-¥900)

Ganko Zushi (☎ 6212 1705; 1-8-24 Dōtombori Chūō-ku; set meals from ¥1000) Part of Kansai's most popular sushi chain, this is a good place for ample sushi sets and a variety of other Japanese favourites.

Gin Sen (☎ 6213 7234; 1-5 Namba Chūō-ku; all-you-can-eat kushikatsu lunch/dinner ¥1980/2980) Gin Sen serves delicious *kushikatsu* (skewers of deep-fried food). It's on the 2nd floor of the Gurukas building.

Imai Honten (☎ 6211 0319; 1-7-22 Dōtombori Chūō-ku; Kake-udon/Kitsune-udon ¥550/735) One of the area's oldest and most revered *udon* (white wheat noodle) specialists.

Kani Dōraku Honten (☎ 6211 8975; 1-6-18 Dōtombori Chūō-ku; lunch/dinner from ¥1600/3000) Like its sister branch in Kita, this crab specialist does all kinds of imaginative things with the unfortunate crustaceans. If the main branch is full, there's an annex just down the road.

Nishiya (☎ 6241 9221; 1-18-18 Higashi Shinsaibashi Chūō-ku; meals from ¥1200) Rustic Osaka landmark serves *udon* noodles and a variety of hearty *nabe* (iron pot) dishes for reasonable prices.

Ume no Hana (☎ 6258 3766; 11th fl, OPA bldg, 1-4-3 Nishi Shinsaibashi, Chūō-ku; dinner ¥5000) Part of an upscale chain that serves a variety of tofu-based dishes.

Zuboraya (☎ 6211 0181; 1-6-10 Dōtombori Chūō-ku; fugu sashimi ¥1800, full dinners from ¥3000) The place to go when you've worked up the nerve to try *fugu* (Japanese pufferfish). Look for the giant *fugu* hanging out front.

MINAMI – INTERNATIONAL

Krungtep (☎ 4708 0088; 1-6-14 Dōtombori Chūō-ku; lunch buffet/dinner ¥980/2000) Dōtombori's most popular Thai place, Krungtep serves fairly authentic versions of the standard favourites such as green curry and fried noodles.

La Bamba (☎ 6213 9612; 2-3-23 Dōtombori Chūō-ku; dinner average ¥2500-3000) Minami's most popular Mexican restaurant, La Bamba serves some mean guacamole and tasty fajitas.

Namaste (☎ 6241 6515; 3-7-28 Minamisemba Chūō-ku; lunch sets/dinner from ¥750/2000) Up in the Shinsaibashi area, this friendly Indian restaurant serves filling set meals at reasonable prices.

Santana (☎ 6211 5181; 2-2-17 Dōtombori Chūō-ku; lunch sets/dinner sets from ¥1000/2000) Santana is our favourite Indian place in Minami, with lots of vegie choices and delicious samosas.

Sleeping

It makes little sense to stay in Osaka with Kyoto just over half an hour away. If you do want to stay in Osaka, however, there are lots of business hotels and regular hotels in both the Kita and Minami areas.

KITA

Hilton Osaka (☎ 6347 7111; fax 6347 7001; 1-8-8 Umeda 1-chōme Kita-ku; s/d & tw from ¥17,400/29,000) Just across from Osaka Station, the Hilton is one of the city's most luxurious hotels, with a swimming pool and business centre.

Hotel Granvia Osaka (☎ 6344 1235; fax 6344 1130; 3-1-1 Umeda Kita-ku; s/d & tw from ¥13,500/21,000) You can't beat this hotel for convenience: it's located directly over Osaka Station. Rooms and facilities are of a high standard.

Hotel Green Plaza Osaka (☎ 6374 1515; fax 6734 1089; 2-5-12 Nakazaki nishi Kita-ku; s/d/tw from ¥7900/17,400/11,400) Drab but economical business hotel that's also fairly close to Osaka Station.

Hotel Hankyū International (☎ 6377 2100; fax 6377 3622; 19-19 Chayamachi Kita-ku; s/d/tw from ¥34,650/46,200/48,510) Osaka's most luxurious hotel; almost all of the rooms have great views over the city.

Hotel New Hankyū (☎ 6372 5101; fax 6374 6885; 1-1-35 Shibata Kita-ku; s/d/tw from ¥15,592/33,495/26,565) Next to Hankyū Umeda Station, this is a decent choice with fairly spacious rooms.

Hotel Sunroute Umeda (☎ 6373 1111; fax 6374 0523; 3-9-1 Toyosaki Kita-ku; s/d/tw from ¥8820/12,600/15,750) Perhaps the best-value business hotel in the area. It's located just north of Hankyū Umeda Station.

New Japan Sauna & Capsule Hotel (☎ 6314 2100; 9-5 Dōyama-chō Kita-ku; male-only capsules ¥2500, sauna from ¥525) Located in one of Kita's busiest entertainment districts, this is the place to stay if you miss the last train.

Umeda OS Hotel (☎ 6312 1271; fax 6312 7283; 2-11-5 Sonezaki Kita-ku; s/tw from ¥8300/11,800) About five minutes south of Osaka Station, this clean modern hotel is more attractive than some of the other choices.

MINAMI

Considering the wealth of dining and entertainment options in the area, the Minami area is probably the best place in Osaka to be based.

Hotel Nikkō Osaka (☎ 6244 1111; fax 6245 2432; 1-3-3 Nishishinsaibashi Chūō-ku; s/d & tw from ¥18,500/28,5000) The Nikkō is one of Osaka's better hotels, with a great selection of restaurants and bars on the premises.

Hotel Riva Nankai (☎ 6213 8281; fax 6213 8640; 2-5-15 Shinsaibashisuji Chūō-ku; s/d/deluxe from ¥11,550/15,750/17,850) Just a short walk from the Dōtombori area, this is the most reasonably priced hotel (as opposed to business hotel) in Minami.

Swissotel Nankai Osaka (☎ 6646 1111; 5-1-60 Namba Chūō-ku; s/d/tw from ¥25,000/28,000/28,000) Located directly above Nankai Namba Station, this clean, modern hotel has large rooms, most of which have great views.

Entertainment

Osaka has a lively nightlife scene, with lots of bars and clubs that see mixed foreign and Japanese clientele. For up-to-date listings of upcoming club and music events, check *Kansai Time Out*. See below for *bunraku* (Japanese puppet) theatre and see right for nō performances.

Although *bunraku* did not originate in Osaka, it was popularised here. Performances are only held at certain times of the year; check with the tourist information offices. Tickets normally start at around ¥2300, and earphones and programme guides in English are available.

KITA

Although Minami is the real nightlife district, there are plenty of good bars and clubs in the neighbourhoods to the south and east of Osaka Station.

Canopy (☎ 6341 0339; 1-11-20 Sonezakishinchi Kita-ku) An intimate café-style bar is a popular spot with expats for after-work snacks and drinks.

Karma (☎ 6344 6181; 1-5-18 Sonezakishinchi Kita-ku) A very long-standing club popular with Japanese and foreigners alike. On weekends they usually host techno events with cover charges averaging ¥2500.

National Bunraku Theatre (☎ 6212 2531; 1-12-10 Nihonbashi Chūō-ku) Osaka's main *bunraku* theatre.

Windows on the World (☎ 6347 7111; 1-8-8 Umeda 1-chōme Kita-ku) For drinks with a view, head to this bar on the 35th floor of the Hilton Osaka. Be warned that there's a ¥2500 per person table charge and drinks average ¥1000.

MINAMI

This is the place for a wild night out – you simply won't believe the number of bars, clubs and restaurants they've packed into the narrow streets and alleys of Dōtombori, Shinsaibashi, Namba and Amerika-Mura. Go on a weekend night and you'll be part of a colourful human parade of Osaka characters – this is one of Japan's best spots for people-watching.

American Beauty (☎ 6484 2299; 2-7-10 Shinsaibashi-suji, Chūō-ku) This small Shinsaibashi bar attracts both foreign and Japanese customers with good rock-and-roll music.

Arc en Ciel (☎ 6646 1119; 5-1-60 Namba Chūō-ku) For something a little swanky, head up to this bar on the 36th floor of the Nankai South Tower Hotel. The view is fantastic and the prices are, too: there's a ¥1500 per person table charge and drinks average ¥1200.

Cellar (☎ 6212 6437; B1 Shin-sumiya bldg, 2-17-13 Nishishinsaibashi, Chūō-ku) Live music is often the draw here at this popular basement bar on the west side of Nishishinsaibashi.

Murphy's (☎ 6282 0677; 1-6-31 Higashishinsaibashi Chūō-ku; per person average ¥1000) One of the oldest Irish-style pubs in Japan, this is a good place to rub shoulders with local expats and young Japanese.

Osaka Nōgaku Hall (☎ 6373 1726; 2-3-17 Nakasakinishi Kita-ku) A five-minute walk east of Osaka Station, the hall holds nō shows about four times a month, some of which are free.

Pig & Whistle (☎ 6213 6911; 2-6-14 Shinsaibashisuji Chūō-ku; drinks from ¥720, food from ¥1100) Like its sister branches in Kita and Kyoto, the Pig is the place to go for a pint and a plate of fish and chips.

SoulFuckTry (☎ 6539 1032; 1-9-14 Minami Horie, Nishi-ku; drinks from ¥700) This interestingly named bar/club describes itself as a soul/disco and that's pretty much what it is.

Shopping

For Osaka's local speciality, electronics, head over to Den Den Town, an area of shops that is almost exclusively devoted to electronic goods. To avoid sales tax, check if the store has a 'Tax Free' sign outside and bring your passport. Most stores are closed Wednesday. Take the Sakaisuji subway line to Ebisu-chō Station and exit at No 1 or No 2 exit. Alternatively, it's a 15-minute walk south of Nankai Namba Station.

KŌBE

☎ 078

Perched on a hillside overlooking Osaka bay, Kōbe is one of Japan's most attractive cities. It's also one of the country's most famous, owing largely to the tragic earthquake of 17 January 1995, which levelled whole neighbourhoods and killed over 6000 people. Fortunately, the city has risen Phoenix-like from the ashes and is now more vibrant than ever.

One of Kōbe's best features is its relatively small size – most of the sights can be reached on foot from the main train stations. Keep in mind that none of these are really must-see attractions; most of what Kōbe has to offer is likely to appeal more to residents than to travellers.

However, Kōbe does have some great restaurants, hip bars and happening clubs and is a good place for a night out in Kansai.

A 20-minute walk north of Sannomiya, the pleasant hillside neighbourhood of **Kitano** is where local tourists come to enjoy the feeling of foreign travel without leaving Japanese soil. The European/American atmosphere is created by the winding streets and *ijinkan* (foreigners' houses) that housed some of Kōbe's early Western residents. Admission to some is free, others cost ¥300 to ¥700; most are open 9am to 5pm.

Kōbe City Museum has a collection of Namban (literally 'southern barbarian') art and occasional special exhibits. Namban art is a school of painting that developed under the influence of early Jesuit missionaries in Japan, who taught Western painting techniques to Japanese students.

Five minutes' walk southeast of Kōbe Station, **Kōbe Harbor Land** is awash with new megamall shopping and dining developments. This may not appeal to foreign travellers the way it does to local youth, but it's still a nice place for a stroll in the afternoon.

Five minutes to the east of Harbor Land you'll find **Meriken Park** on a spit of reclaimed land jutting out into the bay. The main attraction here is the **Kōbe Maritime Museum**, which has a good collection of ship models and displays with some English explanations. Nearby, the **Port Tower** looks like a relic from an earlier age of tourism. It's probably not worth paying to ascend the tower when comparable views are available for free at some of the nearby shopping centres.

Nankinmachi, Kōbe's Chinatown, is not on a par with Chinatowns elsewhere in the world, but it is a good place to wander and have a bite to eat. It's particularly attractive in the evening. See the Eating section later (p167) for details on some of the area's restaurants.

Transport

Sannomiya Station is on the JR Tōkaidō/Sanyō line as well as the private Hankyū line, both of which connect it to Kyoto.

The fastest way between Kōbe and Kyoto is a JR *shinkaisoku* from Kyoto Station (¥1050, 48 minutes).

The Hankyū line, which leaves from Kyoto's Kawaramachi, Karasuma and Ōmiya Stations, is cheaper but less convenient (to/from Kawaramachi limited express ¥590, one hour; change at Osaka's Jūsō or Umeda Stations).

JR Rail Pass holders should also note that Shin-Kōbe Station is on the Tōkaidō/Sanyō *shinkansen* line.

Kōbe is small enough to travel around on foot. The JR, Hankyū and Hanshin railway lines run east–west across Kōbe, providing access to most of Kōbe's more distant sights. A subway line also connects Shin-Kōbe Station with Sannomiya Station (¥200). There is also a city loop bus service that makes a grand circle tour of most of the city's sightseeing spots (¥250 per ride, ¥650 for an all-day pass). The bus stops at both Sannomiya and Shin-Kōbe Stations.

Orientation & Information

Kōbe's two main entry points are Sannomiya and Shin-Kōbe Stations. Shin-Kōbe, in the northeast of town, is where the *shinkansen* pauses. A subway runs from here to the busier Sannomiya Station, which has frequent rail connections with Osaka and Kyoto. It's possible to walk between the two stations in around 15 minutes. Sannomiya (not Kōbe) Station marks the city centre. Before starting your exploration of Kōbe, pick up a copy of the *Kōbe City Map*, at one of the two information centres.

The city's main tourist information office is outside **Sannomiya Station** (☎ 322 0220; ❤ 9am-7pm). There's a smaller counter on the 2nd floor of Shin-Kōbe Station. You'll find an international ATM in the shopping arcade just south of Sannomiya Station. Behind Kōbe City Hall, there's a Citibank with machines that also accept a variety of cards. For second-hand books, try **Wantage Books** (☎ 232 4517; ❤ 10am-5.30pm Mon-Fri), near Shin-Kōbe Station.

KŌBE

0 |━━━━| 200 m
0 |━━━━| 0.1 miles

A   **B**   **C**   **D**

1

To Nunobiki
Haabu-kōen

To Osaka;
Kyoto

33 🏠

Ⓜ Shin-Kōbe

Shin-Kōbe
Ropeway

Tōkaidō Shinkansen Line

22 🏛
● 39

To Himeji;
Okayama;
Hiroshima

2

29 🏠
16 🏛

Kōbe City Subway

17
🏛

To Rokkō Island;
Osaka

Kitano

13 🏛
30 🏠

Yamate-kansen

Jinkan-dōri

Kitano-zaka

Fudō-zaka

20 🏛

3

19 🏛

Hunter-zaka

7
🏛

Hankyū Kōbe Line

Tōkaidō Line

8
🏛
● 1

Community Rd

Tor Rd

11 🏛
37 🏛

Nakayamate-dōri

Higashimon-gai

25 🏛

4

Sannomiya Ⓜ

3 🏛

34 🏛
🏛 Sannomiya

31 🏠

Hanshin Main Line

28 🏛
32 🏛
● 2

Hankyū
Sannomiya

🏛 Hanshin Sannomiya

Ikuta-shin-michi

10 🏛

Ikuta Rd

38
ⓘ

27
🏛

5

Tor Rd

14 🏛 21 🏛
18 🏛

Kōkawa-suji

Sannomiya Sentah Gai

36
🏛

24 🏛

Isogami-kōen

Port Line

35
🏛

4 ●

Flower Rd

Motomachi 🏛

San'yō Line

Hanshin
Motomachi

9 🏛

23 🏛

Kyukyoryuchi

6

To
Himeji

**Nankinmachi
(Chinatown)**

6 ●
15 🏛

To Harbor
Land

26 🏛

12 🏛

To Meriken Park;
Hotel Ōkura Kōbe;
Kōbe Maritime Museum;
Naka Pier;
Port Tower

5 🏛

To Port Island;
Kōbe City
Air Terminal (KCAT)

Sights

Kōbe City Museum (☎ 391 0035; 24 Kyō machi, Chūō-ku; admission ¥200; ⏱ 10am-4.30pm, closed Mon)

Kōbe Maritime Museum (☎ 327 8983; 2-2 Hatoba-chō, Chūō-ku; admission ¥600; ⏱ 10am-4.30pm, closed Mon)

Port Tower (☎ 391 6751; 5-5 Hatoba-chō, Chūō-ku; admission ¥600; ⏱ 9am-8.30pm)

Festival & Events

The **Luminarie festival**, Kōbe's biggest yearly event, is held every evening from 13 to 26 December to celebrate the city's miraculous recovery from the 1995 earthquake (check dates with the Kōbe tourist office as they change slightly every year). The streets southwest of Kōbe City Hall are decorated with countless illuminated metal archways and people flock from all over Kansai to stroll around and enjoy the usual festival food and drink.

Eating

Although Kōbe is more famous for its international cuisine, there are plenty of good Japanese restaurants to be found. The restaurants in this section are open during usual business hours (11am to 2pm and 5pm to 10pm), unless otherwise noted.

JAPANESE

Kintoki (☎ 331 1037; 1-7-2 Motomachi-dōri Chūō-ku; lunch & dinner from ¥500) For a taste of what Japan was like before it got rich, try this atmospheric old shokudō that serves the cheapest food in the city. You can order standard noodle and rice dishes from the menu (plain *soba* – thin, brown buckwheat noodles – or *udon* noodles are ¥250 and a small rice is ¥160) or choose from a variety of dishes laid out on the counter.

Mikami (☎ 242 5200; 2-5-9 Kitano-chō; lunch & dinner from ¥400; ⏱ 11.30am-10pm, closed Sun & public holidays) Try this friendly spot for good-value lunch and dinner sets of standard Japanese fare. Noodle dishes are available from ¥400 and *teishoku* (set-course meals) from ¥600. There is also an English menu.

Tada (☎ 222 1715; 2-9-15 Yamamoto-dōri Chūō-ku; lunch & dinner from ¥650) Casual *okonomiyaki* place in Kitano with counter seating also serves teppanyaki Kōbe beef from ¥1100 for a set.

Yoshinoya (☎ 265 6269; 1-1-12 Ikuta-chō Chūō-ku; dishes from ¥320) Close to Shin-Kōbe Station, this fast food *gyū-don* (beef over rice) specialist is also good for a healthy breakfast.

INTERNATIONAL

Kōbe is most famous for its Indian food and there are lots of places to choose from. There are also lots of trendy café-style spots, including a clutch of restaurants just north of Motomachi Station in the fashionable Tor Rd area. For Chinese food, the natural choice is Nankinmachi (Chinatown), just south of Motomachi Station.

A-1 (☎ 331 8676; 2-2-9 Shimoyamate-dōri Chūō-ku; Kōbe-beef course from ¥6500) This downtown steak specialist is a good spot to try Kōbe beef.

Court Lodge (☎ 222 5504; 1-23-16 Nakayamate-dōri Chūō-ku; lunch & dinner average ¥1000-2000) Right in the heart of Kitano, this Sri Lankan place serves tasty set meals and delicious Ceylon tea.

Gaylord (☎ 251 4359; 1-26-1 Nakayamate-dōri Chūō-ku; lunch/dinner from ¥900/3000) Long-standing Indian restaurant is the place to go for splashier meals and delicious curries.

Kōkaen (☎ 231 7079; 2-21-12 Nakayamate-dōri Chūō-ku; lunch/dinner average ¥1000/4000) Local cognoscenti favour this authentic little Chinese place for its good food and properly gruff owners.

Lois Café (☎ 322 0904; 45 Harima-chō Chūo-ku; dinner from ¥2500) Hip pan-Asian place draws Kōbe's chic young crowd for light meals and conversation.

Modernark Pharm (☎ 391 3060; 3-11-15 Kitanagasa-dōri Chūo-ku; lunch & dinner average ¥900-1500) An open spot popular with Kōbe's chic young things, Modernark Pharm serves tasty sets of Japanese and Western dishes, including burritos and rice dishes.

Motomachi Gyōza-en (☎ 331 4096; 2-8-11 Sakaemachi-dōri Chūo-ku; 6 dumplings ¥380) The best spot in Nankin-machi for Chinese dumplings (that's about all they serve). Try their wonderful *yaki gyōza* (fried dumplings) at lunch or dinner. At dinner they also make *sui gyōza* (steamed dumplings). Use the vinegar, soy sauce and miso on the table to make a dipping sauce. The red sign is in Japanese only, so you may have to ask someone to point out the store.

Nailey's (☎ 231 2008; 2-8-12 Kanou-chō Chūo-ku; coffee from ¥400, lunch/dinner from ¥900/1200) A hip little café that serves espresso, light lunches and dinners. This is also a good spot for an evening drink.

Native (☎ 242 7677; 2-9-1 Kanou-chō Chūo-ku; dinner from ¥1500) An interesting little restaurant that serves creative, modern Japanese fare.

Patisserie Tooth Tooth (☎ 334 1350; 3-2-17 Kitana-gasa-dōri Chūo-ku; cakes/light meals from ¥380/900) Near Motomachi Station, this fashionable European-style café/restaurant does a variety of light meals.

Upwards (☎ 230 8551; 1-7-16 Yamamoto-dōri Chūo-ku; lunch & dinner from ¥1000) This fashionable eatery in Kitano serves light Italian fare in an airy, open space. Another good spot for a drink in the evening.

Wakoku (☎ 262 2838; 1-1 Kitano-chō Chūo-ku, 3F Shin Kōbe Oriental Ave; lunch/dinner from ¥2500/6800) Our top choice for Kōbe beef. It's an elegant place that serves absolutely top-quality beef.

Weekend (☎ 332 3131; 3-12-3 Kitanagasa-dōri Chūo-ku; lunch from ¥800) Weekend is typical of the cool cafés that are popping up all over Kōbe. It's a good spot for a sandwich, a drink or a full meal.

Sleeping

Green Hill Hotel Kōbe (☎ 222 0909; fax 222 1139; 2-8-3 Kano-chō Chūo-ku; s/tw from ¥8925/15,330) The rooms here are clean and well kept, making it another good business hotel choice.

Green Hill Hotel Urban (☎ 222 1221; 2-5-16 Kano-chō Chūo-ku; s/d & tw from ¥4500/9000) Probably the best-value business hotel in Kōbe.

Hotel Ōkura Kōbe (☎ 333 0111; fax 333 6673; 2-1 Hatoba-chō Chūo-ku; s/d & tw from ¥19,635/31,185) On the waterfront behind Meriken Park, this is the most elegant hotel in town with fine rooms and spacious common areas.

Hotel Tor Road (☎ 391-6691 fax 391-6570; 3-1-19 Nakaya-mate-dōri Chūo-ku; s/d & tw from ¥8662/15,592) A good, inexpensive business hotel not far from Motomachi Station.

Kōbe Washington Hotel Plaza (☎ 331 6111; fax 331 6651; 2-11-5 Shimoyamate-dōri Chūo-ku; s/d & tw from ¥8100/17,500) Close to Sannomiya Station, this hotel has small but clean rooms.

Shin-Kōbe Oriental Hotel (☎ 291 1121; fax 291 1154; 1 Kitano-chō Chūo-ku; s/d & tw from ¥15,015/26,565) Towering above Shin-Kōbe Station, this hotel commands the best views of the city.

Entertainment

Kōbe has a relatively large foreign community and a number of bars that see mixed Japanese and foreign crowds. For Japanese-style drinking establishments, try the *izakaya* in the neighbourhood between the JR tracks and Ikuta-jinja. Also bear in mind that a lot of Kōbe's nightlife is centred on the city's many cafés, most of which transform into bars come evening.

Munchen Club (☎ 335 0170; 47 Akashi-chō Chūo-ku) A decent German-style pub that draws its share of foreign residents. It's close to Daimaru department store.

Polo Dog (☎ 331 3944) A short walk from Sannomiya Station, this is a small casual bar at home with foreigners.

HIMEJI

☎ 0792

It's worth the long trip out to see Himeji-jō, unanimously acclaimed as the most splendid Japanese castle still standing.

Himeji can easily be visited as a day trip from Kyoto. A couple of hours at the castle plus the 10- to 15-minute walk from the station is all the time you really need. Other attractions include Himeji's history museum and Kōko-en, a fine garden next to the castle.

There's a **tourist information counter** (☎ 85 3792) at the station, on the ground floor to the right as you come off the escalator. Between 10am and 3pm English-speaking staff are on duty and can help with hotel/ryokan reservations.

Himeji-jō is the most magnificent of the handful of Japanese castles that survive in their original (nonconcrete) form. Although there have been fortifications in Himeji since 1333, this castle was built in 1580 by Toyotomi Hideyoshi and enlarged some 30 years later by Ikeda Terumasa.

The castle has a five-storey main *donjon* (keep) and three smaller *donjons*, and the entire structure is surrounded by moats and defensive walls punctuated by rectangular, circular and triangular openings for firing guns and shooting arrows at attackers.

English-speaking guides are sometimes available and can really add a lot to your tour of the castle. Unfortunately, appointments aren't accepted and it's hit or miss whether any will be available on the day of your visit – ask at the ticket office of the castle and hope for the best. The guide service is free.

The **Hyōgo Prefectural Museum of History** is a well-organised museum that has good displays on Himeji-jō and other castles around Japan. In addition to the displays on castles, the museum covers the main periods of Japanese history with some English explanations. At 11am, 2pm and 3.30pm you can even try on a suit of samurai armour or a kimono. The museum is a five-minute walk north of the castle.

Just across the moat on the west side of Himeji-jō, you'll find **Kōko-en**, a reconstruction of the former samurai quarters of the castle in a garden setting. There are nine separate Edo-style gardens, two ponds, a stream, a tea arbour (¥500 for *matcha* tea)

Transport

The best way to get to Himeji from Kyoto is a *shinkai-soku* on the JR Tōkaidō line (¥2210, one hour and 20 minutes).

You can also reach Himeji from Kyoto via the Tōkaidō/Sanyō *shinkansen* line and this is a good option for JR Rail Pass holders.

On the way to Himeji, take a look out the train window at the new Akashi Kaikyō Bridge. Its 3910m span links the island of Honshū with Awaji-shima, making it the longest suspension bridge in the world. It comes into view on the south side of the train about 15km west of Kōbe.

and the restaurant, **Kassui-ken**, where you can enjoy lunch while gazing over the gardens. If you'd like to visit Kōko-en in conjunction with the castle, you can buy a combination ticket to both here for ¥720.

Nada-no-Kenka Matsuri (p170)

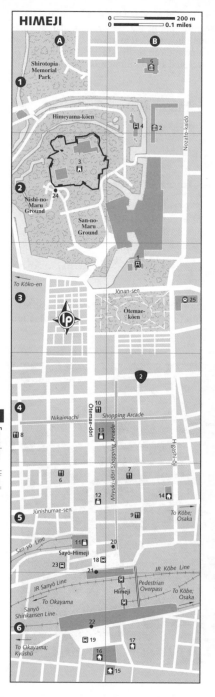

HIMEJI

| 0 | 200 m |
| 0 | 0.1 miles |

Sights & Information

Himeji-jō (☎ 85 1146; 68 Honmachi; admission ¥600; ☯ 9am-5pm, last admission 4pm, 5pm in summer)

Hyōgo Prefectural Museum of History (☎ 88 9011; 68 Honmachi; admission ¥200; ☯ 10am-5pm, last admission 4.30pm, closed Mon)

Kōko-en (☎ 89 4120; 68 Honmachi; admission ¥300; ☯ 9am-4.30pm, 9am-5.30pm in summer)

Festivals & Events

The **Nada-no-Kenka Matsuri**, held on 14 and 15 October, involves a conflict between three *mikoshi* (portable shrines) that are battered against each other until one smashes. The festival is held about five minutes' walk from Shirahamanomiya Station (10 minutes from Himeji Station on the Sanyō-Dentetsu line). You should try to go on the second day when the festival reaches its peak – the action starts around noon.

Eating

The food court in the underground mall at JR Himeji Station has all the usual Western and Japanese dishes. It's just to the right as you exit the north ticket gate of the station.

Bistro Angelot (☎ 26 1113; 23 Tatemachi; lunch from ¥900) Casual French/Italian place serving a good daily lunch special.

Excursions – Himeji

Fukutei (☎ 23 0981; 75 Kamei-chō; lunch/dinner ¥1400/5000; 🕒 Fri-Wed) If you want something a little nicer for lunch or dinner in Himeji, try this *kaiseki* specialist. From 11am to 2pm, try their mini-*kaiseki* course (¥1400).

Morijū (☎ 23 2517; 126 Uomachi; meals from ¥2500) An upscale *unagi* (eel) specialist that also serves a variety of oyster dishes in winter.

Sekishin (☎ 22 3842; 301 Ekimae-chō; rice/tonkatsu ¥200/550) The locals line up outside this hole-in-the-wall joint for tasty *tonkatsu* (pork cutlets). You might also try their special *tonjiru* (miso soup with bits of fatty pork). Look for the white curtains with red kanji.

Tonkatsu Musashi (☎ 82 6257; 62 Nikaimachi; meals from ¥700) A very casual *tonkatsu* specialist that's on the way to the castle.

Sleeping

Himeji Washington Hotel Plaza (☎ 25 0111; 98 Higashiekimae-chō; fax 25 0133; s/d from ¥6754/13,508) The small clean rooms in this hotel make it about the best hotel option in Himeji.

Hotel Himeji Plaza (☎ 81 9000; fax 84 3549; 158 Toyozawa-chō; s/tw from ¥6000/13,800) Although cheaper than the Himeji Washington Hotel Plaza, this hotel is slightly less appealing.

Hotel Sun Garden Himeji (☎ 22 2231; fax 24 3731; 100 Minamiekimae-chō; s/d & tw ¥9500/17,900) The ritziest place in town with clean, newish rooms and a convenient location just outside the station.

Tōyoko Inn (☎ 84-1045; 97 Minamiekimae-chō; s/d & tw from ¥5980/8190) This new business hotel is a good choice if you want to be close to the station.

MIYAMA-CHŌ

☎ 0771

If you yearn for a glimpse of old rural Japan, head to lovely Miyama-chō, a town nested in the Kitayama mountains of northern Kyoto-fu.

The 'town' is composed of several village clusters spread over a large area. These picturesque hamlets are home to an abundance of traditional *kayabuki-yane* (thatched-roof) farmhouses thatched with a thick roof of long *susuki* (pampas grass) reeds.

Miyama-chō has become a popular home for artists, and is also gaining attention from outdoor enthusiasts for its excellent hiking, camping and kayaking on the Yura-gawa. It is possible to travel to Miyama-chō as a day trip from Kyoto, but it makes a much nicer overnight trip.

The Japanese-language *Map Kyoto*, available at the Kyoto Tourism Federation above Kyoto Station, covers the Miyama-chō area.

Rice fields, Miyama-chō (above)

Transport

Miyama-chō is about 50km due north oϊ Kyoto over a series of mountain passes. There are no train lines to Miyama-chō, so you either have to rent a car, hitch or take a series of buses from Kyoto.

To get to Kitamura by bus, take a JR bus from in front of Kyoto Station to Shimonaka. At Shimonaka transfer to a Miyama-chō-ei bus to Agake. From Agake, take another Miyama-chō-ei bus bound for Chimiguchi and get off at Kitamura (entire trip ¥2320, 2½ hours).

From Kitamura, you can catch a Miyama-chō-ei bus onward to Chimiguchi, where you can catch another bus to Sasari (for Ashiu get off at Deai and walk the last kilometre into the village). Needless to say, the complexity and cost of this route makes either renting a car or hitching look awfully attractive.

The best road to Miyama-chō is Rte 162 (Shūzankaidō), though there is a lovely (but time-consuming) alternative route via Kurama in the north of Kyoto and over Hanase-tōgei Pass. Serious cyclists should be able to reach the area via either route by pedalling for about five arduous hours.

Another option is to take Kyoto bus 32 from Kyoto's Demachiyanagi Station to the last stop, Hirogawara (¥1050, 90 minutes), and hike over Sasari-tōge Pass. From Hirogawara follow the road to the pass and then take the hiking trail down into Ashiu (you'll probably need the hiking map – see below for details). The hike notwithstanding, this is probably the easiest route into Ashiu since it involves only one bus.

Those intent on seeing a lot of Miyama-chō without renting a car can combine the two bus routes described above to make one grand traverse of the area. Take the aforementioned buses all the way to Sasari from Kyoto Station, hike over the pass and return to Kyoto by bus from Hirogawara (or vice-versa). Note that the road over the pass is closed in winter, when it makes a great snowshoe or cross-country ski route.

ASHIU

The quiet village of **Ashiu** sits on the far eastern edge of Miyama-chō. The main attraction of Ashiu is the 4200-hectare virgin forest that lies to the east of the village. Safeguarded under the administration of Kyoto University's Department of Agriculture, this is about the only remaining virgin forest in all of Kansai.

The best way to sample the beauty of Ashiu's forest is to hike up into the gorge of the Yura-gawa. Lonely Planet's *Hiking in Japan* guide details a four-day hike up the river. Those with less time can do shorter day trips up the gorge. Hikers should get hold of Shōbunsha's Japanese-language *Kyoto Kitayama 2* map, part of their Yama-to-Kōgen Chizu series (available at bigger bookshops in Kyoto).

KITAMURA

Miyama-chō's star attraction is **Kitamura** (North Village) a small hamlet boasting a cluster of some 50 thatched-roof farmhouses. In 1994 the village was designated a national preservation site, and the local government has been generously subsidising the exorbitant cost of rethatching the roofs (at an average cost of ¥6 million – more than US$50,000!).

There's not much to do in the village except walk around and admire the old houses.

Eating

Morishige (☎ 75 1086; 15 Taninoshita, Uchikubo, Miyama-chō; noodle dishes from ¥650) A thatched-roof place that serves simple but tasty noodle dishes and *nabe* dishes.

Yurui (☎ 76 0741; Hayashi Morisato Miyama-chō; mochimugi-udon ¥1500, tororo-gohan ¥1500) A wonderfully elegant restaurant occupying a fine thatched-roof house. It's about half an hour north of the centre of Miyama-chō by car. Reservations are required.

Sleeping

There are a number of interesting places to stay in the Miyama-chō area. It's best to have a Japanese person call to make reservations at these places since few lodge owners speak English. Some owners will pick up guests in Hirogawara, the most convenient access point to Miyama-chō.

Matabe (☎ 77 0258; Kita Miyama-chō Kita-kuwada-gun; per person incl 2 meals ¥7875) This quaint *minshuku* in Kitamura is in a traditional thatched-roof house.

Miyama Heimat Youth Hostel (☎ /fax 75 0997; 57 Nakasai Obuchi Miyama-chō; members/nonmembers ¥3360/4410, dinner ¥1050, breakfast ¥630) One of the cheaper options in the area. This simple youth hostel is located in a thatched-roof house and it's on the road to Ōno Dam.

Yama-no-le (☎ 77 0290; Ashiu Miyama-chō Kita-kuwada-gun; per person ¥1700) The only place to stay in Ashiu – other than camping – is in this impressive lodge. There are no meals served but there are simple cooking facilities. It's a few minutes on foot from the forest trailhead.

Directory

Directory

TRANSPORT

Kyoto has an excellent public transportation system. Most visitors will find that they use the city bus for most of their getting around, but there are also two subway lines, three private train lines and a huge fleet of taxis. Furthermore, being largely flat, Kyoto is a great city for bicycling, and it's perfectly feasible to rent or buy a bicycle on your first day in the city and never have to resort to the public transportation system.

AIR

While there is no international or domestic airport in Kyoto, the city is within easy reach of both Osaka's Itami airport (domestic flights) and Kansai International Airport (KIX). Of course, there are other ways to get to and from Kyoto, including ferries from Shanghai (p177) and trains from other parts of the country (p179).

Airlines

The major airline offices in Kyoto are All Nippon Airways and Japan Airlines. Their ☎ 0120 numbers are toll free.

All Nippon Airways (ANA; Map pp228-9; international ☎ 0120-029 333, domestic ☎ 0120-029 222; www.ana .co.jp/eng/; near JR Osaka Station; ☺ 9am-6pm Mon-Fri, 9am-5pm Sat & Sun)

Japan Airlines (JAL; Map pp228-9; international ☎ 0120-255 931, domestic ☎ 0120-255 971; www.jal.co.jp/en/; Karasuma-Oike; ☺ 9.30am-5.30pm)

Most foreign airlines have offices in Osaka. The ☎ 0120 numbers are toll free.

Air Canada (☎ 0120-048 048)

Air France (☎ 06-6641 1411)

Air New Zealand (☎ 0120-300 747)

Alitalia (☎ 06-6341 3951)

American Airlines (☎ 0120-000 860)

Cathay Pacific Airways (☎ 0120-355 747)

Delta Air Lines (☎ 0120-333 742)

Garuda Indonesia (☎ 06-6635 3222)

KLM-Royal Dutch Airlines (☎ 0120-868 862)

Korean Air (☎ 06-6264 3311)

Lufthansa Airlines (☎ 0724-56 5222)

Northwest Airlines (☎ 0120-120 747)

Qantas Airways (☎ 0120-207 020)

Scandinavian Airlines (☎ 0120-678 101)

Swissair (☎ 0120-667 788)

Thai Airways International (☎ 06-6202 5161)

United Airlines (☎ 0120-114 466)

Airports
KANSAI INTERNATIONAL AIRPORT (KIX)

Built on an artificial island and opened in 1994, **KIX** (www.kansai-airport.or.jp/english/) is now the first port of call for many visitors to Japan. With over 690 weekly departures, it handles flights to 76 cities and 32 countries worldwide, and chances are you can fly straight into KIX rather than flying into Tokyo's Narita and then having to make connections onward to Kyoto (overland or via nearby Osaka International Airport, better known as Itami).

Itami airport has frequent flights to/from Tokyo (about 70 minutes) but unless you are very lucky with connections you'll probably find it more convenient and cheaper to take the *shinkansen* (bullet train).

The trip between KIX and Kyoto can be quite expensive and time consuming; if you are flying domestically and have a choice of airports, always choose Itami.

It's sometimes cheaper to fly into Tokyo's Narita airport than into KIX. As a rule, it will cost about ¥15,000 and take around five hours to get from Narita to Kyoto. Thus, you'd have to save at least ¥30,000 and have plenty of time and energy to spare to consider Narita as your gateway to Kansai/Kyoto. Of course, if you're interested in seeing other parts of Japan, Narita might well be the gateway of choice.

At KIX there are information counters throughout the complex that have English-speaking staff. There is also the **main tourist information counter** (☎ 0724-56 6025; 1st fl, International Arrivals Hall; ☺ 9am-9pm) which is operated by the Osaka prefectural government. It's roughly in the centre of the international arrivals hall.

After clearing customs, it is a short walk to public transport (straight out the doors for buses and up the escalators or elevators for train connections). KIX offers short-term and long-term baggage storage for ¥350 to ¥1000 per day, depending on the size of the bag. You pay the bill when you pick up your bag.

If you don't want to lug your bags all the way to Kyoto, there are several luggage delivery services located in the arrivals hall.

For international departures, there are shower and dayroom facilities, costing ¥1200. These are available only to those who have cleared passport control and transit passengers.

TO/FROM KIX

Osaka Airport Transport (☎ 06-6844 1124; www .okkbus.co.jp/eng/) runs direct limousine buses between Kyoto and KIX (adult/child ¥2300/1150, 105 minutes). There are pick-up and drop-off points on the southern side of Kyoto Station (Map pp230-1; in front of Avanti department store), Kyoto ANA Hotel (Map pp222–4) and Keihan Sanjō Station (Map pp228–9). At KIX, the buses leave from the kerb outside the international arrivals hall.

There's always the possibility of a delay in traffic, so we don't really recommend this route when you're leaving Kyoto. It's only marginally cheaper than an unreserved seat on the *haruka*.

The fastest, most convenient way between KIX and Kyoto is the special JR *haruka* airport express, which makes the trip in about 75 minutes for ¥3490. Most seats are reserved on this train, but there are usually two cars with unreserved seats costing ¥2980. Unreserved seats are almost always available, so you don't usually need to purchase tickets in advance. First and last departures from KIX to Kyoto are at 6.29am and 10.18pm Monday to Friday (6.41am at weekends); first and last departures from Kyoto to KIX are at 5.46am and 8.16pm.

If you have time to spare, you can save some money by taking the *kankū kaisoku* (Kansai airport express) between the airport and Osaka Station and taking a regular *shinkaisoku* (special rapid train) to/from Kyoto (p180). The total journey by this route takes about 90 minutes with good connections, and costs ¥1800. The downside is that you will have to carry your baggage from one train to another at Osaka Station.

For those travelling on Japanese airlines (JAL and ANA), there is an advance check-in counter inside the JR ticket office in Kyoto Station (Map pp230–1). This service allows you to check-in with your luggage at the station – a real boon for those with heavy bags.

Lastly, perhaps the most convenient option is the MK Taxi Sky Gate Shuttle limousine van service (☎ 702 5489; www.mk-group.co.jp /english/shuttle/top.htm), which will drop you off anywhere in Kyoto for ¥3000 (simply go to their counter at the south end of the arrivals hall of KIX and they will do the rest). In the reverse direction (Kyoto to the airport) it is necessary to make reservations two days in advance and they will pick you up anywhere in Kyoto and drop you at the airport. These days, many seasoned travellers and Kyotoites use this option since you don't have to lug your bags through the train station. A similar service is offered by Yasaka Taxi (☎ 803 4800).

OSAKA ITAMI AIRPORT

Itami airport is the main airport for domestic flights in and out of Kansai. It is closer to Kyoto and is easier to travel to/from the city. We suggest if you have a choice of flying into KIX or Itami, always choose Itami. You'll find an information counter with English-speaking staff in the main arrivals hall.

There are several luggage-delivery services in the arrivals hall in case you don't want to carry your bags all the way to Kyoto.

TO/FROM OSAKA ITAMI AIRPORT

Osaka Airport Transport (☎ 06-6844 1124; www .okkbus.co.jp/eng/) runs frequent airport limousine buses (¥1370, one hour) between Kyoto Station and Itami. There are less frequent pick-ups/drop-offs at some of Kyoto's main hotels. The Kyoto Station stop is in front of Avanti department store (Map pp230–1) and the Itami stop is outside the arrivals hall – buy your tickets from the machine near the bus stop. Allow extra time in case of traffic. You can also take the MK Taxi Sky Gate Shuttle limousine van service (☎ 702 5489; www .mk-group.co.jp/english/shuttle2/top.htm) to/from the city for ¥2000.

Domestic Air Services

The larger airports in Japan have regular flights to/from Osaka. For most cities in Honshū (the main island of Japan), including Tokyo, Nagoya and Hiroshima, it is usually faster, cheaper and more convenient to travel by *shinkansen* (bullet train; p179).

Domestic airfares can be rather expensive and tend to vary little between carriers. ANA and JAL offer tickets at up to 50% off if you purchase a month or more in advance, with smaller discounts for purchases made one to three weeks in advance.

The following are typical one-way prices for flights between Osaka (Itami or KIX) and several major cities in Japan.

Destination	One-way (¥)
Fukuoka	18,300
Kagoshima	22,800
Kōchi	15,000
Kumamoto	19,800
Matsuyama	14,300
Nagasaki	21,800
Naha	28,800
Niigata	24,800
Sapporo	35,300
Sendai	26,300
Tokyo	18,800

BICYCLE

Kyoto is a great city to explore on a bicycle. With the exception of outlying areas, it's mostly flat and there is a new bike path running the length of the Kamo-gawa.

Unfortunately, Kyoto must rank near the top in having the world's worst public facilities for bike parking (hence the number of bikes you see haphazardly locked around the city) and many bikes end up stolen or impounded during regular sweeps of the city (in particular near entrances to train/subway stations). If your bike does disappear, check for a poster in the vicinity (in both Japanese and English) indicating the time of seizure and the inconvenient place you'll have to go to pay the ¥2000 fine and retrieve your bike. Note that the city does not impound bicycles on Sundays or holidays, so you can park pretty much at will on those days.

If you don't want to worry about your bike being stolen or impounded, we recommend using one of the city-run bicycle/motorcycle parking lots. There is one on Kiyamachi-dōri midway between Sanjō-dōri and Shijō-dōri, on the east side of the street, and another near Kyoto Station (from the north side of the station, go west past the Central Post Office and it's on your right). These places charge ¥150 per day (buy a ticket from the machine on your way in or out).

For hardcore cyclists touring Japan, or for anyone looking for equipment or a pro-

fessional tune-up, drop by **Takenaka** (Map pp216-18; ☎ 256 4863), a small, but first-rate bike shop near the southeastern corner of the Imperial Palace Park.

Hire

Tour Club (Map pp230-1; ☎ 353 6968; www .kyotojp.com) rents large-frame and regular bicycles for ¥800, with a ¥3000 deposit, see p139. Bicycles can be picked up between 8am and 9.30pm. They offer a similar deal at their sister inn, Budget Inn (p139).

Another great place to rent a bike is the **Kyoto Cycling Tour Project** (KCTP; Map pp230-1; ☎ 467 5175; www.kctp.net). The folks here rent mountain bikes (¥1500 per day), which are perfect for getting around Kyoto. Bicycles can be delivered upon request (¥500) or you can pick them up at their shop. KCTP also conducts a variety of bicycle tours of Kyoto, which are an excellent way to see the city (check the website for details).

Near Sanjō Station on the Keihan line, **Kitazawa Bicycle Shop** (Map pp228-9; ☎ 771 2272; per hr ¥200, per day ¥1000; ☺ 8am-5pm) rents out bicycles with discounts for rentals over three days. It's a 200m walk north of the station next to the river on the east side.

Nearby, **Rental Cycle Yasumoto** (Map pp228-9; ☎ 751 0595; Kawabata-dōri, north of Sanjō-dōri; ☺ 9am-5pm), offers a similar deal.

Most rental outfits require you to leave ID such as a passport or driver's licence.

Purchase

If you plan on spending more than a week or so exploring Kyoto by bicycle, it might make sense to purchase a used bicycle. A simple *mama chari* (shopping bike) can be had for as little as ¥3000. Try the used cycle shop **Ei Rin** (Map pp219-21; ☎ 752 0292; Imadegawa-dōri) near Kyoto University. Otherwise, you'll find a good selection of used bikes advertised for sale on the message board at **Kyoto International Community House** (Map pp225-7; ☎ 752 3010; Sakyō-ku, Awataguchi).

BOAT
Domestic Ferries

Domestic overnight ferries are an excellent way to save time and one night's accommodation costs.

Osaka and Kōbe are the main ports for ferries between Kansai and Shikoku, Kyūshū and Okinawa. There are a range of fares available to/from Osaka and Kōbe.

Destination	Cost (¥)
Beppu (Kyūshū)	7400
Imabari (Shikoku)	4170
Kōchi (Shikoku)	4610
Matsuyama (Shikoku)	5200
Naha (Okinawa)	15,750

Note that from Naha there are ferries onward to Taiwan (¥15,750, 19 hours).

From the cities north of Kyoto on the Sea of Japan you can also catch ferries as far north as Hokkaidō. Two popular routes, with daily departures, are Maizuru to Otaru (¥6710, 29 hours) and Tsuruga to Otaru (¥7420, 36 hours).

The TIC (p192) can provide detailed information on various routes and up-to-date schedules.

International Ferries

There are regular ferries running between Kansai and Korea or China. There is no international departure tax when leaving Japan by boat.

SOUTH KOREA

Kampu Ferry Service (Japan ☎ 0832-24-3000, Korea ☎ 051-464-2700; www.kampuferry .co.jp/) operates the Shimonoseki–Pusan ferry service. There are daily departures at 7pm from Shimonoseki and Pusan, arriving at the other end at 8.30am (the next day). One-way fares range from ¥8500 to ¥18,000. There's a 10% discount on return fares.

An international high-speed hydrofoil service known as the 'Beetle' that is run by JR Kyūshū (Japan ☎ 092-281-2315, Korea ☎ 051-465-6111) connects Fukuoka with Pusan in Korea, taking about three hours (¥13,000, twice daily). The Camellia line (Japan ☎ 092-262-2323, Korea ☎ 051-466-7799; www.camellia-line.co.jp/ in Japanese) also has a regular daily ferry service between Fukuoka and Pusan (¥9000, 14½ hours).

CHINA

The **Japan China International Ferry company** (Japan ☎ 06-6536-6541; www.fune.co.jp/chinjif /index.html in Japanese) connects Shanghai and Osaka/Kōbe. A 2nd-class ticket is around US$180. A similar service is provided by the **Shanghai Ferry Company** (Japan ☎ 06-6243-6345, China ☎ 021-6537-5111; www.shanghai-ferry.co.jp/ in Japanese).

The **China Express Line** (Japan ☎ 078-321-5791, China ☎ 022-2420-5777; www.celkobe

.co.jp/) operates a ferry between Kōbe and Tanggu (near Tianjin). Ferries leave from Kōbe every Thursday at noon, arriving in Tanggu the next day. Economy/1st-class tickets cost US$200/US$300.

Orient Ferry Ltd (Japan ☎ 0832-32-6615, China ☎ 0532-389-7636; www.orientferry .co.jp/ in Japanese) runs between Shimonoseki and Qingdao, China, with two departures per week. The cheapest one-way/ return tickets cost ¥18,000/34,200.

BUS
Long-Distance Buses

The JR Dream Bus runs nightly between Kyoto Station and Tokyo (either to the Yaesu-guchi long-distance bus stop, which is next to Tokyo Station, or to Shinjuku long-distance bus terminal, which is on the west side of Shinjuku Station). The trip takes about eight hours. There are departures in both directions at 10pm and 11pm, arriving at 6am and 7am respectively; from Kyoto, these depart from the northern side of Kyoto Station, adjacent to the city bus terminal. Tickets are ¥8180 one way; if you're returning within one week a return ticket works out cheaper at ¥14,480.

Although it's possible to just show up and get a seat, reservations and advance purchase are recommended. Contact **JR buses** (☎ 341 0489; www.jrbuskanto.co.jp/mn/ce index.html) or go to the ticket counters in most JR stations, or the main bus information centre in front of Kyoto Station. Most local travel agents can issue tickets in a few minutes for a nominal fee.

Other JR options to/from Kyoto include Kanazawa (one way/return ¥4060/7310, four hours), Tottori (¥3870/6970, four hours), Hiroshima (¥6620/11,720, 7¾ hours), Nagasaki (¥11,310/20,380, 11 hours) and Kumamoto (¥10,800/19,440, 11 hours).

City Buses

Kyoto has an intricate network of bus routes providing an efficient way of getting around at moderate cost. Many of the routes used by visitors have announcements in English. The core timetable for buses is between 7am and 9pm, though a few run earlier or later.

The main bus terminals are Kyoto Station on the JR and Kintetsu lines, Sanjō Station on the Keihan line, Karasuma-Shijō Station on the Hankyū and Karasuma lines, and Kitaōji

Station on the Karasuma line. The bus terminal at Kyoto Station is on the north side and has three main departure bays (departure points are indicated by the letter of the bay and number of the stop within that bay).

The TIC stocks the *Bus Navi: Kyoto City Bus Sightseeing Map*, which is a good map of the city's main bus lines. This map is not exhaustive. If you can read a little Japanese, pick up a copy of the regular (and more detailed) Japanese bus map available at major bus terminals throughout the city, including the main bus information centre in front of Kyoto Station.

Bus stops usually display a map of destinations from that stop on the top section. On the bottom section there's a timetable for the buses serving that stop. Unfortunately, all of this information is in Japanese, and nonspeakers will simply have to ask locals for help.

Entry to the bus is usually through the back door and exit is via the front door. Inner-city buses charge a flat fare (¥220), which you drop into the clear plastic receptacle on top of the machine next to the driver on your way out. A separate machine gives change for ¥100 and ¥500 coins or ¥1000 notes.

On buses serving the outer areas, you take a numbered ticket *(seiri-ken)* when entering. When you leave, an electronic board above the driver displays the fare corresponding to your ticket number (drop the *seiri-ken* into the ticket box with your fare).

To save time and money, you can buy a *kaisū-ken* (book of five tickets) for ¥1000. There's also a one-day card *(shi-basu senyo ichinichi jōshaken cādo)* valid for unlimited travel on city buses that costs ¥500. A similar pass (*Kyoto kankō ichinichi jōsha-ken*) that allows unlimited use of the bus and subway costs ¥1200. A two-day bus/subway pass *(Kyoto kankō futsuka jōsha-ken)* costs ¥2000. *Kaisū-ken* can be purchased directly from bus drivers. The other passes and cards can be purchased at major bus terminals and at the **main bus information centre** (Map pp230–1). Also, be sure to see the Kansai Thru Pass entry (p181).

The main bus information centre is located in front of Kyoto Station. Here, you can pick up bus maps, purchase bus tickets and passes (on all lines, including highway buses), and get additional information. Nearby, there's an English/Japanese bus information computer terminal; just enter your intended destination and it will tell you the correct bus and bus stop.

Three-digit numbers written against a red background denote loop lines: bus 204 runs around the northern part of the city and No 205 and 206 circle the city via Kyoto Station. Buses with route numbers on a blue background take other routes.

When heading for locations outside the city centre, be careful which bus you board. Kyoto city buses are green, Kyoto buses are tan and Keihan buses are red and white.

CAR & MOTORCYCLE

The Meishin Expressway runs between Nagoya and Kōbe. The best access to Kyoto is from the Kyoto–Minami off-ramp (it will leave you on Rte 1, a few kilometres south of the city centre). Kyoto is also accessible from Osaka on Rte 1, Nishinomiya (Kōbe area) on Rte 171, from the western hills on Rte 9, or from the north (Sea of Japan) on the Shūzan Kaidō (Rte 162).

Kyoto's heavy traffic and narrow roads make city driving difficult and stressful. You will almost always do better on a bicycle or public transport. Unless you have specific needs, don't even entertain the idea of renting a car to tour the city – it's far more cost and headache than any traveller needs (plus parking ticket fines start at ¥15,000!).

Remember, driving is on the left-hand side in Japan and a litre of petrol costs between ¥120 and ¥150.

Hire

It makes sense to rent a car if you plan to explore certain rural areas that aren't serviced by train lines. One such place is Miyama-chō (p171).

There are several car-rental agencies in Kyoto. You will need to produce an International Driving Permit and if you cannot find a local to assist you with the paperwork, speaking a little Japanese will help greatly.

Nissan Rent-a-Car (Map pp230–1) has an office directly in front of Kyoto Station. **Matsuda Rent-a-Car** (Map pp222–4; ☎ 361 0201) is close to the intersection of Kawaramachi-dōri and Gojō-dōri.

Rates vary greatly and it's a good idea to shop around, but expect to spend at least ¥6500 per day for an ultracompact sedan, or around ¥10,000 for a regular sedan. Daily rates decrease if you rent for several days.

Motorcycles are a quick but dangerous way to get around town or do some countryside touring. **Sakaguchi Shōkai** (Map pp214–15;

☎ 791 6338; Nakamachi Iwakura) in the Iwakura area (northern Kyoto) rents a variety of bikes ranging from 50cc scooters (per day ¥3200) to 400cc 'ninja' speed machines (¥14,600).

Driving Licence & Permits

Travellers from most nations are able to drive in Japan with an International Driving Permit backed up by their own regular licence. The international permit is issued by your national automobile association and costs around US$5 in most countries. Make sure that it is endorsed for cars and motorcycles if you're licensed for both. For motorbikes up to 250cc (including scooters), the same combination will suffice. Anything over 250cc will require a special motorcycle-licence rating and corresponding stamp in the international permit.

Travellers from Switzerland, France and Germany (and others whose countries are not signatories to the Geneva Convention of 1949 concerning international driver's licences) are not allowed to drive in Japan on a regular international licence. Rather, travellers from these countries must have their own licence backed by an authorised translation of the same licence. These translations can be made by their country's embassy or consulate in Japan or by the Japan Automobile Federation.

If you do decide to drive, you might want to pick up a copy of *Rules of the Road,* available from the **Japan Automobile Federation** (www .jaf.or.jp in Japanese).

TAXI

Taxis are a convenient, though expensive, way of getting from place to place about town. A taxi can usually be flagged down in most parts of the city at any time. There are also a large number of *takushī noriba* (taxi stands) in town, outside most train/subway stations, department stores etc. Remember, there is no need to touch the back doors of the cars at all – the opening/closing mechanism is controlled by the driver.

Fares start at ¥630 for the first 2km. The exception is **MK Taxi** (☎ 721 2237), where fares start at ¥580. Regardless of which taxi company you use, there's a 20% surcharge for rides between midnight and 6am.

MK Taxi also provides tours of the city with English-speaking drivers. For a group of up to four people, prices start at ¥13,280 for three hours.

Two other companies that offer a similar tour service, English-speaking drivers and competitive prices are **Kyōren Taxi Service** (☎ 672 5111) and the **Keihan Taxi Service** (☎ 602 8162).

TRAIN

Kyoto is reached from most places in Japan by JR (Japan's main train company), but there are also several private lines connecting Kyoto with Nagoya, Nara, Osaka and Kōbe. Where they exist, private lines are always cheaper than JR.

In transport information in the listings of this book we have included either the common name for the train station, or the closest bus stop. The train station names are made up of a shortened reference to the train or subway line and then the station name, eg Keihan Shijō Station is the Shijō Station on the Keihan Main Line. Note that there are some exceptions to this, such as the Karasuma and Tōzai subway lines, where we generally state both the line and the station.

Subway

Kyoto has two efficient subway lines, which operate from 5.30am to 11.30pm. The minimum fare is ¥200 (children ¥100).

The quickest way to travel between the north and south of the city is the Karasuma subway line. The line has 15 stops and runs from Takeda in the far south, via Kyoto Station, to the Kyoto International Conference Hall (Kokusaikaikan Station) in the north.

The east–west Tōzai subway line traverses Kyoto from Nijō Station in the west, meeting the Karasuma subway line at Karasuma-Oike Station, and continuing east to Sanjō Keihan, Yamashina and Rokujizō, in the east and southeast.

To/From Other Parts of Japan
KŌBE

Kobe's Sannomiya Station is on the JR Tōkaidō/Sanyō line as well as the Hankyū line, both of which connect it to Kyoto. The fastest way between Kōbe and Kyoto Station is a JR *shinkaisoku* (¥1050, 48 minutes).

The Hankyū line, which stops at Kawaramachi (¥590, one hour limited express), Karasuma and Ōmiya Stations in Kyoto, is cheaper but less convenient; change at Osaka's Jūsō or Umeda Stations.

JR Rail Pass holders should also note that Shin-Kōbe Station is on the Tōkaidō/Sanyō *shinkansen* line.

KYŪSHŪ

Kyoto is on the JR Tōkaidō/Sanyō *shinkansen* line, which runs to Hakata Station in Fukuoka, northern Kyūshū (¥15,210, just under four hours). Other places to pick up the train along this route include Shimonoseki (¥13,960, three hours), Hiroshima (¥10,790, 1¾ hours) and Okayama (¥7330, one hour).

NAGOYA

The *shinkansen* (¥5340, 44 minutes) goes to/from Nagoya. You can save around half the cost by taking regular express trains, but you will need to change trains at least once and can expect the trip to take about three hours.

NARA

Unless you have a Japan Rail Pass, the best option is the Kintetsu line (sometimes written in English as the Kinki Nippon railway), which links Nara (Kintetsu Nara Station) and Kyoto (Kintetsu Kyoto Station). There are direct limited express trains (¥1110, 35 minutes) and ordinary express trains (¥610, 45 minutes), which may require a change at Saidai-ji.

The JR Nara line also connects JR Nara Station with Kyoto Station. Your best bet between the two cities is a *kaisoku* (rapid train; ¥690, 46 minutes) but departures are often few and far between.

THE NORTH

Kyoto can be reached from the northern cities of Kanazawa and Fukui by the JR Hokuriku and Kosei lines, which run along the west coast of Biwa-ko. From Sea of Japan cities, such as Obama and Maizuru, you can take the JR Obama line to Ayabe and then change to the San-in line coming from Kinosaki.

OSAKA

Other than the *shinkansen*, the fastest way between Osaka Station and Kyoto Station is a JR *shinkaisoku* (¥540, 29 minutes).

There is also the cheaper private Hankyū line, which runs between Umeda Station in downtown Osaka and Kawaramachi (¥390, 40 minutes limited express), Karasuma and Ōmiya Stations in Kyoto.

Alternately, you can take the Keihan line between Yodoyabashi Station in Osaka and Demachiyanagi, Marutamachi, Sanjō (¥400, 45 minutes limited express), Shijō or Shichijō Stations in Kyoto.

If you arrive in Osaka at the Osaka-kō or Nan-kō ferry ports, you will find convenient subway connections to JR Osaka Station, Keihan Yodoyabashi Station or the Hankyū Umeda Station. From these stations there are convenient rail connections onward to Kyoto.

From Osaka's Itami airport, take the Osaka monorail to Minami Ibaraki (¥380, 30 minutes) and connect to the Hankyū Kyoto line for Kawaramachi (¥310, about 30 minutes). Of course, it's much easier to take a bus from Itami to Kyoto (p175).

TOKYO

The JR *shinkansen* is the fastest and most frequent rail link; the *hikari* super-express (¥13,220 one way, two hours and 50 minutes) goes to/from Tokyo Station.

By regular express train (¥7980, around eight hours), the trip involves at least two – and possibly three or four – changes along the way.

Buying a Ticket

All stations are equipped with automatic ticket machines, which are simple to operate. Destinations and fares are all posted above the machines in both Japanese and English and once you've figured out the fare to your destination, just insert your money and press the yen amount. Most of these machines accept paper currency in addition to coins (usually just ¥1000 notes). If you've made a mistake, press the red *tori-keshi* (cancel) button. There's also a help button to summon assistance.

Train Passes
JAPAN RAIL PASS

One of Japan's few real travel bargains is the Japan Rail Pass. The pass lets you use any JR service for seven days for ¥28,300, 14 days for ¥45,100 or 21 days for ¥57,700. Green Car (1st class) passes are ¥37,800, ¥61,200 and ¥79,600 respectively. The pass cannot be used for the new super-express Nozomi *shinkansen* service, but is valid for everything else. The only surcharge levied on the Japan Rail Pass is for overnight sleepers. Since a reserved-seat Tokyo–Kyoto *shinkansen* ticket costs ¥13,220, you only have to travel Tokyo–Kyoto–Tokyo once to make the seven-day almost pay itself off.

The pass can only be bought overseas at JAL and ANA offices and major travel agencies. It can only be used by those with a short-stay visa (you'll need to show your passport), which means it *cannot* be used by foreign residents of Japan.

The clock starts to tick on the pass as soon as you validate it, which can be done at JR Travel Service Centres located in most major train stations and at Narita and Kansai airports if you're intending to jump on a JR train immediately. Don't validate it if you're just going into Tokyo or Kyoto and intend to hang around the city for a few days. The pass is valid *only* on JR services; you will still have to pay for private train services.

For more details on the pass, as well as overseas purchase locations, check out JR East (www.jreast.co.jp/e/index.html).

JR WEST KANSAI PASS

A great deal for those who only want to explore the Kansai area, this pass covers unlimited travel on JR lines between most major Kansai cities, such as Himeji, Kōbe, Osaka, Kyoto and Nara. It also covers JR trains to/from Kansai airport but does not cover any *shinkansen* lines. A one-day pass costs ¥2000 and a four-day pass costs ¥6000 (children are half-price). These can be purchased at the same places as the San-yō Area Pass, which is a similar pass, that also entitles you to discounts at station rent-a-car offices. Like the San-yō Area Pass, the Kansai Area Pass can only be used by those with a temporary visitor visa. For more information on this pass, see the website of JR West (www.westjr .co.jp/english/english/index.html).

KANSAI THRU PASS

This new pass is a real boon to travellers who plan to do a fair bit of exploration in the Kansai area. It enables you to ride on city subways, private railways and city buses in Kyoto, Nara, Osaka, Kobe, and Wakayama. It also entitles you to discounts at many attractions in the Kansai area. A two-day pass costs ¥3800 and a three-day pass costs ¥5000. It is available at the Kansai airport travel counter on the first floor of the international arrivals hall and at the main bus information centre in front of Kyoto Station, among others. For more information, visit the site of Kansai Thru Pass (www.surutto.com/conts/ticket/3dayeng/).

SEISHUN JŪHACHI KIPPU

If you don't have a Japan Rail Pass, one of the best deals going is a five-day *Seishun Jūhachi Kippu* (literally a 'Youth 18 Ticket'). Despite the ticket's name, it can be used by anyone of any age. Basically, for ¥11,500 you get five one-day tickets valid for travel anywhere in Japan on JR lines. The only catches are that you can't travel on *tokkyū* (express) or *shinkansen* trains and each ticket must be used within 24 hours. However, even if you only have to make a return trip, say, between Tokyo and Kyoto, you'll be saving a lot of money.

The tickets are intended to be used during Japanese university holidays. There are three periods of sales and validity: spring – sold from 20 February to 31 March and valid for use between 1 March and 10 April; summer – sold from 1 July to 31 August and valid for use between 20 July and 10 September; winter – sold from 1 December to 10 January and valid for use between 20 December and 20 January. Note that these periods are subject to change. For more details, ask at any JR ticket window or JNTO-operated TIC.

Discount Ticket Shops

Known as *kakuyasu-kippu-uriba* in Japanese, these stores deal in discounted tickets for trains, buses, domestic plane flights, ferries and a host of other things like cut-rate stamps and phonecards. Typical savings on *shinkansen* tickets are between 5% and 10%, which is good news for long-term residents who are not eligible for Japan Rail Passes. Discount ticket agencies are found around train stations in medium and large cities. The best way to find one is to ask at the *kōban* (police box) outside the station.

In Kyoto Station, you'll find Tōkai Discount Ticket Shop (Map pp230-1; ☎ 344 0330 north side, 662 6640 south side; ☻ north side: 9.30am-7.30pm Mon-Fri, 10am-7pm Sat, Sun & holidays, south side: 10am-7.30pm Mon-Fri, 10am-7pm Sat, Sun & holidays). In the Excursions chapter (p149), discount ticket shops are listed on the maps of Himeji (p170), Kita (pp158-9) and Kōbe (pp166-7).

Left Luggage

There are coin lockers in train stations in Kyoto. Small/medium/large lockers cost ¥300/400/600 for 24 hours. Otherwise, in Kyoto Station there is an *ichiji-nimotsu-azukari* (luggage-storage office) that charges ¥410 per piece of luggage for up to six days, after which the daily rate increases to ¥820. Luggage can be stored for a total of 15 days and there is a size limit (within two metres across and up to 30kg). The office is on the B1 floor near the centre ticket gate.

PRACTICALITIES

ACCOMMODATION

In this guide, accommodation listings have been organised alphabetically and by neighbourhood. Mid-range to high-end options are listed within the main part of each neighbourhood's sleeping options. Budget options follow under the Cheap Sleeps heading. For further information, see Sleeping (p136).

BUSINESS HOURS

Shops in town are typically open from 10am to 7pm or 8pm. Shopping on Sunday, the only free day for most working Japanese, should be avoided if you've got an aversion to crowds.

Kyoto's six major department stores are open from 10am to 7.30pm and each closes one day a week. If one is closed you stand a good chance of finding another one open close by.

Although most companies technically operate on a 9am to 5pm, five-day work week, many stay in business on Saturday morning as well. Banks are open Monday to Friday from 9am to 3pm, and are closed on Saturday, Sunday and national holidays.

For those late-night cravings, beer and cigarette vending machines shut down after 11pm, though there are 24-hour convenience stores all over town, some of which stock alcohol and tobacco.

For details on post office opening hours, see p190.

CHILDREN

Japan is a great place to travel with children; it's safe, clean and extremely convenient. It's possible to book cots in most proper hotels (as opposed to 'business hotels') and nappy-changing tables are available in the bathrooms of most hotels and in some train stations. Nappies and baby formula are widely available in supermarkets, department stores and convenience stores.

Breastfeeding in public is generally not done in Japan. Child-care facilities are usually available in department stores – ask at the information counter when you enter. Otherwise, child-care facilities are generally geared to locals only and are hard to access for short-term visitors.

In general, the cost of public transport is half-price for children under 12. Likewise, many of the city's attractions and hotels also offer discounted rates for children.

For more information on child-centred activities in Kyoto, see the boxed text, 'Kyoto for Children', on p66.

CLIMATE

Without a doubt, the best times to visit Kyoto are the climatically stable seasons of spring (March to May) and autumn (late September to November).

The highlight of spring is cherry-blossom season, which usually arrives in Kyoto in early April. Bear in mind, though, that the blossoms are notoriously fickle, blooming any time from late March to mid-April.

Autumn is an equally good time to travel, with pleasant temperatures and soothing autumn colours. The shrines and temples of Kyoto look stunning against a backdrop of blazing leaves, which usually peak between late October and mid-November.

Of course, the Japanese are well aware that Kyoto is most beautiful at these times, and the main attractions can be packed with local tourists. Likewise, accommodation can be hard to find; if you do come at these times, be sure to book well in advance.

Travelling in either winter or summer is a mixed bag. Mid-winter (December to February) weather can be quite cold (but not prohibitively so), while the sticky summer months (June to August) can turn even the briefest excursion out of the air-con into a soup bath.

June is the month of Japan's rainy season, which varies in intensity from year to year; some years there's no rainy season to speak of, other years it rains virtually every day.

For more information on the best times to visit Kyoto, see p8.

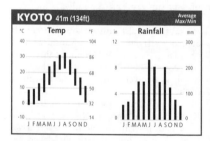

COURSES

There's more to Kyoto than just temples, shrines and parks: there are several places to get hands-on experience in traditional arts and crafts including tea ceremony, Japanese *washi* paper, textiles, ceramics and calligraphy. This is only a partial list of what's available. The people at the TIC can help with requests for more specialised activities.

Kyoto International Community House (KICH; Map pp225-7; ☎ 752 3010; Sakyō-ku, Awataguchi) offers an intriguing variety of introductory courses in Japanese culture, open to all for observation (free) and participation. The cost is ¥500 per class, ¥3000 per three-month semester. It also offers Japanese-language as well as calligraphy classes. Other courses are occasionally offered in the tea ceremony and *koto* (a Japanese string instrument). For more on KICH, see p192.

Ai-Zome Dyeing

In the Nishijin area, **Aizen-Kōbō** (Map pp216-18; ☎ 441 0355; Nakasuji-dōri-Ōmiya nishi iru; ⏰ 10am-5.30pm Mon-Fri, 10am-4pm Sat & Sun; 5min walk from Imadegawa-Ōmiya bus stop) dyes indigo-blue *ai-zome* fabrics in a charming *kyō-machiya* (wooden townhouse). You can observe and try your hand at tie-dyeing a handkerchief (¥2000) or scarf (¥6300) in about an hour. Reservations should be made a few days in advance.

Braiding

Kyoto's most famed braid-maker, **Adachi Kumihimo-kan** (Map pp216-18; ☎ 432 4113; Demizu-dōri-Karasuma nishi iru; classes ¥2000-5000; ⏰ 9am-noon, 1-4pm Mon-Fri & 1st Sat of month; 5min walk from Subway Marutamachi Station) has a gallery of fine items on display. Here you can weave your own braid on wooden hand looms. It takes about two hours, and the cost depends on the length of the class and what you make. Delicately woven *kyō-kumihimo* (Kyoto-style braidwork) was developed in the Heian period for fastening kimono, but gradually spread to other ornamental applications. Today the braid is again most commonly used as *obi-jime* (the tie for kimono sashes). Reservations in Japanese are necessary.

Doll-Making

In about four hours at **Honke Katsura** (Map pp228-9; ☎ 221 6998; Takakura-dōri-Sanjō kudaru; cost ¥10,500; ⏰ 10am-6pm, Feb-Nov only, closed Mon; 10min walk from Keihan Sanjō Station) you can learn to paint the face on and assemble a hand-crafted *kyō-ningyō* doll. Advance reservations in Japanese are necessary.

Handwoven Textiles

In Nishijin, **Orinasu-kan** (Map pp216-18; ☎ 431 0020; Kamigyō-ku, Daikoku-chō; cost incl museum admission ¥5000; ⏰ 10am-4pm; 15min walk from Karasuma subway line, Imadegawa Station) offers traditional weaving workshops. The cost is for a three-hour course and you can take home your handmade fabric. Reservations in Japanese are required one week in advance.

Japanese Language

Kyoto is a good place to study Japanese. **Kawara Juku** (Map pp228-9; ☎ 231 1608) is a friendly little school that offers three-month part-time courses for ¥85,000. Courses start in April, September and January. They also offer a summer intensive course for the same price. Joining a class here is a great way to meet people when you're new in town.

Metalwork

Kyō-zōgan is a damascene technique of laying fine metals onto figures engraved on brass and can be tried at **Amita-honten** (Map pp225-7; ☎ 761 7000; Okazaki Heian-jingū Kita; ⏰ 9am, 10am & 2pm Mar-Nov, closes at 5.30pm Dec-Feb; 3min walk from Kumanojinja-mae bus stop, bus 206 from Kyoto Station), just beside the Kyoto Handicraft Center on Marutamachi-dōri. The cost of making a small pendant is ¥3500 and it takes about an hour (it will be sent to you one week later).

Paper Fans

You can learn to design your own *kyō-sensu* paper fan in about 90 minutes at **Kyōsen-dō** (Map pp230-1; ☎ 371 4151; www.kyosendo .co.jp/english/index.html; Higashinotōin-dōri-Shomen agaru; cost ¥2200; sessions 9am, 10.30am, 1pm & 5pm Mon-Fri, 10am, 1pm & 3pm Sat & Sun; 10min walk from Kyoto Station). Reservations in Japanese are necessary a few days in advance. Your fan will be sent to a Japanese address a month later (no overseas deliveries).

Paper-Making

Rakushi-kan (Map pp228-9; ☎ 251 0078; ra kushikan@kami-kyo.to; Takoyakushi-dōri-Muromachi nishi iru; ¥1000-1300; ⏰ 10am-7pm Tue-Sun; 5min walk from Karasuma subway line, Karasuma-Oike Station) offers papermaking workshops on Thursday, Friday and Saturday, with sessions at 1pm, 2pm,

3pm and 4pm. The one-hour course costs from ¥1000 for making sheets of *washi*, business cards or postcards. Reservations in Japanese should be made a week in advance and courses are held for groups of five or more.

Tea Ceremony

At **Urasenke Chadō Research Center** (Map pp216-18; ☎ 431 6474; Horikawa-dōri-Teranouchi; admission ¥500; ☼ 9.30am-4pm Tue-Sun; 5min walk from Horikawa Teranouchi bus stop), it's possible to watch a 20-minute tea-making procedure *(temae)* during the Urasenke Foundation's quarterly art exhibitions. You can sample a bowl of *matcha* (powdered green tea) and a sweet (included in the cost of visiting the centre's gallery).

Vegetable-Dyeing

In Ōhara, **Ōhara Kōbō** (Map p233; ☎ 744 3138; Ōhara Kusao-chō; cost ¥500-3000; ☼ 10am-5pm Thu-Tue; 5min walk from the Ōhara bus stop) offers a chance to dye fabrics using vivid plant and vegetable dyes *(kusaki-zome)*. The time and cost depend on the item; choose from a handkerchief (¥500), scarf (¥3000) or plain woollen yarn (enough to knit one sweater ¥8000); if you bring your own wool to dye, the cost is ¥5000. Advance reservations in Japanese are required, and the process takes from two to four hours.

Yūzen-Dyeing

At the **Kodai Yūzen-en Gallery** (Map pp222-4; ☎ 823 0500; Takatsuji-dōri-Inokuma; cost incl museum admission ¥500; ☼ 9am-4pm; 5min walk from Horikawa Matsubara bus stop) there are facilities to try Yūzen stencil-dyeing in about 40 minutes. You can choose from various items to dye, such as a handkerchief (¥1050) or necktie (¥4200).

Offering similar activities is **Yūzen Cultural Hall** (Yūzen Bunka Kaikan; Map pp214-15; ☎ 311 0025; Nishikyogoku-Mameda; cost incl museum admission ¥400; ☼ 9am-4pm Mon-Sat; 6min walk from Hankyū line Nishikyōgoku Station). In about 20 minutes you can stencil-dye a hankie (¥450 to ¥800) or try hand painting (¥2100). The workshop closes for one hour at lunch (noon to 1pm) and you must arrive by 4pm.

CULTURAL CENTRES

There are British, German, French and Italian cultural centres, listed respectively below, in Kyoto. All have libraries, sponsor art exhibitions, organise lectures and seminars relating to their respective country, and participate in cross-cultural exchange programmes.

British Council (☎ 229 7151; Karasuma-dōri-Nishikikōji; ☼ 10am-8pm Mon-Fri, 10am-5pm Sat, closed Sun & public holidays)

Goethe Institute Kyoto (Map pp219-21; ☎ 761 2188; Kawabata-dōri, south of Imadegawa-dōri; ☼ 9am-5pm Mon-Fri, closed Sat-Sun & public holidays)

Institut Franco-Japonais du Kansai (Map pp219-21; ☎ 761 2105; Higashiōji-dōri, south of Imadegawa-dōri; ☼ 9.30am-7pm Tue-Fri, 9.30-am-6.30pm Mon & Sat, closed Sun)

Instituto Italiano di Cultura di Kansai (Map pp219-21; ☎ 761 4356; Higashiōji-dōri, south of Imadegawa-dōri; ☼ 11am-7pm Mon-Fri, 11am-6pm Sat, closed Sun & public holidays)

CUSTOMS

Customs allowances include the usual tobacco products, plus three 760mL bottles of alcohol, 57g of perfume, and gifts and souvenirs up to a value of ¥200,000 or its equivalent. The alcohol and tobacco allowances are available only for those who are aged 20 or older. The penalties for importing drugs are severe. Pornography (magazines, videos etc) in which pubic hair or genitalia are visible is illegal in Japan and will be confiscated by customs officers.

There are no limits on the import of foreign or Japanese currency. The export of foreign currency is also unlimited but a ¥5 million limit exists for Japanese currency.

DISABLED TRAVELLERS

Although Kyoto has made some attempts at making public facilities more accessible, its narrow streets and the terrain of sights such as temples and shrines make it a challenging city for people with disabilities, especially for those confined to wheelchairs.

If you are going to travel by train and need assistance, ask one of the station workers as you enter the station. Try asking: '*Karada no fujiyuū no kata no tame no sharyō wa arimasu ka?*' ('Are there any train carriages for disabled travellers?').

There are carriages on most lines that have areas set aside for those in wheelchairs. Those with other physical disabilities can use one of the seats set aside near the train exits, called *yūsen-zaseki*. You'll also find these seats near the front of buses; usually they're a different colour from the regular seats.

MK Taxi (☎ 721 2237) can accommodate wheelchairs in many of its cars and is an attractive possibility for anyone interested in touring the city by cab. Facilities for the visually impaired include musical pedestrian lights at many city intersections and raised bumps on railway platforms for guidance.

AD-Brain (the same outfit which publishes the monthly *Kyoto Visitor's Guide*) has produced a basic city map for disabled people and senior citizens showing wheelchair-access points in town and giving information on public transport access etc. The map is available at the TIC. You might also try contacting the **Disabled Welfare** (☎ 251 2385) section at Kyoto City Hall, or the **Kyoto City Association for Disabled Persons** (☎ 822 0770 in Japanese), which publishes the very detailed *Handy Map* guidebook on local facility accessibility, presently in Japanese only.

The most useful information for disabled visitors to Japan is provided by the **Japanese Red Cross Language Service Volunteers** (☎ 3438-1311; http://accessible.jp.org; c/o Volunteers Division, Japanese Red Cross Society, 1-1-3 Shiba Daimon, Minato-ku, Tokyo 105-8521).

DISCOUNT CARDS

An international youth hostel card is useful if you plan to stay in hostels in Kyoto or Japan. Student cards are also handy and Japan is one of the few places left in Asia where a student card can be useful. Officially, you should be carrying an ISIC (International Student Identity Card) to qualify for a discount (usually for entry to places of interest), but in practice you will often find that any youth or student card will do the trick. There are a variety of discounts available in Japan for seniors over the age 65. In almost all cases a passport will be sufficient proof of age, so seniors' cards are rarely worth bringing.

ELECTRICITY

The Japanese electric current is 100V AC, an odd voltage not found elsewhere in the world, though most North American electrical items, designed to run on 117V, will function reasonably well on the Japanese current. While Tokyo and eastern Japan are on 50 Hz, Kyoto and the rest of western Japan are on a cycle of 60 Hz.

Identical to North American plugs, Japanese plugs are of the flat, two-pronged

Bringing Guide Dogs to Japan

Japanese regulations on importing live animals are very strict, and are not waived for guide dogs. Dogs brought from countries in which rabies has been eradicated need not be quarantined, provided their owners can show a *yushutsu shōmeisho* (exportation certificate). Dogs arriving from countries in which rabies occurs will be placed into quarantine for up to six months, unless their owners can supply an exportation certificate, veterinary examination certification and written proof of rabies vaccination.

variety. Both transformers and plug adaptors are readily available in Kyoto's Teramachi-dōri electronics district (p128).

EMBASSIES & CONSULATES
Tokyo

Most countries have embassies in Tokyo (area code ☎ 03), some of which are listed below.

Australia (☎ 5232 4111; www.dfat.gov.au/missions /countries/jp.html; 2-1-14 Mita, Minato-ku)

Canada (☎ 5412-6200; www.dfait-maeci.gc.ca/ni-ka /tokyo-en.asp; 7-3-38 Akasaka, Minato-ku, Tokyo)

China (☎ 3403 3380; 3-4-33 Moto-Azabu, Minato-ku)

France (☎ 5420 8800; www.ambafrance-jp.org in French; 4-11-44 Minami-Azabu, Minato-ku)

Germany (☎ 5791-7700; www.germanembassy-japan .org; 4-5-10 Minami Azabu, Minato-ku)

Ireland (☎ 3263 0695; www.embassy-avenue.jp/ireland /index_eng.html; 2-10-7 Koji-machi, Chiyoda-ku)

Netherlands (☎ 5401 0411; www.oranda.or.jp/index /english/index.html; 3-6-3 Shiba-kōen, Minato-ku)

New Zealand (☎ 3467 2271; www.nzembassy.com /home.cfm; 20-40 Kamiyamachō, Shibuya-ku)

South Korea (☎ 3452 7611; 1-2-5 Minami-Azabu, Minato-ku)

UK (☎ 3265 5511; www.uknow.or.jp/be_e; 1 Ichibanchō, Chiyoda-ku)

USA (☎ 3224 5000; http://tokyo.usembassy.gov/; 1-10-5 Akasaka, Minato-ku)

Osaka

Several countries also have consulates in Osaka (area code ☎ 06).

Australia (☎ 6941 9271; 2-1-61 Shiromi, Chūō-ku)

Canada (☎ 6212 4910; 12F, Dai-san Shoho Bldg, 2-2-3 Nishi-Shinsaibashi, Chūō-ku)

China (☎ 6445 9473; 3-9-2 Utsubo Honmachi, Nishi-ku, Osaka)

France (☎ 4790-1500; 1-2-27 Shiromi, Chūō-ku, Osaka)

Germany (☎ 6440 5070; 35F, Umeda Sky Bldg, Tower East, 1-1-88 Ōyodo-naka, Kita-ku)

Netherlands (☎ 6944 7272; 33F, Twin 21 Mid-Tower, 2-1-61 Shiromi, Chūō-ku)

New Zealand (☎ 6942 9016; 28F, Twin 21 Mid-Tower, 2-1-61 Shiromi, Chūō-ku)

UK (☎ 6281 1616; 19F, Seiko Osaka Bldg, 3-5-1 Bakuro-machi, Chūō-ku)

USA (☎ 6315 5900; 2-11-5 Nishi-Tenma, Kita-ku)

EMERGENCY

Although most emergency operators in Kyoto don't speak English, they will refer you to someone who does. Be sure to have your address handy when calling for assistance. Japan Helpline is a service that provides assistance to foreigners living in Japan.

Ambulance	☎ 119
Fire	☎ 119
Japan Helpline	☎ 0120-461 997
Police	☎ 110

Kōban (police boxes) are small police stations typically found at city intersections. Most can be recognised by the small, round red lamp outside. They are a logical place to head in an emergency, but remember that the police may not always speak English.

GAY & LESBIAN TRAVELLERS

With the possible exception of Thailand, Japan is Asia's most enlightened nation with regard to the sexual preferences of foreigners. Same-sex couples probably won't encounter many problems travelling in Japan. However, some travellers have reported problems when checking into love hotels with a partner of the same sex. Apart from this, it's unlikely that you'll run into difficulties, but it does pay to be discreet in rural areas.

While there is a sizable gay community in Kyoto and a number of establishments where gays do congregate, they will take a fair amount of digging to find. There's a more active scene in Osaka, and many of Kyoto's gay residents make the trip there.

Gay Scene Japan (http://members.tripod.co.jp/GSJ) might be helpful when planning your trip. It's a fun and useful site with information specifically aimed at gay and lesbian travellers.

HEALTH

Your health while travelling will depend on your predeparture preparations, your day-to-day health care and how you handle any medical problem or emergency that does develop. However, looking after your health in Japan should pose few problems, since hygiene standards are high and medical facilities are widely available, though expensive (see opposite). There are very few health risks in Japan to speak of, aside perhaps from an overabundance of secondary smoke.

No immunisations are required for Japan though despite the very low risk factor, you may want to consider vaccinations against Hepatitis A and B. The former is transmitted by contaminated food and drinking water and the latter is spread through contact with infected blood, blood products or body fluids. It is also wise to keep up-to-date with your tetanus, diphtheria and polio shots (boosters are recommended every 10 years). Tap water is safe to drink and the food is almost uniformly prepared with high standards of hygiene. It is advisable to take out some form of health insurance.

HOLIDAYS

The following public holidays are observed in Kyoto.

Ganjitsu (New Year's Day) 1 January

Seijin-no-hi (Coming-of-Age Day) 2nd Sunday in January

Kenkoku Kinem-bi (National Foundation Day) 11 February

Shumbun-no-hi (Spring Equinox) 20 or 21 March

Midori-no-hi (Green Day) 29 April

Kempō Kinem-bi (Constitution Day) 3 May

Kokumin-no-Saijitsu (Adjoining Holiday Between Two Holidays) 4 May

Kodomo-no-hi (Children's Day) 5 May

Umi-no-hi (Marine Day) 20 July

Keirō-no-hi (Respect-for-the-Aged Day) 15 September

Shūbun-no-hi (Autumn Equinox) 23 or 24 September

Taiiku-no-hi (Sports Day) 2nd Monday in October

Bunka-no-hi (Culture Day) 3 November

Kinrō Kansha-no-hi (Labour Thanksgiving Day) 23 November

Tennō Tanjōbi (Emperor's Birthday) 23 December

INTERNET ACCESS

If you plan on bringing your laptop with you to Kyoto, first make sure that it is compatible with Japanese current (100V AC; 50Hz in eastern Japan and 60Hz in western Japan, including Kyoto). Most laptops function just fine on Japanese current. Second, check to see if your plug will fit Japanese wall sockets (Japanese plugs are flat two pin, identical to most ungrounded North American plugs). Both transformers and plug adaptors are readily available in electronics districts like Kyoto's Teramachi-dōri (p128).

Modems and phone jacks are similar to those used in the USA (RJ11 phone jacks). Conveniently, many of the grey IDD pay phones in Japan have a standard phone jack and an infrared port so that you can log on to the Internet just about anywhere in the country.

Kyoto has no shortage of Internet cafés, though rates are much higher than other countries in the region (per half hour is around ¥250). If necessary, the TIC can recommend additional places to log on.

C. Coquet (Map pp216-18; ☎ 212 0882; Shimogoryō-mae-chō 631; with drink/food order Internet free; ⏰ 9am-10pm, closed Thu) This new restaurant/café is a great place to log on, and you can do it with your own machine if you don't want to use the machines provided.

Kyoto International Community House (KICH; Map pp225-7; ☎ 752 3512; Sakyō-ku, Awataguchi; per 30 min ¥200) The machines here have Japanese keyboards and you are limited in the sites you can visit, but it's a fairly cheap place to log on.

Kyoto Prefectural International Center (Map pp230-1; ☎ 342 5000; 9th fl, Kyoto Station bldg; per 15 min ¥100; ⏰ 10am-6pm) One of the cheaper places in town. In addition to using the machines provided, you can also log on with your own machine here. It's closed on the second and fourth Tuesday of each month.

MAPS

Available free at the TIC and all JNTO offices, the *Tourist Map of Kyoto-Nara* fulfils most mapping needs and includes a simplified map of the subway and bus systems. *Walking Tour Courses in Kyoto* details five good walks in and around Kyoto. Also available is the *Bus Navi: Kyoto City Bus Sightseeing Map*, which has detailed information on bus routes in the city and some of the major stops written in both English and Japanese.

There are many other useful maps for sale at local English-language bookshops, some of which are practical for excursions outside Kyoto. Shōbunsha's *Tourist Map of Kyoto, Nara, Osaka and Kōbe* is the best privately produced map of these cities.

Serious hikers should pick up Shōbunsha's *Kyoto Kitayama 1* and *Kyoto Kitayama 2* maps, part of their *Yama-to-Kōgen Chizu* series. These two maps cover Kyoto's northern Kitayama mountains in exquisite detail, showing all hiking trails and topographical features. Unfortunately, they are written entirely in Japanese. The maps can be found at most local bookshops.

Kyoto Bus company's *Kyoto Kitayama/Hira-san* map, available free at its Kyoto Demachiyanagi office (which is located next to Eizan-Dentetsu Demachiyanagi Station) is another good map of Kitayama hikes. Again, it's all in Japanese.

MEDICAL SERVICES

Medical care in Japan is relatively expensive. Although the cost of a basic consultation is cheap (about ¥3000) the costs really start to add up with any further examinations, especially with the tendency of Japan's doctors to over-prescribe medication. If you do need to visit a hospital in Kyoto, it is not usually necessary to have cash in hand; most hospitals will admit people on a pay-later basis. Credit cards are rarely accepted.

Clinics

For non-emergency medical care in Kyoto, the **Japan Baptist Hospital** (Map pp219-21; ☎ 781 5191; ⏰ 8.30am-11am & 1-3.45pm, closed Sat afternoon, Sun & holidays) is popular with foreign residents and has some English-speaking doctors. It's in northeast Kyoto; to get there, take bus 3 from Shijō Kawaramachi Station on the Hankyū line and get off at the Shibuse-chō stop (last stop). It's a short walk up the hill.

There are several other hospitals and clinics around town, including the following.

Kyoto City Hospital (Map pp222-4; ☎ 311 5311; Higashi-takada-chō 1-2, Mibu, Nakagyō-ku)

Kyoto Prefectural University Hospital (Map pp219-21; ☎ 251 5111; Hirokoji-agaru, Kawaramachi-dōri, Kamigyō-ku)

Tomita Maternity Clinic (Map pp222-4; ☎ 221 1202; Sanjō-agaru, Shinmachi-dōri, Nakagyō-ku)

For additional hospitals, the TIC (p192) has lists of English-speaking doctors and hospitals in Kyoto. You can also find information on hospitals with English-speaking doctors by visiting the website of the **Kyoto City International Foundation** (www.kcif.or.jp/en /benri/03_02.html).

Directory – Practicalities

Emergency Rooms

For an emergency clinic open on Sunday and public holidays, try the **Kyoto Holiday Emergency Clinic** (Map pp216-18; ☎ 811 5072). For emergency dental problems call the **Kyoto Holiday Emergency Dental Clinic** (Map pp222-4; ☎ 812 8493) or **Igarashi Dental Clinic** (Map pp214-15; ☎ 392 0993).

MONEY

The Japanese postal system has recently linked its ATMs to the international Cirrus and Plus networks, so money is no longer the issue it once was for travellers to Japan. Of course, it always makes sense to carry some foreign cash and some credit cards just to be on the safe side. For those without credit cards, it would be a good idea to bring some travellers cheques as a back up.

For details on costs in Kyoto, see p13, and for current exchange rates, see the inside front cover.

ATMs

Automatic teller machines are almost as common as vending machines in Kyoto. Unfortunately, most of these do not accept foreign-issued cards. Even if your card displays the Visa or MasterCard logo, most ATMs will only accept Japan-issued versions of these cards.

Luckily, you don't have to rely on these since the Japanese postal system has recently linked all of its ATMs to the international Cirrus and Plus cash networks (as well as some credit card networks), making life a breeze for foreign travellers to Japan. You'll find postal ATMs in most large post offices. Most postal ATMs are open 9am to 5pm Monday to Friday, 9am to 12.30pm on Saturday, and are closed on Sunday and holidays. If you need cash outside these hours, try the Kyoto **central post office** (Map 10; next to Kyoto Station; ☯ 12.05am-8pm Sun, 7am-11.55pm Mon, 12.05am to 11.55pm Tue-Sat).

Note that the postal ATMs are a little tricky to use: first press 'English Guidance' on the left of the screen, then press 'Other', then choose your transaction and you're away.

There are several international ATMs in town that accept foreign-issued cards (see Credit Cards, opposite). You'll find an **international ATM** (Map pp230-1; ☯ 10am-9pm) in the Kyoto Tower Hotel on the B1 floor, and in the middle of town is another **international ATM** (Map pp228-9; ☯ 7am-11pm) in the Zest Underground Shopping Arcade, 200m west of the Oike-Kawaramachi intersection, near exit 7.

Citibank (Map pp222–4) has a 24hr ATM that accepts most foreign-issued cards. Note that only holders of Japan-issued Citibank cards can use the ATM after hours.

Internet Resources

There's no better place to start your Web explorations than the website of **Lonely Planet** (www.lonelyplanet.com). Here you'll find succinct summaries on travelling to most places on earth, postcards from other travellers and the Thorn Tree bulletin board, where you can ask questions before you go or dispense advice when you get back. You can also find travel news and updates to many of our most popular guidebooks, and the 'subwwway' section links you to the most useful travel resources elsewhere on the Web.

Other websites with useful Japan and Kyoto information and links:

Japan National Tourist Organization (www.jnto.go.jp) Japan's main national tourist authority.

Japan Weather Association (www.jwa.or.jp/fcst/00305e.html) Daily weather information.

Japanese Traffic Guide (www.jorudan.co.jp/english/norikae/e-norikeyin.html) A brilliant site for getting transport information in the Kyoto area.

JNTO Sightseeing Maps of Kyoto (www.jnto.go.jp/eng/spn/kyoto/sightseeing/index.html) Download maps of Kyoto to help find your way around town.

JR East (www.jreast.co.jp/e/index.html) Information on rail travel in Japan, with details on the Japan Rail Pass.

Kansai Time Out (www.kto.co.jp) Monthly English-language magazine for the Kansai area.

Kyoto Shimbun News (www.kyoto-np.co.jp/kp/english/index.html) Kyoto's main newspaper.

Kyoto Temple Admission Fees (www.templefees.com) These change from time to time, so it's best to get the latest info.

Kyoto Visitor's Guide (www.kyotoguide.com) Lot's of Kyoto-specific information.

Changing Money

You can change cash or travellers cheques at any 'Authorised Foreign Exchange Bank' (signs will always be displayed in English) or at some of Kyoto's larger hotels and department stores. Main post offices will also cash travellers cheques. Rates vary little, if at all, between banks (even the exchange counters at the airport offer rates comparable to those offered by downtown banks).

In Kyoto, most major banks are located near the Shijō-Karasuma intersection, two stops north of Kyoto Station on the Karasuma subway line. Of these, **UFJ Bank** (Map pp228-9; ☎ 211 4583) is the most convenient for changing money and buying travellers cheques. There's also a branch of **Citibank** (Map pp222–4), which has an international ATM in its lobby.

Credit Cards

Do not rely on credit cards in Japan. While department stores, top-end hotels and *some* fancy restaurants do accept cards, most businesses in Japan do not. Cash-and-carry is still very much the rule in Japan. Among places that accept credit cards, you'll find Visa most useful, followed by MasterCard and American Express.

For cash advances of amounts up to ¥40,000, any of the ATMs mentioned previously should suffice. For larger amounts, Visa cardholders can also get cash advances at the 1st floor Hankyū department store branch of **Mitsui Sumitomo Bank** (Map pp228-9; ☎ 223 2288).

Currently there is no representation for international cardholders in Kyoto, and for inquiries it is often best to call the number in your home country on the back of your card, or try the offices in Tokyo. The telephone numbers (area code ☎ 03) of the Tokyo offices:

American Express (toll free ☎ 0120-020 120 24hr)

MasterCard (☎ 03-5728 5200)

Visa (☎ 03-5251 0633, toll free ☎ 0120-133 173)

Currency

The currency in Japan is the yen (¥), and banknotes and coins are easily identifiable. There are ¥1, ¥5, ¥10, ¥50, ¥100 and ¥500 coins, and ¥1000, ¥5000 and ¥10,000 banknotes. The ¥1 coin is of lightweight aluminium, and the ¥5 (known to bring good luck) and ¥50 coins have a hole in the middle. There has also been talk of introducing a new ¥2000 note; keep your eyes peeled for them.

Travellers Cheques

Travellers cheques are fairly commonplace in Japan nowadays, though they can only be cashed at banks, major post offices and some hotels. It is not possible to use foreign currency travellers cheques in stores and restaurants. In most cases the exchange rate for travellers cheques is slightly better than cash. In order to cash travellers cheques or make cash advances at banks, you will need to show your passport or a valid Alien Registration Card.

NEWSPAPERS & MAGAZINES

There are three English-language daily newspapers in Japan: the *Japan Times,* the *Daily Yomiuri* and the *Asahi Shimbun/International Herald Tribune* (a joint publication published by the Asahi Shimbun corporation). All of these can be found at the bookshops listed in Shopping chapter (p128), at most major hotels and at some newspaper stands in train and subway stations.

Another excellent source of information on Kyoto and the rest of the Kansai area is *Kansai Time Out,* a monthly English-language what's on magazine (¥300). For short-term visitors, new arrivals and even long-term expats, *Kansai Time Out* is a useful resource. Apart from lively articles, it has a large section of announcements and ads for employment, travel agencies, clubs, lonely hearts etc. It's available at Maruzen (p134) and Kinokuniya (p130) bookshops.

Those with more eclectic interests should keep an eye out for the praiseworthy *Kyoto Journal,* which publishes in-depth articles on Asian culture and issues, as well as artwork by Kyoto residents and others. It's also available at local bookshops.

The monthly *Kyoto Visitor's Guide* is the best source of information on cultural and tourist events. It's available free at the TIC (p192), Maruzen bookshop (p130), the Kyoto International Community House, (p192) and most major hotels.

PHARMACIES

Pharmacies can be found in any neighbourhood in the city and are easily spotted by their colourful outdoor displays of shampoo and other pharmaceutical products.

PHOTOGRAPHY

For amateur and professional photography supplies including slide film, black-and-white film and all the latest gadgets, Kyoto's best shop is **Medic** (Map pp228-9; ☎ 256 6651), on the west side of Kawaramachi-dōri, about 50m north of Sanjō-dōri. It also offers reliable processing services.

Another popular place to have print film developed is at the Yellow Camera chain (with several branches in Kyoto), easy to spot by its all-yellow façade. One-hour processing tends to be slightly more expensive than overnight, but it is offered at many local shops. Japanese labs usually print on what's called *sābisu saizu* (service size), which is about two-thirds of the standard size in most countries (four by six inches). Unless you're happy with this size, ask to have your photos printed on *hagaki* (postcard) sized paper.

For black-and-white film or slide processing, the best option is **Horiuchi Color** (Map pp228-9; ☎ 223 5321; Yanaginobamba-dōri, Oike-sagaru).

POST

Most local post offices are open Monday to Friday from 9am to 5pm, and some are also open on Saturday from 9am to 12.30pm. Kyoto's **central post office** (Map pp230-1; ☎ 365 2467; ⏰ 9am-7pm Mon-Fri, 9am-5pm Sat, 9am-12.30pm Sun & holidays), is on the north side of Kyoto Station. Poste restante mail can be collected here. There's a service counter on the south side of the building open 24 hours per day for air mail, small packages, and special express mail services.

Nakagyō post office (Map pp228-9; ☎ 255 1112) at the Nishinotōin-Sanjō crossing is open until 7pm on weekdays, but is closed at weekends. There is a 24-hour service window on the west side of the building.

The airmail rate for postcards is ¥70 to any overseas destination; aerograms cost ¥90. Letters weighing less than 10g cost ¥90 to other countries within Asia, ¥110 to North America, Europe or Oceania (including Australia and New Zealand) and ¥130 to Africa and South America. One peculiarity of the Japanese postal system is that you will be charged extra if your writing runs over onto the address side (the right side) of a postcard.

All post offices provide a reliable international Express Mail Service (EMS), which is as good or better than private express shipping services.

RADIO

Kyoto's best station with bilingual broadcasts and decent music is Alpha station (89.4 FM), but there are several other Kansai stations worth checking out:

76.5 FM Cocolo Multilingual.

80.2 FM 802 Japanese and English.

85.1 FM Osaka Japanese and English.

89.9 Kiss FM Kōbe Japanese and English.

SWIMMING

You can swim in the **Kamo-gawa** in the summer. The best spot is about one kilometre north of Kamigamo-jinja; just look for all the people. Keep in mind that swimming here is not without hazard and people have drowned swimming in this river. Parents should keep a close eye on their kids. If you'd prefer to swim in a pool, **Tosuikai** (☎ 761 1275; Marutamachi-dōri; ⏰ 10am-3pm Mon-Sat, noon-5pm Sun) allows nonmembers to use their pools for ¥1100 per visit.

TAXES & REFUNDS

There is a 5% consumption tax on retail purchases in Japan. Visitors on a short-stay visa can, however, avoid this tax on purchases made at major department stores and duty-free stores such as the Kyoto Handicraft Center (p129). For a refund on purchases, check first that the department store has a service desk for tax refunds. When you make a purchase the tax will be included; take the purchase, receipt and your passport to the service desk for an immediate refund.

If you eat at expensive restaurants and stay at 1st-class accommodation, you will encounter a service charge, which varies from 10% to 15%. A tax of 5% is added to restaurant bills exceeding ¥5000 or for hotel bills exceeding ¥10,000. This means it might be cheaper to ask for separate bills.

TELEPHONE

The area code for greater Kyoto is ☎ 075; unless otherwise indicated, all numbers in this book fall into this area. Japanese telephone codes consist of an area code plus a local code and number. You do not dial the area code when making a call in that area. When dialling Japan from abroad, the country code is ☎ 81, followed by the area code (drop the 0) and the number. Area codes for some of the main cities:

City	Area Code (☎)
Fukuoka/Hakata	092
Hiroshima	082
Kōbe	078
Matsuyama	0899
Nagasaki	0958
Nagoya	052
Nara	0742
Narita	0476
Osaka	06
Sapporo	011
Sendai	022
Tokyo	03
Yokohama	045

Local Calls

The Japanese public telephone system is very well developed. There are a great many public phones and they work almost 100% of the time.

Local calls from pay phones cost ¥10 per minute; unused ¥10 coins are returned after the call is completed but no change is given on ¥100 coins.

In general it's much easier to buy a *terefon kādo* (telephone card) when you arrive rather than worry about always having coins on hand. Phonecards are sold in ¥500 and ¥1000 denominations (the latter earns you an extra ¥50 in calls) and can be used in most green or grey pay phones. They are available from vending machines and convenience stores, come in a myriad of designs and are also a collectable item.

Directory Assistance

For local directory assistance dial ☎ 104 (the call costs ¥100), or for assistance in English ring ☎ 0120-364 463 from 9am to 5pm weekdays. For international directory assistance dial ☎ 0057.

International Calls

The best way to make an international phone call from Japan is to use a prepaid international phonecard (see right).

Paid overseas calls can also be made from grey international ISDN phones. These are usually found in phone booths marked 'International & Domestic Card/Coin Phone'. Unfortunately, these are very rare; try looking in the lobbies of top-end hotels and at airports. Calls are charged by the unit, each of which is six seconds, so if you don't have much to say you could phone home for just ¥100. Collect (reverse-charge) overseas calls can be made from any pay phone.

You can save money by dialling late at night. Economy rates, with a discount of 20%, apply from 7pm to 11pm on weekdays and to 11pm at weekends and holidays. From 11pm to 8am a discount rate brings the price of international calls down by 40%. Note that it is also cheaper to make domestic calls by dialling outside the standard hours.

To place an international call through the operator, dial ☎ 0051 (international operators all seem to speak English). To make the call yourself, dial ☎ 001 010 KDDI, ☎ 0041 010 ITJ, or ☎ 0033 010 NTT – there's very little difference in their rates – then the international country code, the local code and the number.

Another option is to dial ☎ 0039 plus your country code for home country direct, which takes you straight through to a local operator in the country dialled. You can then make a reverse-charge call or a credit-card call with a telephone credit card valid in that country.

PREPAID INTERNATIONAL PHONECARDS

Because of the lack of pay phones from which you can make international phone calls in Japan, the easiest way to make an international phone call is to buy a prepaid international phonecard. With the exception of the IC Card, which can only be used with special orange IC phones, these phonecards can be used with any regular pay phone in Japan.

Global Card Only available at discount ticket shops (p181) and some guesthouses.

IC Cards These cards – which are sold from machines that accompany IC card phone – can only be used with IC card phones.

KDDI Superworld Card Can be purchased at almost any convenience store in Japan.

Renting a Phone

Several outfits specialise in short-term mobile (cell) phone rentals for travellers and businesspeople. Rentafone Japan (☎ 080-3240 9183; www.rentafonejapan.com) rents phones for ¥3500 per week and offers free delivery of the phone to your accommodation. Phone charges are extra and are billed at cost.

TIME

Kyoto local time is nine hours ahead of GMT/UTC. There is no daylight-saving time. When it's noon in Kyoto, it's 7pm (the day before) in Los Angeles, 10pm (the day before) in Montreal and New York, 3am (the same day) in London, 4am in Frankfurt, Paris and Rome, 11am in Hong Kong, 1pm in Melbourne, and 3pm in Wellington.

TOURIST INFORMATION
Local Tourist Offices

The best source of information on Kyoto is the **Kyoto Tourist Information Center** (TIC; Map pp230-1; ☎ 344 3300; ☺ 10am-6pm, closed 2nd & 4th Tue & 29 Dec–3 Jan) located on the 9th floor of the Kyoto Station building. To get there from the main concourse of the station, take the west escalator to the 2nd floor, enter Isetan department store, take an immediate left, look for the elevator on your left and take it to the 9th floor. It's right outside the elevator, inside the **Kyoto Prefectural International Center** (Map pp230–1). There is a Welcome Inn Reservation counter at the TIC, which can help with accommodation bookings.

The **Kyoto City Tourist Information Center** (Map pp230-1; ☎ 343 6656; 2nd fl Kyoto Station bldg; ☺ 8.30am-7pm), is located at the top of the west escalator which leaves from the main concourse. Although it's geared towards Japanese visitors, English speakers are usually on hand and can be of great assistance when the TIC is closed.

On the 9th floor of the Kyoto Station building, the **Kyoto Tourism Federation** (Map pp230-1; ☎ 371 2226; ☺ 9.30am-6pm, closed 2nd & 4th Tue & 29 Dec–3 Jan) distributes information on outlying destinations in *Kyoto Prefecture* (it has very little on the city itself). Although most literature is only in Japanese, it's worth stopping by to pick up a free map of Kyoto-fu if you plan a trip to outlying areas of the prefecture.

Kansai International Airport has a **tourist information counter** (☎ 0724-56 6025; ☺ 9am-9pm) on the 1st floor of the international arrivals hall. Staff here can provide information on Kyoto, Kansai and Japan.

Japan National Tourist Organization (JNTO) Offices Abroad

JNTO has several offices overseas.

Australia (☎ 02-9232 4522; Level 33, Chifley Tower, 2 Chifley Square, Sydney, NSW 2000)

Canada (☎ 416-366 7140; 165 University Ave, Toronto, Ontario M5H 3B8)

France (☎ 01 42 96 20 29; 4 rue de Ventadour, 75001 Paris)

Germany (☎ 069 20353; Kaiserstrasse 11, 60311 Frankfurt am Main 1)

UK (☎ 020-7734 9638; Heathcoat House, 20 Savile Row, London W1X 1AE)

USA Los Angeles (☎ 213-623 1952; Ste 1470, 515 South Figueroa St, CA 90017); New York (☎ 212-757 5640; Ste 1250, One Rockefeller Plaza, NY 10020); San Francisco (☎ 415-292 5686; 1 Daniel Burnham Court, Suite 250C, CA 94109)

TRAVEL AGENCIES

Kyoto has several good central travel agencies that can arrange discount air tickets, car rental, accommodation as well as other services. These include **No 1 Travel** (Map pp228-9; ☎ 251 6970; Shinkyōgoku-dōri, Shijō-agaru).

USEFUL ORGANISATIONS
Kyoto International Community House

An essential stop for those planning a long-term stay in Kyoto is the **Kyoto International Community House** (KICH; Map pp225-7; ☎ 752 3010; Sakyō-ku, Awataguchi; ☺ 9am-9pm Tue-Sun). It can also be quite useful for short-term visitors. It's closed Tuesday if the Monday is a national holiday.

Services include typewriter/computer rental; sending and receiving faxes, and a library with maps, books, newspapers and magazines from around the world. Perhaps most useful for residents, however, is the noticeboard, which has messages regarding work, accommodation, rummage sales and so on. They've also just introduced Internet service (¥200 for 30 minutes).

While you're there you can pick up a copy of their excellent *Guide to Kyoto* map and their *Easy Living in Kyoto* book (but note that both of these are intended for residents). You can also chill out in the lobby and watch CNN news.

If you would like to meet a Japanese family at home, you can also make arrangements through KICH. Let them know at least one day (preferably two days) in advance.

See p182 for information on cultural demonstrations and classes held at KICH.

KICH is in eastern Kyoto about 500m west of Nanzen-ji. You can walk from Sanjō

Keihan Station in about 20 minutes. Alternately, take the Tōzai subway from downtown and get off at Keage Station, from which it's a five-minute walk downhill.

VISAS

Most visitors who are not planning to engage in any remunerative activities while in Japan are exempt from obtaining visas and will be issued a *tanki-taizai* visa (short-stay visa) on arrival.

Stays of up to six months are permitted for citizens of Austria, Germany, Ireland, Mexico, Switzerland and the UK. Citizens of these countries will almost always be given a 90-day short-stay visa on arrival, which can usually be extended for another 90 days at immigration bureaus in Japan (see right).

Citizens of the USA, Australia and New Zealand are granted 90-day short-stay visas, while stays of up to three months are permitted for citizens of Argentina, Belgium, Canada, Denmark, Finland, France, Iceland, Israel, Italy, The Netherlands, Norway, Singapore, Spain, Sweden and a number of other countries.

As well as the information following on visas and regulations, you should check with your nearest Japanese embassy or go to the website of the Japanese Ministry of Foreign Affairs (www.mofa.go.jp/).

Working-Holiday Visas

Australians, Canadians and New Zealanders between the ages of 18 and 25 (the age limit can be pushed up to 30) can apply for a working-holiday visa. This visa allows a six-month stay and two six-month extensions. It aims to enable young people to travel extensively during their stay, and for this reason employment is supposed to be part time or temporary, although in practice many people work full time.

A working-holiday visa is much easier to obtain than a working visa and is popular with Japanese employers. Single applicants must have the equivalent of A$2500 (C$2005) of funds and a married couple A$5000 (C$4010), and all applicants must have an onward ticket from Japan. For details, inquire at the nearest Japanese embassy or consulate (p185).

Working Visas

It is not as easy as it once was to get a work visa for Japan. Ever-increasing demand has prompted much stricter work-visa require-ments. Arriving in Japan and looking for a job is really quite a tough proposition these days, although people still do it. There are legal employment categories for foreigners that specify standards of experience and qualifications.

Once you find an employer in Japan who is willing to sponsor you it is necessary to obtain a Certificate of Eligibility from the nearest immigration office. The same office can then issue you your working visa, which is valid for either one or three years. The whole procedure usually takes two to three months.

Visa Extensions

With the exception of those nationals whose countries have reciprocal visa exemptions and who can stay for six months, 90 days or three months is the limit for most nationalities. To extend a short-stay visa beyond the standard 90 days or three months, apply at the Kyoto branch of the **Osaka Immigration Bureau** (Map pp225-7; ☎ 752 5997; 4th fl, Dai Ni Chihō Godochosha Bldg, 34-12 Higashi Marutamachi, Kawabata Higashi-iru, Sakyō-ku). You must provide two copies of an Application for Extension of Stay (available at the bureau), a letter stating the reasons for the extension and supporting documentation, as well as your passport. There is a processing fee of ¥4000; be prepared to spend well over an hour completing the process.

The Kyoto branch is best reached from Marutamachi Station on the Keihan line. To get there take the No 4 exit, turn left and continue east past a church to the second traffic light. The bureau is in the five-storey building on your left.

The **Osaka Immigration Bureau** (☎ 06-6774 3409) has an English-language visa information line at its Osaka headquarters, though you can usually have most questions about visas answered in English by calling the Kyoto branch. Both offices are open Monday to Friday from 9am to noon and 1pm to 4pm.

Alien Registration Card

Anyone – and this includes tourists – who stays for more than 90 days is required to obtain an Alien Registration Card (Gaikokujin Torokushō). This card can be obtained at the municipal office of the city, town or ward in which you're living but moving to another area requires that you re-register within 14 days.

You must carry your Alien Registration Card at all times as the police can stop you and ask to see the card. If you don't have the card, you may be taken back to the station and will have to wait there until someone fetches it for you.

WOMEN TRAVELLERS

The major concern, 'Will I be physically safe?' is less of a worry in Japan than many other countries. Statistics show low rates of violent crimes against women, although some Japanese women's organisations and media attribute this to under-reporting.

The biggest hazard for many women travellers is that of adopting a too casual disregard for normal safety precautions while in Japan. Many women, lulled by Japan's reputation for safety, mistakenly assume that nothing can happen to them. This, unfortunately, is false.

Although some expats will assure you that it's safe to walk the streets of any Japanese city alone at night, ignore this and follow your common sense: keep to streets with heavier foot traffic, stay in groups etc. Western women who are alone on foot are easy targets for verbal harassment or worse by passing male motorists. Walking solo along highways in remote rural areas at any time of day and hitchhiking are definitely advised against.

It is the rare (or super streetwise) woman who stays in Japan for any length of time without encountering some type of sexual harassment. Apparently some men find that words are not enough to express how they feel, as flashers and cruder exhibitionists are not uncommon.

Statistics on reported rape are low, but it is estimated that actual rates are significantly higher. If you or someone you know is raped, you should seek immediate medical help and report the matter to the police. Be forewarned, though, that police and medical personnel can be quite unhelpful, even accusatory. Insist on receiving the appropriate medical care (STD tests, antibiotic booster shot, morning after pill) and, as appropriate, filing a police report.

If you do have a problem and find the local police unhelpful, you can call the **Human Rights Center Information Line** (☎ 03-3581 2302) in Tokyo.

There are a variety of helpful contacts and women's services in Kyoto, and the **YWCA** (Map pp216-18; ☎ 431 0351) is a good place to begin. The YWCA offers a free telephone consultation service for foreign women in English, as well as Spanish, Thai, Tagalog and Chinese, on Monday from 1pm to 4pm and Thursday from 3pm to 6pm. You can also arrange long-term accommodation here. There is a useful book of Kansai area contacts for women on display in the lobby.

Recently the Kyoto police launched a **women's telephone consultation service** (☎ /fax 411 0110; 🕑 9am-5pm Mon-Fri, send fax after 5pm) staffed by local policewomen. There are English-speaking staff, and though they're not always on duty, you can arrange a time to call back to speak with one of them (you may have to have a Japanese speaker make the initial call).

Finally, an excellent resource for women setting up in Japan is Caroline Pover's book *Being A Broad in Japan,* which can be found in bookstores and ordered from her website at www.being-a-broad.com.

WORK

Kyoto's popularity makes it one of Japan's most difficult cities in which to find work. Despite this fact and increasingly strict immigration policies, there is a relatively quick turnaround of many resident foreigners, so it is often just a case of being patient until something comes up. If you are planning to make a go of it in Kyoto, you'll need to have enough money to survive for three months or so (around US$6000).

Many who would prefer to live in Kyoto end up commuting to jobs in Osaka or other neighbouring cities, at least until they find something closer to home. Apart from teaching English, other popular jobs include bar hostessing (mainly women), work in restaurants and bars, and carpentry.

The best place to look for work is in *Kansai Time Out,* followed by the *Kansai Flea Market,* and the jobs listing at the KICH (p192; you can also post messages and offer your service as a private tutor at the KICH). The Monday edition of the *Japan Times* also has a small Kansai employment section. Word-of-mouth is also a great way to find work in Kyoto – you could try dropping any of the *gaijin*-friendly bars listed in the Entertainment chapter (p122).

Language

Language

It's true – anyone can speak another language. Don't worry if you haven't studied languages before or that you studied a language at school for years and can't remember any of it. It doesn't even matter if you failed English grammar. After all, that's never affected your ability to speak English! And this is the key to picking up a language in another country. You just need to start speaking.

Learn a few key phrases before you go. Write them on pieces of paper and stick them on the fridge, by the bed or even on the computer – anywhere that you'll see them often.

You'll find that locals appreciate travellers trying their language, no matter how muddled you may think you sound. So don't just stand there, say something! If you want to learn more Japanese than we've included here, pick up a copy of Lonely Planet's comprehensive but user-friendly *Japanese Phrasebook*.

PRONUNCIATION

Pronounce double consonants with a slight pause between them, so that each is clearly audible. Vowel length affects meaning, so make sure you distinguish your short and long vowels clearly. Certain vowel sounds (like **u** and **i**) aren't pronounced in some words, but are included as part of the official Romanisation system (which employs a literal system to represent Japanese characters). In the following words and phrases these 'silent' letters are shown in square brackets to indicate that they aren't pronounced.

a	short, as the 'u' in 'run'
ā	long, as the 'a' in 'father'
e	short, as in 'red'
ē	long, as the 'ei' in 'rein'
i	short, as in 'bit'
ī	long, as in 'marine'
o	short, as in 'pot'
ō	long, as the 'aw' in 'paw'
u	short, as in 'put'
ū	long, as in 'rude'

SOCIAL
Meeting People

Hello/Hi.
konnichi wa   こんにちは。
Goodbye.
sayōnara   さようなら
Yes.
hai   はい。
No.
iie   いいえ。

Please.
(when offering something)
dōzo   どうぞ。
(when asking a favour or making a request)
onegai shimasu   お願いします。
Thank you (very much).
(dōmo) arigatō   (どうも)ありがとう
(gozaimas[u])   (ございます)。
You're welcome.
dō itashimash[i]te   どういたしまして。
Excuse me. (to get attention or to get past)
sumimasen   すみません。
Sorry.
gomen nasai   ごめんなさい。

What's your name?
o-namae wa nan des[u] ka?
お名前は何ですか?
My name is …
watashi no namae wa … des[u]
私の名前は…です。
Do you speak English?
eigo ga hanasemas[u] ka?
英語が話せますか?
Do you understand?
wakarimash[i]ta ka?
わかりましたか?
Yes, I do understand.
hai, wakarimash[i]ta
はい、わかりました。
No, I don't understand.
iie, wakarimasen
いいえ、わかりません。

Could you please …?
… kuremasen ka?
…くれませんか?

repeat that
kurikaeshite
繰り返して
speak more slowly
motto yukkuri hanashite
もっとゆっくり話して
write it down
kaite
書いて

Going Out

What's on ...?
... wa nani ga arimas[u] ka?
…は何がありますか?

locally
kinjo ni   近所に
this weekend
konshū no   今週の週末
  shūmatsu
today
kyō   今日
tonight
konya   今夜

Where can I find ...?
doko ni ikeba ... ga arimas[u] ka?
どこに行けば…がありますか?

clubs
kurabu   クラブ
gay venues
gei no basho   ゲイの場所
Japanese-style pubs
izakaya   居酒屋
places to eat
shokuji ga   食事ができる所
  dekiru tokoro
pubs
pabu   パブ

Is there a local entertainment guide?
jimoto no entāteimento gaido wa
  arimas[u] ka?
地元のエンターテイメントガイドは
  ありますか?

PRACTICAL
Question Words

Who?
dare?/donata?   だれ?/どなた? (polite)
What?/What is this?
nan?/nani?   何?/なに?
Which?
dochira?   どちら?
When?
itsu?   いつ?

Where?
doko?   どこ?
How?
dono yō ni?   どのように?
How much does it cost?
ikura des[u] ka? いくらですか?

Numbers

0	zero/rei	ゼロ/零
1	ichi	一
2	ni	二
3	san	三
4	shi/yon	四
5	go	五
6	roku	六
7	shichi/nana	七
8	hachi	八
9	ku/kyū	九
10	jū	十
11	jūichi	十一
12	jūni	十二
13	jūsan	十三
14	jūshi/jūyon	十四
15	jūgo	十五
16	jūroku	十六
17	jūshichi/jūnana	十七
18	jūhachi	十八
19	jūku/jūkyū	十九
20	nijū	二十
21	nijūichi	二十一
22	nijūni	二十二
30	sanjū	三十
40	yonjū	四十
50	gojū	五十
60	rokujū	六十
70	nanajū	七十
80	hachijū	八十
90	kyūjū	九十
100	hyaku	百
200	nihyaku	二百
300	sambyaku	三百
1000	sen	千

Days

Monday	getsuyōbi	月曜日
Tuesday	kayōbi	火曜日
Wednesday	suiyōbi	水曜日
Thursday	mokuyōbi	木曜日
Friday	kinyōbi	金曜日
Saturday	doyōbi	土曜日
Sunday	nichiyōbi	日曜日

Banking

I'd like to ...
... o onegai shimas[u]
…をお願いします。

cash a cheque
kogitte no genkinka
小切手の現金化
change a travellers cheque
toraberāz[u] chekku no genkinka
トラベラーズチェックの現金化
change money
ryōgae
両替

Where's …?
… wa doko des[u] ka?
…はどこですか?
  an ATM
  ētīemu
  ATM
  a foreign exchange office
  gaikoku kawase sekushon
  外国為替セクション

Post

Where is the post office?
yūbin kyoku wa doko des[u] ka?
郵便局はどこですか?

I want to send a/an …
… o okuritai no des[u] ga
…を送りたいのですが。
  letter
  tegami   手紙
  parcel
  kozutsumi   小包
  postcard
  hagaki   はがき

I want to buy a/an …
… o kudasai
…をください。
  aerogram
  earoguramu   エアログラム
  envelope
  fūtō   封筒
  stamp
  kitte   切手

Phones & Mobiles

I want to …
…tai no des[u] ga
…たいのですが。
  buy a phonecard
  terefon kādo o kai
  テレフォンカードを買い
  call (Singapore)
  (shingapōru) ni denwa shi
  (シンガポール)に電話し

make a (local) call
(shinai) ni denwa shi
(市内)に電話し
reverse the charges
korekuto-kōru de denwa shi
コレクトコールで電話し

I'd like a …
… o onegai shimas[u]
…をお願いします。
  charger for my phone
  keitaidenwa no jūdenki
  携帯電話の充電器
  mobile/cell phone for hire
  keitaidenwa no rentaru
  携帯電話のレンタル
  prepaid mobile/cell phone
  puripeido no keitaidenwa
  プリペイドの携帯電話
  SIM card for your network
  shimukādo
  SIMカード

Internet

Where's the local Internet café?
intānetto-kafe wa doko des[u] ka?
インターネットカフェはどこですか?

I'd like to …
… shitai no des[u] ga
…したいのですが。
  check my email
  īmēru o chekku
  Eメールをチェック
  get Internet access
  intānetto ni akses[u]
  インターネットにアクセス

Transport

When's the … (bus)?
… (bas[u]) wa nan-ji des[u] ka?
…(バス)は何時ですか?
  first
  shihatsu no   始発の
  last
  saishū no   最終の
  next
  tsugi no   次の

What time does it leave?
kore wa nan-ji ni demas[u] ka?
これは何時に出ますか?
What time does it get to …?
kore wa … ni nan-ji ni tsukimas[u] ka?
これは...に何時に着きますか?

Is this taxi available?
kono tak[u]shī wa kūsha des[u] ka?
このタクシーは空車ですか？
Please put the meter on.
mētā o irete kudasai
メーターを入れてください。
How much is it to …?
… made ikura des[u] ka?
…までいくらですか？
Please take me to (this address).
(kono jūsho) made onegai shimas[u]
(この住所)までお願いします。

FOOD

breakfast
chōshoku   朝食
lunch
chūshoku   昼食
dinner
yūshoku   夕食
snack
kanshoku   間食
to eat
tabemas[u]   食べます
to drink
nomimas[u]   飲みます

Can you recommend a …?
doko ka ii … o shitte imas[u] ka?
どこかいい…を知っていますか？
  bar
  bā   バー
  café
  kafe   カフェ
  restaurant
  restoran   レストラン

Is service included in the bill?
sābis[u] ryō komi des[u] ka?
サービス料込みですか？

For more detailed information on food and dining out, see Eating on p101 or Food & Drink on p27.

EMERGENCIES

Help!
tas[u]kete!
たすけて！
It's an emergency!
kinkyū des[u]!
緊急です。
Call the police!
keisatsu o yonde!
警察を呼んで。

Call a doctor!
isha o yonde!
医者を呼んで。
Call an ambulance!
kyūkyūsha o yonde!
救急車を呼んで。
Could you please help?
tas[u]kete kudasai?
たすけてください。
Where's the police station?
keisatsusho wa doko des[u] ka?
警察署はどこですか？

HEALTH

Where's the nearest …?
kono chikaku no … wa doko des[u] ka?
この近くの…はどこですか？
  (night) chemist
  (nijūyojikan   (24時間営業の)薬局
    eigyō no) yakkyoku
  doctor
  isha   医者
  hospital
  byōin   病院

I need a doctor (who speaks English).
(eigo ga dekiru) o-isha-san ga hitsuyō des[u]
(英語ができる)お医者さんが必要です。

I'm allergic to …
watashi wa … arerugī des[u]
私は…アレルギーです。
  antibiotics
  kōsei busshitsu   抗生物質
  aspirin
  as[u]pirin   アスピリン
  bees
  hachi   蜂
  nuts
  nattsurui   ナッツ類
  penicillin
  penishirin   ペニシリン

Symptoms

I have …
watashi wa … ga arimas[u]
私は…があります。
  diarrhoea
  geri   下痢
  a headache
  zutsū   頭痛
  nausea
  hakike   吐き気
  a pain
  itami   痛み

Glossary

ageya – traditional banquet hall used for entertainment, which flourished during the Edo period
Amida Nyorai – Buddha of the Western Paradise
ANA – All Nippon Airways

bashi – bridge (also *hashi*)
ben – dialect, as in *Kyoto-ben*
bentō – boxed lunch or dinner, usually containing rice, vegetables and fish or meat
biwa – Japanese lute
bosatsu – a bodhisattva, or Buddha attendant, who assists others to attain enlightenment
bugaku – dance pieces played by court orchestras in ancient Japan
bunraku – classical puppet theatre that uses life-size puppets to enact dramas similar to those of *kabuki*

chadō – see *sadō*
cha-kaiseki – a *kaiseki* meal that accompanies a tea ceremony
chanoyu – tea ceremony; see also *sadō*
chō – city area (for large cities) sized between a *ku* and *chōme*
chōme – city area of a few blocks

dai – great; large
Daibutsu – Great Buddha
daimyō – domain lords under the *shōgun*
dera – temple (also *ji* or *tera*)
dōri – street

fugu – poisonous pufferfish, elevated to *haute cuisine*
futon – cushion-like mattress that is rolled up and stored away during the day

gagaku – music of the imperial court
gaijin – foreigner; the contracted form of gaikokujin (literally, 'outside country person')
gawa – river (also *kawa*)
geiko – Kyoto dialect for *geisha*
geisha – a woman versed in the arts and other cultivated pursuits who entertains guests
gū – shrine

haiden – hall of worship in a shrine
haiku – 17-syllable poem
hakubutsukan – museum
hanami – cherry-blossom viewing
hashi – bridge (also *bashi*); chopsticks
higashi – east
hiragana – phonetic syllabary used to write Japanese words
honden – main building of a shrine
hondō – main building of a temple (also *kondō*)

ikebana – art of flower arrangement
irori – open hearth found in traditional Japanese homes
ITJ – International Telecom Japan
izakaya – Japanese pub/eatery

ji – temple (also *tera* or *dera*)
jingū – shrine (also *jinja* or *gū*)
Jizō – bodhisattva who watches over children
JNTO – Japan National Tourist Organization
jō – castle (also *shiro*)
JR – Japan Railways

kabuki – form of Japanese theatre that draws on popular tales and is characterised by elaborate costumes, stylised acting and the use of male actors for all roles
kaiseki – Buddhist-inspired, Japanese *haute cuisine*; called *cha-kaiseki* when served as part of a tea ceremony
kaisoku – rapid train
kaiten-zushi – automatic, conveyor-belt sushi
kamikaze – literally, 'wind of the gods'; originally the typhoon that sank Kublai Khan's 13th-century invasion fleet and the name adopted by Japanese suicide bombers in the waning days of WWII
kampai – cheers, as in a drinking toast
kanji – literally, 'Chinese writing'; Chinese ideographic script used for writing Japanese
Kannon – Buddhist goddess of mercy
karaoke – a now famous export where revellers sing along to taped music, minus the vocals
karesansui – dry-landscaped rock garden
kawa – river
kayabuki-yane – traditional Japanese thatched-roof farmhouse
KDD – Kokusai Denshin Denwa
ken – prefecture, eg Shiga-ken
kimono – traditional outer garment that is similar to a robe
kita – north
KIX – Kansai International Airport
Kiyomizu-yaki – a distinctive type of local pottery
ko – lake
kōban – local police box
kōen – park
koma-inu – dog-like guardian stone statues found in pairs at the entrance to *Shintō* shrines
kondō – main building of a temple
koto – 13-stringed zither-like instrument
ku – ward
kura – traditional Japanese warehouse
kyōgen – drama performed as comic relief between *nō* plays, or as separate events
kyō-machiya – see *machiya*
kyō-obanzai – see *obanzai*
kyō-ryōri – Kyoto cuisine
Kyoto-ben – distinctive Japanese dialect spoken in Kyoto

LDP – Liberal Democratic Party
live house – a small concert hall where live music is performed

machi – city area (for large cities) sized between a *ku* and *chōme*

machiya – traditional wooden townhouse, called *kyō-machiya* in Kyoto

maiko – apprentice *geisha*

mama-san – older women who run drinking, dining and entertainment venues

matcha – powdered green tea served in tea ceremonies

matsuri – festival

mikoshi – portable shrine carried during festivals

minami – south

minshuku – Japanese equivalent of a B&B

minyō – traditional Japanese folk music

Miroku – Buddha of the Future

mizu shōbai – the world of bars, entertainment and prostitution (also known as *water trade*)

momiji – Japanese maple trees

momiji-gari – viewing of the changing autumn colours of trees

mon – temple gate

mōningu setto – morning set of toast and coffee served at cafés

mura – village

Nihon – Japanese word for Japan; literally, 'source of the sun' (also known as *Nippon*)

ningyō – doll

niō – temple guardians

Nippon – see *Nihon*

nishi – west

nō – classical Japanese mask drama performed on a bare stage

noren – door curtain for restaurants, usually labelled with the name of the establishment

NTT – Nippon Telegraph & Telephone Corporation

o- – prefix used as a sign of respect (usually applied to objects)

obanzai – Japanese home-style cooking (the Kyoto variant of this is sometimes called *kyō-obanzai*)

obi – sash or belt worn with *kimono*

Obon – mid-August festivals and ceremonies for deceased ancestors

okiya – old-style *geisha* living quarters

onsen – mineral hot spring with bathing areas and accommodation

o-shibori – hot towels given in restaurants

pachinko – vertical pinball game that is a Japanese craze

pink salon – seedy hostess bars (pink is the Japanese equivalent of blue, as in pornography)

Raijin – god of thunder

ryokan – traditional Japanese inn

ryōri – cooking; cuisine (see also *kyō-ryōri*)

ryōtei – traditional-style, high-class restaurant; *kaiseki* is typical fare

sabi – a poetic ideal of finding beauty and pleasure in imperfection; often used in conjunction with *wabi*

sadō – tea ceremony, or 'The Way of Tea'

sakura – cherry blossoms

salaryman – male employee of a large firm

sama – a suffix even more respectful than *san*

samurai – Japan's traditional warrior class

san – a respectful suffix applied to personal names, similar to Mr, Mrs or Ms but more widely used

sen – line, usually railway line

sencha – medium-grade green tea

sensu – folding paper fan

sentō – public bath

setto – set meal; see also *teishoku*

Shaka Nyorai – Historical Buddha

shakuhachi – traditional Japanese bamboo flute

shamisen – three-stringed, banjo-like instrument

shi – city (to distinguish cities with prefectures of the same name)

shidare-zakura – weeping cherry tree

shinkaisoku – special rapid train

shinkansen – bullet train (literally, 'new trunk line')

Shintō – indigenous Japanese religion

shiro – castle

shodō – Japanese calligraphy; literally, 'the way of writing'

shōgun – military ruler of pre-Meiji Japan

shōjin-ryōri – Zen vegetarian cuisine

shokudō – Japanese-style cafeteria/cheap restaurant

shukubō – temple lodging

soba – buckwheat noodles

tatami – tightly woven floor matting on which shoes should not be worn

teishoku – set meal in a restaurant

tera – temple (also *dera* or *ji*)

TIC – Tourist Information Center (usually refers to Kyoto Tourist Information Center)

tokkyū – limited express train

torii – entrance gate to a *Shintō* shrine

tsukemono – Japanese pickles

ukiyo-e – woodblock prints; literally, 'pictures of the floating world'

wabi – a Zen-inspired aesthetic of rustic simplicity

wagashi – traditional Japanese sweets that are served with tea

wasabi – spicy Japanese horseradish

washi – Japanese paper

water trade – see *mizu shōbai*

yakuza – Japanese mafia

yudōfu – bean curd cooked in an iron pot; common temple fare

Zen – a form of Buddhism

zōgan – damascene ware

Behind the Scenes

THE LONELY PLANET STORY

The story begins with a classic travel adventure: Tony and Maureen Wheeler's 1972 journey across Europe and Asia to Australia. There was no useful information about the overland trail then, so Tony and Maureen published the first Lonely Planet guidebook to meet a growing need.

From a kitchen table, Lonely Planet has grown to become the largest independent travel publisher in the world, with offices in Melbourne (Australia), Oakland (USA) and London (UK). Today Lonely Planet guidebooks cover the globe. There is an ever-growing list of books and information in a variety of media. Some things haven't changed. The main aim is still to make it possible for adventurous travellers to get out there – to explore and better understand the world.

At Lonely Planet we believe travellers can make a positive contribution to the countries they visit – if they respect their host communities and spend their money wisely. Every year 5% of company profit is donated to charities around the world.

THIS BOOK

This 3rd edition of *Kyoto* was updated by Chris Rowthorn. He updated the 2nd edition, too. Mason Florence wrote the 1st edition. Marc Peter Keane wrote the boxed text 'My Favourite Gardens', which appears in the Neighbourhoods chapter. This guide was commissioned in Lonely Planet's Melbourne office and produced by the following people:

Commissioning Editor Rebecca Chau
Coordinating Editor Carolyn Boicos
Coordinating Cartographer Jacqueline Nguyen
Layout Designer Sonya Brooke
Editors & Proofreaders Margedd Heliosz, Nancy Ianni & Fionnuala Twomey
Assisting Cartographer Tim Lohnes
Assisting Layout Designers Yvonne Bischofberger, Michael Ruff & Wibowo Rusli
Indexer Carolyn Boicos
Cover Designer Julie Rovis
Cover Artwork Sonya Brooke
Layout Manager Adriana Mammarella
Managing Cartographer Corinne Waddell
Managing Editor Darren O'Connell
Project Managers Andrew Weatherill & Celia Wood
Language Content Coordinator Quentin Frayne

Thanks to Stefanie Di Trocchio, Adrian Persoglia, Nicholas Stebbing, Ryan Evans, Gerard Walker and Glenn Beanland.

Cover photographs The first cherry blossoms of the season at Higashi Hongan-ji, Oliver Strewe/Lonely Planet Images (top); Traditional torii at Fushimi-Inari-taisha, Izzet Keribar/Lonely Planet Images (bottom); Geisha holding parcel at Nanzen-ji, Frank Carter/Lonely Planet Images (back).

Internal photographs by Phil Weymouth/Lonely Planet Images except for p69 (#1), p71 (#1, #3, #4) Frank Carter/Lonely Planet Images, p71 (#2) Simon Charles Rowe/Lonely Planet Images, p73 Chris Rowthorn. All images are the copyright of the photographers unless otherwise indicated. Many of the images in this guide are available for licensing from Lonely Planet Images: www.lonelyplanet images.com.

THANKS
CHRIS ROWTHORN

Chris would like to thank the following people: Toshiko Doi; the tireless Keiko Hagiwara for her fantastic input; Anthony and Denise Weersing for their excellent restaurant picks, among many other things; Paul Carty for great restaurant info and much besides; Divyam for providing the perfect retreat; Masako Nakamura and Matsumiya-san for their great restaurant picks; Shaheed Rupani for his brilliant Kyoto nightlife picks; K.S. and H.S. for their great input, computer assistance and Kyoto information; Kishimoto Yorihiku for his great Osaka restaurant picks and a fantastic sushi dinner; and all the readers of Lonely Planet *Japan* books who sent in letters and emails with information about Japan – your input really helps and I've tried to use as much of it as possible! Finally, I would like to thank folks inhouse at Lonely Planet for their hard work on this guide: Rebecca Chau, Carolyn Boicos, Corinne Waddell and Jacqueline Nguyen.

OUR READERS

Many thanks to the travellers who used the last edition and wrote to us with helpful hints, useful advice and interesting anecdotes:

Melissa Addy, Riccardo Albertini, Ahmed Ali, Claudia B, Judy Barnsley, Darren Bauer, Patty Beauchamp, Erin Betlock, Inge Bley-Hiersemenzel, Patrick Boyle, Kim Bradford-Watts, Rosemarie Brickley, Andrea Broglia, Felix Burkei, Rod Byatt, Pierre-Luigi Camedda, Silvia Campanelli, Carianne Carleo-Evangelist, Ian Chamberlin, Sui-Fung Chan, Lim Huck Chin, Leonard Cogan, Erin Corry, Thomas Danielsen, Shobha Rani Dash, Alard de Boer, Erwin de Kock, Silvia Di Lucia, Sarah Dolman, Rachael Dunlop, James Embry, Paul Engels, Liz Evans, Walter Falk, Nils Ferry, Adrian Fischer, Tony Fitzcarl, Signe Foersom, Josep Maria Font, Tricia Foster Jones, Diodato Francesco, Louise Frost, Cecilia Fujishima, Roey Gafter, Helene Gagnon, Judith Geelen, John Gibb, Hana Gilbert, Denis Giraud, Stephen Glade,

Tim Gomersall, Vicky Hallion, Catherine Hancorne, Karla Hawke, Wesley J Hayter, Charles Heydt, Richard Holt, Benjamin Houssa, James Howard, Nicolas Karman, Louise Kiely, Carina Knoll, Danai Kuangparichat, Craig Kuykendall, Kai Lingemann, Roy Yu-Ching Lo, Jennifer Lui, Diane Mackin, Nici Matlock, Toru Matsubayashi, Corey Don McDaniel, Prue McKay, James P Menath, Sam Meyer, Shinji Nakajima, Elaine Ng, Robin O'Donoghue, Merikay Olson, Jude Page, David Palmer, Stacey Pearl, Emile Phaneuf, Peter Quarry, Roderick Rees, Sarah Riches, Paul Rivers, Thomas Rohlich, Catherine Rose, Daniel Ryntjes, Xavier Sales, Ben Salzberg, Dante Schmidt, Matthias Seidl, Shahid Shaikh, Faye Shelton, Mark Silverberg, Trevor Skingle, Roger Smith, Frieda Sorber, Maartje Swart, Andra Sydorko-Flock, Yvonne Tan, Ryan Taylor, Lily Toh, Franky Tseng, Robert van der Kleij, Hans van der Veen, Iain Varley, NA Walker, Eddie Wall, Raymond Wan, David W Warren, Stephanie Weng, Jayne West, Simon White, Julien Wilk, Stevey Wong, Jitka Zelenkova

SEND US YOUR FEEDBACK

We love to hear from travellers – your comments keep us on our toes and help make our books better. Our well-travelled team reads every word on what you loved or loathed about this book. Although we cannot reply individually to postal submissions, we always guarantee that your feedback goes straight to the appropriate authors, in time for the next edition. Each person who sends us information is thanked in the next edition – and the most useful submissions are rewarded with a free book.

To send us your updates – and find out about Lonely Planet events, newsletters and travel news – visit our award-winning website: www.lonelyplanet.com /feedback.

Note: We may edit, reproduce and incorporate your comments in Lonely Planet products such as guidebooks, websites and digital products, so let us know if you don't want your comments reproduced or your name acknowledged. For a copy of our privacy policy visit www.lonelyplanet.com/privacy.

Notes

Index

See also separate indexes for Eating (p209–10), Shopping (p210) and Sleeping (p210).

000 map pages
000 photographs

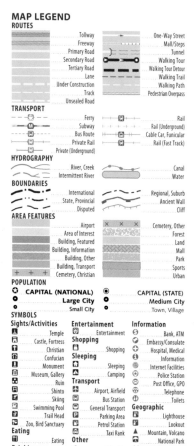

MAP LEGEND

ROUTES

Tollway	One-Way Street
Freeway	Mall/Steps
Primary Road	Tunnel
Secondary Road	Walking Tour
Tertiary Road	Walking Tour Detour
Lane	Walking Trail
Under Construction	Walking Path
Track	Pedestrian Overpass
Unsealed Road	

TRANSPORT

Ferry	Rail
Subway	Rail (Underground)
Bus Route	Cable Car, Funicular
Private Rail	Rail (Fast Track)
Private (Underground)	

HYDROGRAPHY

River, Creek	Canal
Intermittent River	Water

BOUNDARIES

International	Regional, Suburb
State, Provincial	Ancient Wall
Disputed	Cliff

AREA FEATURES

Airport	Cemetery, Other
Area of Interest	Forest
Building, Featured	Land
Building, Information	Mall
Building, Other	Park
Building, Transport	Sports
Cemetery, Christian	Urban

POPULATION

CAPITAL (NATIONAL)	CAPITAL (STATE)
Large City	Medium City
Small City	Town, Village

SYMBOLS

Sights/Activities
Temple
Castle, Fortress
Christian
Confucian
Monument
Museum, Gallery
Ruin
Shinto
Skiing
Swimming Pool
Trail Head
Zoo, Bird Sanctuary

Eating
Eating

Drinking
Drinking
Café

Entertainment
Entertainment

Shopping
Shopping

Sleeping
Sleeping
Camping

Transport
Airport, Airfield
Bus Station
General Transport
Parking Area
Petrol Station
Taxi Rank

Other
Other Site
Picnic Area
Wheelchair Access

Information
Bank, ATM
Embassy/Consulate
Hospital, Medical
Information
Internet Facilities
Police Station
Post Office, GPO
Telephone
Toilets

Geographic
Lighthouse
Lookout
Mountain, Volcano
National Park
Pass, Canyon
River Flow
Waterfall

Map Section

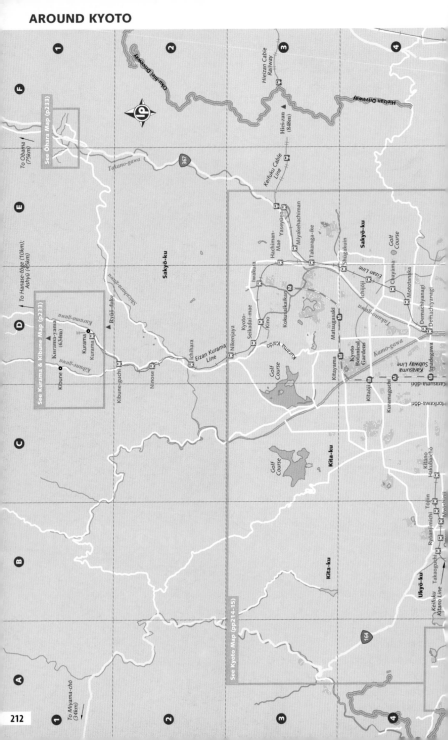

To Miyama-chō
(34km)

Kita-ku

Ukyō-ku

Kita-ku

Golf
Course

Golf
Course

Golf
Course

See Kyoto Map (pp214-15)

Ryōanjimichi Tōjin

Takaoguchi

Keifuku
Kitano Line

164

Kitano
Hakubaichō

Mochiii

Honkawa-dōri

Karasuma-dōri

Karasuma
Subway Line

Kitaōji

Kuramaguchi

Kyoto
Botanical
Gardens

Kitayama

Imadegawa

Demachiyanagi

Demachiyanagi

Matsugasaki

Ichijōji

Mototanaka

Chayama

Kamo-gawa

Takano-gawa

Eizan Line

Shūgakuin

Sakyō-ku

Golf
Course

Ichihara

Nikenjaya

Kyoto-
Seikadai-mae

Kino

Kokusaikaikan

Iwakura

Hachiman-
Mae

Yaseyūen

Miyakehachiman

Takaraga-ike

Kurama Kaidō

Eizan Kurama
Line

Ninose

Kibune-guchi

Ryūbi-daké

Kurama
Kurama

Kurama-yama
(634m)

Kibune-gawa

Kurama-gawa

Kibune

See Kurama & Kibune Map (p233)

To Hanase-tōge (10km);
Ashiyū (45km)

Shizuhara-gawa

Sakyō-ku

367

Takano-gawa

Kurama-gawa

To Ohara
(7.5km)

See Ohara Map (p233)

Ōhi-Hiei Driveway

Hiei-zan
(848m)

Keifuku Cable
Line

Hieizan Cable
Railway

Hieizan Driveway

Sakyō-ku

Golf
Course

KYOTO

SIGHTS & ACTIVITIES

Entsū-ji 円通寺	1	E1
Fujinomori-jinja 藤森神社	2	E7
Fushimi Momoyama-jō 伏見桃山城	3	E8
Fushimi-Inari-taisha 伏見稲荷大社	4	E6
Gekkeikan Sake Ōkura Museum		
月桂冠大倉記念館	5	D8
Jizō-in 地蔵院	6	A5
Jōnan-gū 城南宮	7	D7
Katsura Rikyū Imperial Villa 桂離宮	8	B5
Kōryū-ji 広隆寺	9	B4
Matsuo-taisha 松尾大社	10	A5
Myōshin-ji 妙心寺	11	B3
Ninna-ji 仁和寺	12	B3
Renge-ji 蓮華寺	13	F1
Ryōan-ji 龍安寺	14	B3
Saihō-ji 西芳寺	15	A5
Sampō-in 三宝院	16	B3
Taizō-in 退蔵院	17	B3
Tōei Uzumasa Movie Village		
東映太秦映画村	18	B4
Yūzen Cultural Hall		
京都友禅文化会館	19	C5

EATING

Genya 玄屋	20	D8
Kizakura Kappa Country		
カッパ天国 黄桜酒場	21	D8
Sancho サンチョ	22	D8
Teuchidon Kendonya		
手打ちうどんけんどん屋	23	E6
Uosaburō 魚三楼	24	D8

SHOPPING

Pulse Plaza パルスプラザ	25	D7

SLEEPING

Teradaya 寺田屋	26	D8
Utano Youth Hostel		
宇多野ユースホステル	27	B3

TRANSPORT

Sakaguchi Shōkai 坂口商会	28	E1

INFORMATION

Ark Dental Clinic 仁科歯科医院	29	E8
Igarashi Dental Clinic 五十嵐歯科	30	B6

See pp220-1

Shimogamonaka-dōri

Kūrama Kaidō

Midori-ike

40
15

Kitayama
63

Kitaōji-dōri

67

Kamo-gawa

56
3

25

Kyoto Botanical Gardens

42

Kitayama-dōri

Kitayama-Ōhashi

32
45

Kamigamo-Yamabata-sen

Karasuma Subway Line

Kitaōji

Otani University

Kitaōji-dōri

47

19

Horikawa-dōri

Kitayama-dōri

Dai... (5 color)

6
7

8

Funapka Higashi-dōri

5
69

52

24
43

Kita-ku

4

38

Senbon-dōri

17

10

23

65

Hidari Daimonji
(Daimonji Okuribi)
Fire Festival Character)

NORTHEAST KYOTO (pp220-1)

NORTHEAST KYOTO

1

2

3

4

F

Miyakehachiman

E

15

10

1

14

Sakyō-ku

Takaraga-ike

D

Shūgakuin

35

Shirakawa-dōri

39

Eizan Line

Ichijōji

Kitaōji-dōri

Hō
(Daimonji Okuribi
Fire Festival Characters)

33

42

Kawabata-dōri

Kitayama-dōri

C

Takara-ga-ike

Takara-ga-ike-kōen

17

Kyoto Institute of
Technology

Takano
Crossing

Kitaōji-dōri

49

Takano-gawa

Suzu-harai-ga-gawa

8

Matsugasaki

B

45

Myō
(Daimonji Okuribi
Fire Festival Characters)

51

Shimogamohon-dōri

Kitaōji-dōri

Shimogamohon-dōri

21

A

Mizoro-ike

See pp216-17

1

2

3

4

Shimogamo-dōri

Kawaramachi-dōri

Kamo-gawa (Tōkai-kawa)

Kawaramachi-dōri

Gojō Ōhashi

Gojō Ōbashi

Teramachi-dōri

Shinkyōgoku Covered Arcade

Teramachi Covered Arcade

Kyoto-Shiyakusho-mae

Sanjō-dōri

Rokkaku-dōri

Nishiki-kōji (Nishiki Market)

Shijō-dōri

Ayakōji-dōri

Bukkōji-dōri

Takatsuji-dōri

Matsubara-dōri

Gokomachi-dōri

Tominokōji-dōri

Fuyachō-dōri

Gojō-dōri

See Downtown Kyoto Map (p229)

Sakaimachi-dōri

Karasuma-Oike

Oike-dōri

Tōzai Subway Line

Sakaimachi-dōri

Karasuma Oike

Yanaginobanba-dōri

Sakaimachi-dōri

Ainomachi-dōri

Takakura-dōri

Manjūji-dōri

Karasuma-Gojō Crossing

Marutamachi

Karasuma-dōri

Karasuma Subway Line

Karasuma Shijō

Karasuma-dōri

Gojō

Ryōgaemachi-dōri

Muromachi-dōri

Takeyamachi-dōri

Ebisugawa-dōri

Koromonotana-dōri

Nijō-dōri

Kamaza-dōri

Nishinotōin-dōri

Yōbai-dōri

Marutamachi-dōri

Oshikōji-dōri

Abura-no-kōji-dōri

Ogawa-dōri

Tōzai Subway Line

Takoyakushi-dōri

Nishikikōji-dōri

Shijō-dōri

Horikawa-dōri

Nijōjō-mae

Horikawa-dōri

Higashi-dōri

Nijōjō

Aneyakōji-dōri

Sanjō-dōri

Rokkaku-dōri

Ōmiya

Shijō-Ōmiya

Kuromon-dōri

Ōmiya-dōri

Takatsuji-dōri

Gojō-dōri

Nakagyō-ku

Keifuku Arashiyama Line

Mibu-dōri

Tanbaguchi

Nijō

Nijō

Sagano Line (San-in Main Line)

Sanjō-dōri

Hankyū Kyoto Line

See pp216-17

Sanjō Guchi

Keifuku Arashiyama Line

Sai

Saiin

Nishōji-dōri

222

Scale: 0–400 m / 0–0.2 miles

Map labels:

Kawabata-dōri
Keihan Main Line
Shichijō
Shichijō-Ōhashi
Shiokōji-bashi
Nara Line
Tōfukuji
Higashiyama-bashi
Tobakaidō
See pp226-7

Kawaramachi-dōri
Kamijūzūyachō-dōri
Shōsei-en
Shimojūzūyachō-dōri
Rokujō-dōri
Tōkaidō Main Line
(Biwako Line & Kosei Line)
Tōkaidō Shinkansen Line
Kujō-dōri
36
Kawaramachi-dōri

Higashinotōin-dōri
Karasuma-dōri
Kyoto
Kyoto
Takeda Kaidō
Kujō
Karasuma-dōri
ōji

Matoba-dōri
Hanayachō-dōri
Shichijō-dōri
Shichōji-dōri
Nishinotōin-dōri
Karasuma Subway Line
Minami-ku

See Kyoto Station Area (p231)

Horikawa-dōri
Hachijō-dōri
Tōji
Tōji
Aburanokōji-dōri
Kintetsu Kyoto Line
ōji

Ōmiya-dōri
Toji-dōri
24

Umekōji-kōen
Hachijō-dōri
13

Shimabara
Shimogyō-ku
9
32
Shichijō-dōri
Tōkaidō Main Line (Kyoto Line)
Tōkaidō Shinkansen Line

12
14
Sagano Line
(San-in Main Line)
Minami-ku
Kujō-dōri

5

Nishōji

Higashiyama-ku

Higashiyama-ku

Biwa-ko Sosui Canal

Tōzai Subway Line

Higashiyama Driveway

Pedestrian Tunnel

Keage

Shirakawa-dōri

Sanjō-dōri

Maruyama-kōen

Ninen-zaka

Kiyomizu-michi

Niōmon-dōri

Higashiyama

Shimonzen-dōri

Shinbashi-dōri

Gion

Shinbashi

Nawate-dōri

Hanami-kōji

Furumonzen-dōri

Yasaka-dōri

Ishibei-kōji

Higashioji-dōri

Yamatooji-dōri

Miyagawa-chō

Kamo-gawa

Kawabata-dōri

Shijō-dōri

Kawaramachi-dōri

Pontochō

Kawaramachi

Shinkyōgoku Covered Arcade

Teramachi Covered Arcade

Sanjō Covered Arcade

Teramachi-dōri

Kawaramachi-Oike Crossing

Tōzai Subway Line

Kyoto-Shiyakusho-mae

See Downtown Kyoto Map (p229)

Higashiyama-Sanjō Crossing

Sanjō Keihan

Sanjō

Nijō-dōri

Reisen-dōri

Higashitakeyachō-dōri

Higashiyama-Marutamachi Crossing

Higashioji-dōri

Keihan Main Line

Niōmon-dōri

Higashioji-dōri

Nijō-dōri

Okazaki-kōen

Marutamachi-dōri

Marutamachi

Higashiyama-Marutamachi Crossing

Kawabata-Marutamachi Crossing

Marutamachi-bashi

Niō-Ohashi

Kawaramachi-Marutamachi Crossing

DOWNTOWN KYOTO

KYOTO STATION AREA (p231)

KYOTO STATION AREA

0 ▭▭ 200 m
0 ▭▬▬ 0.1 miles

Sakyamachi-dō
Toiyamachi-dōri
9 ●
Kawabata-dōri
Shichijō
10
38

Kelhan Main Line
Shichijō-Ohashi
Shichijō-Ohashi Crossing
Shichijō-dōri
Shiokōji-bashi
Shiokōji-dōri

Kamo-gawa
Nara Line
Tōkaidō Main Line (Biwako Line) & Kōsei Line
Tōkaidō Shinkansen Line
F
E
35
34
40

Kawaramachi-dōri
29

Kawaramachi Crossing
Shimojuzuyachō-dōri
Shōkō-en
7 ●
Takakura-dōri
18
13
D
32

Kamijuzuyachō-dōri
Rokujō-dōri
24
37
36
Higashinotōin-dōri
14
48
41
20
Karasuma-dōri
Karasuma Subway Line
Karasuma-Shichijō Crossing
Kyoto
15
27
19
45
Kyoto
Karasuma Subway Line
46
1
22
3
8
52
Muromachi-dōri
9 28
44
Shiokōji-dōri
31
12 11 2 51 50 16
Kyoto
Hanayachō-dōri
49
42
C
Shichijō-dōri
30
Shimogyō-ku
25
Shōmen-dōri
Kitaōji-dōri
Nishinotōin-dōri
17
43
B
Higashinakasuji-dōri
39
26
Kintetsu Kyoto Line
Hachijō-dōri
23
2 ●
5
Horikawa-dōri
33
Shichijō Horikawa Crossing
Tōkaidō Main Line (Kyoto Line)
Tōkaidō Shinkansen Line
A
4

231

0 _____ 200 m
0 _____ 0.1 miles

A **B** **C** **D**

① ② ③ ④ ⑤ ⑥

SIGHTS & ACTIVITIES
Adashino Nembutsu-ji
化野念仏寺 1 A2
Daihikaku Senkō-ji
大悲閣千光寺 2 B4
Daikaku-ji 大覚寺 3 C2
Giō-ji 祇王寺 4 B3
Hōrin-ji 法輪寺 5 C5
Iwatayama Monkey Park
岩田山自然遊園地 6 C5
Jōjakkō-ji 常寂光寺 7 B3
Kameyama-kōen
亀山公園 8 B4

Nison-in 二尊院 9 B3
Nonomiya-jinja
野宮神社 10 C4
Ōkōchi-sansō Villa
大河内山荘 11 B4
Rakushisha 落柿舎 12 B3
Seiryō-ji 清涼寺 13 C3
Takiguchi-dera
滝口寺 14 B3
Tenryū-ji 天竜寺 15 C4
Tenryū-ji North Gate
天竜寺北門 16 C4
Togetsu-kyō 渡月橋 17 C5

*Torii-gata
(Daimonji Okuribi
Yaki Fire Festival Character)*

Osawa-no-ike

Ukyō-ku

Shin-marutamachi-dōri

Sagano Line (San-in Main Line)

Saga
Arashiyama

Okura-ike

Sagano Kankō Line

Ō-gawa

Torokko
Saga

Keifuku Arashiyama Line

Torokko
Arashiyama

Sagaekimae

Rokuō

Kameyama-kōen

Keifuku
Arashiyama

Sanjō-dōri

Hozu-gawa

Katsura-gawa

Nakanoshima-kōen

Iwatayama
Monkey Park

Arashiyama

Hankyu Arashiyama Line

EATING
Ayu Chaya Hiranoya
鮎茶屋平野屋 18 A2
Gyātei ぎゃあてい 19 C4
Kushi-tei 串串 20 C4
Seizansō-dō 西山艸堂 21 C4
Shigetsu 篩月 ....(see 15)
Sunday's Sun
サンデーズサン 22 D5
Togetsu-tei 渡月亭 23 C5
Yoshida-ya よしだや 24 C4
Yudōfu Sagano
湯豆腐嵯峨野 25 C4

SLEEPING
Arashiyama Benkei Ryokan
嵐山辨慶旅館 26 C5
Hotel Ran-tei ホテル嵐亭 27 C5
Minshuku Arashiyama
民宿嵐山 28 D4
Rankyō-kan Ryokan
旅館嵐峡館 29 B4
Rokuō-in 鹿王院 30 D4

INFORMATION
Convenience Store
コンビニエンスストア 31 C4

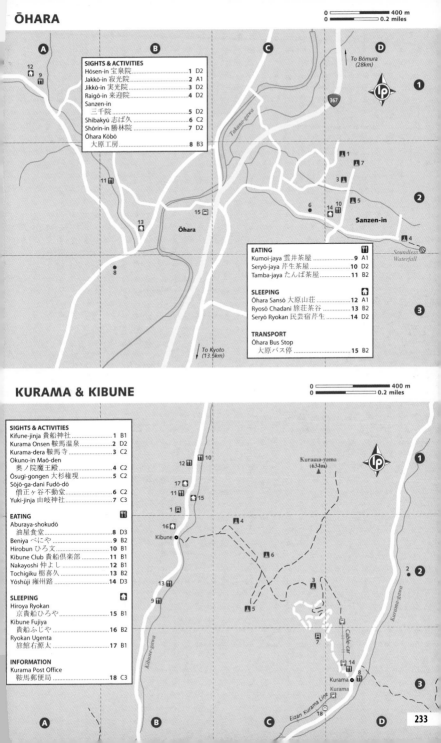

ŌHARA

0 — 400 m
0 — 0.2 miles

SIGHTS & ACTIVITIES
Hōsen-in 宝泉院..................................1 D2
Jakkō-in 寂光院..................................2 A1
Jikkō-in 実光院...................................3 D2
Raigō-in 来迎院..................................4 D2
Sanzen-in
三千院...5 D2
Shibakyū 志ばく..................................6 C2
Shōrin-in 勝林院..................................7 D2
Ōhara Kōbō
大原工房...8 B3

To Bōmura
(28km)

Takano-gawa

367

Ōhara

Sanzen-in

Soundless
Waterfall

EATING
Kumoi-jaya 雲井茶屋.........................9 A1
Seryō-jaya 芹生茶屋.........................10 D2
Tamba-jaya たんば茶屋.....................11 B2

SLEEPING
Ōhara Sansō 大原山荘......................12 A1
Ryosō Chadani 旅荘茶谷...................13 D2
Seryō Ryokan 民芸宿芹生..................14 D2

TRANSPORT
Ōhara Bus Stop
大原バス停..15 B2

To Kyoto
(13.5km)

KURAMA & KIBUNE

0 — 400 m
0 — 0.2 miles

SIGHTS & ACTIVITIES
Kifune-jinja 貴船神社...........................1 B1
Kurama Onsen 鞍馬温泉.....................2 D2
Kurama-dera 鞍馬寺...........................3 C2
Okuno-in Maō-den
奥ノ院魔王殿......................................4 C2
Ōsugi-gongen 大杉権現......................5 C2
Sōjō-ga-dani Fudō-dō
僧正ヶ谷不動堂..................................6 C2
Yuki-jinja 由岐神社.............................7 C3

EATING
Aburaya-shokudō
油屋食堂...8 D3
Beniya べにや....................................9 B2
Hirobun ひろ文...................................10 B1
Kibune Club 貴船倶楽部....................11 B1
Nakayoshi 仲よし................................12 B1
Tochigiku 栃喜久.................................13 B2
Yōshūji 雍州路....................................14 D3

SLEEPING
Hiroya Ryokan
京貴船ひろや......................................15 B1
Kibune Fujiya
貴船ふじや..16 B2
Ryokan Ugenta
旅館右源太...17 B1

INFORMATION
Kurama Post Office
鞍馬郵便局...18 C3

Kurama-yama
(63.4m)

Kibune

Kibune-gawa

Kurama-gawa

Cable-car

Kurama

Eizan Kurama Line

233

KYOTO RAIL SYSTEM

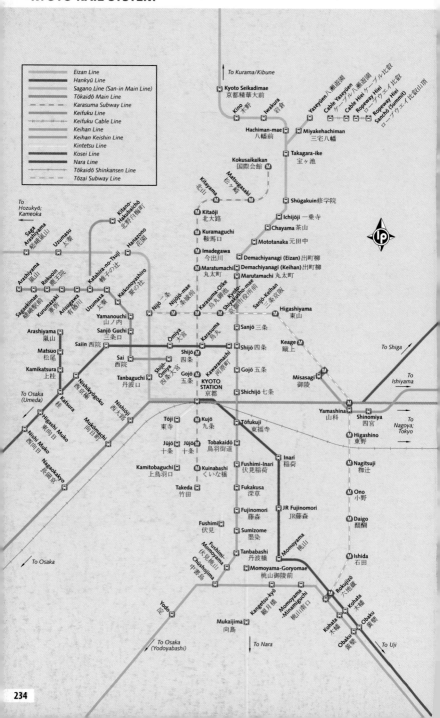